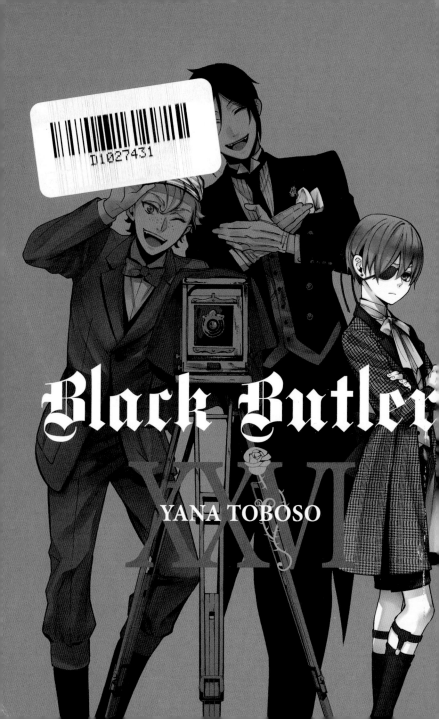

Black Butler

XXVI

YANA TOBOSO

Contents

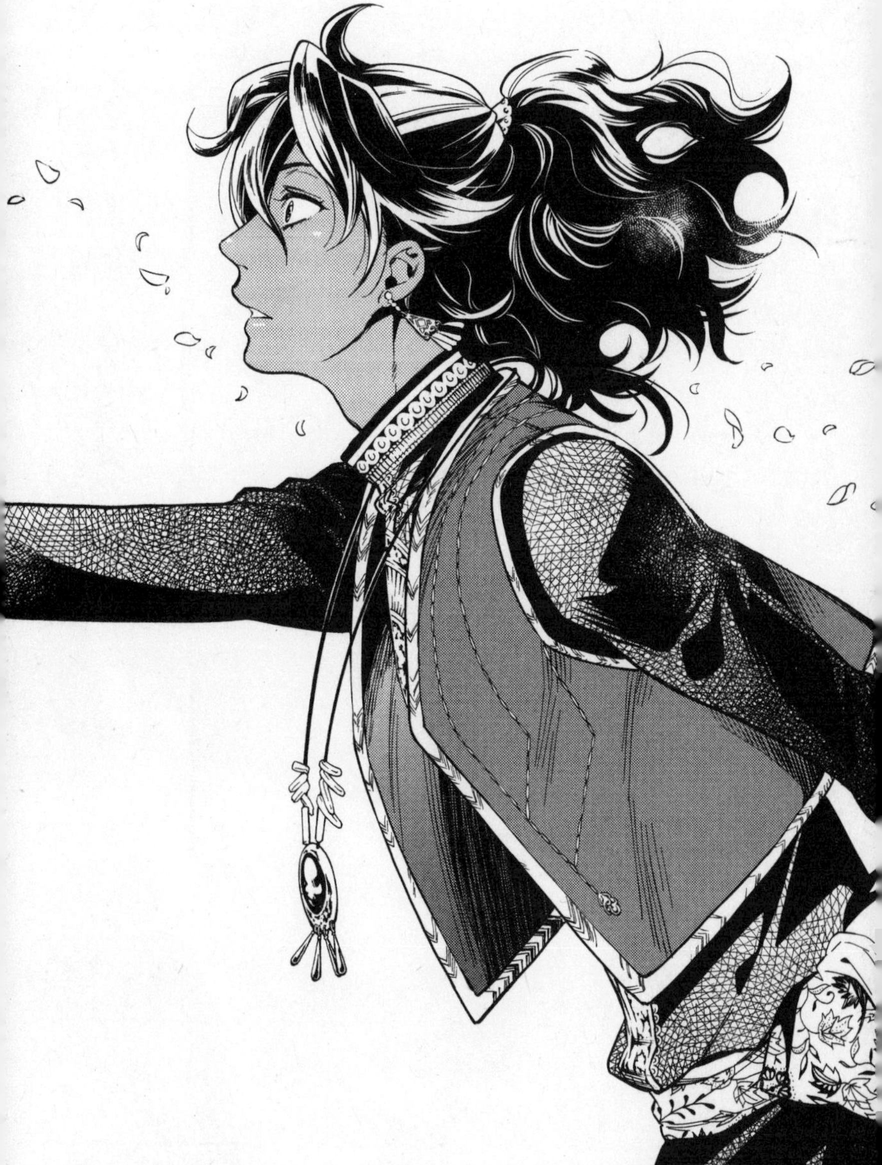

CHAPTER 127

In the morning : The Butler, Commending

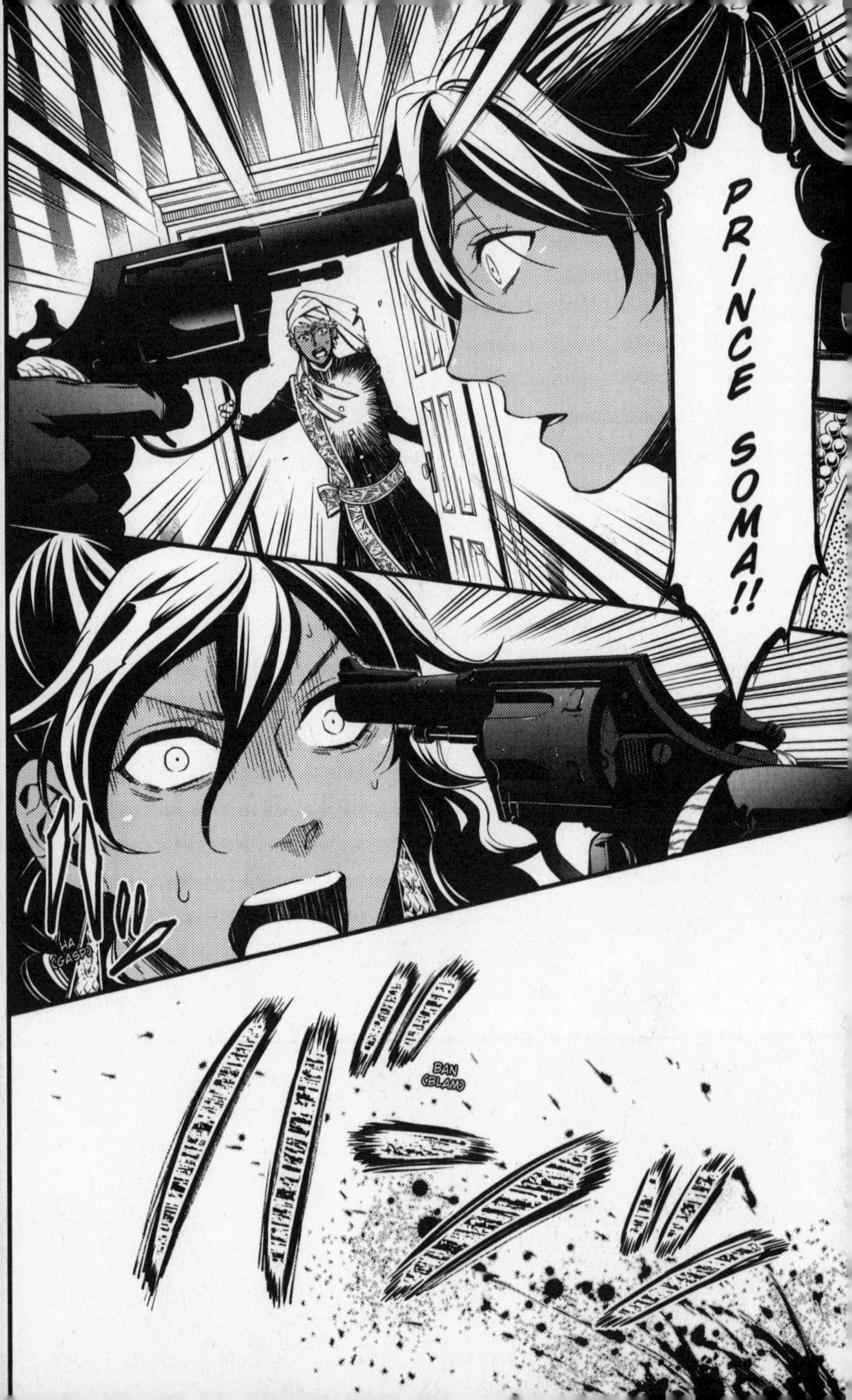
PRINCE SOMA!!
HA (GASP)
BAN (BLAM)

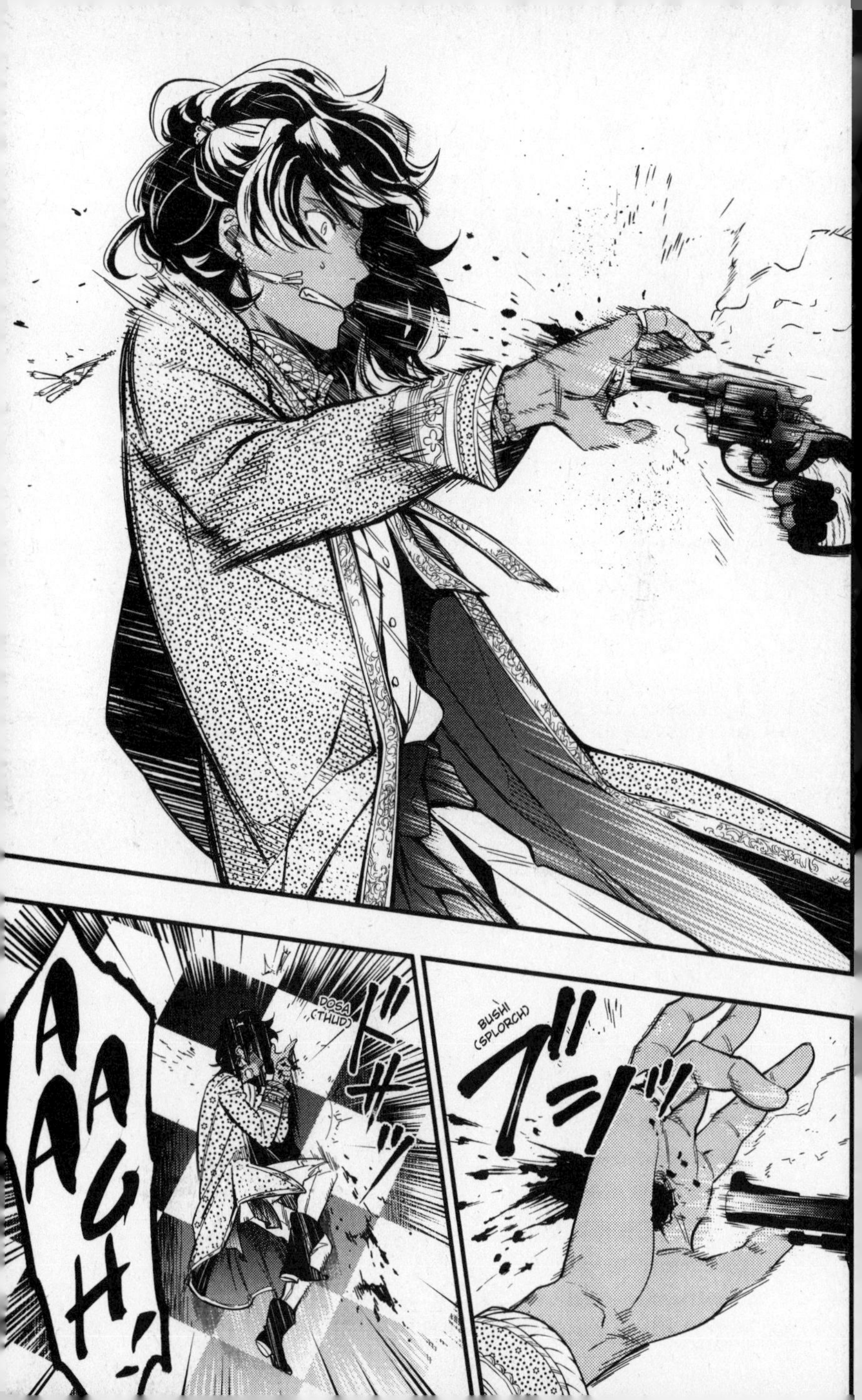
BUSHI
(SPLORCH)
DOSA
(THUD)
AAAUGH!

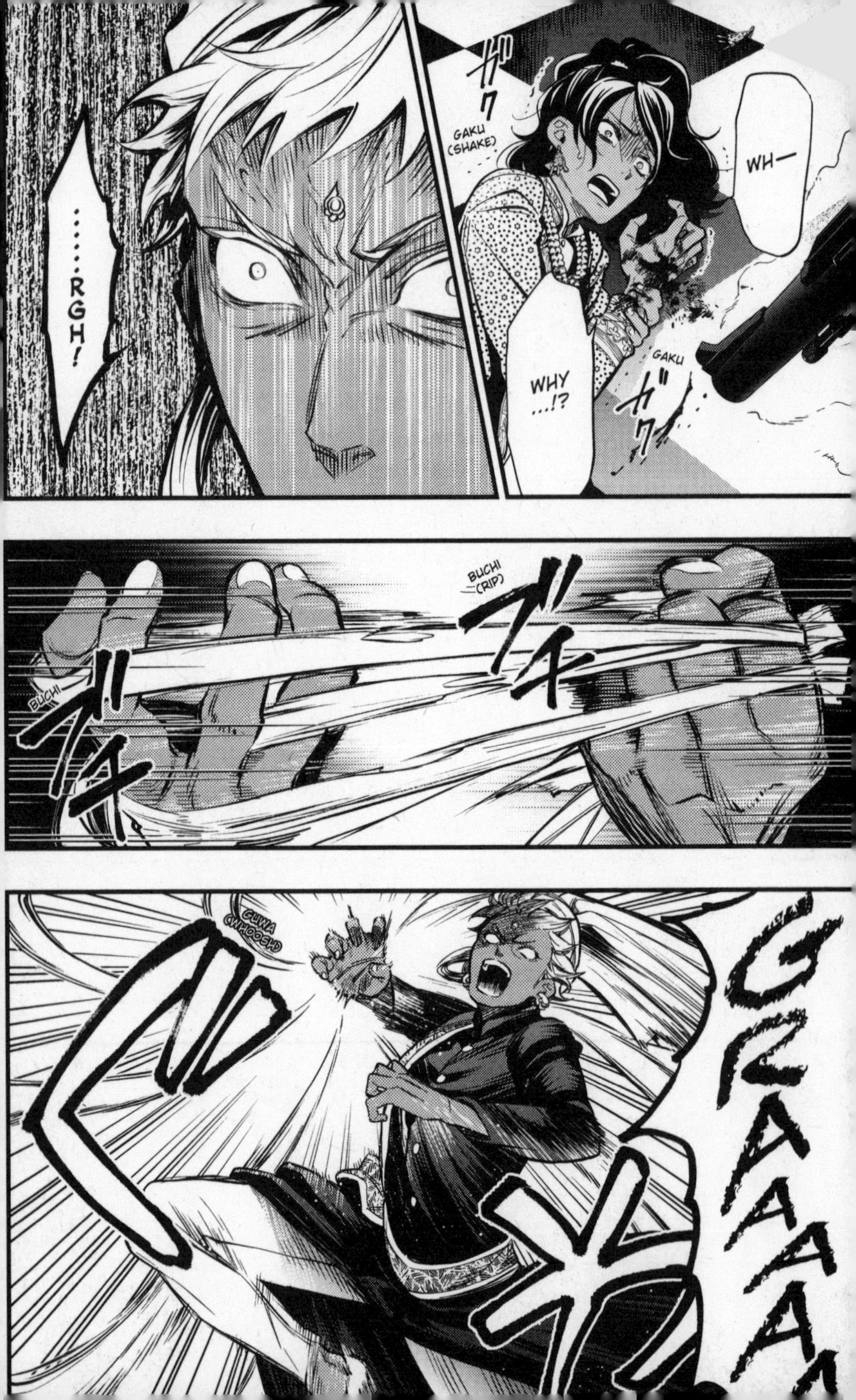
WH—
GAKU (SHAKE)
WHY ...!?
GAKU
......RGH!
BUCHI (RIP)
BUCHI
GWA (WHOOSH)
GRAAAAA

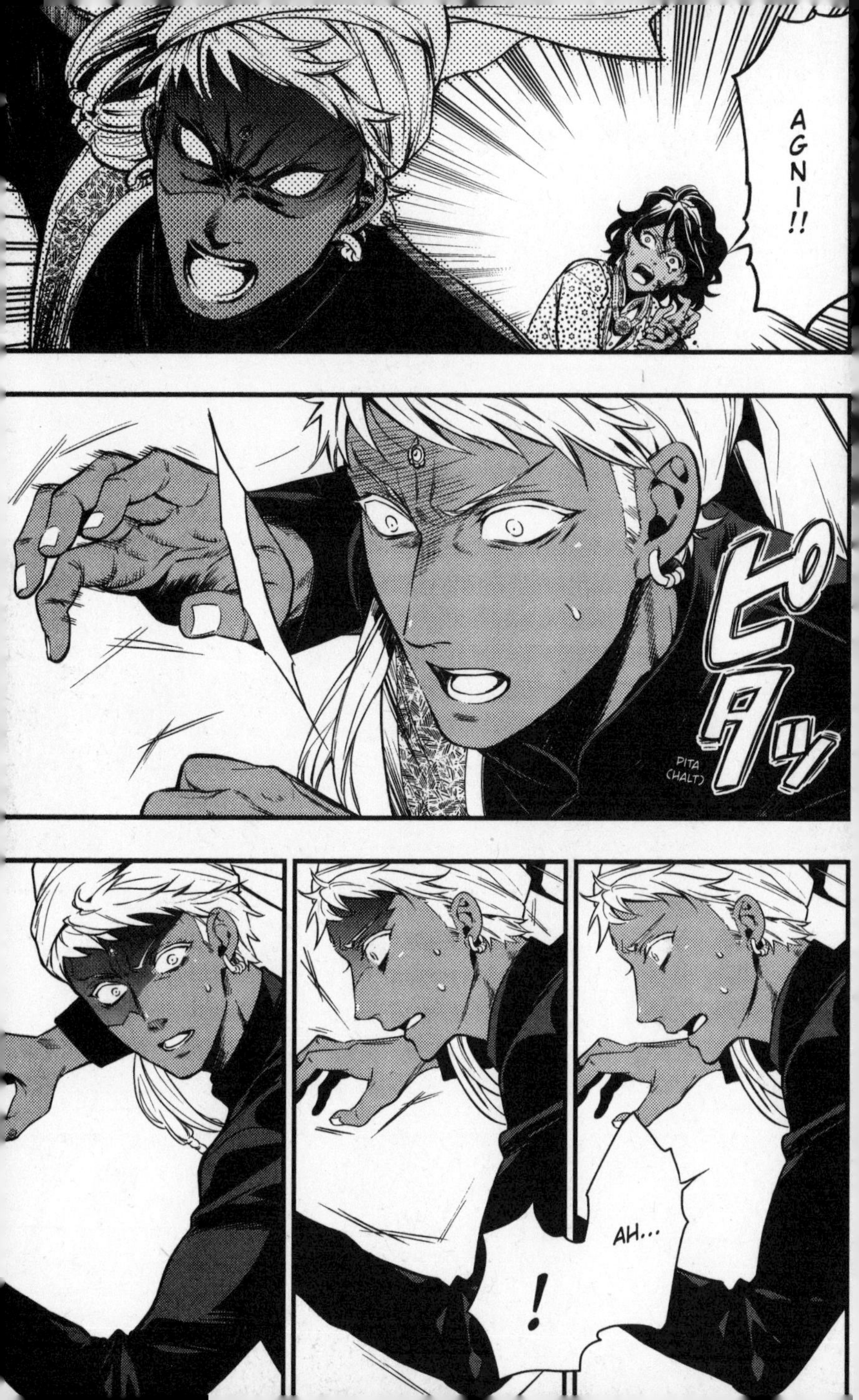
AGNI!!
ピタッ
PITA (HALT)
AH...
!

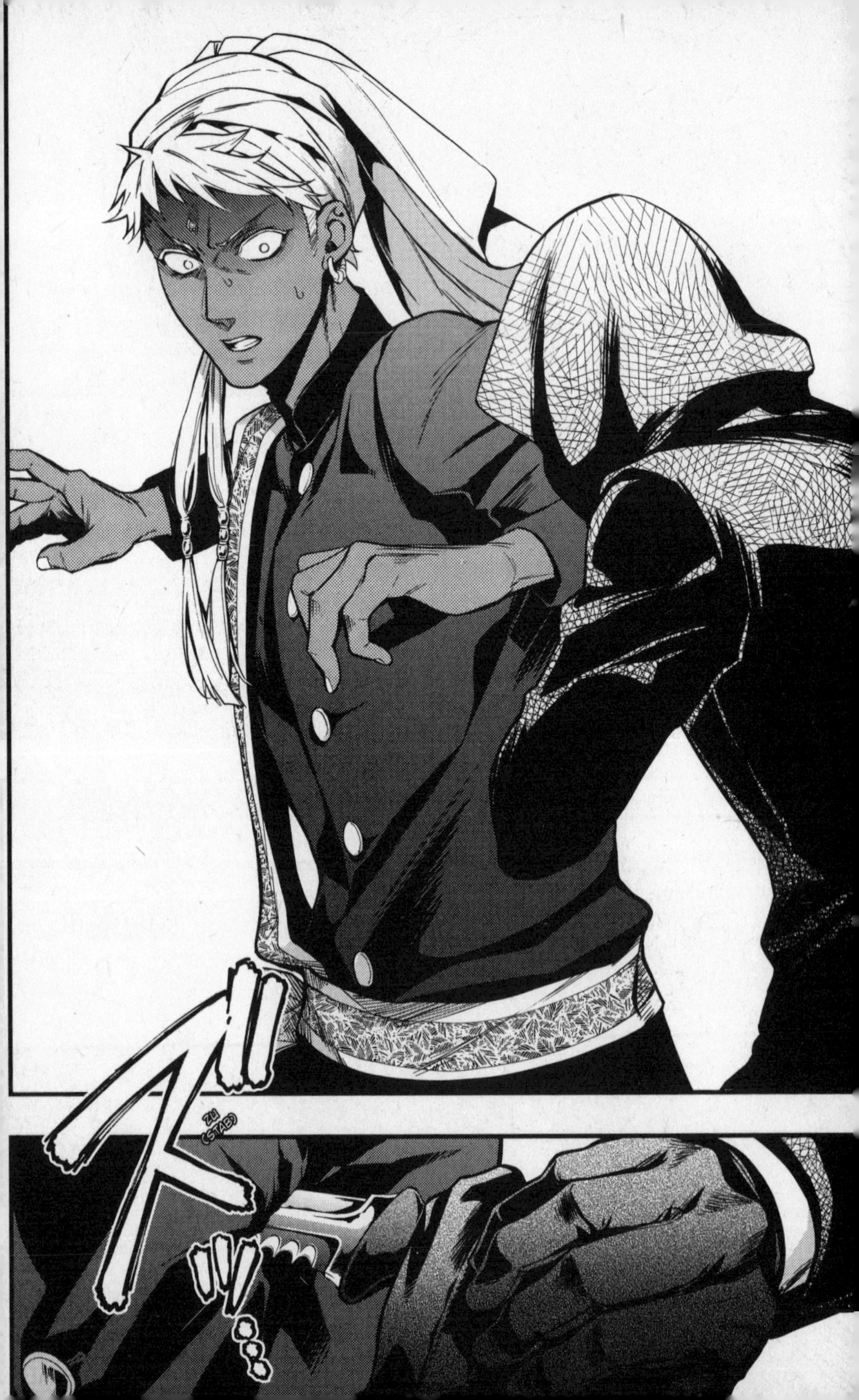
ZU
(STAB)

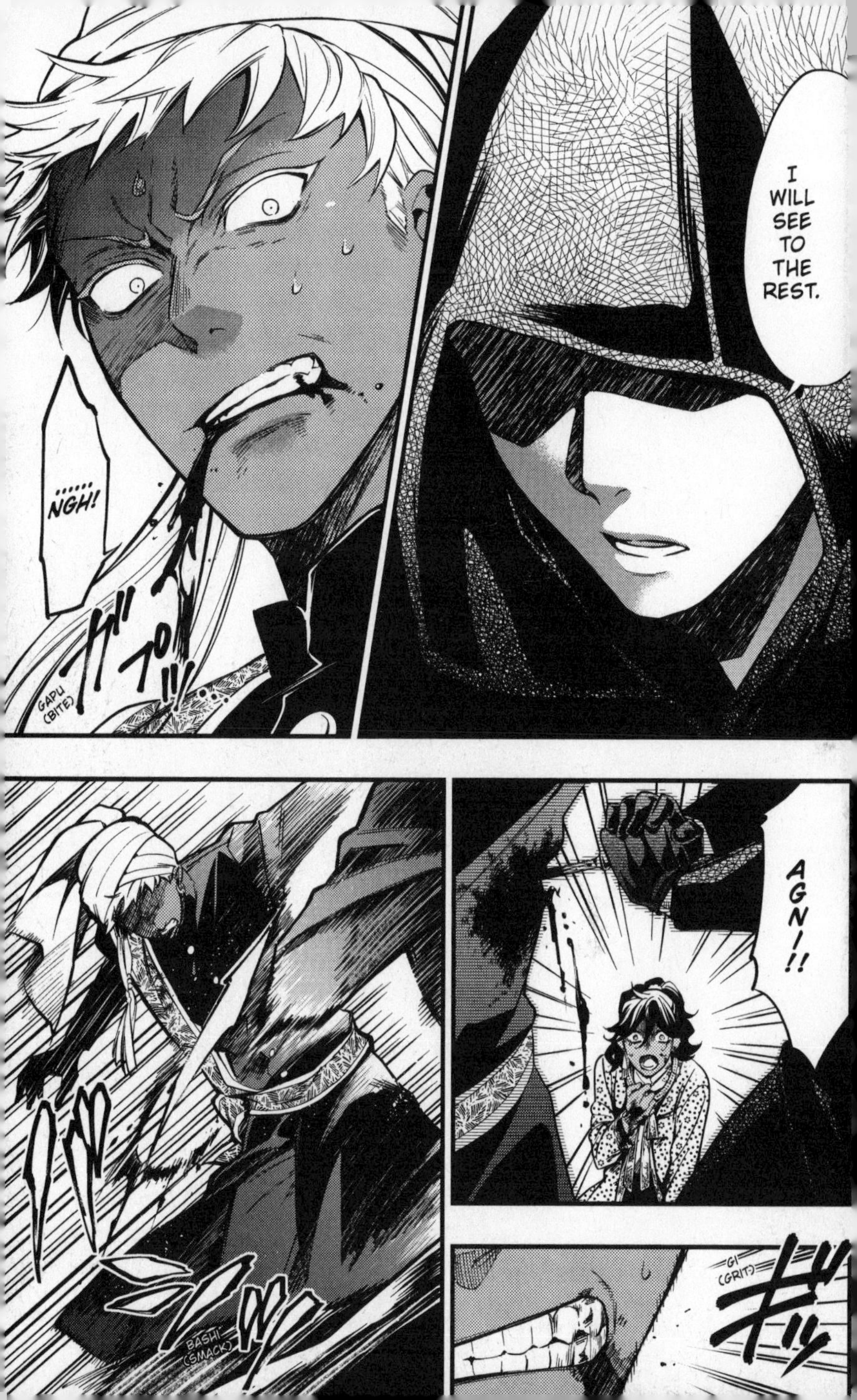
I WILL SEE TO THE REST.
……NGH!
GAPU (BITE)
AGNI!!
GI (GRIT)
BASHI (SMACK)

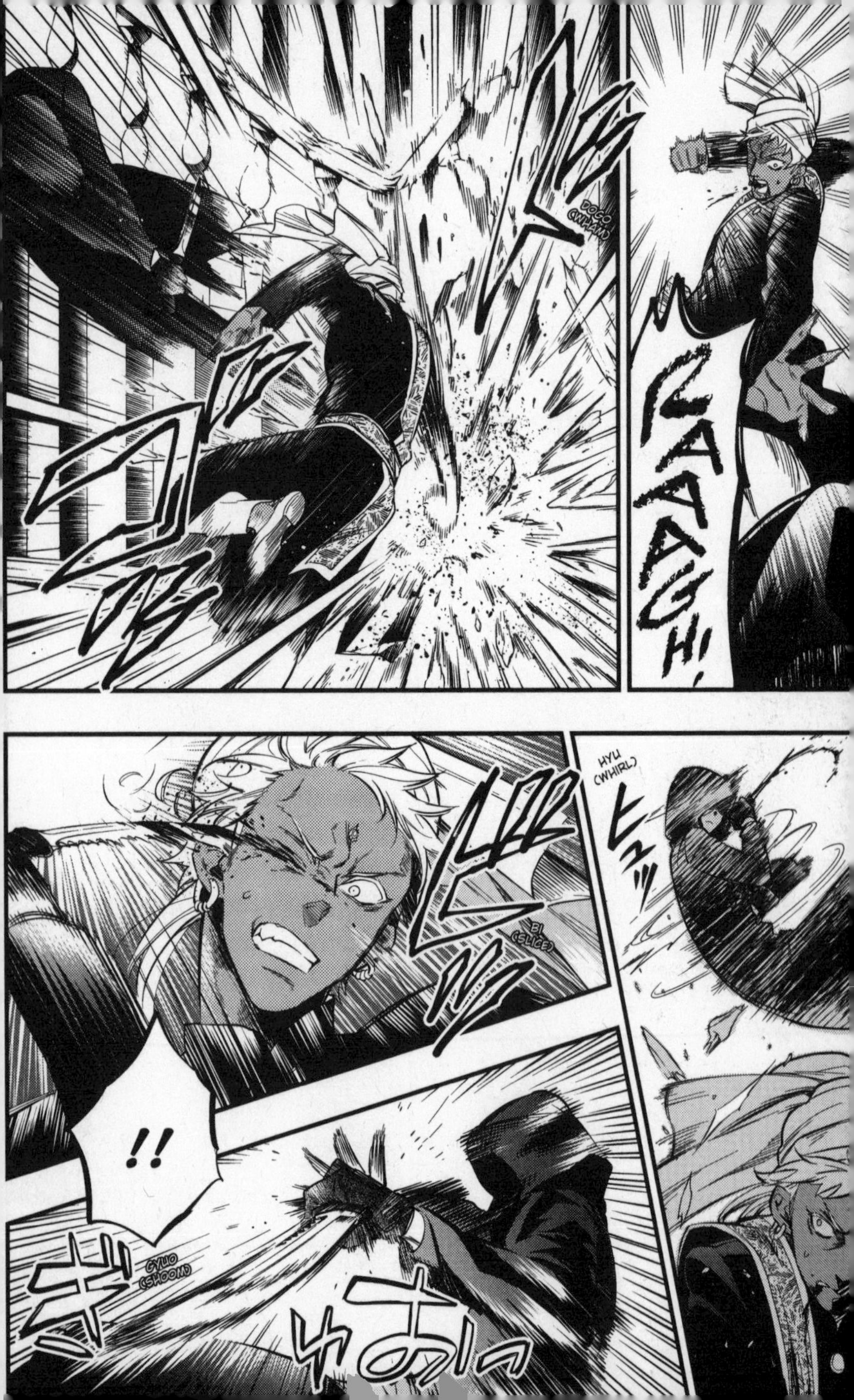
KAAAGH!
DOGO (WHAM)
HYU (WHIRL)
BI (SLICE)
!!
GYUO (SHOOM)

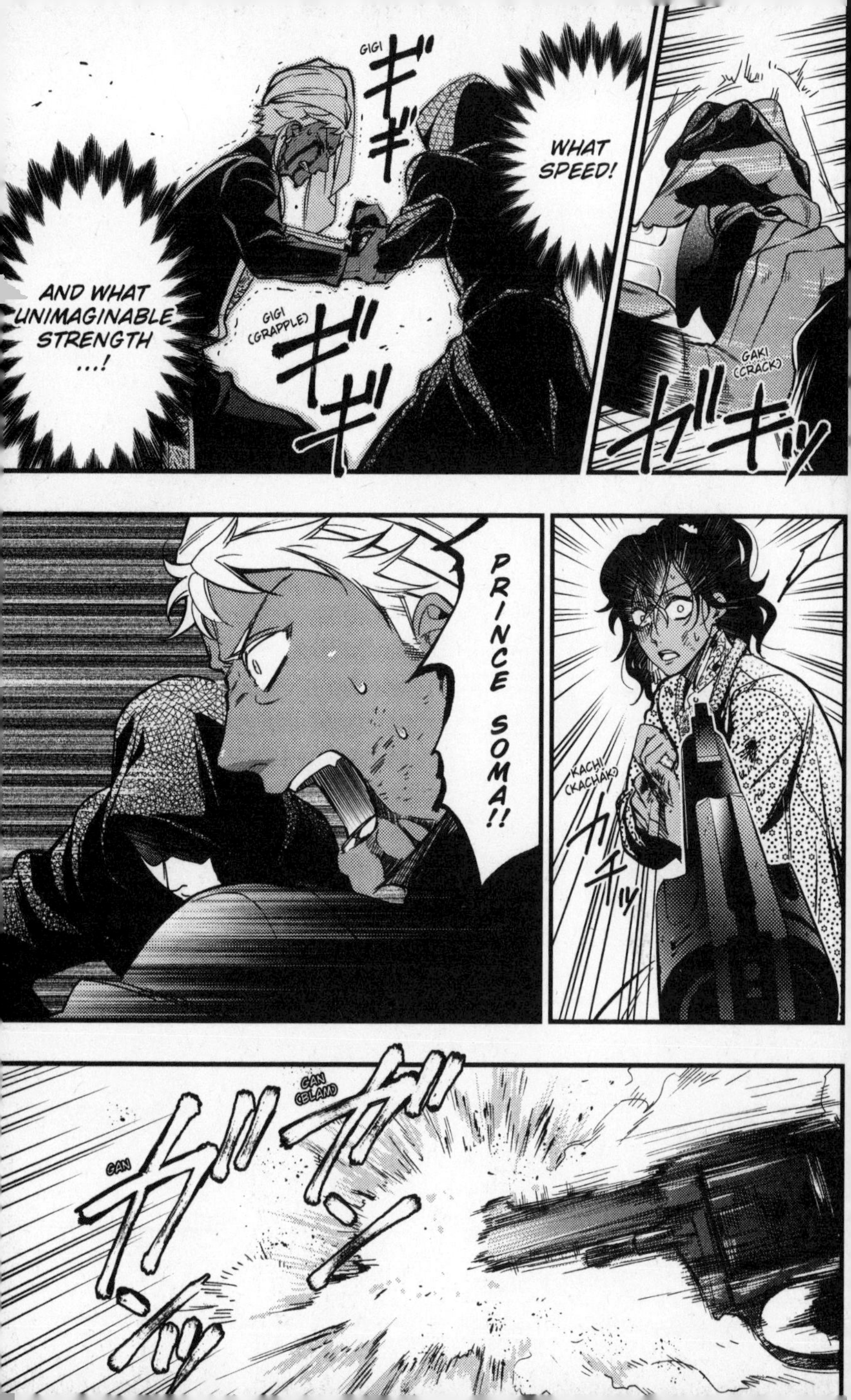
GAKI (CRACK)
WHAT SPEED!
GIGI
AND WHAT UNIMAGINABLE STRENGTH ...!
GIGI (GRAPPLE)
KACHI (KACHAK)
PRINCE SOMA!!
GAN (BLAM)
GAN

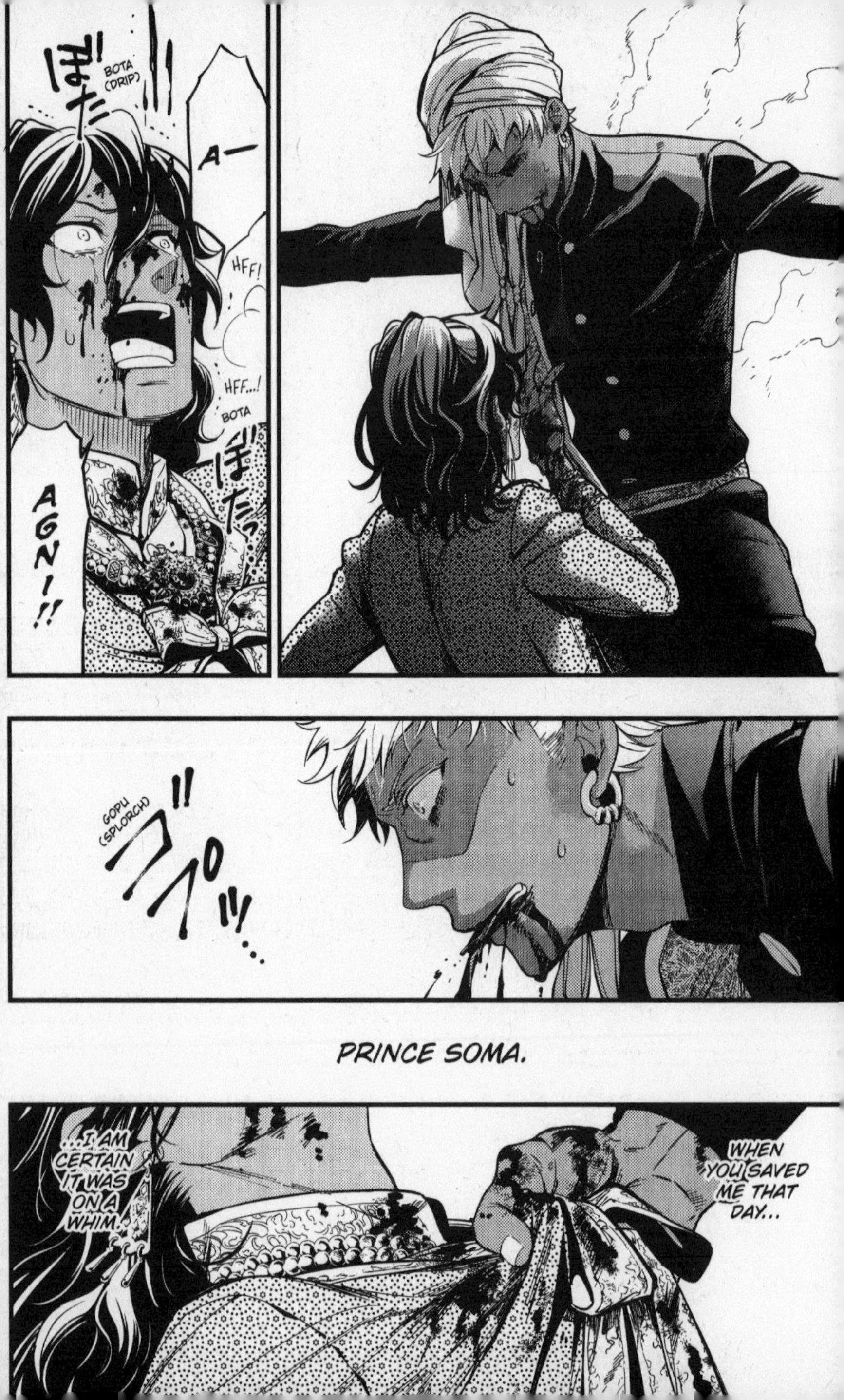
A—
ぼた
BOTA (DRIP)
HFF!
HFF...!
BOTA
ぼたっ
AGNI!!
GOPU (SPLORCH)
ゴプッ...
PRINCE SOMA.
WHEN YOU SAVED ME THAT DAY...
...I AM CERTAIN IT WAS ON A WHIM.

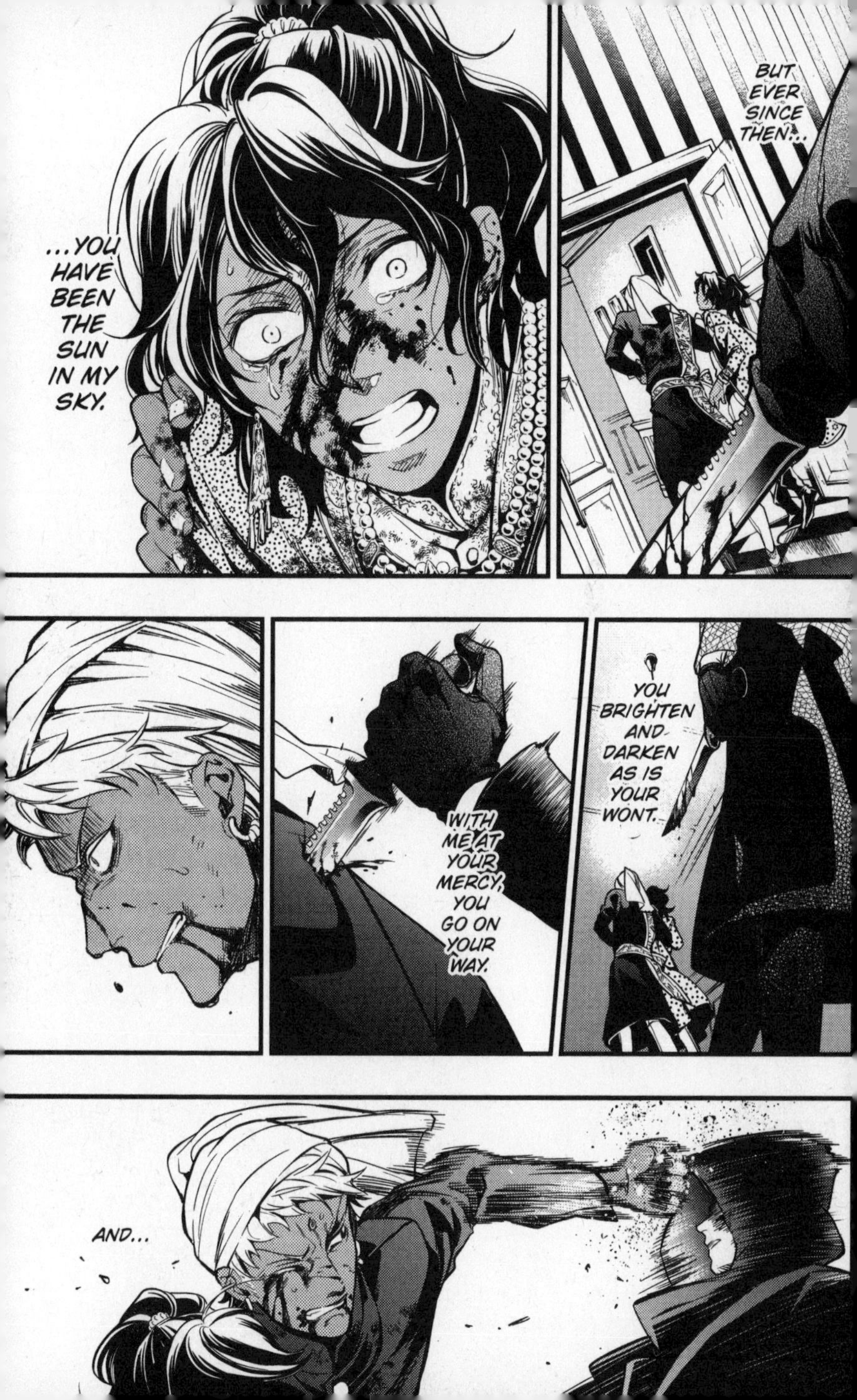
BUT EVER SINCE THEN...
...YOU HAVE BEEN THE SUN IN MY SKY.
YOU BRIGHTEN AND DARKEN AS IS YOUR WONT.
WITH ME AT YOUR MERCY, YOU GO ON YOUR WAY.
AND...

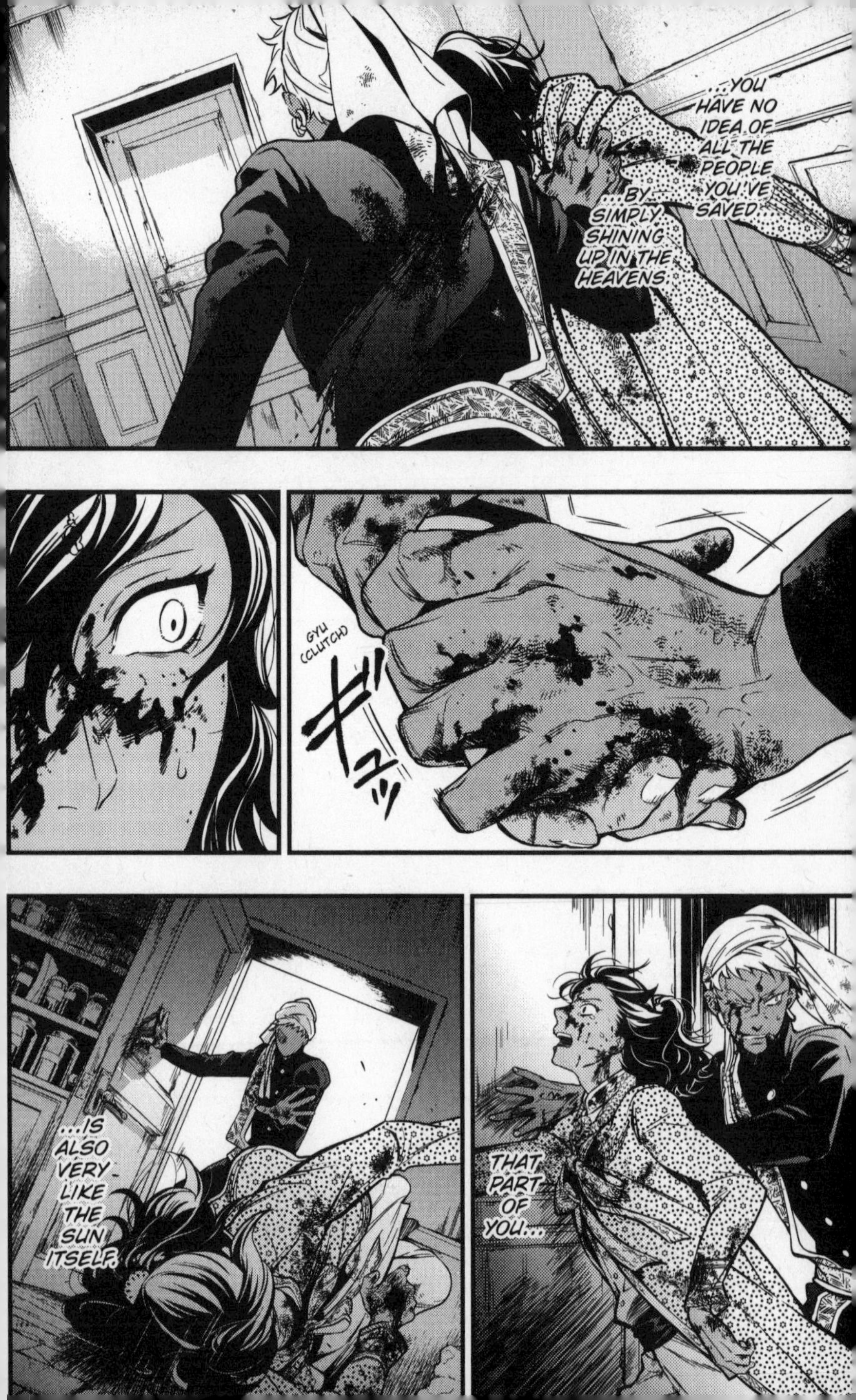
...YOU HAVE NO IDEA OF ALL THE PEOPLE YOU'VE SAVED
...BY SIMPLY SHINING UP IN THE HEAVENS.
GYU (CLUTCH)
ギュッ
THAT PART OF YOU...
...IS ALSO VERY LIKE THE SUN ITSELF.

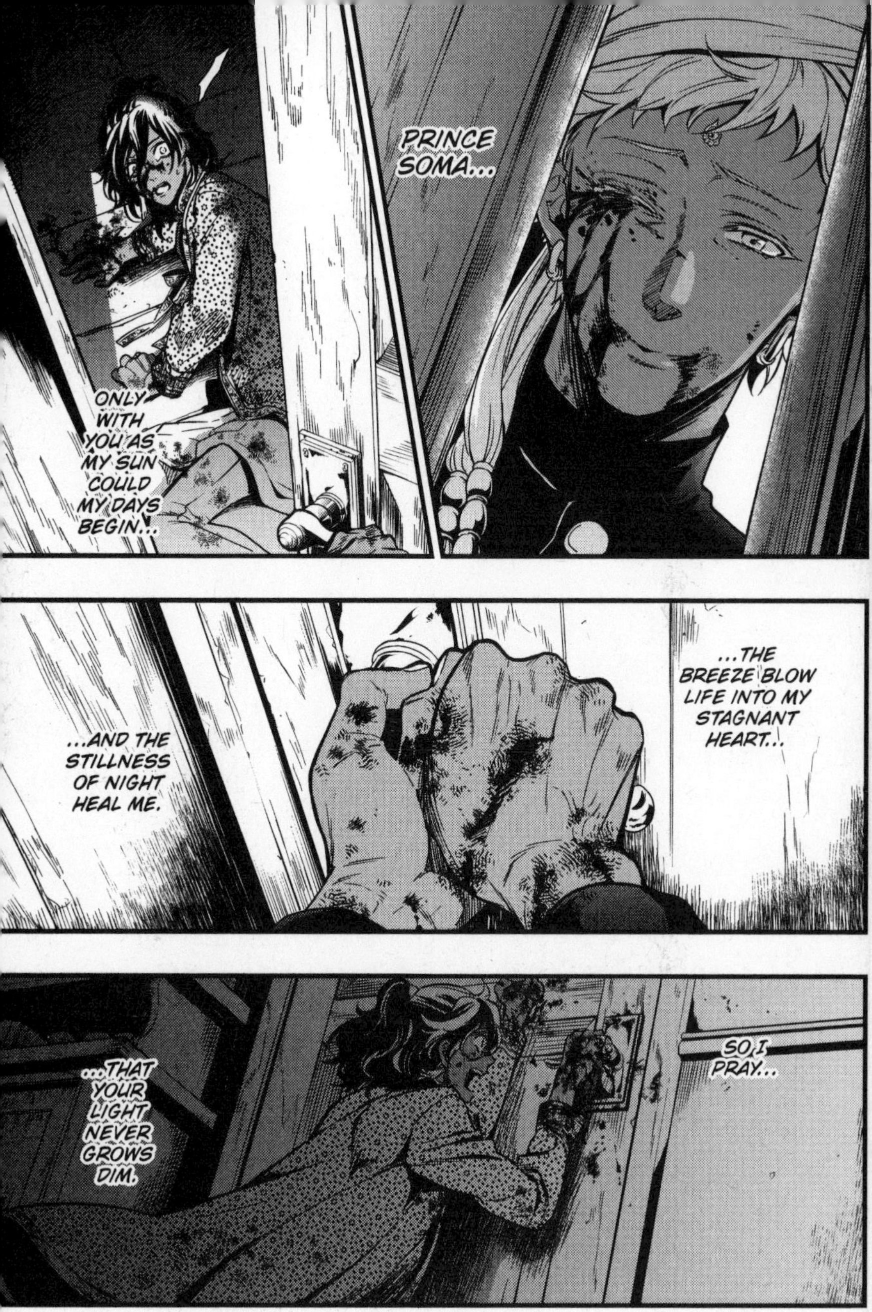
PRINCE SOMA...
ONLY WITH YOU AS MY SUN COULD MY DAYS BEGIN...
...THE BREEZE BLOW LIFE INTO MY STAGNANT HEART...
...AND THE STILLNESS OF NIGHT HEAL ME.
SO I PRAY...
...THAT YOUR LIGHT NEVER GROWS DIM.

AS LONG AS YOU KEEP SHINING BRIGHTLY, I KNOW...

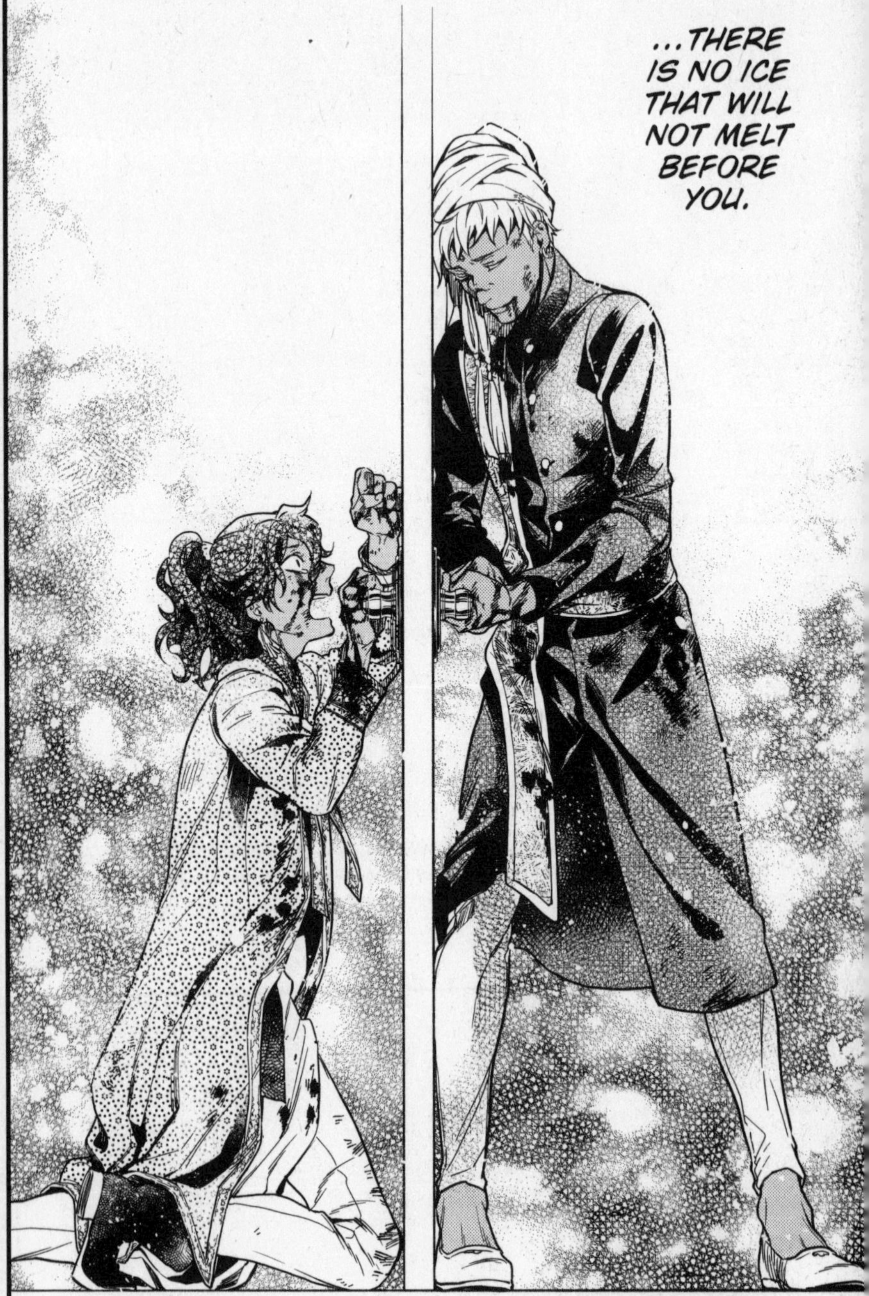
...THERE IS NO ICE THAT WILL NOT MELT BEFORE YOU.

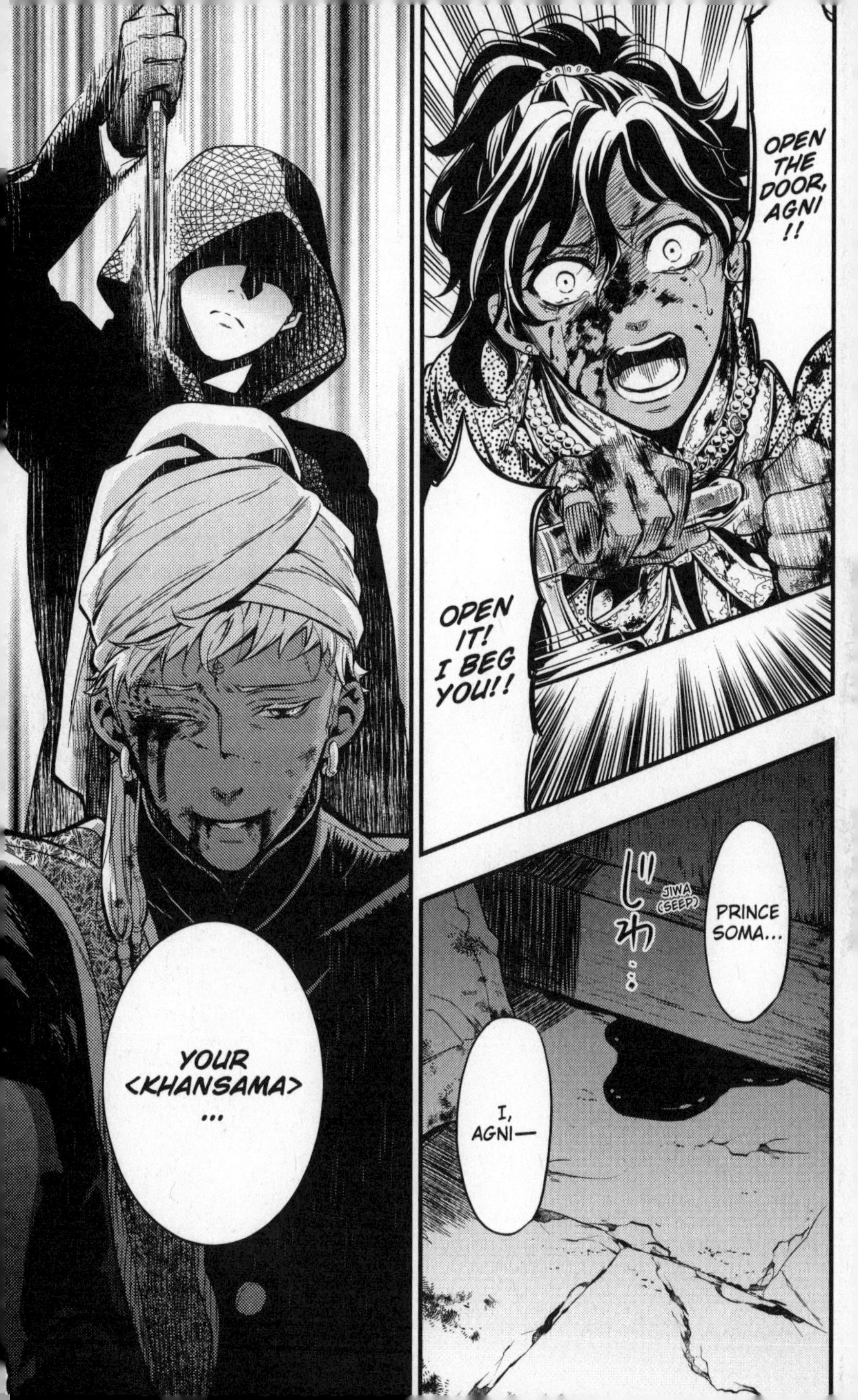
OPEN THE DOOR, AGNI!!
OPEN IT! I BEG YOU!!
じわ…
JIWA (SEEP)
PRINCE SOMA...
I, AGNI—
YOUR <KHANSAMA>...

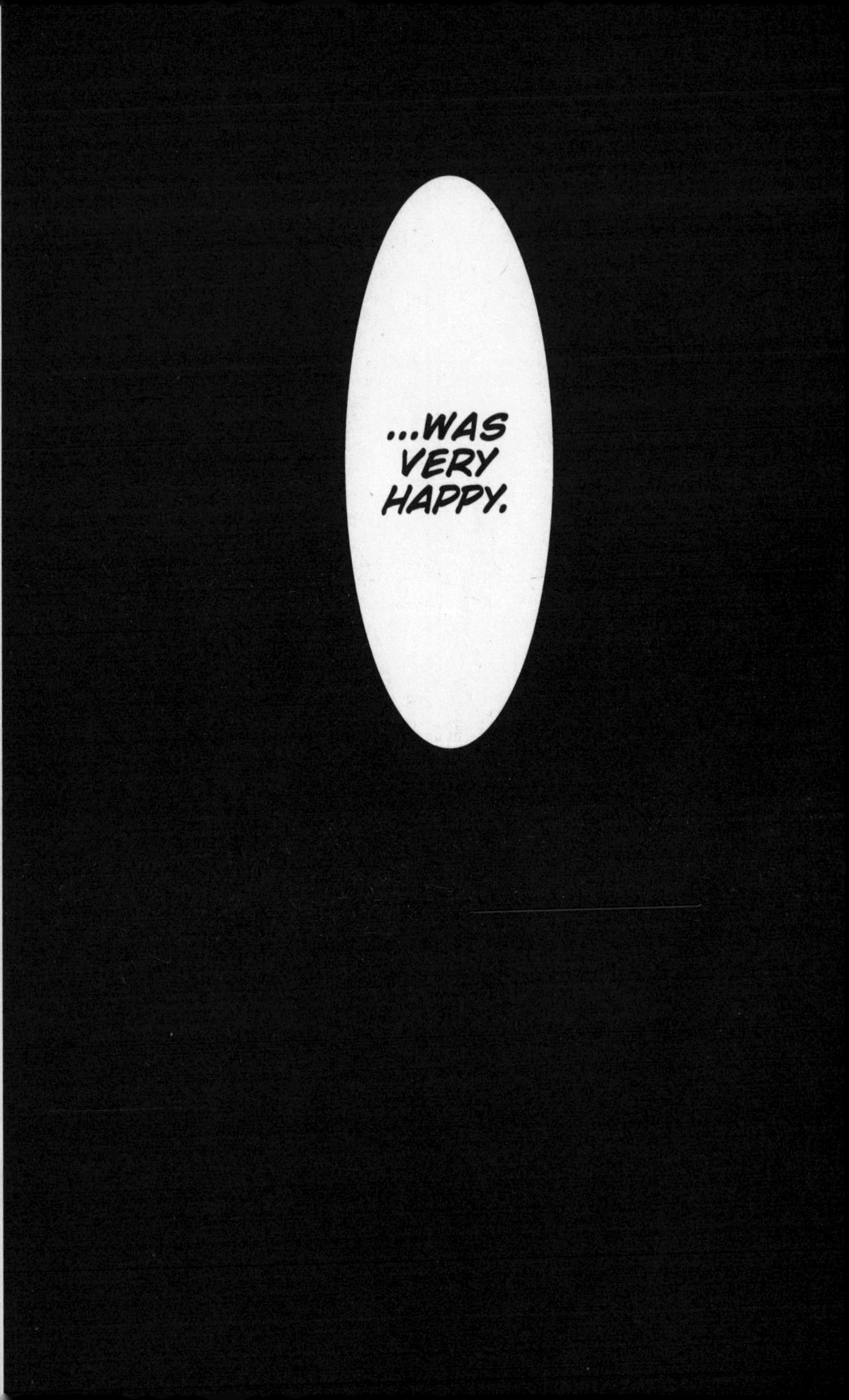
...WAS VERY HAPPY.

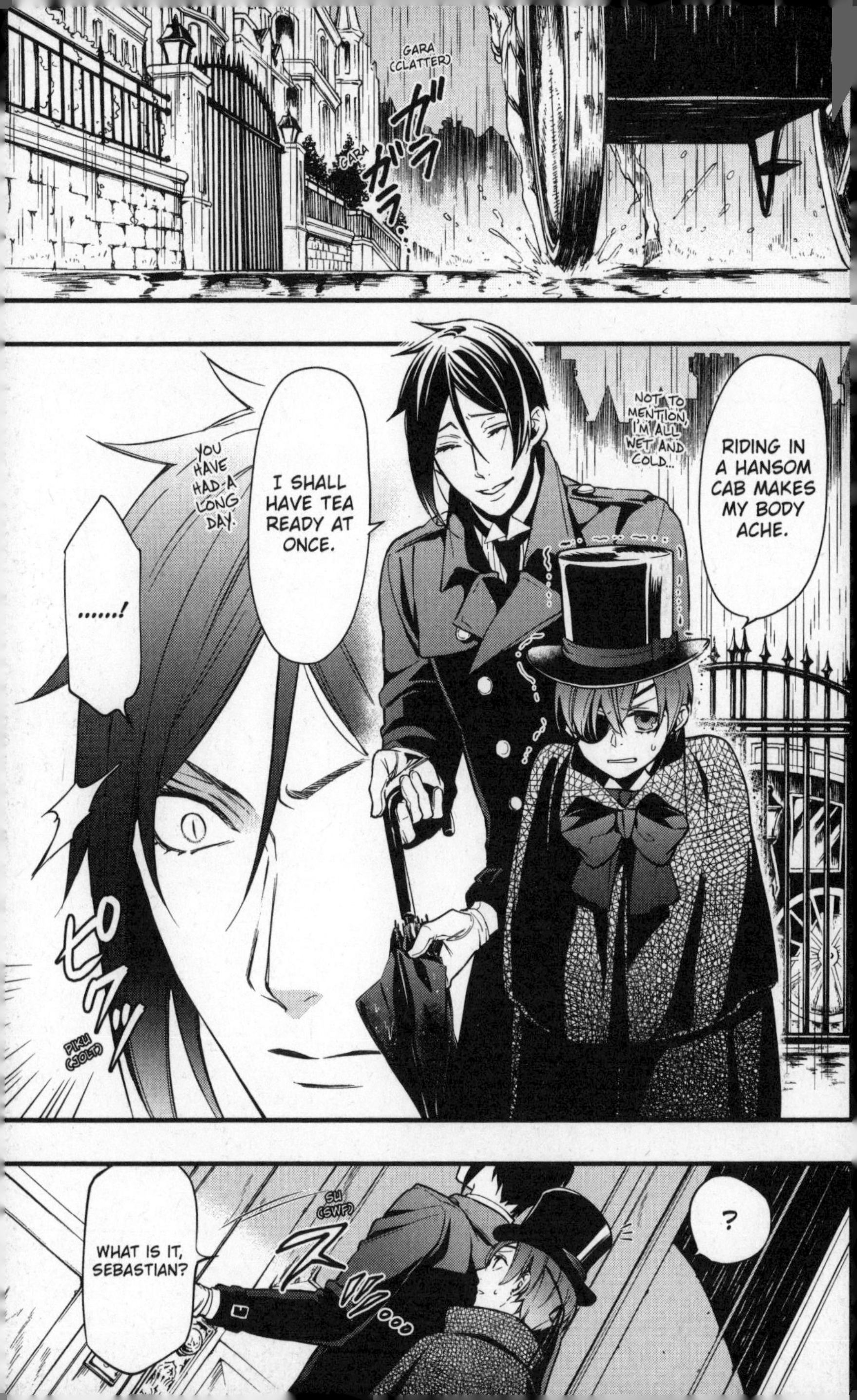
GARA (CLATTER)
ガラ
GARA
ガラ…
RIDING IN A HANSOM CAB MAKES MY BODY ACHE.
NOT TO MENTION, I'M ALL WET AND COLD...
I SHALL HAVE TEA READY AT ONCE.
YOU HAVE HAD A LONG DAY.
......!
ピクッ
PIKU (JOLT)
?
SU (SWF)
ス
WHAT IS IT, SEBASTIAN?

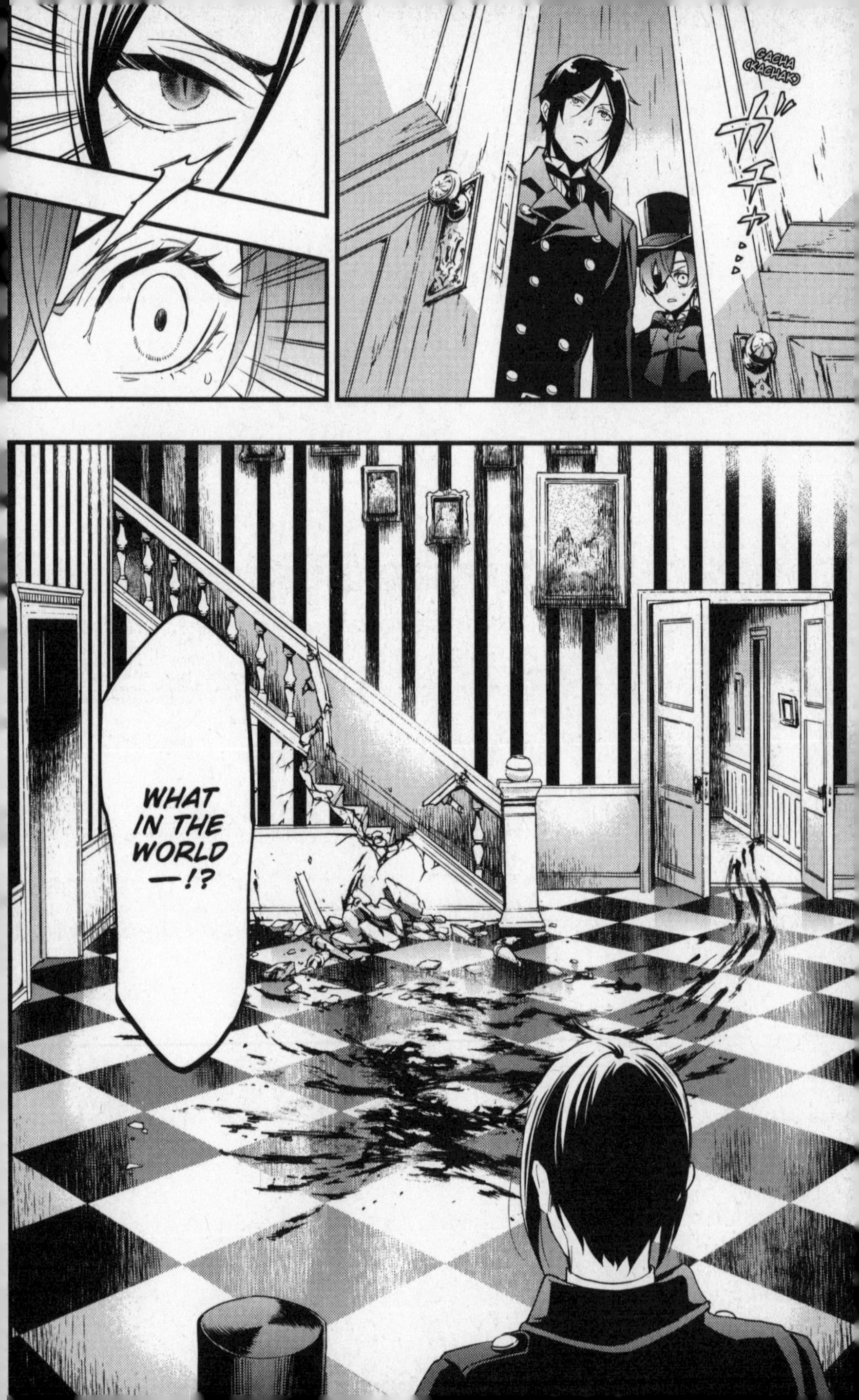
GACHA (KACHAK)
ガチャ…
WHAT IN THE WORLD —!?

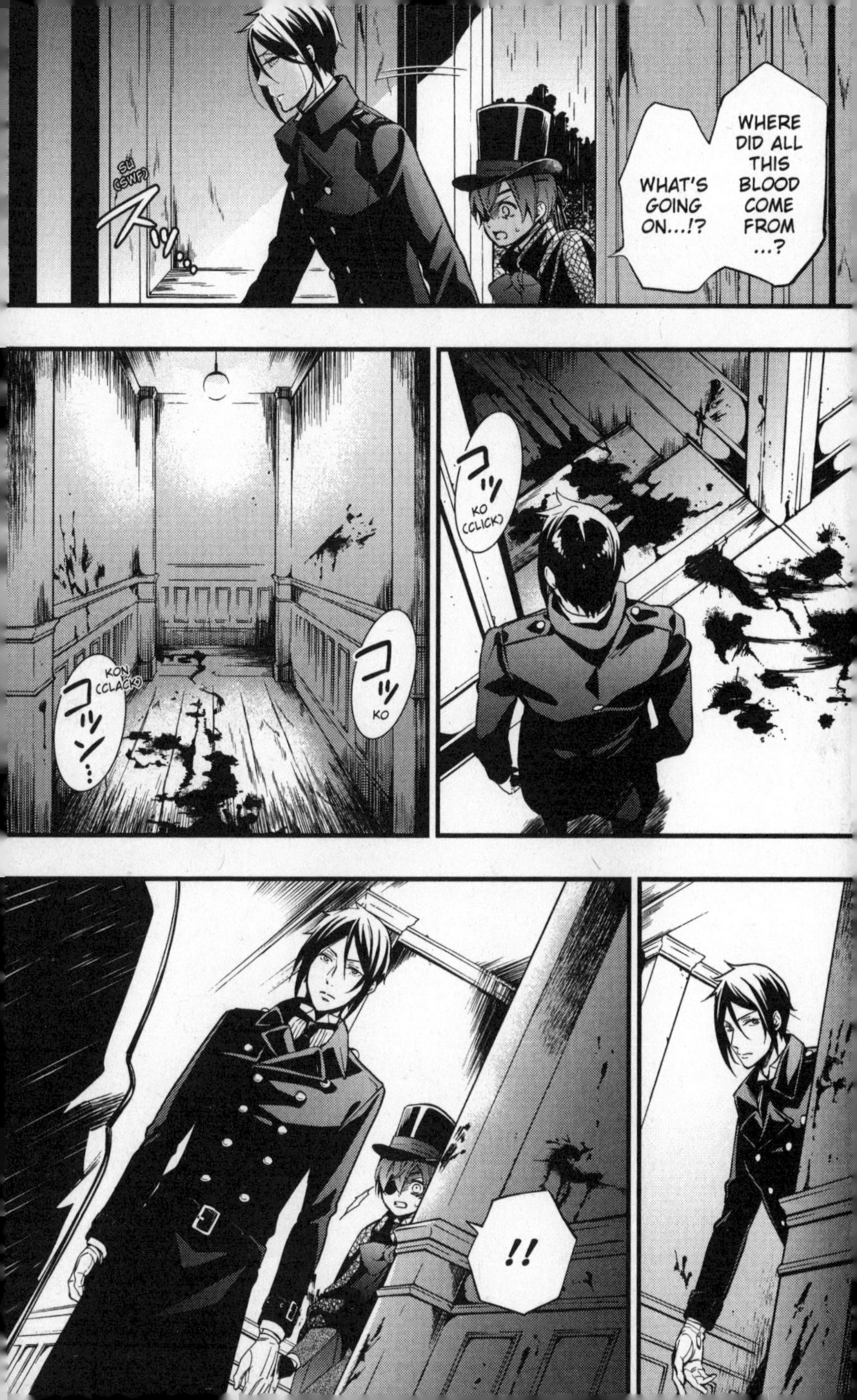
WHERE DID ALL THIS BLOOD COME FROM ...?
WHAT'S GOING ON...!?
スッ…
SU (SWF)
コッ
KO (CLICK)
コッ
KO
コッン…
KON (CLACK)
!!

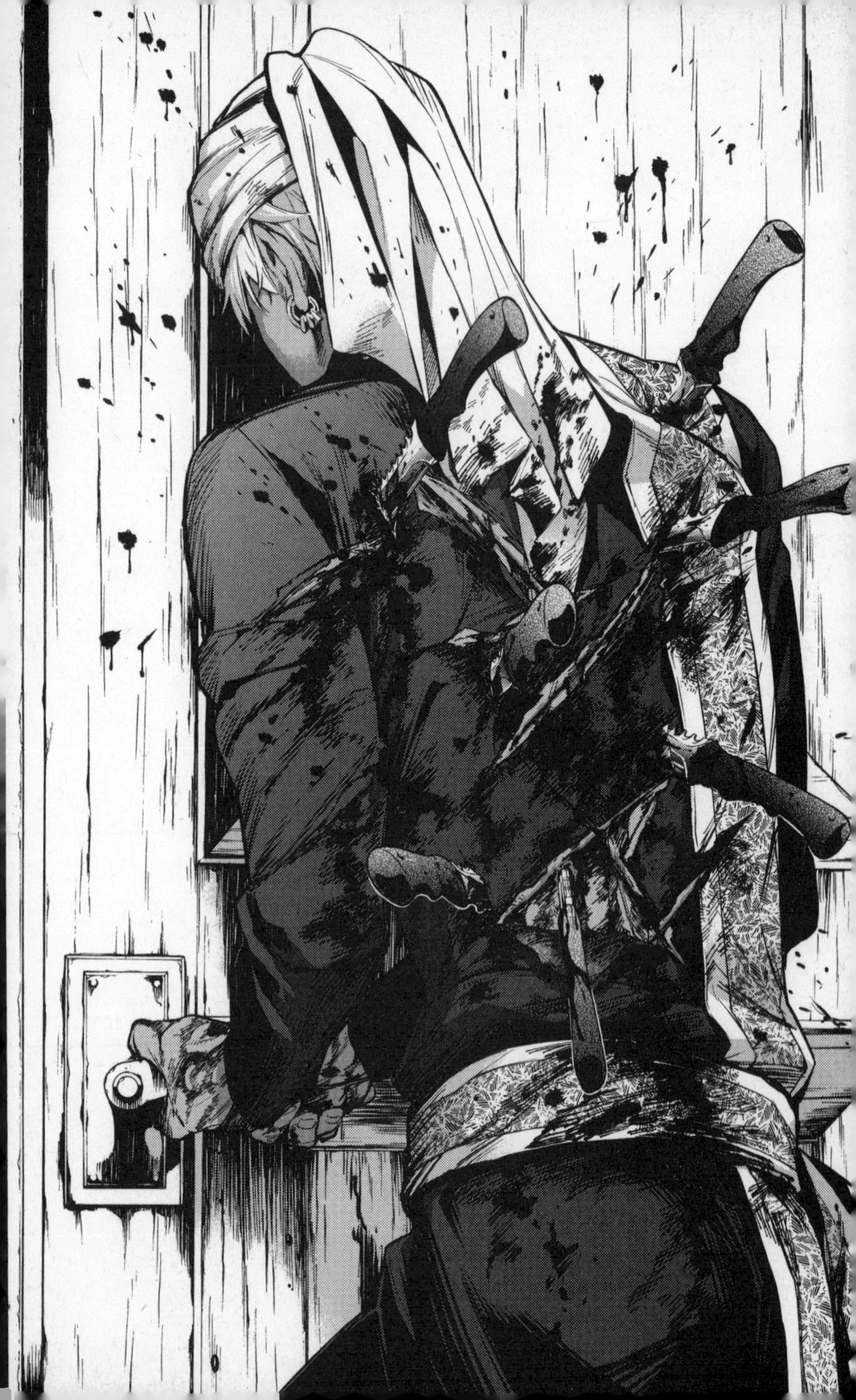

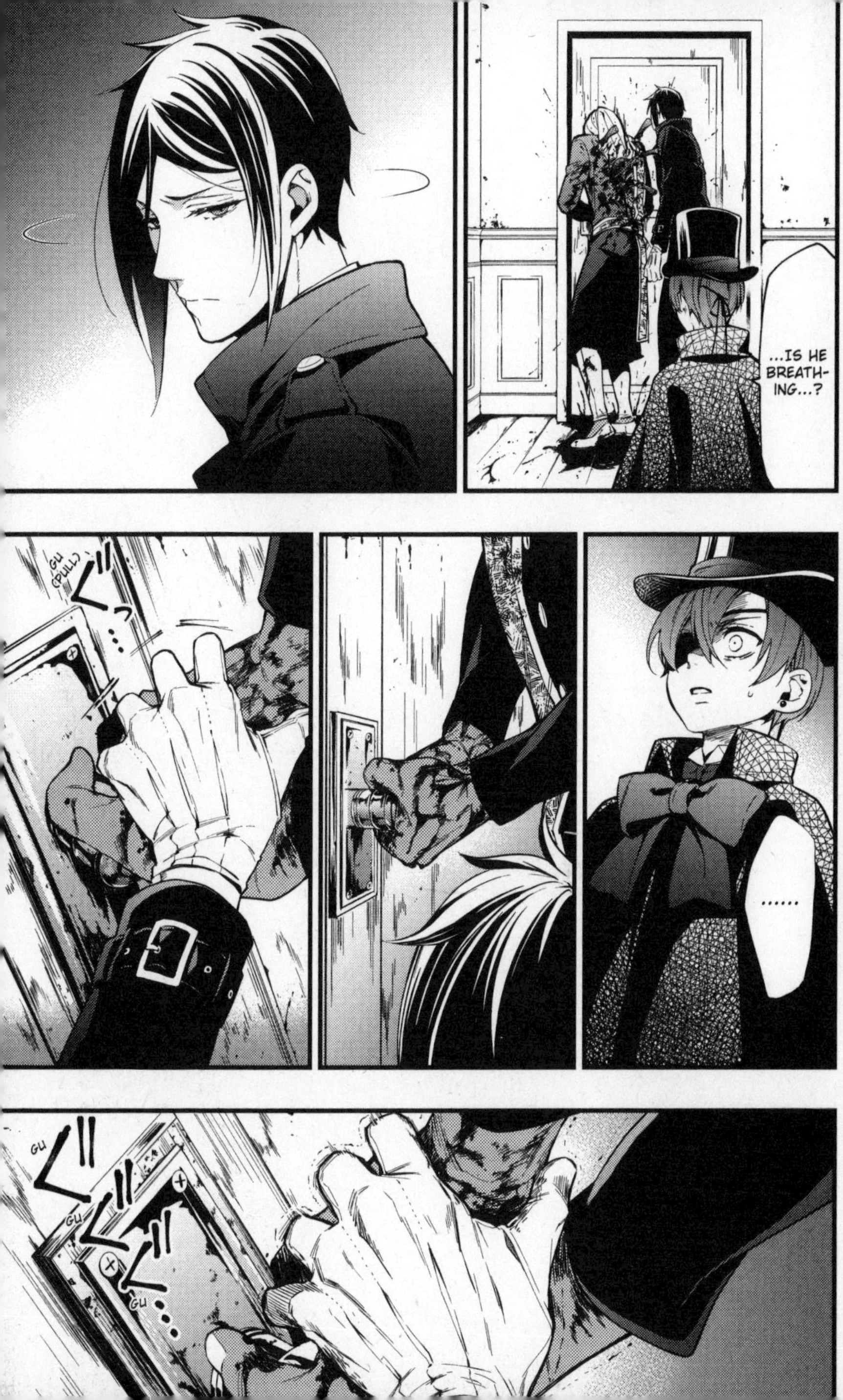
...IS HE BREATHING...?
......
GU (PULL)
GU
GU
GU

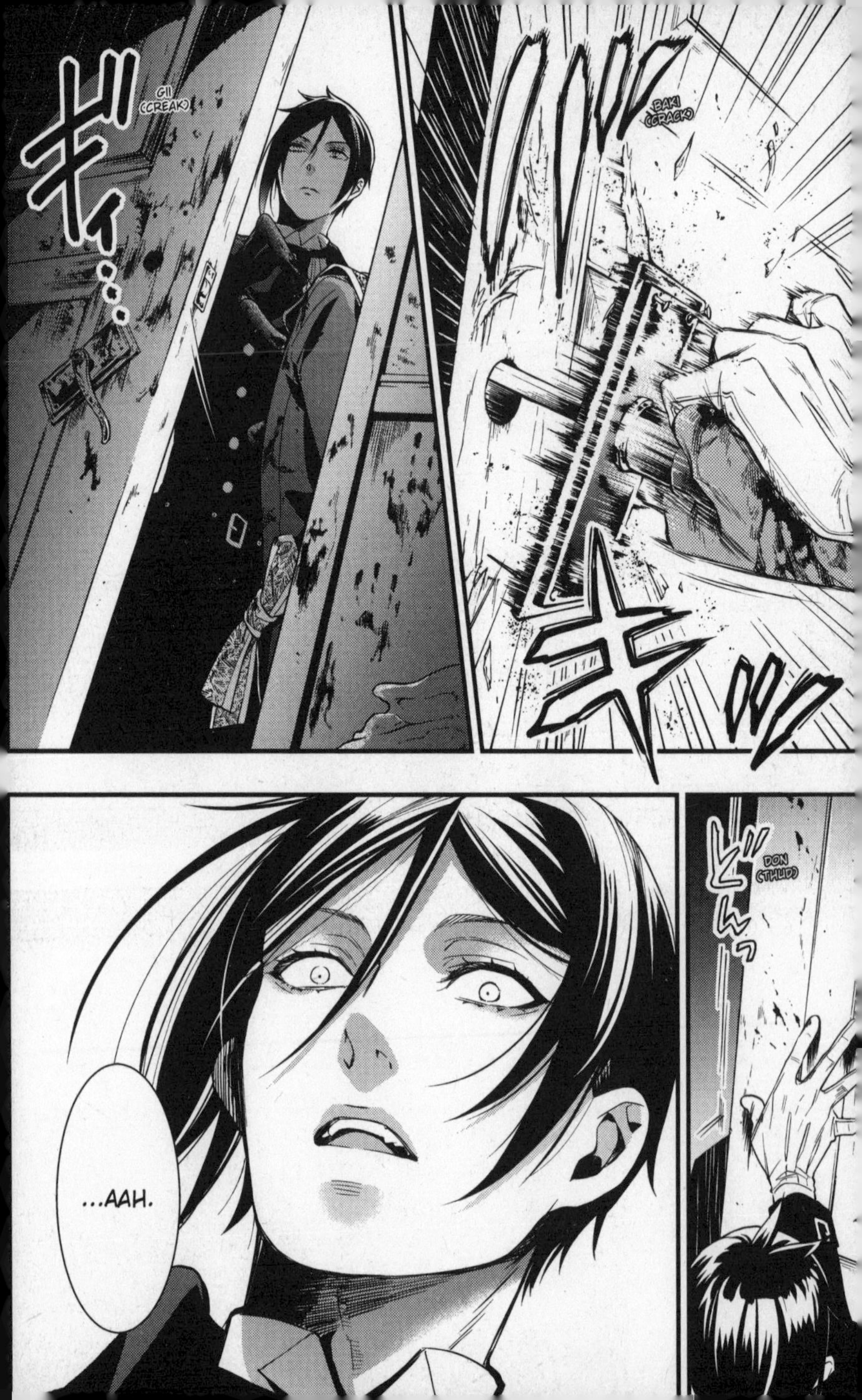
BAKI (CRACK)
GII (CREAK)
DON (THUD)
...AAH.

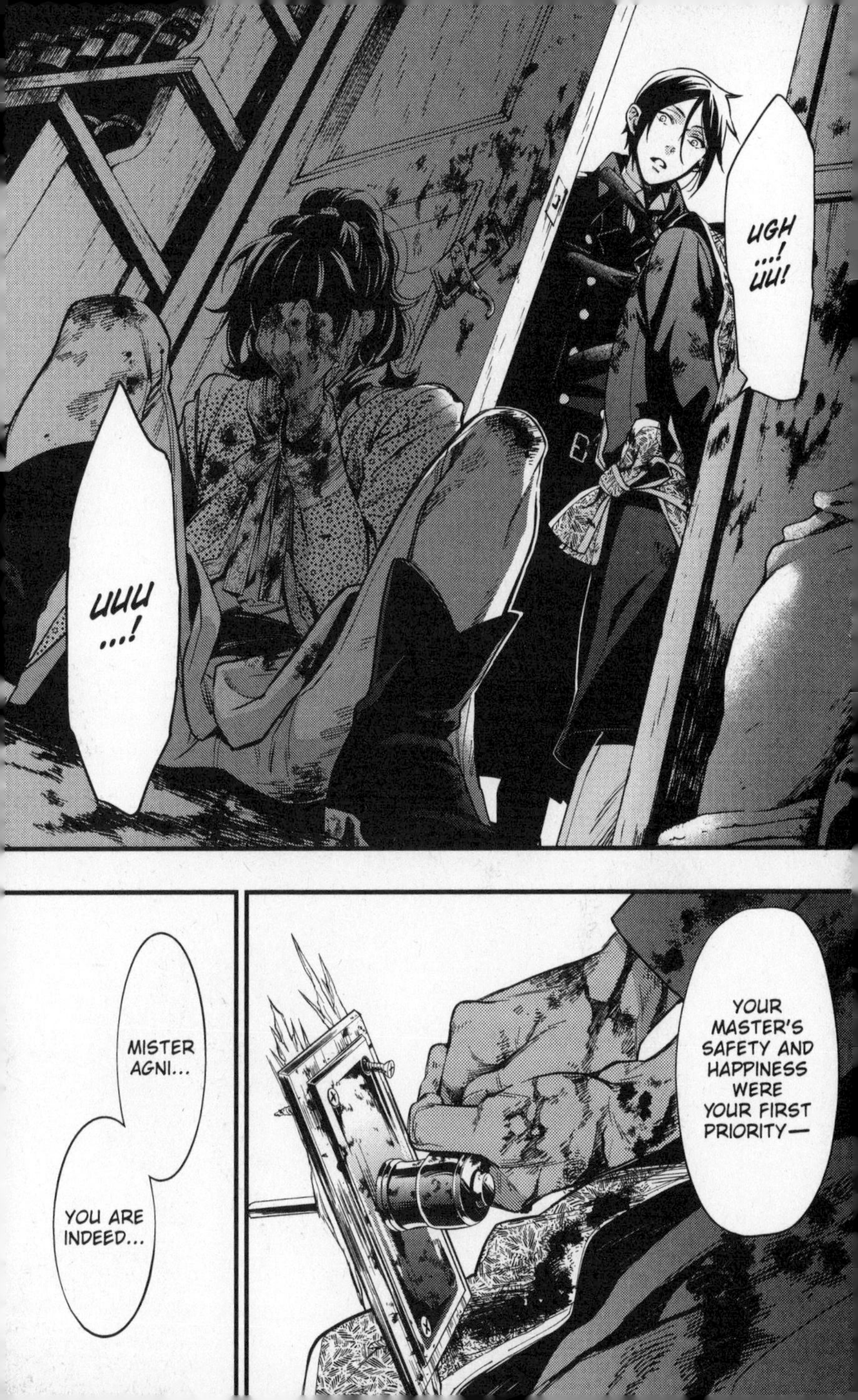
UGH ...! UU!
UUU ...!
YOUR MASTER'S SAFETY AND HAPPINESS WERE YOUR FIRST PRIORITY—
MISTER AGNI...
YOU ARE INDEED...

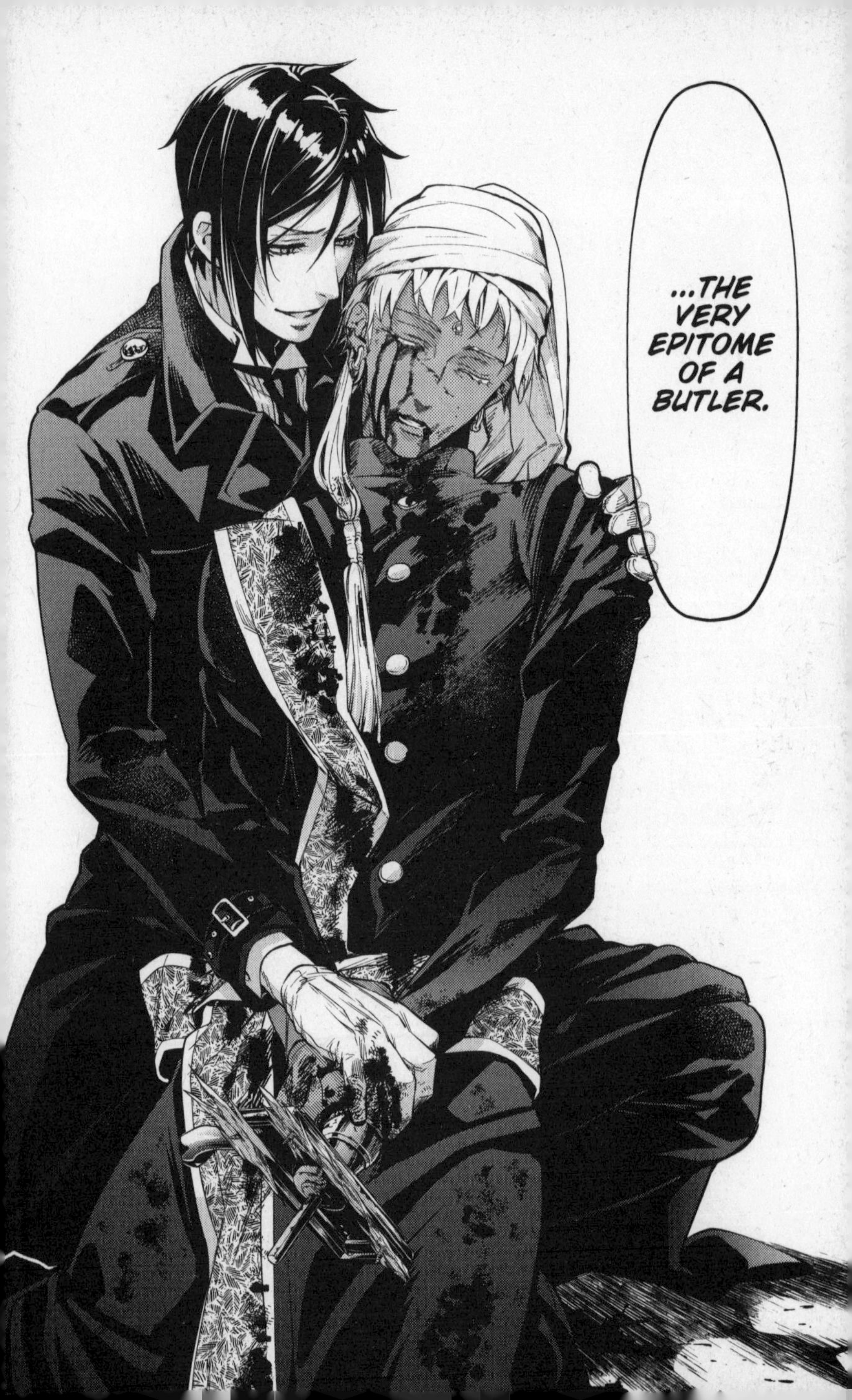
...THE VERY EPITOME OF A BUTLER.

Black Butler

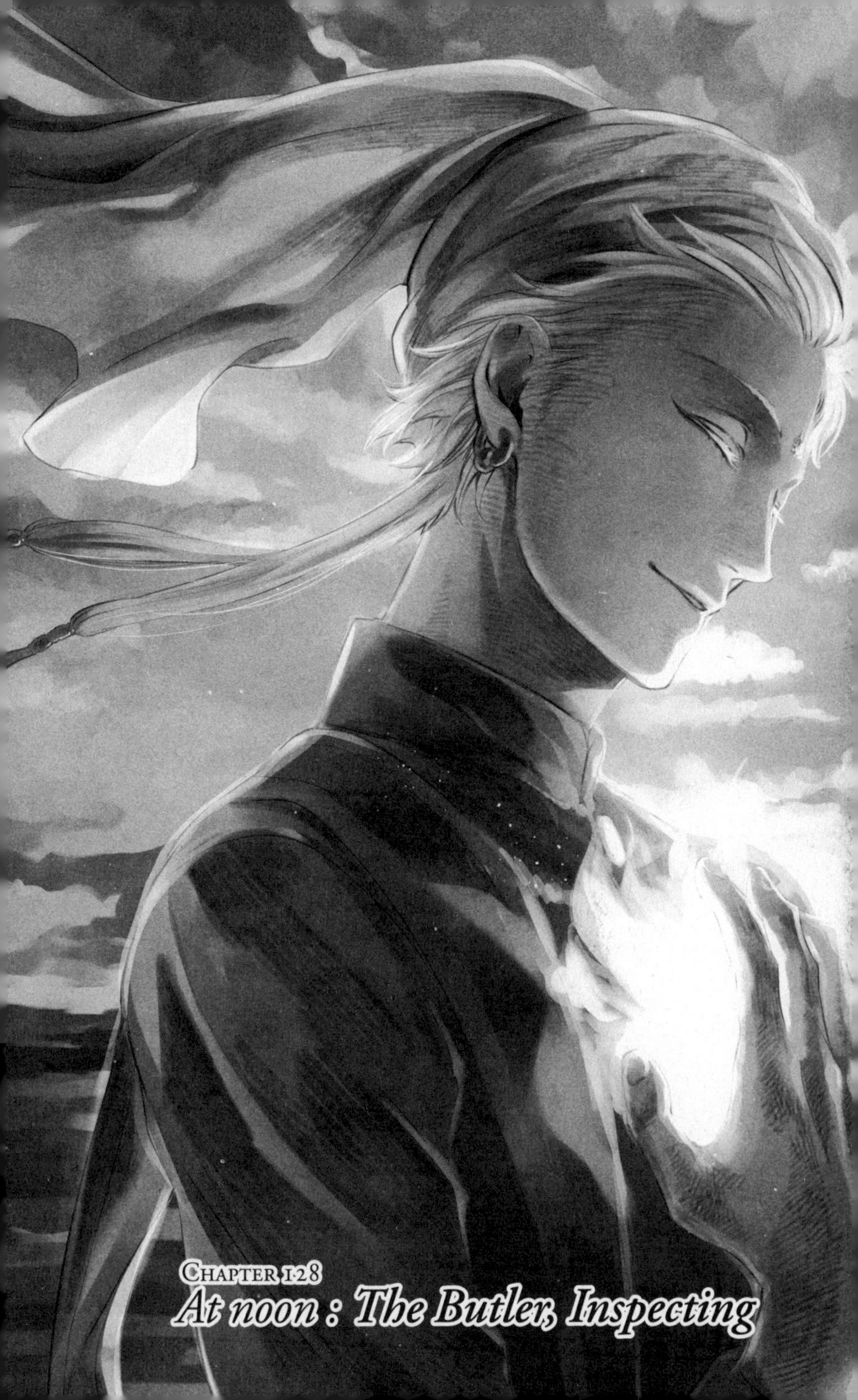
Chapter 128
At noon : The Butler, Inspecting

Black Butler

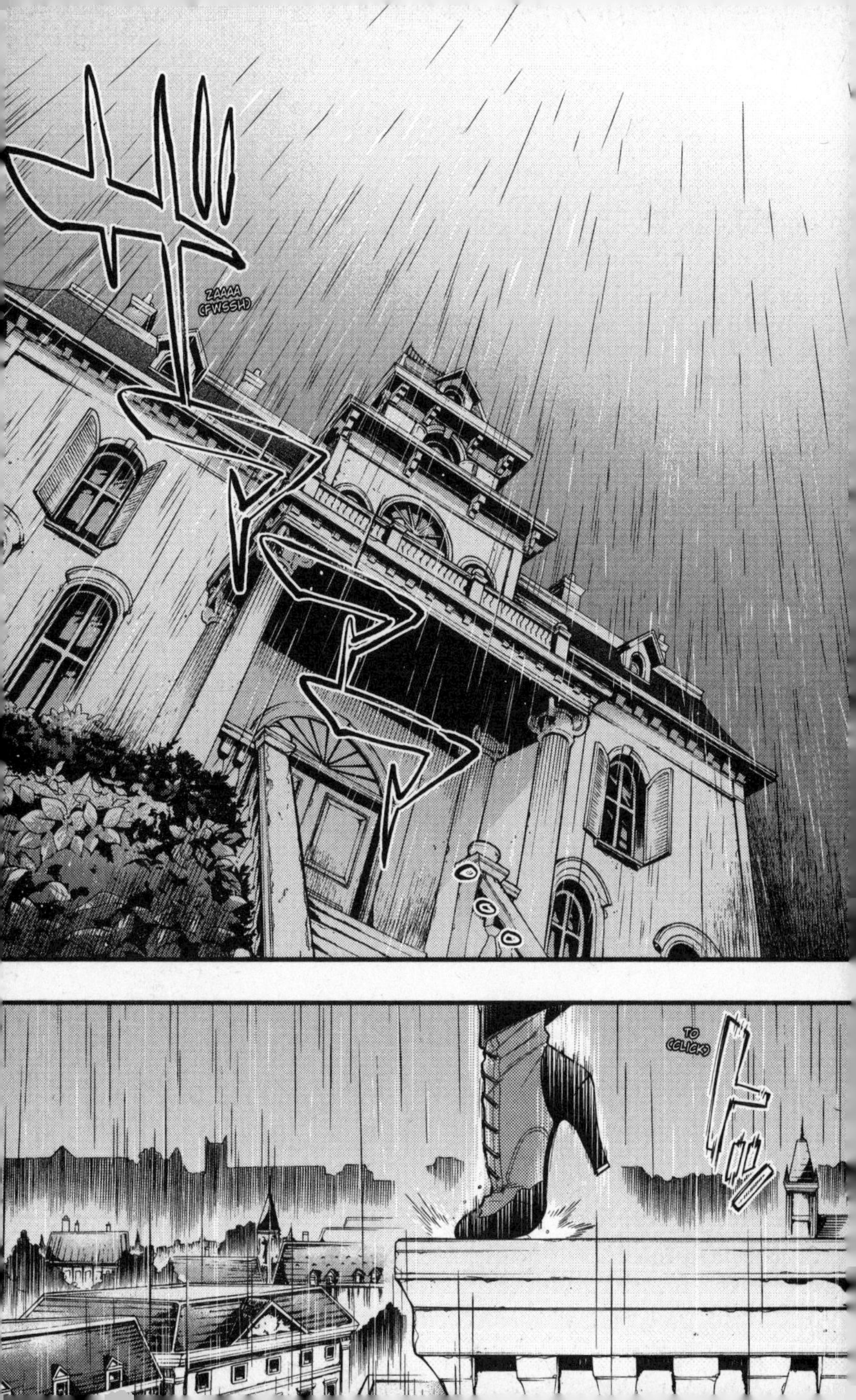
ZAAAA
(FWSSH)
TO
(CLICK)

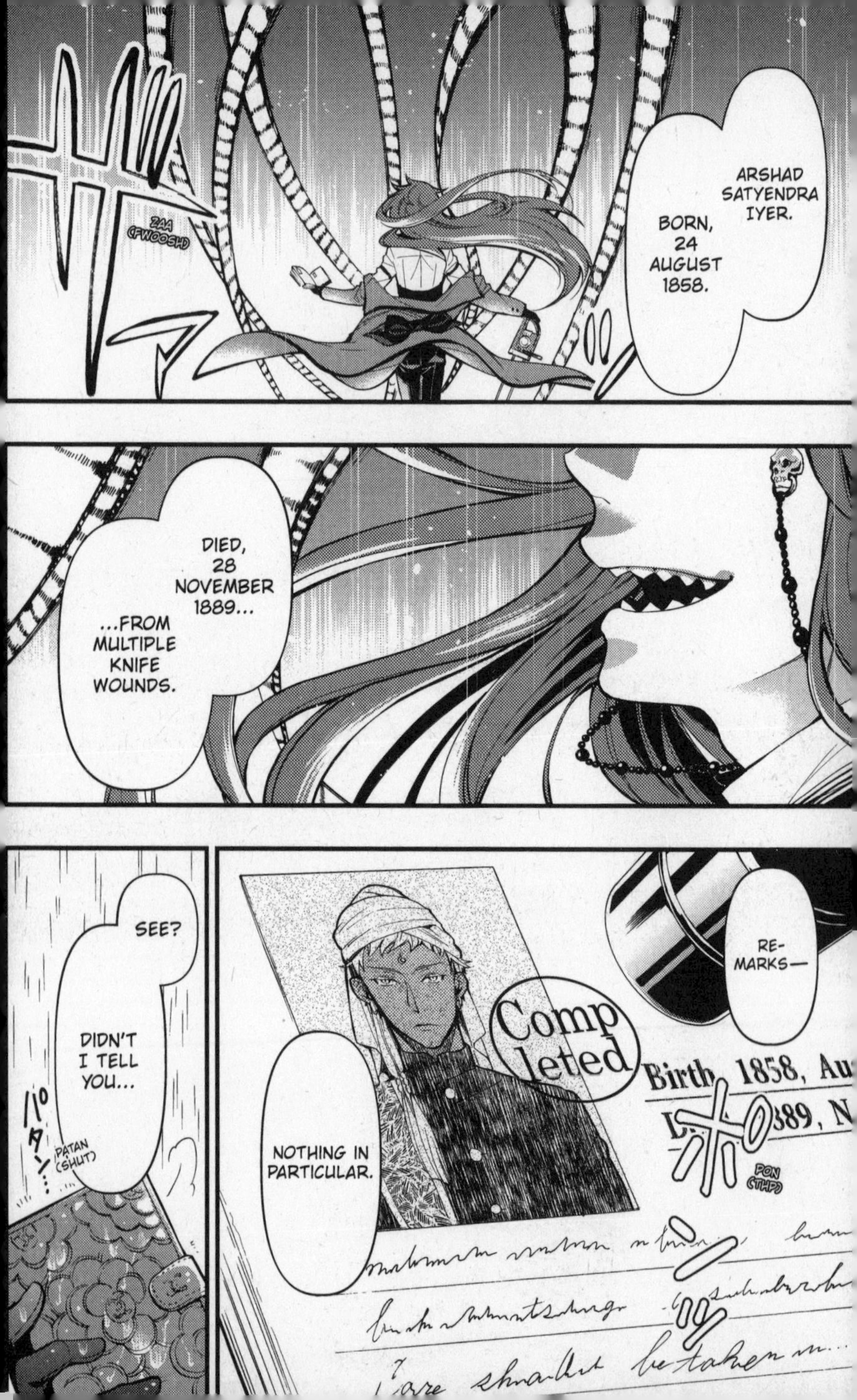
ARSHAD SATYENDRA IYER.
BORN, 24 AUGUST 1858.
ZAA (FWOOSH)
DIED, 28 NOVEMBER 1889...
...FROM MULTIPLE KNIFE WOUNDS.
RE-MARKS—
Completed
Birth, 1858, Au
389, N
NOTHING IN PARTICULAR.
PON (THP)
SEE?
DIDN'T I TELL YOU...
PATAN (SHUT)

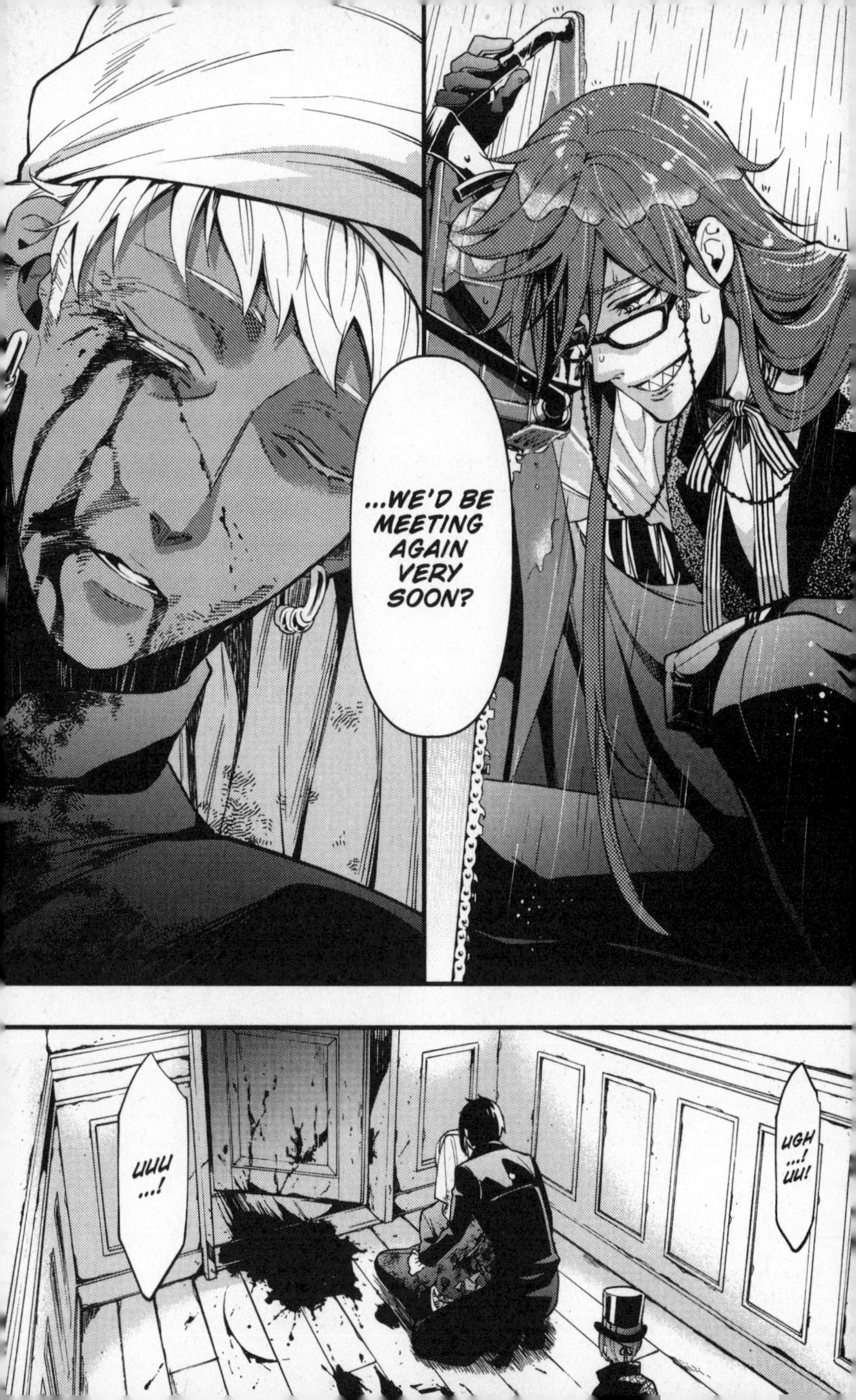
...WE'D BE MEETING AGAIN VERY SOON?
UGH ...! UU!
UUU ...!

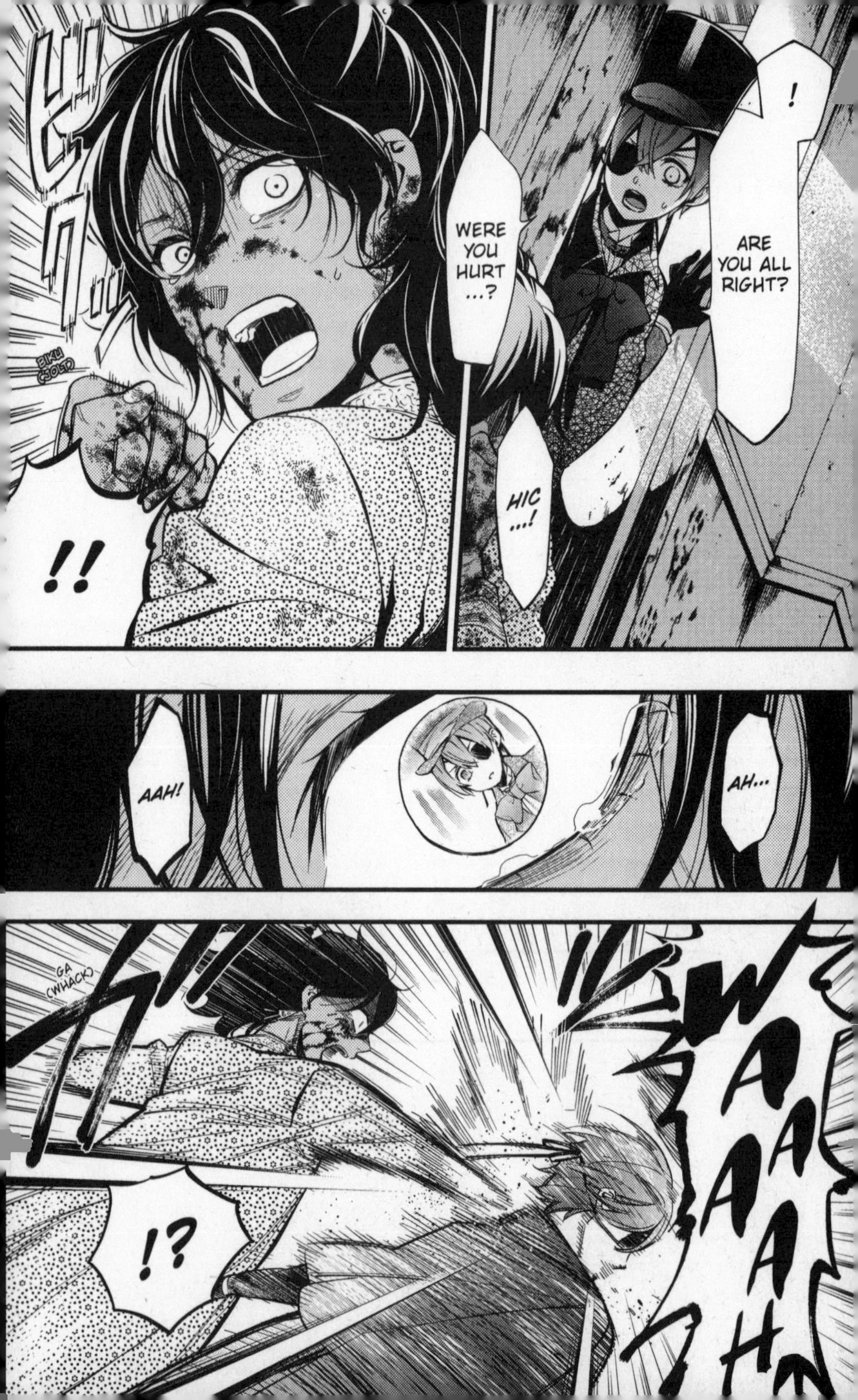
!
ARE YOU ALL RIGHT?
WERE YOU HURT ...?
HIC ...!
BIKU (JOLT)
!!
AH...
AAH!
WAAAAAH
GA (WHACK)
!?

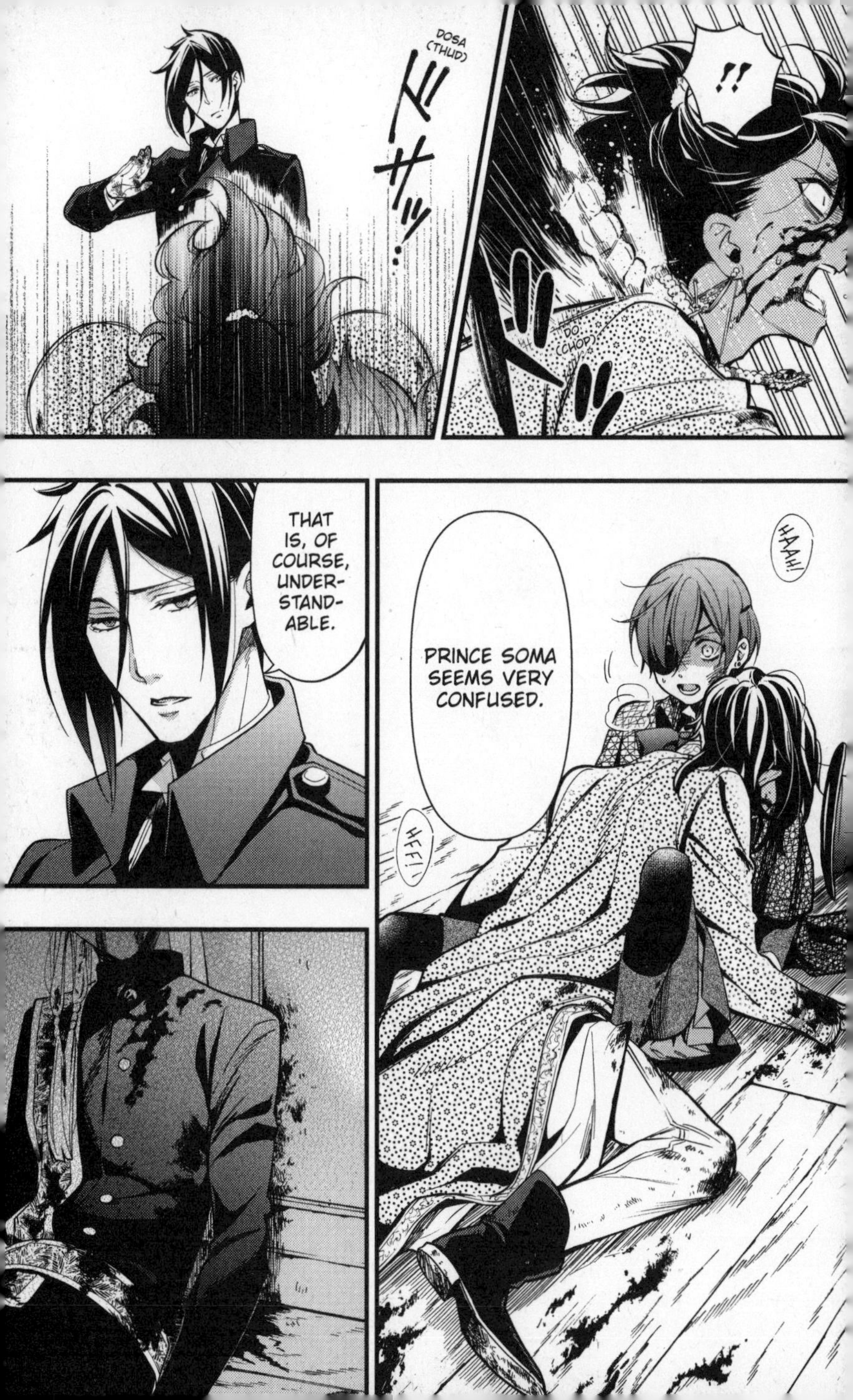
!!
DO (CHOP)
DOSA (THUD)
HAAH!
PRINCE SOMA SEEMS VERY CONFUSED.
HFF!
THAT IS, OF COURSE, UNDER-STAND-ABLE.

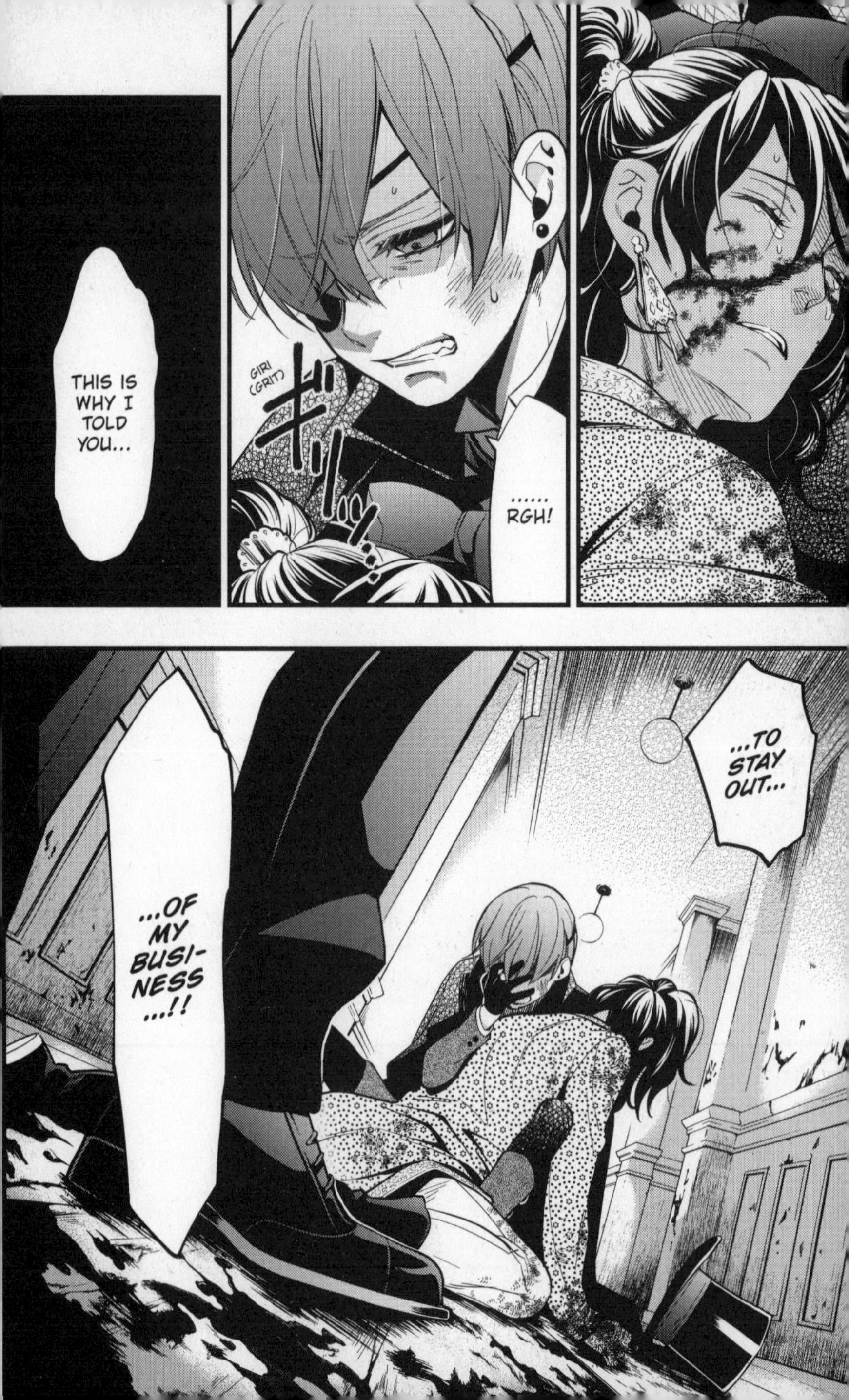
GIRI (GRIT)
......RGH!
THIS IS WHY I TOLD YOU...
...TO STAY OUT...
...OF MY BUSI-NESS...!!

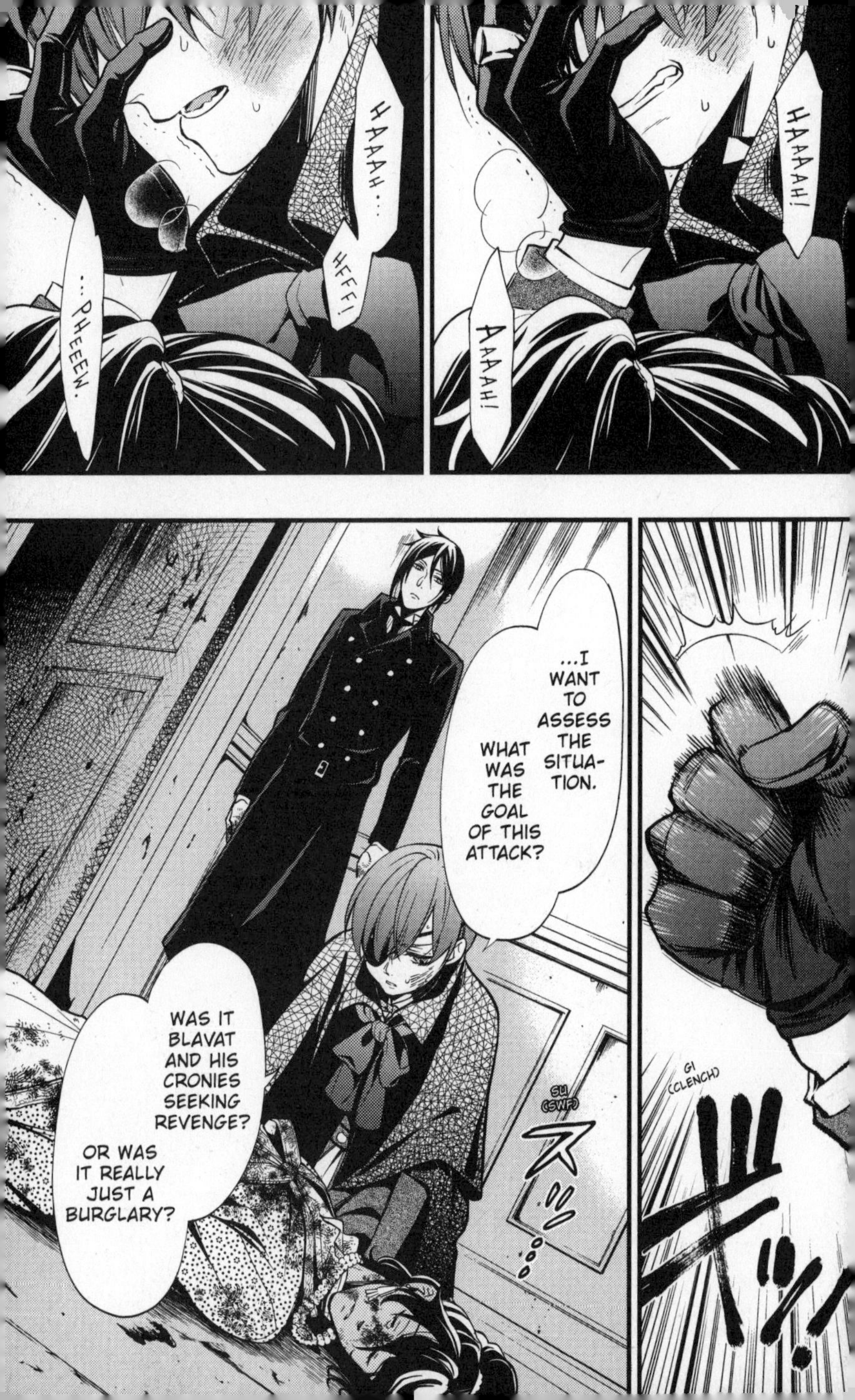
HAAAAH!
AAAAH!
HAAAH...
HFFF!
...PHEEEW.
GI (CLENCH)
...I WANT TO ASSESS THE SITUATION.
WHAT WAS THE GOAL OF THIS ATTACK?
SU (SWF)
WAS IT BLAVAT AND HIS CRONIES SEEKING REVENGE?
OR WAS IT REALLY JUST A BURGLARY?

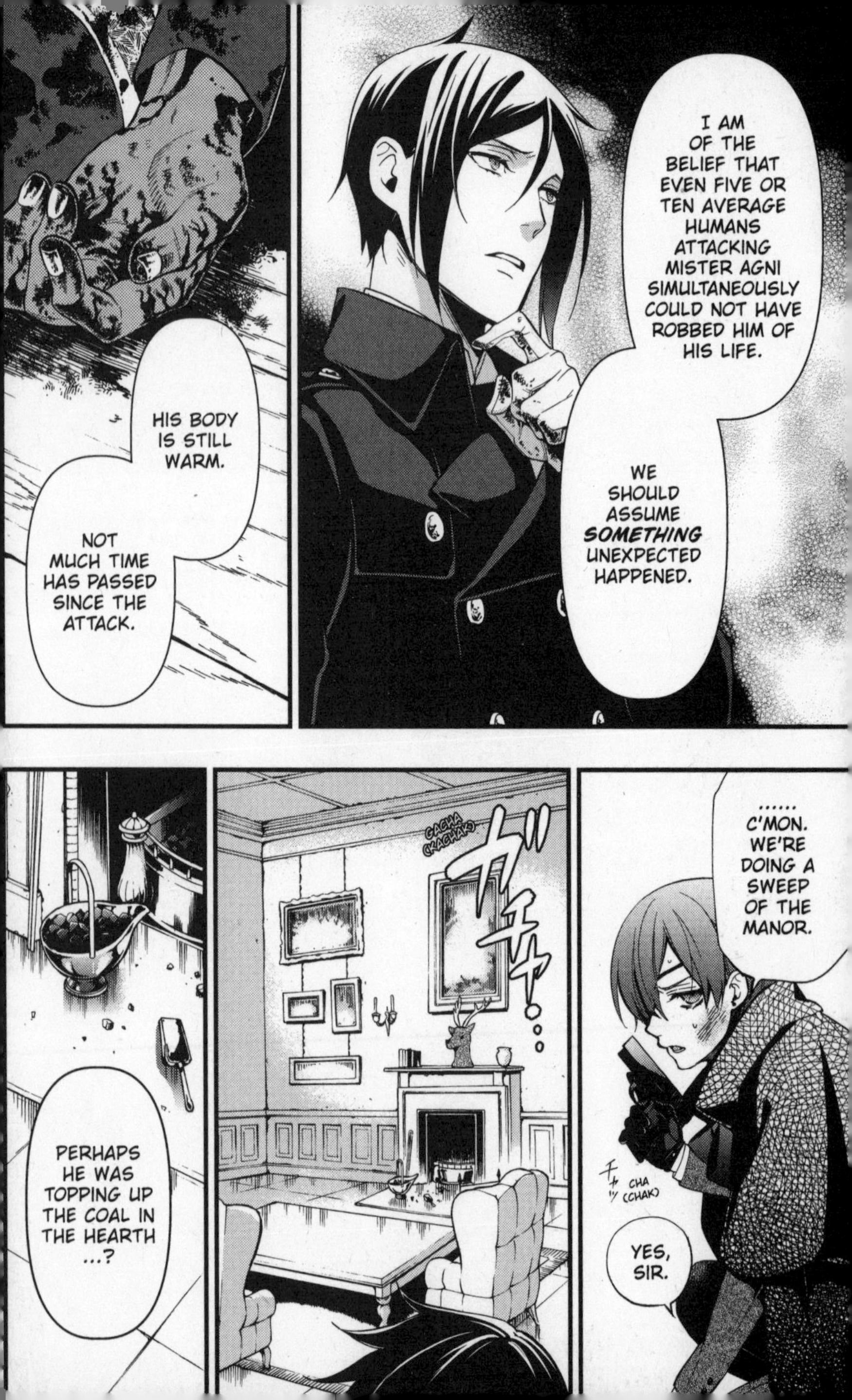
I AM OF THE BELIEF THAT EVEN FIVE OR TEN AVERAGE HUMANS ATTACKING MISTER AGNI SIMULTANEOUSLY COULD NOT HAVE ROBBED HIM OF HIS LIFE.
WE SHOULD ASSUME *SOMETHING* UNEXPECTED HAPPENED.
HIS BODY IS STILL WARM.
NOT MUCH TIME HAS PASSED SINCE THE ATTACK.
...... C'MON. WE'RE DOING A SWEEP OF THE MANOR.
CHA (CHAK)
YES, SIR.
GACHA (KACHAK)
PERHAPS HE WAS TOPPING UP THE COAL IN THE HEARTH ...?

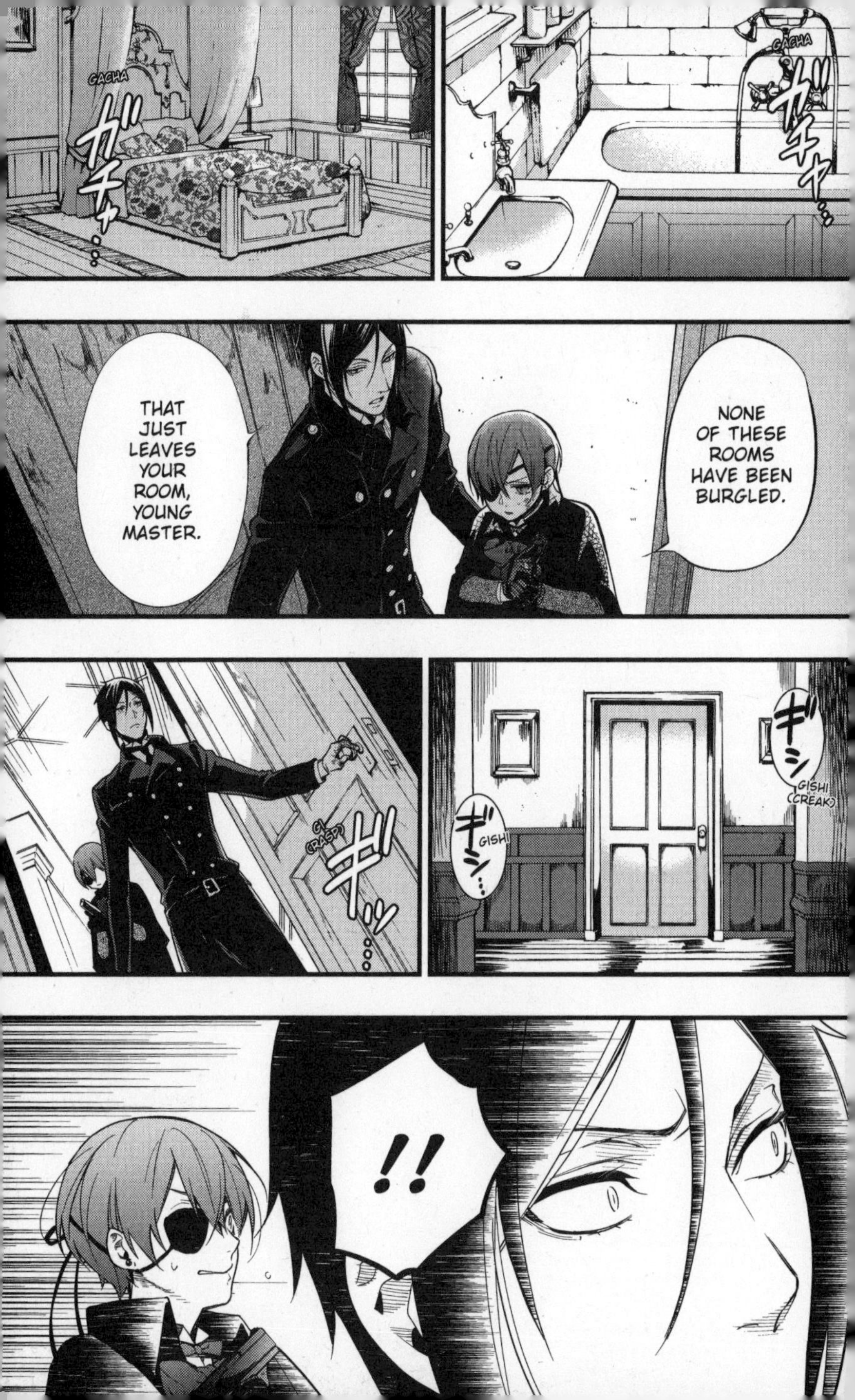

GACHA
ガチャ…
GACHA
ガチャ…
NONE OF THESE ROOMS HAVE BEEN BURGLED.
THAT JUST LEAVES YOUR ROOM, YOUNG MASTER.
ギシ
GISHI (CREAK)
ギシ…
GISHI
GI (RASP)
ギッ…
!!

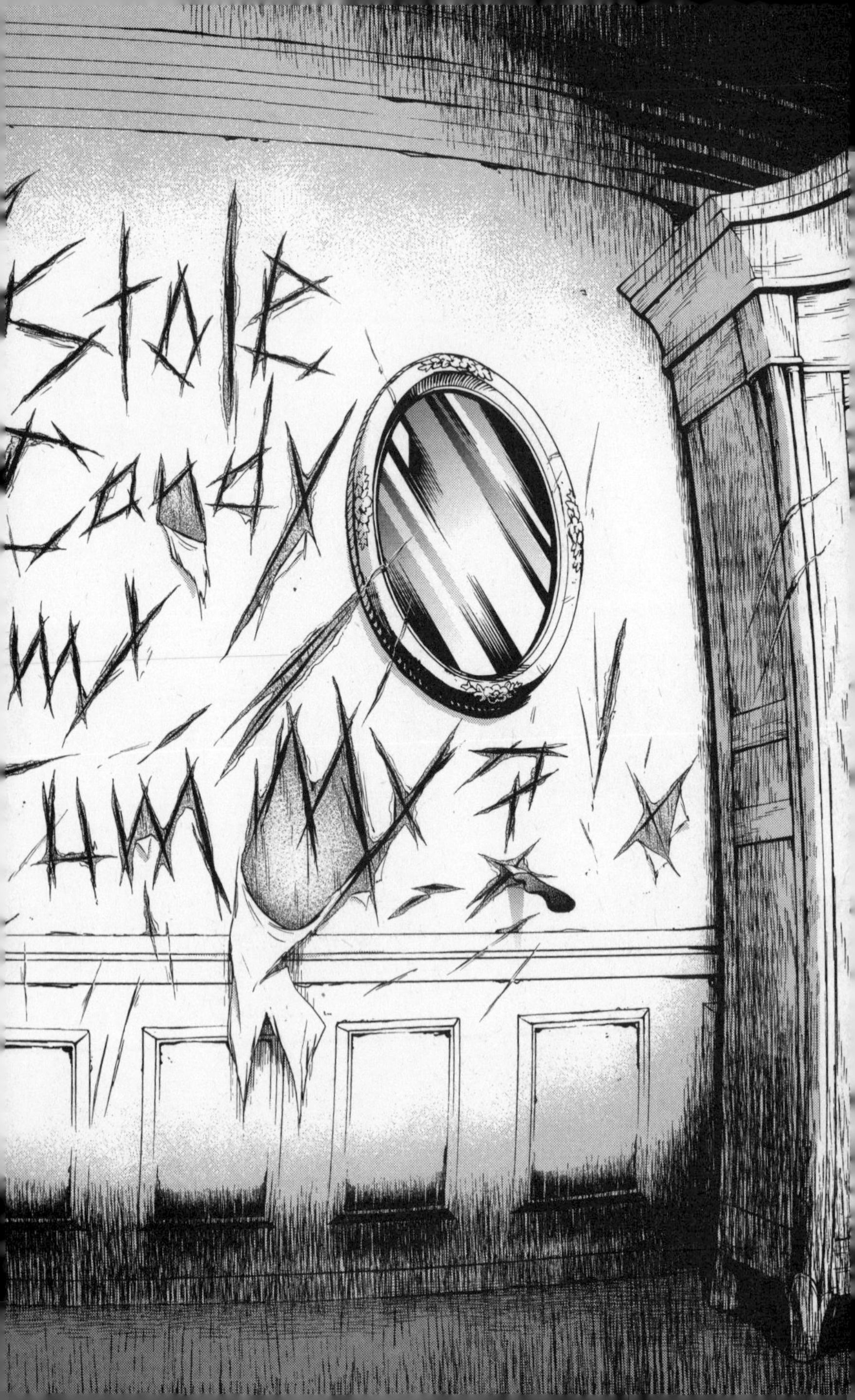
stole
candy

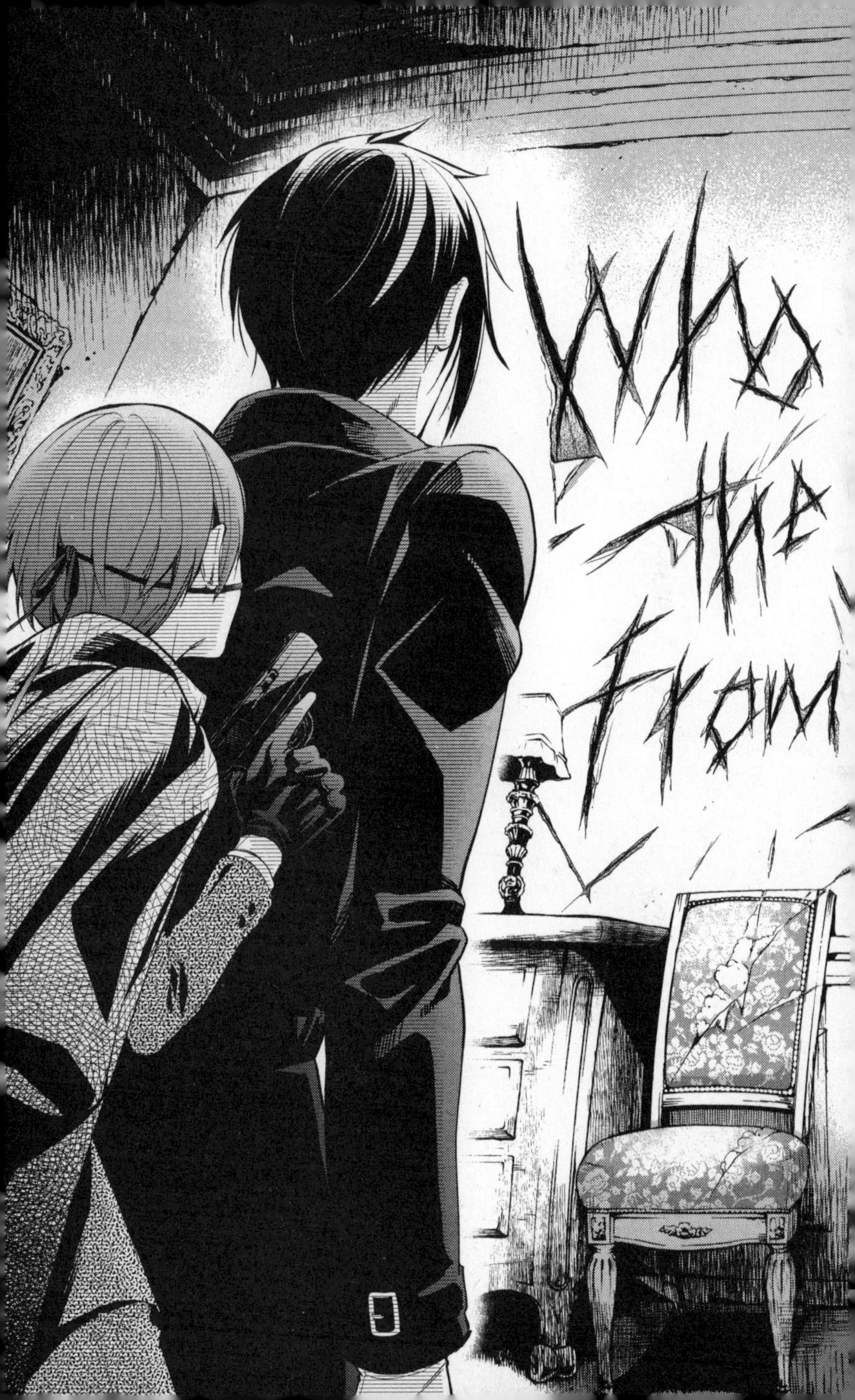
Who
the
from

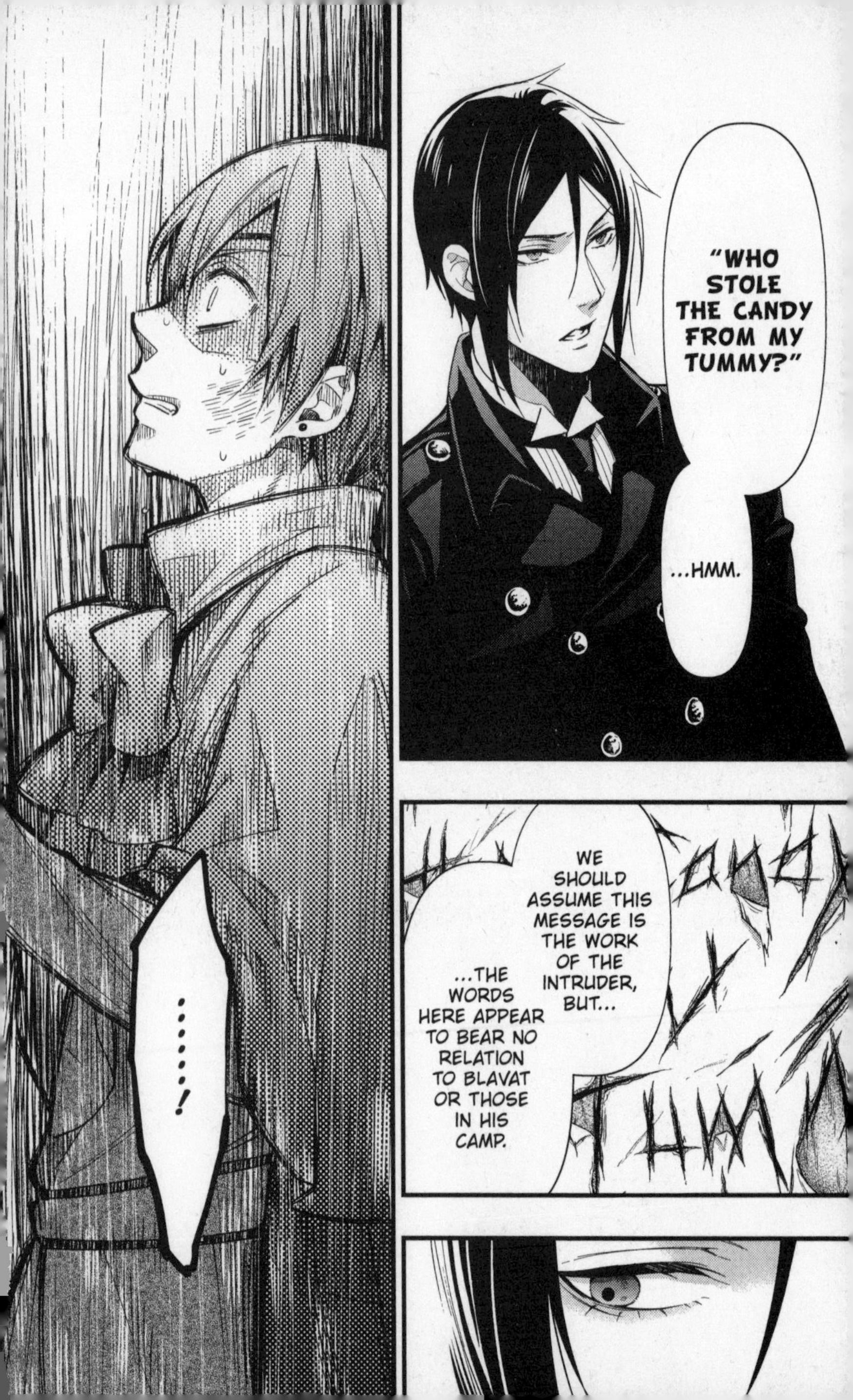
"WHO STOLE THE CANDY FROM MY TUMMY?"
...HMM.
WE SHOULD ASSUME THIS MESSAGE IS THE WORK OF THE INTRUDER, BUT...
...THE WORDS HERE APPEAR TO BEAR NO RELATION TO BLAVAT OR THOSE IN HIS CAMP.
......!

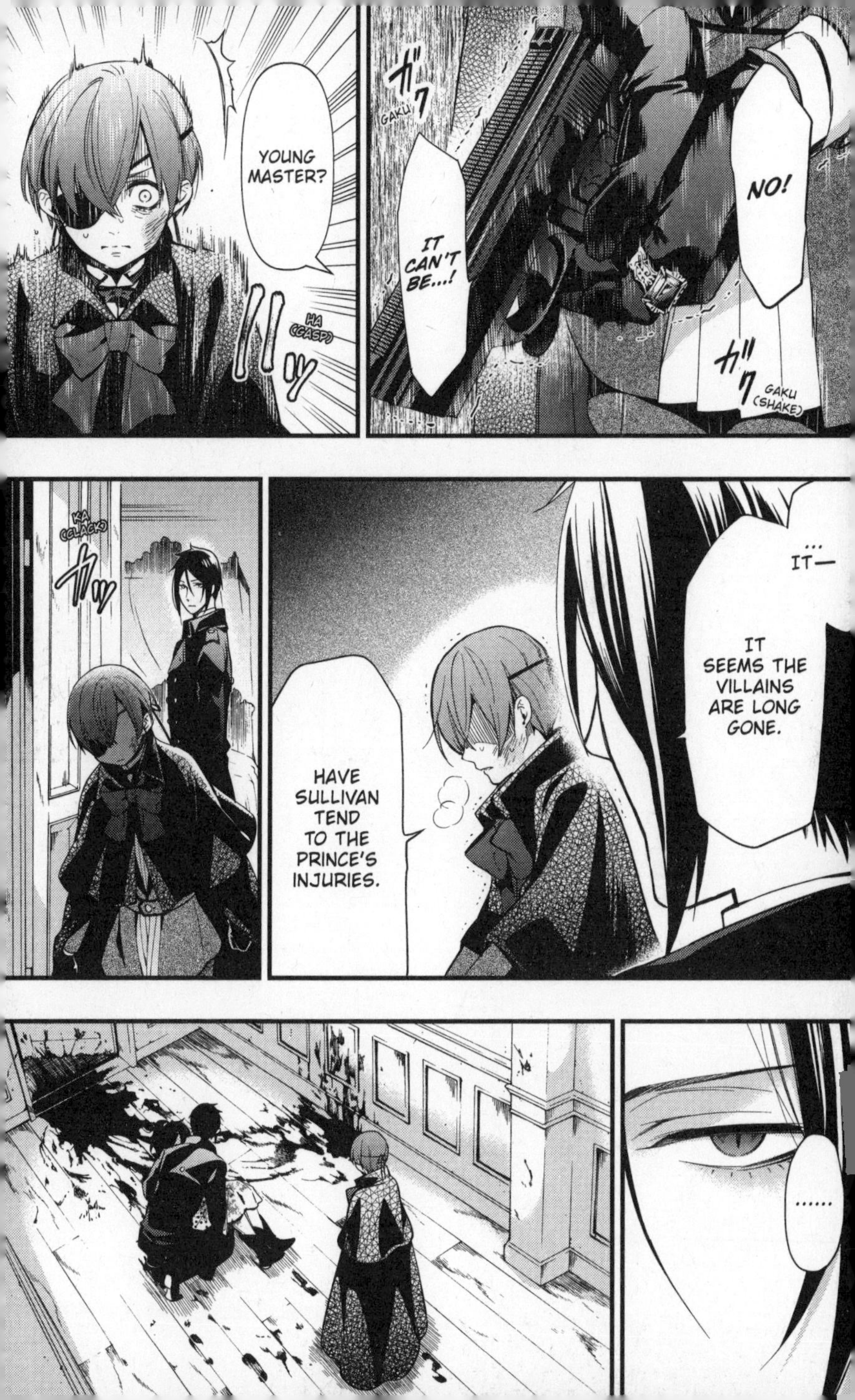
NO!
GAKU (SHAKE)
IT CAN'T BE...!
GAKU
YOUNG MASTER?
HA (GASP)
... IT—
IT SEEMS THE VILLAINS ARE LONG GONE.
HAVE SULLIVAN TEND TO THE PRINCE'S INJURIES.
KA (CLACK)
......

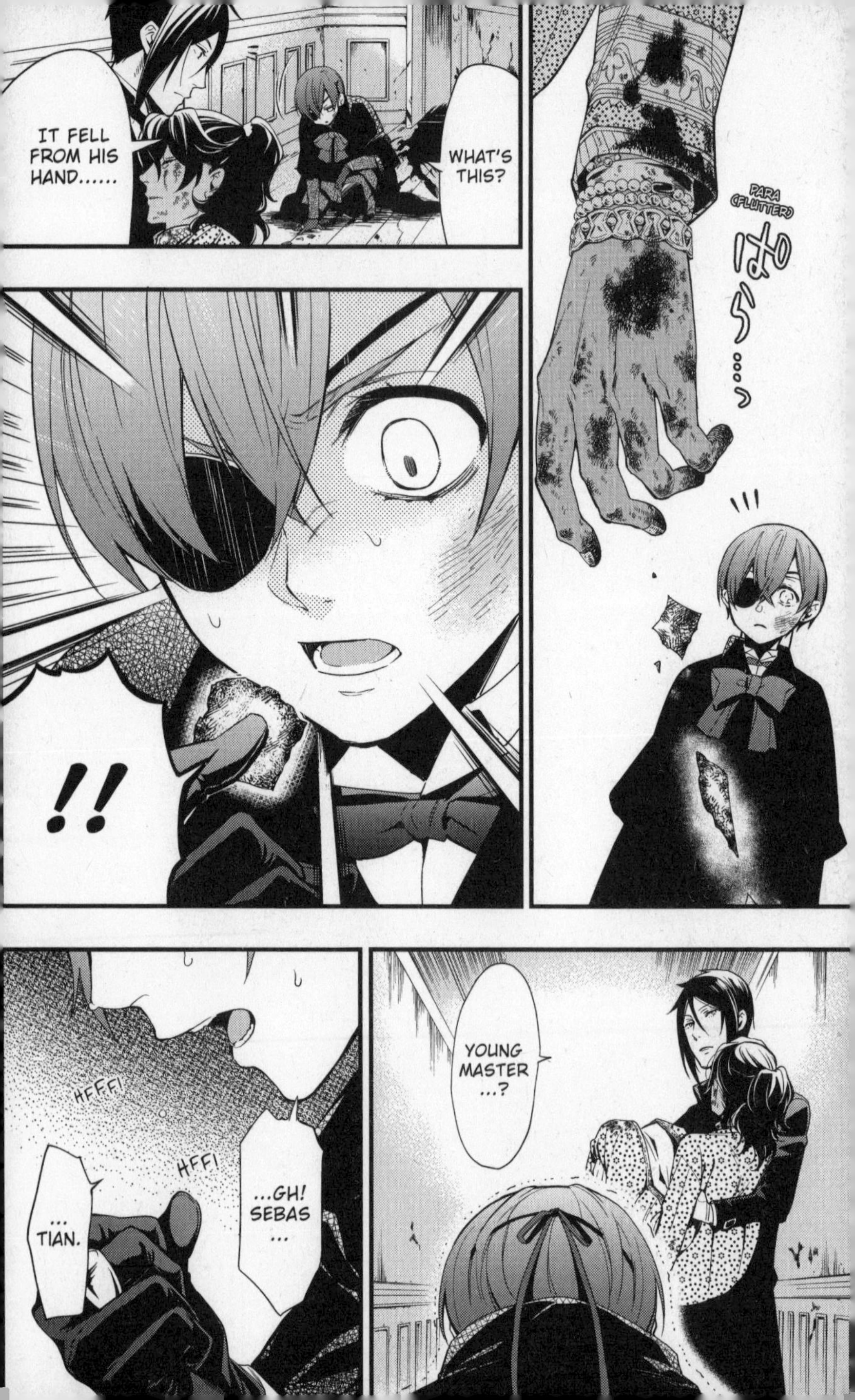
PARA (FLUTTER)
ぱら…
WHAT'S THIS?
IT FELL FROM HIS HAND......
!!
YOUNG MASTER ...?
HFFF!
...GH! SEBAS ...
HFF!
... TIAN.

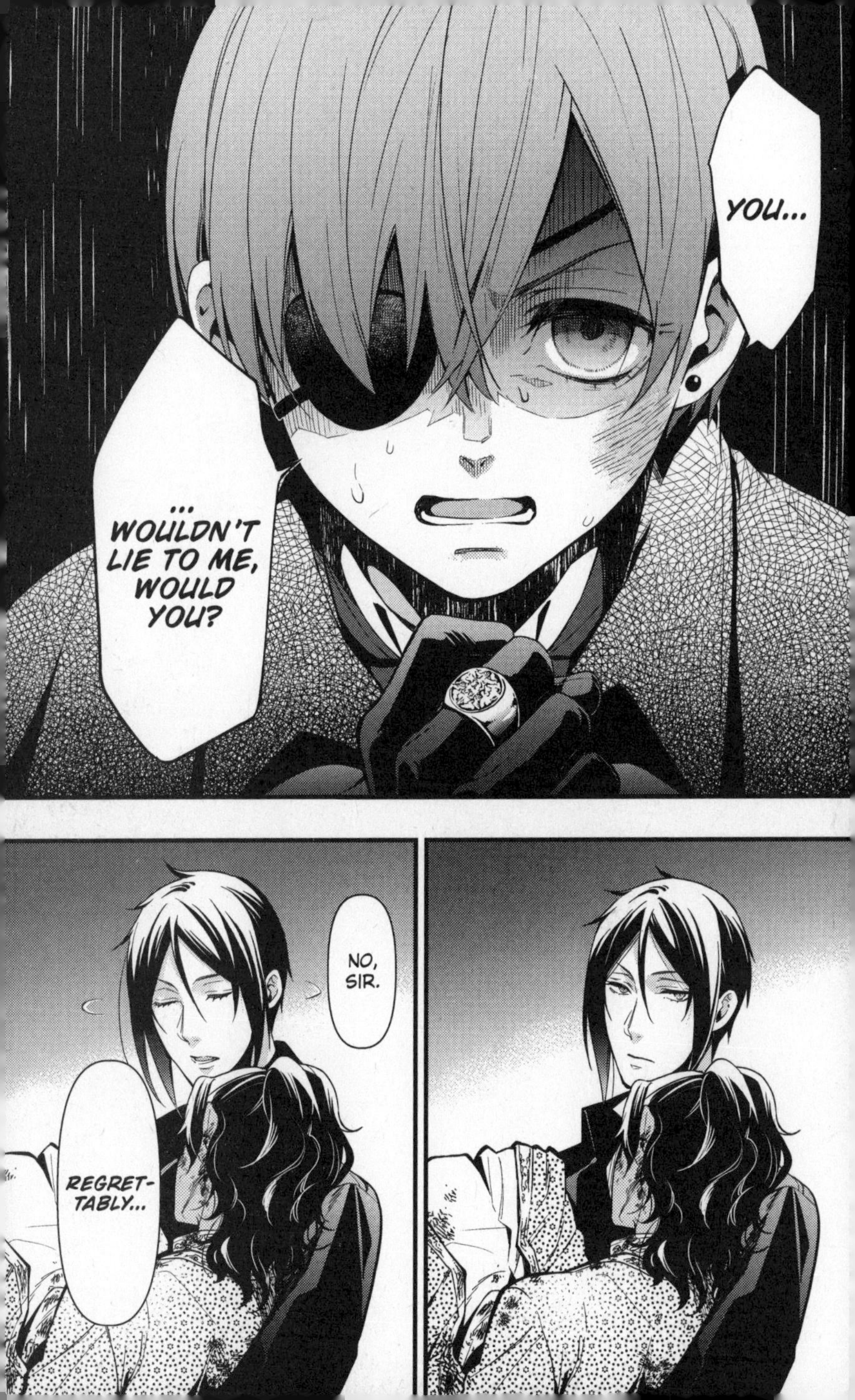
YOU...
...WOULDN'T LIE TO ME, WOULD YOU?
NO, SIR.
REGRET-TABLY...

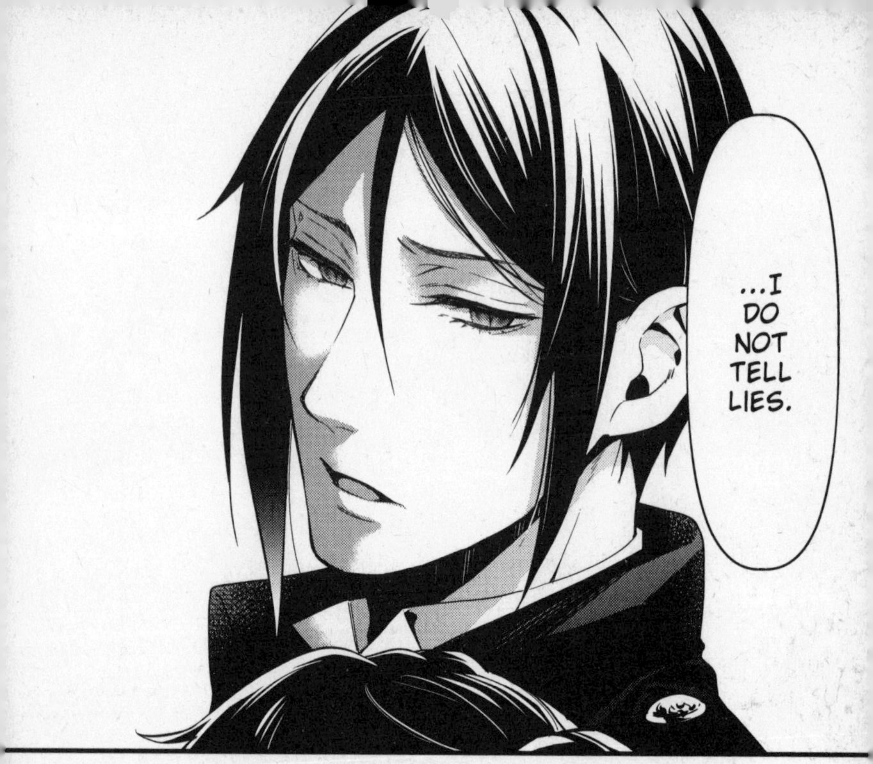
...I DO NOT TELL LIES.
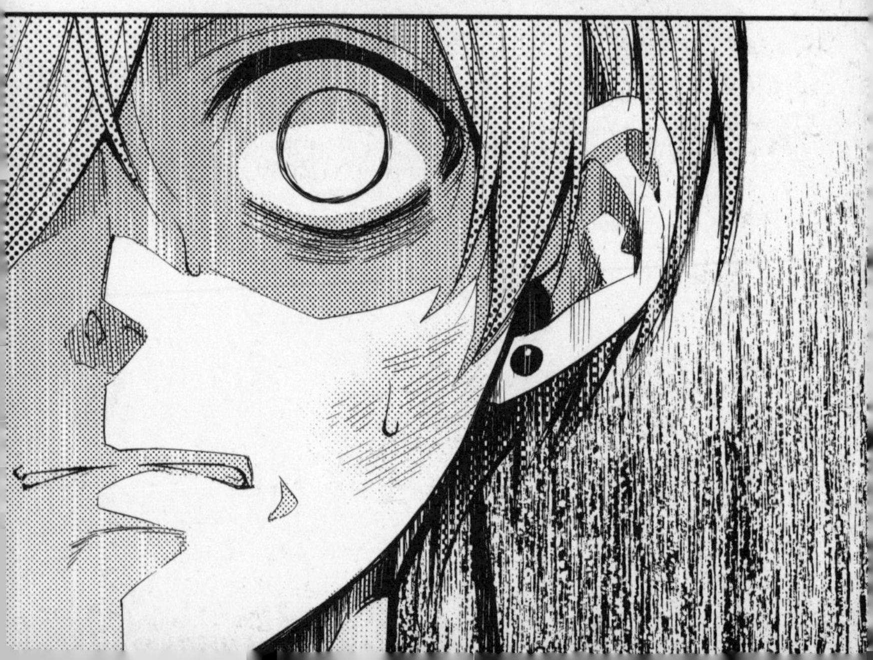

Black Butler

CHAPTER 1·29
In the afternoon : The Butler, Bedevilled

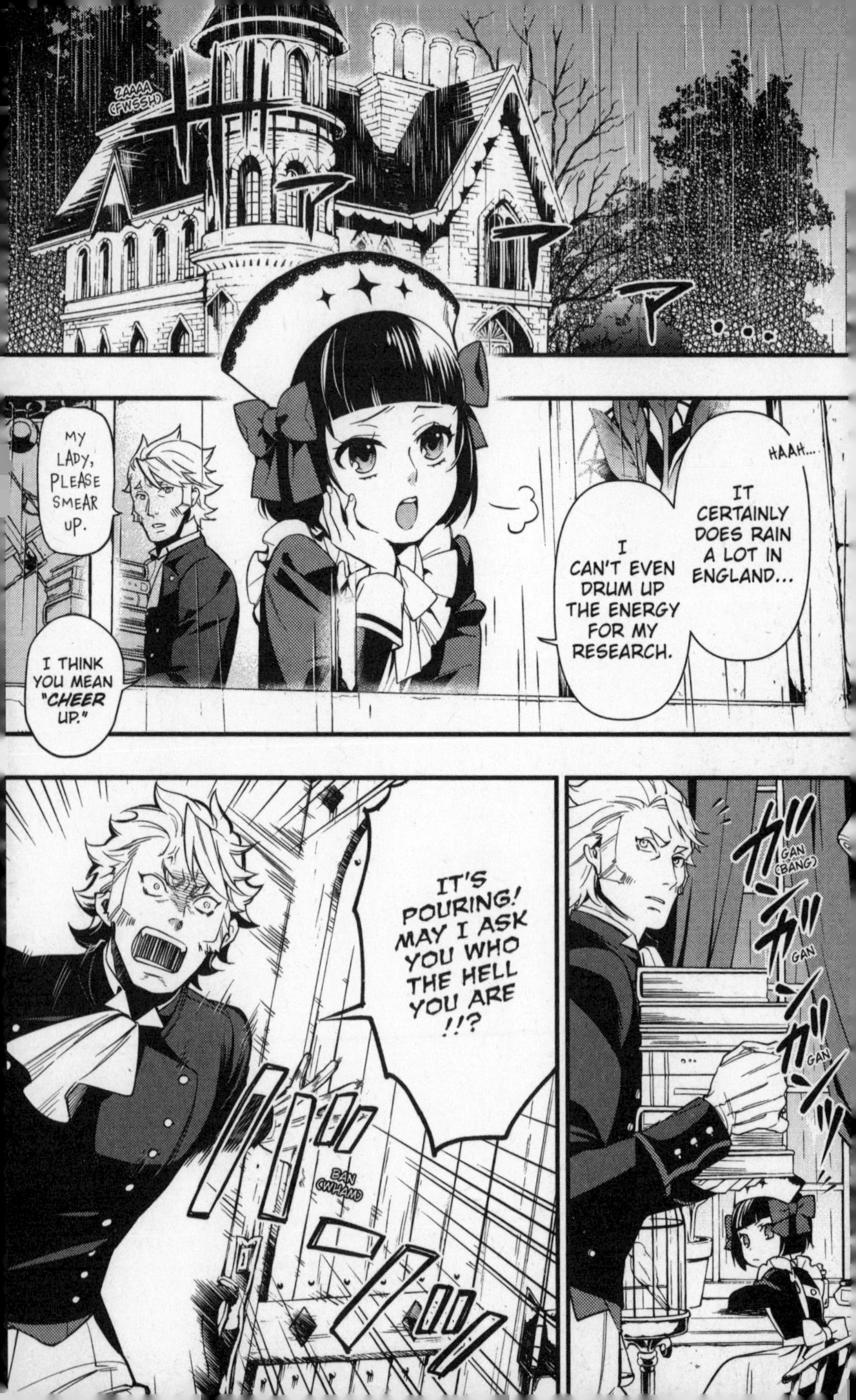
ZAAAA (FWSSH)
HAAH...
IT CERTAINLY DOES RAIN A LOT IN ENGLAND...
I CAN'T EVEN DRUM UP THE ENERGY FOR MY RESEARCH.
MY LADY, PLEASE SMEAR UP.
I THINK YOU MEAN "CHEER UP."
GAN (BANG)
GAN
GAN
...
IT'S POURING! MAY I ASK YOU WHO THE HELL YOU ARE!!?
BAN (WHAM)

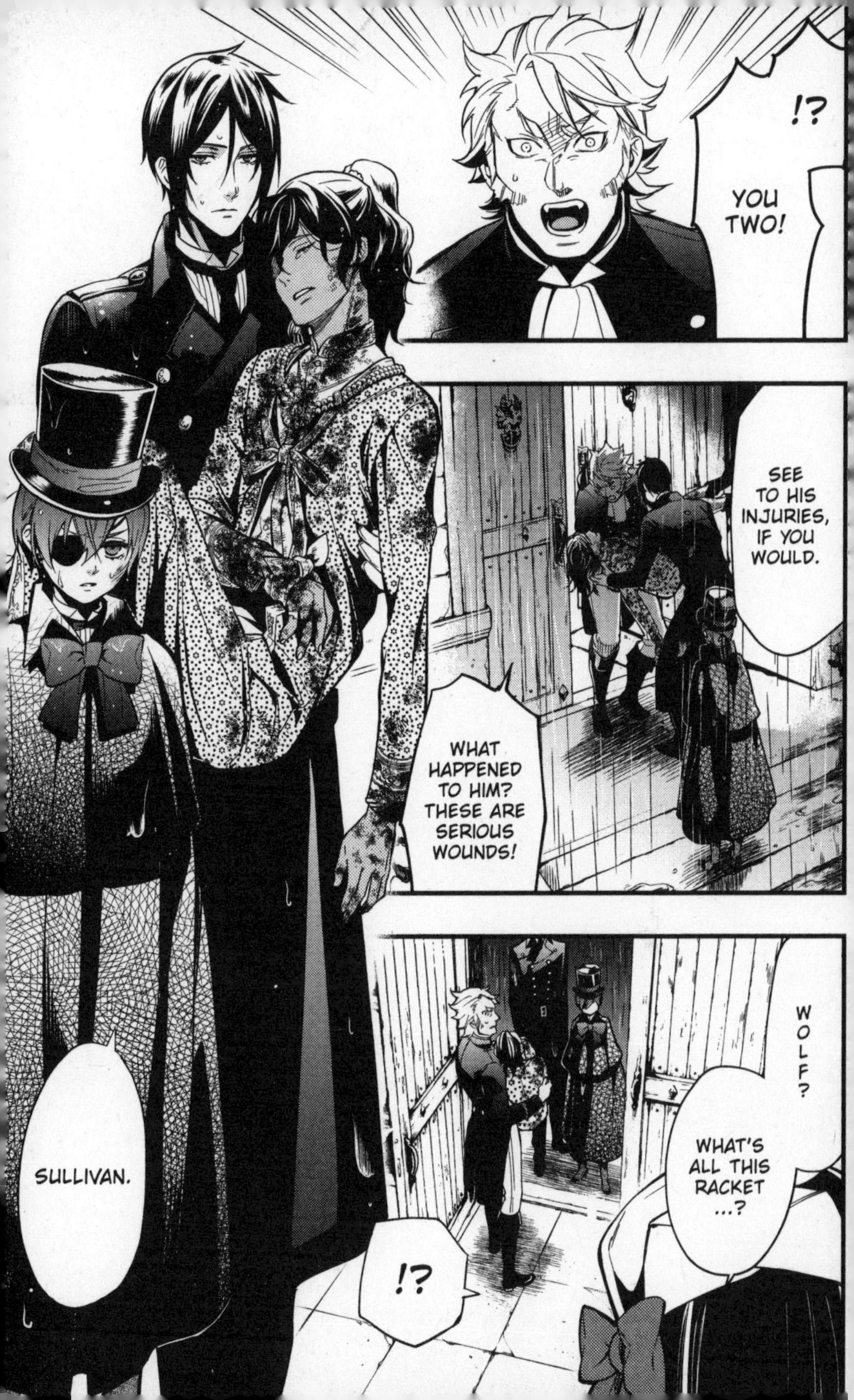
!?
YOU TWO!
SEE TO HIS INJURIES, IF YOU WOULD.
WHAT HAPPENED TO HIM? THESE ARE SERIOUS WOUNDS!
WOLF?
WHAT'S ALL THIS RACKET ...?
!?
SULLIVAN.

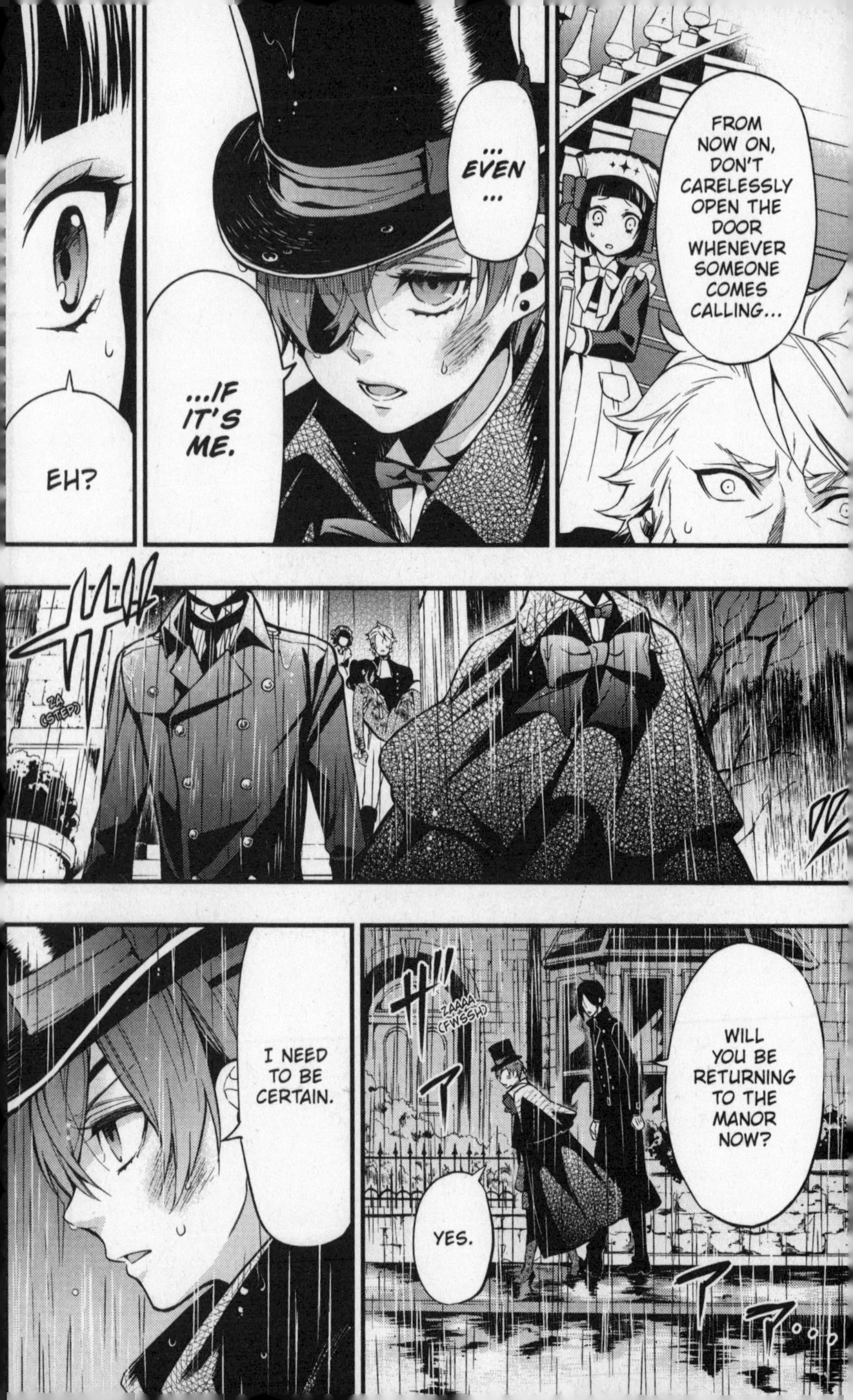
FROM NOW ON, DON'T CARELESSLY OPEN THE DOOR WHENEVER SOMEONE COMES CALLING...
...EVEN...
...IF IT'S ME.
EH?
ZA (STEP)
WILL YOU BE RETURNING TO THE MANOR NOW?
ZAAAA (FWSSH)
YES.
I NEED TO BE CERTAIN.

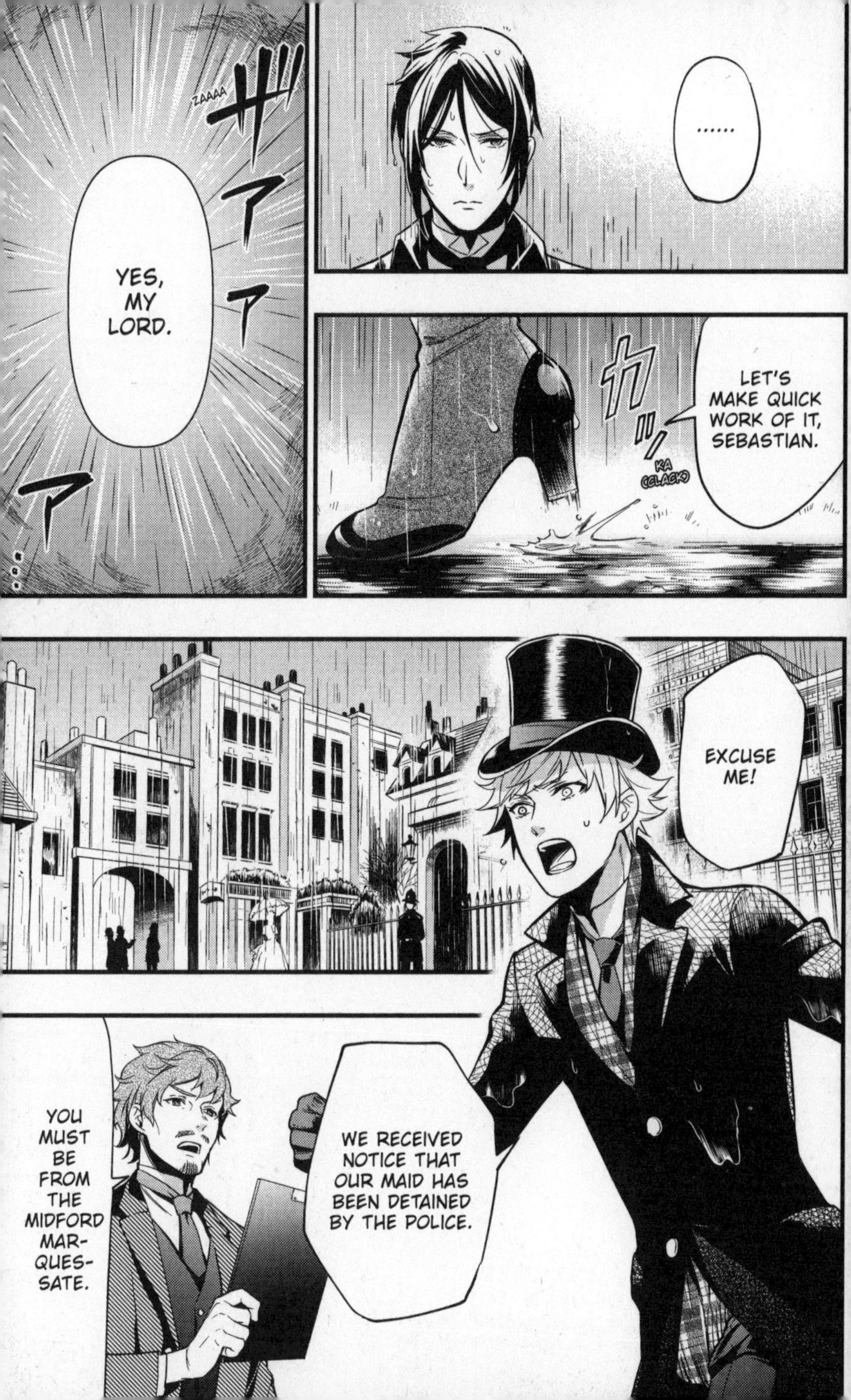

......
LET'S MAKE QUICK WORK OF IT, SEBASTIAN.
KA (CLACK)
ZAAAA
YES, MY LORD.
EXCUSE ME!
WE RECEIVED NOTICE THAT OUR MAID HAS BEEN DETAINED BY THE POLICE.
YOU MUST BE FROM THE MIDFORD MAR-QUES-SATE.

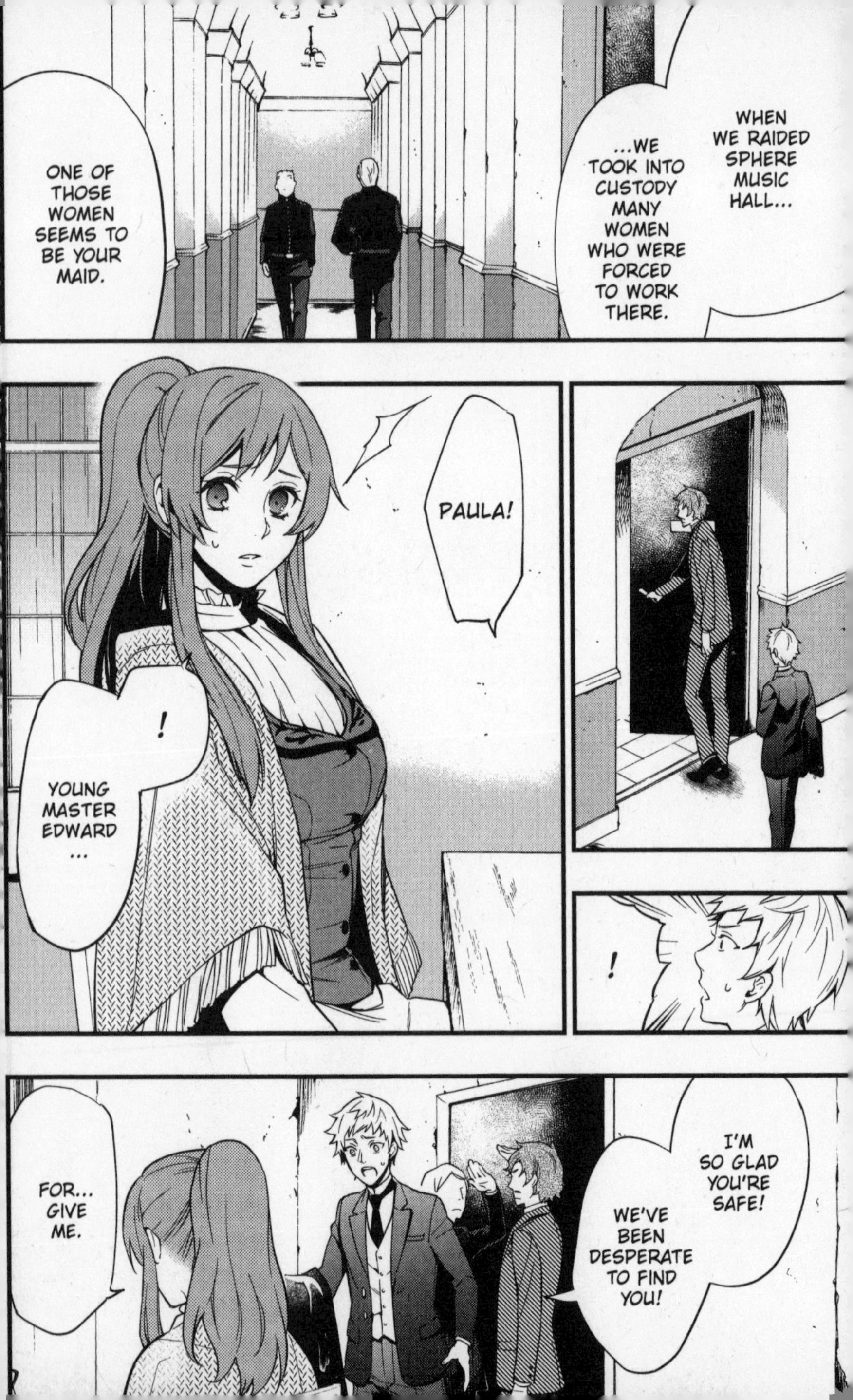
WHEN WE RAIDED SPHERE MUSIC HALL...
...WE TOOK INTO CUSTODY MANY WOMEN WHO WERE FORCED TO WORK THERE.
ONE OF THOSE WOMEN SEEMS TO BE YOUR MAID.
!
PAULA!
!
YOUNG MASTER EDWARD...
I'M SO GLAD YOU'RE SAFE!
WE'VE BEEN DESPERATE TO FIND YOU!
FOR... GIVE ME.

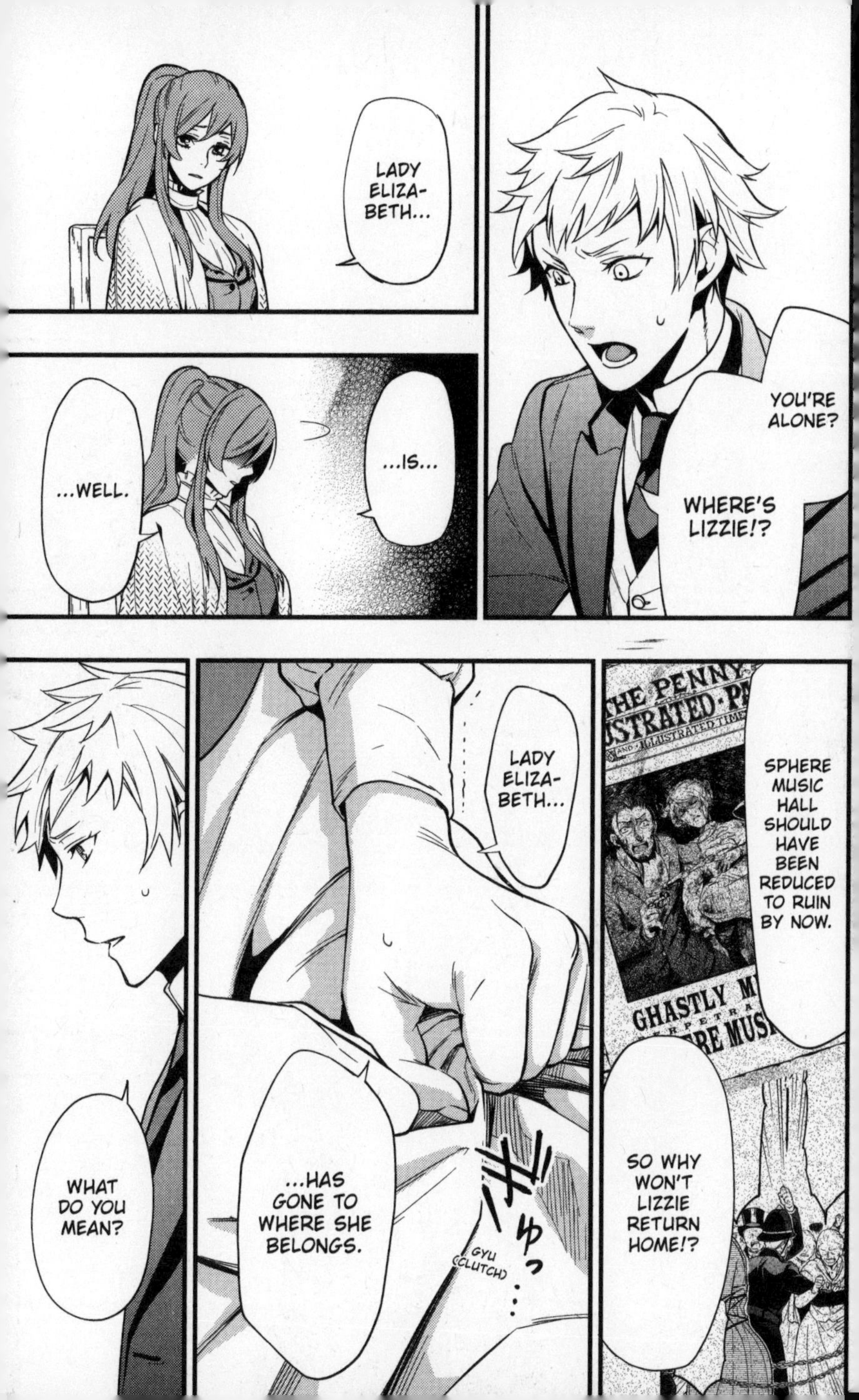
YOU'RE ALONE?
WHERE'S LIZZIE!?
LADY ELIZA-BETH...
...IS...
...WELL.
SPHERE MUSIC HALL SHOULD HAVE BEEN REDUCED TO RUIN BY NOW.
SO WHY WON'T LIZZIE RETURN HOME!?
LADY ELIZA-BETH...
...HAS GONE TO WHERE SHE BELONGS.
ぎゅっ
GYU (CLUTCH)
WHAT DO YOU MEAN?

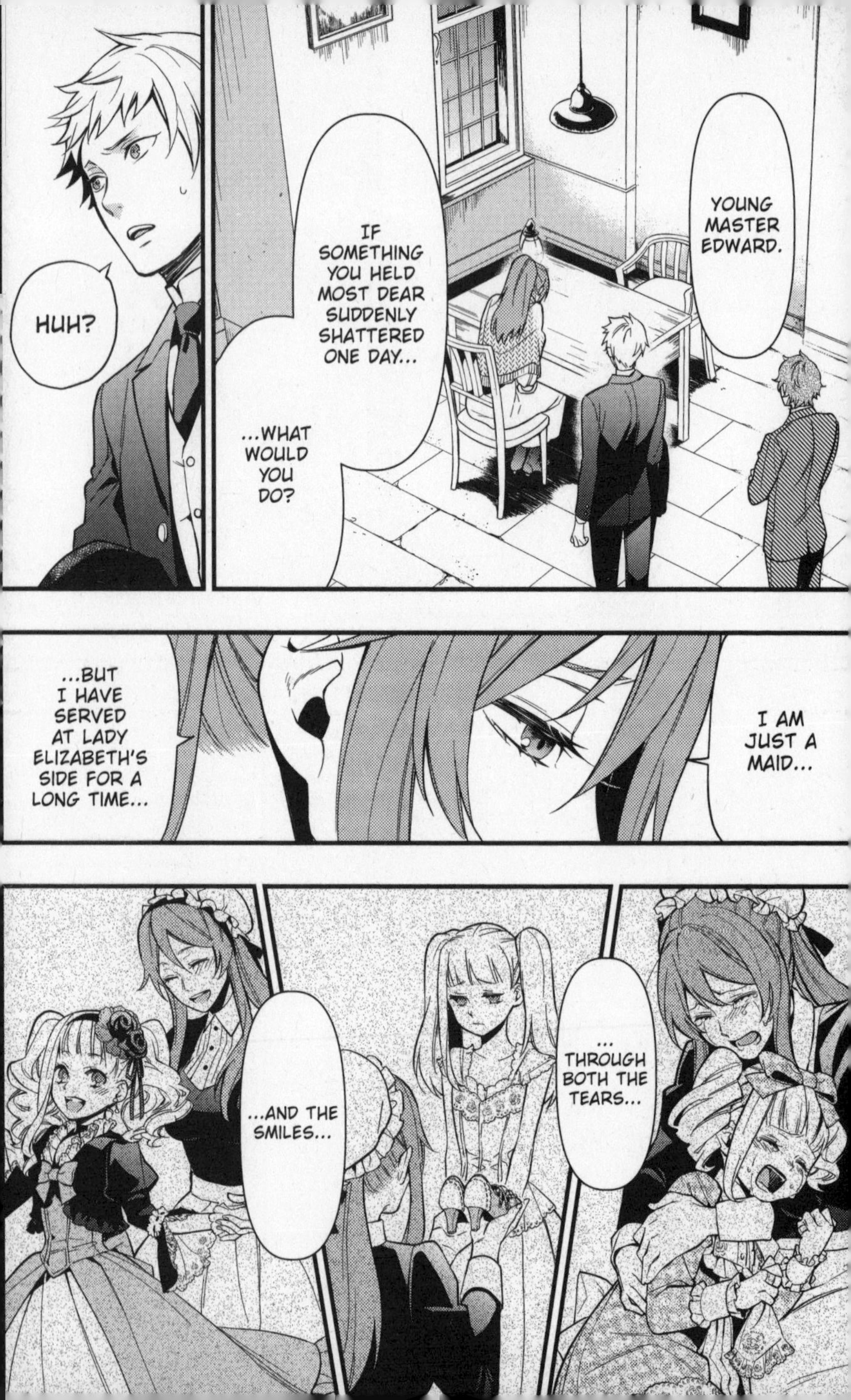
YOUNG MASTER EDWARD.
IF SOMETHING YOU HELD MOST DEAR SUDDENLY SHATTERED ONE DAY...
...WHAT WOULD YOU DO?
HUH?
I AM JUST A MAID...
...BUT I HAVE SERVED AT LADY ELIZABETH'S SIDE FOR A LONG TIME...
...THROUGH BOTH THE TEARS...
...AND THE SMILES...

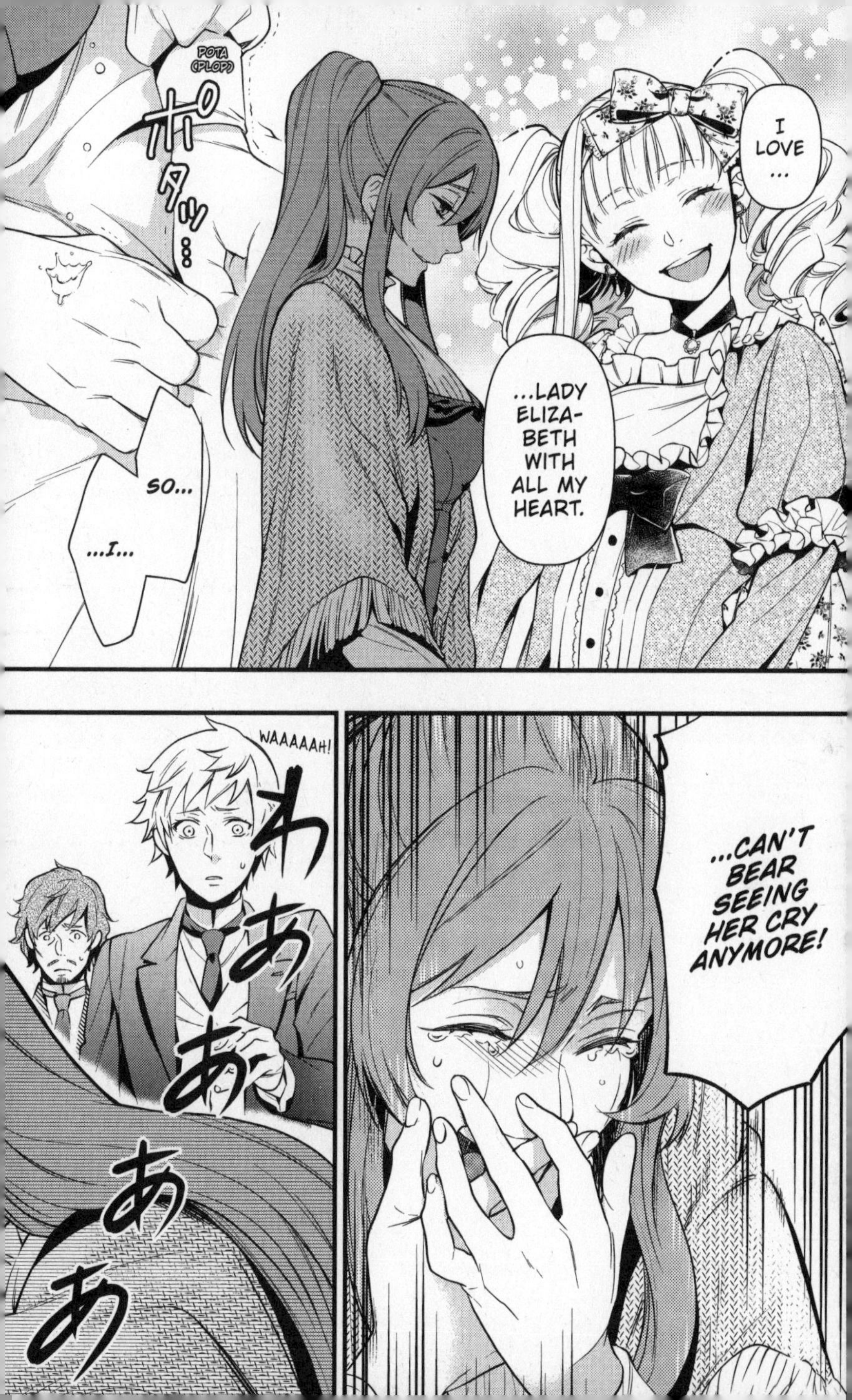
I LOVE...
...LADY ELIZABETH WITH ALL MY HEART.
POTA (PLOP)
ポタッ..
SO...
...I...
...CAN'T BEAR SEEING HER CRY ANYMORE!
WAAAAAH!
わあああ

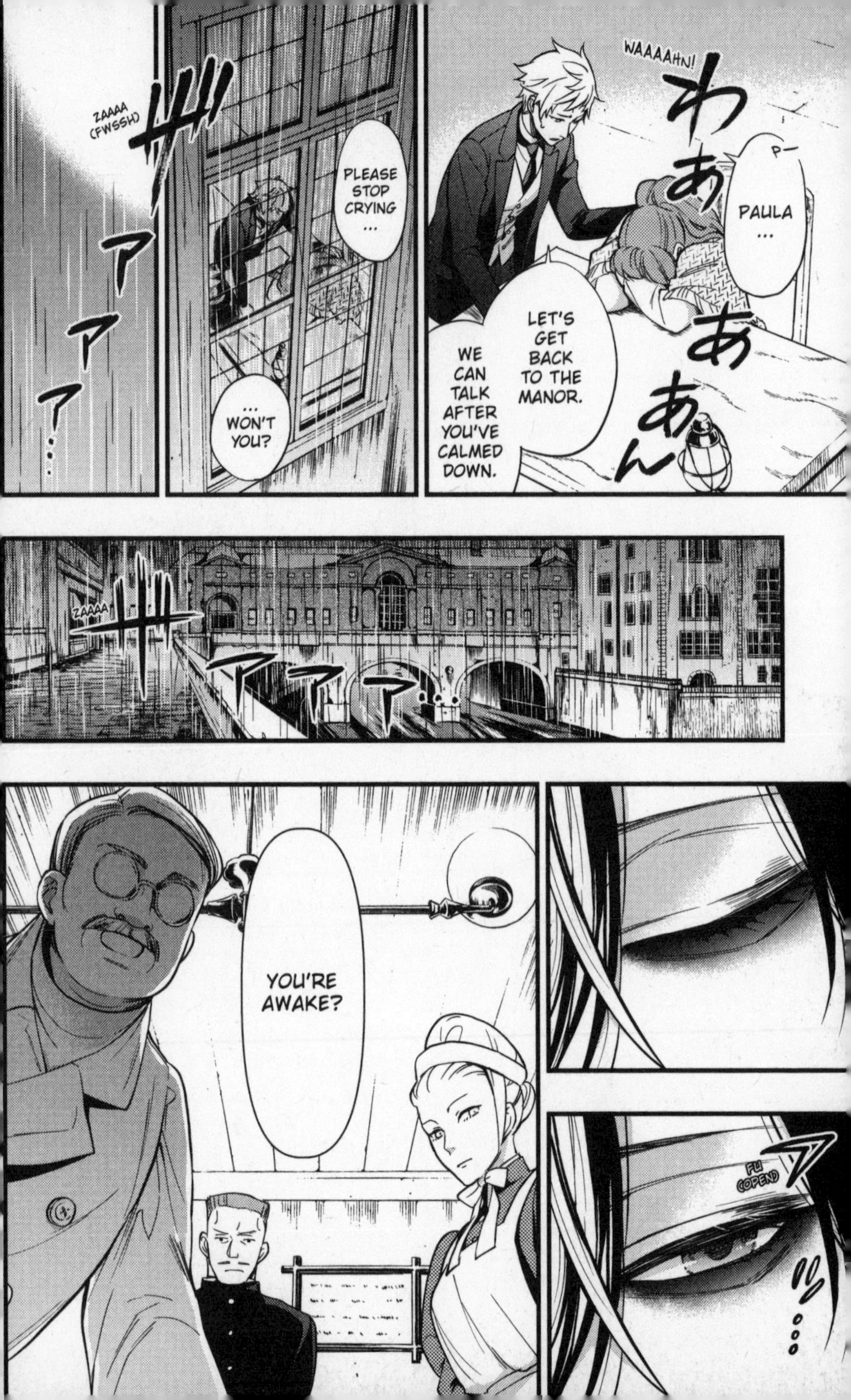
WAAAAHN!
わあああん
P— PAULA ...
LET'S GET BACK TO THE MANOR.
WE CAN TALK AFTER YOU'VE CALMED DOWN.
PLEASE STOP CRYING ...
... WON'T YOU?
ZAAAA (FWSSH)
ZAAAA
FU (OPEN)
YOU'RE AWAKE?

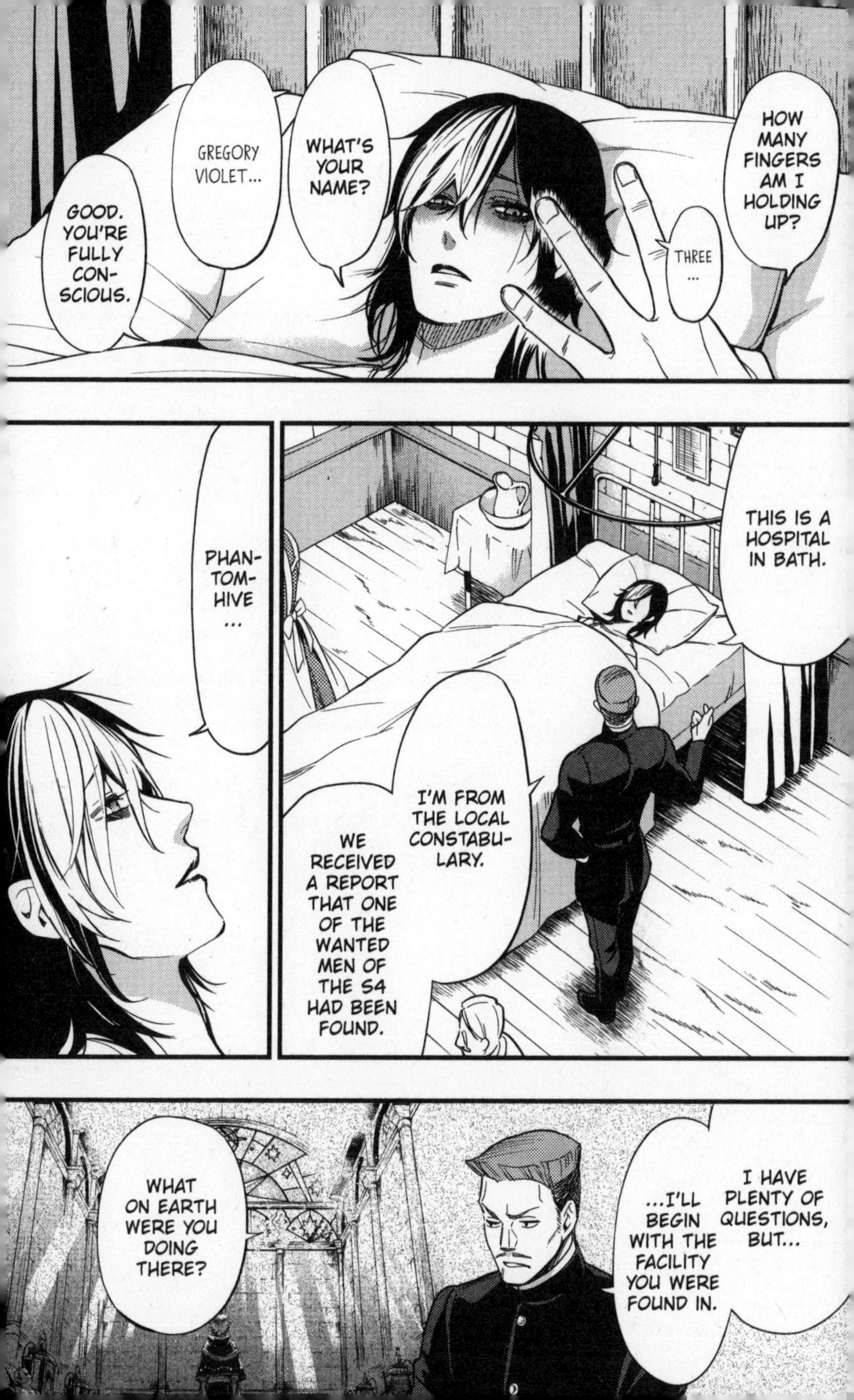
HOW MANY FINGERS AM I HOLDING UP?
THREE...
WHAT'S YOUR NAME?
GREGORY VIOLET...
GOOD. YOU'RE FULLY CON-SCIOUS.
THIS IS A HOSPITAL IN BATH.
I'M FROM THE LOCAL CONSTABU-LARY.
WE RECEIVED A REPORT THAT ONE OF THE WANTED MEN OF THE S4 HAD BEEN FOUND.
PHAN-TOM-HIVE...
I HAVE PLENTY OF QUESTIONS, BUT...
...I'LL BEGIN WITH THE FACILITY YOU WERE FOUND IN.
WHAT ON EARTH WERE YOU DOING THERE?

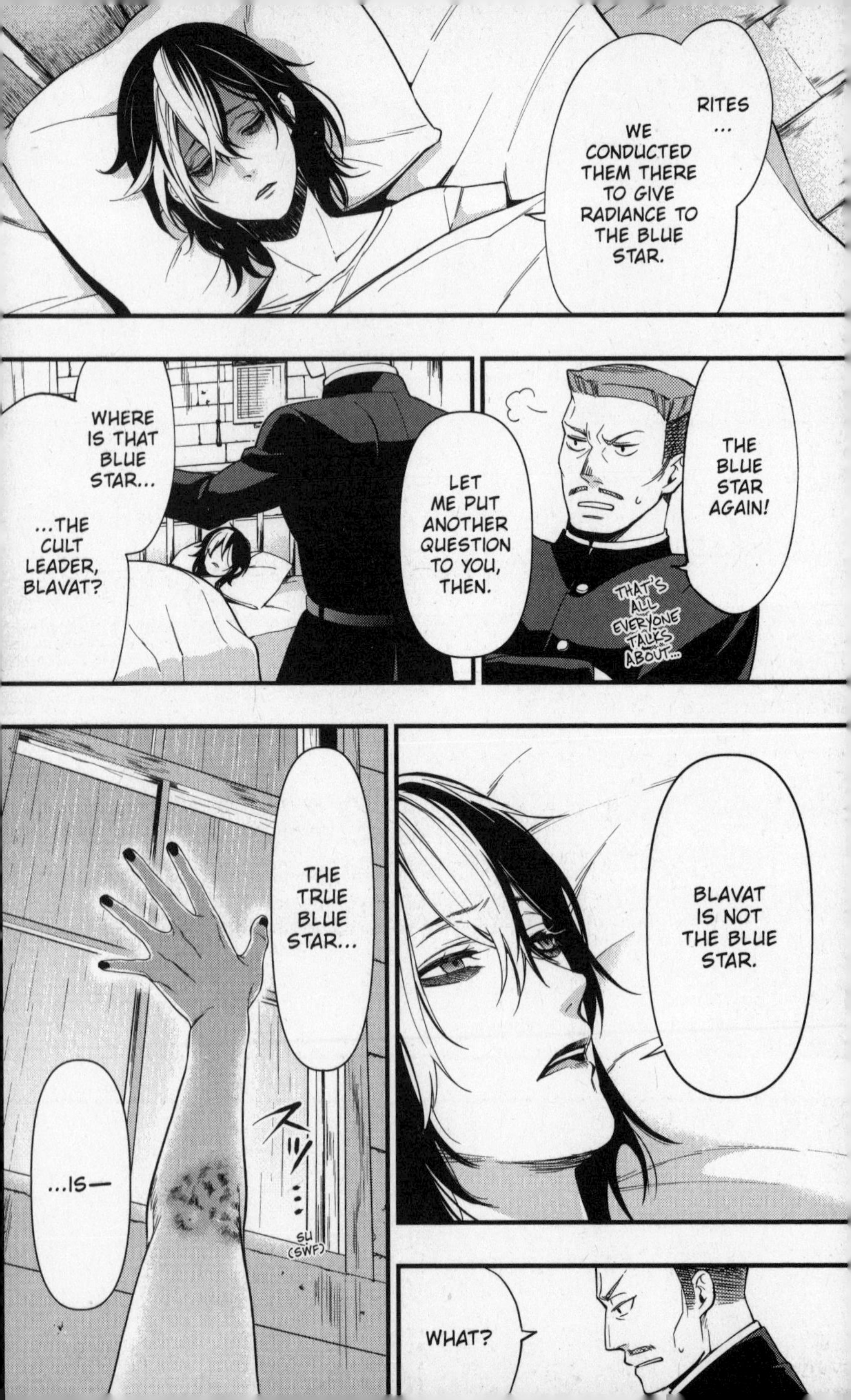

RITES ...
WE CONDUCTED THEM THERE TO GIVE RADIANCE TO THE BLUE STAR.
THE BLUE STAR AGAIN!
THAT'S ALL EVERYONE TALKS ABOUT...
LET ME PUT ANOTHER QUESTION TO YOU, THEN.
WHERE IS THAT BLUE STAR...
...THE CULT LEADER, BLAVAT?
BLAVAT IS NOT THE BLUE STAR.
WHAT?
THE TRUE BLUE STAR...
...IS—
SU (SWF)

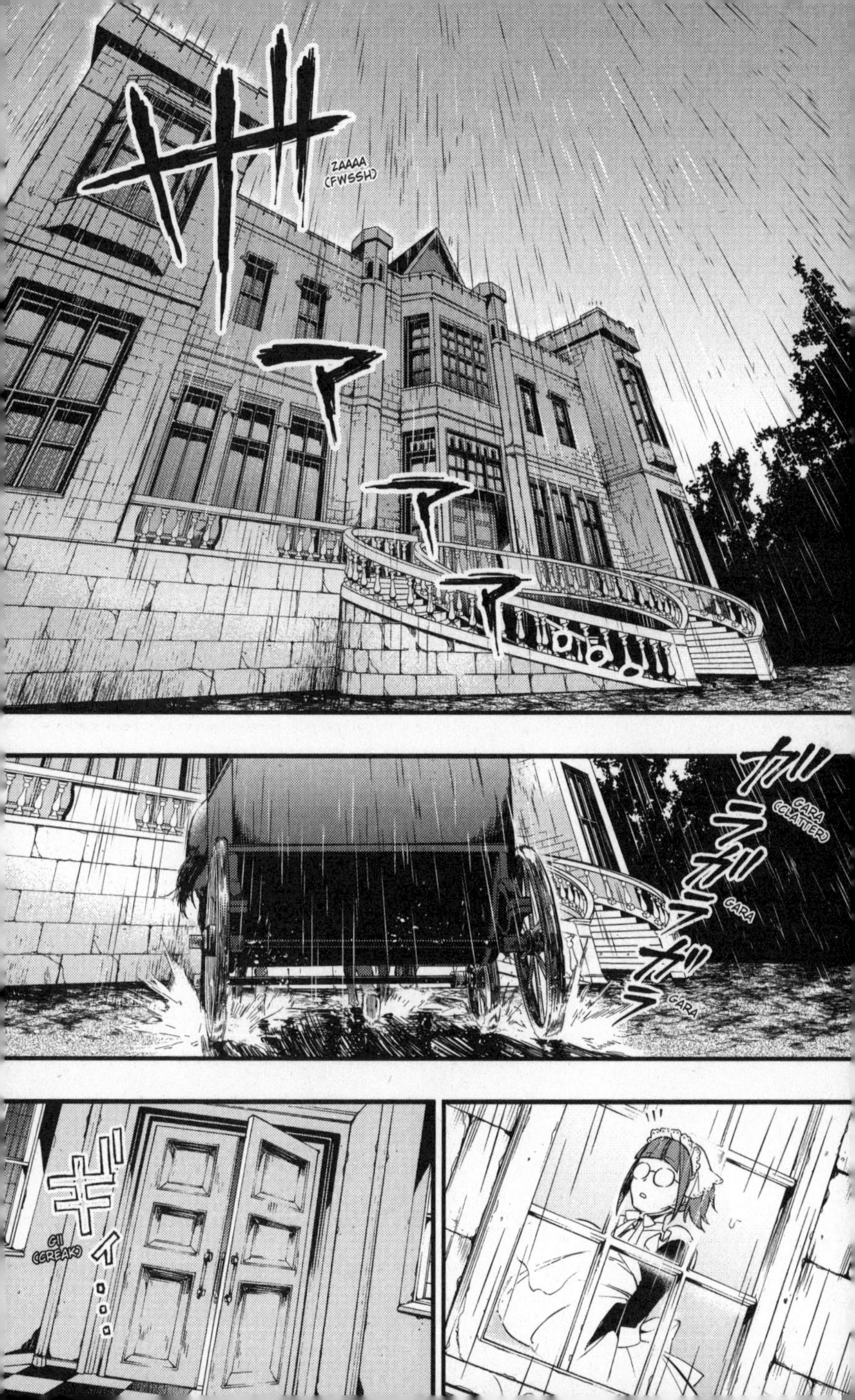
ZAAAA
(FWSSH)
GARA
(CLATTER)
GARA
GARA
GII
(CREAK)

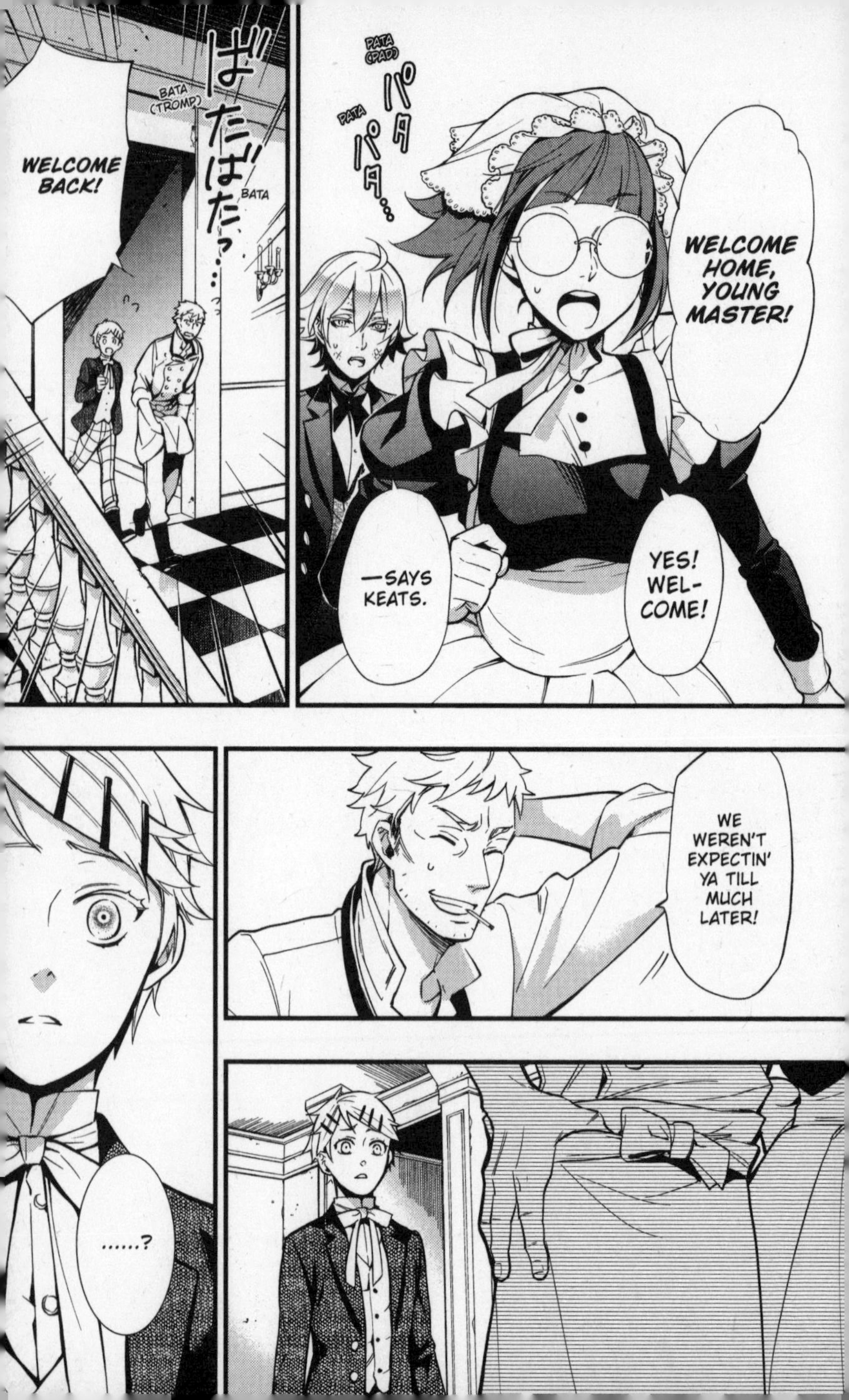
PATA (PAD)
パタ
PATA
パタ…
WELCOME HOME, YOUNG MASTER!
YES! WEL-COME!
—SAYS KEATS.
BATA (TROMP)
ばたばたっ…
BATA
WELCOME BACK!
WE WEREN'T EXPECTIN' YA TILL MUCH LATER!
......?

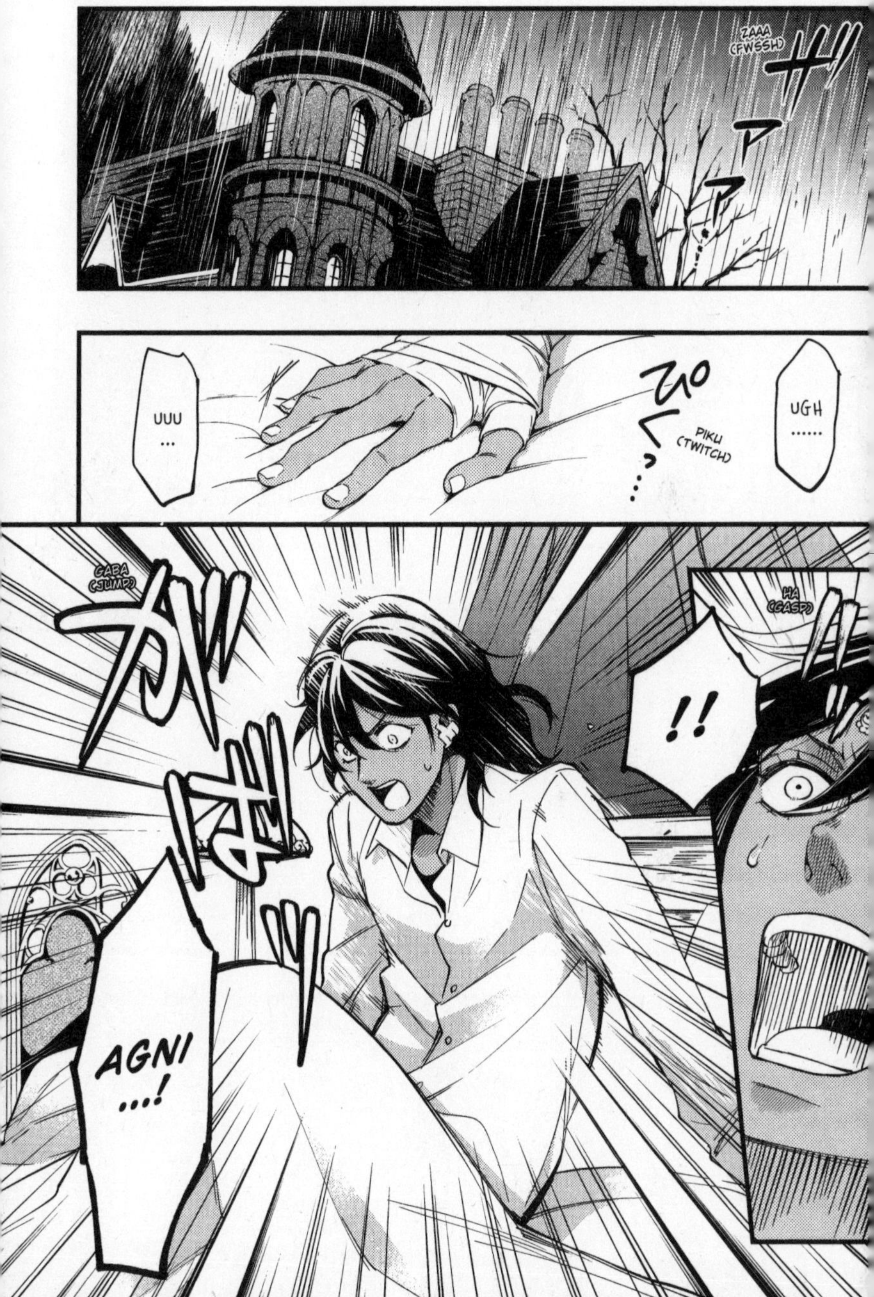
ZAAA (FWSSH)
UGH ......
PIKU (TWITCH)
UUU ...
HA (GASP)
!!
GABA (JUMP)
AGNI ...!

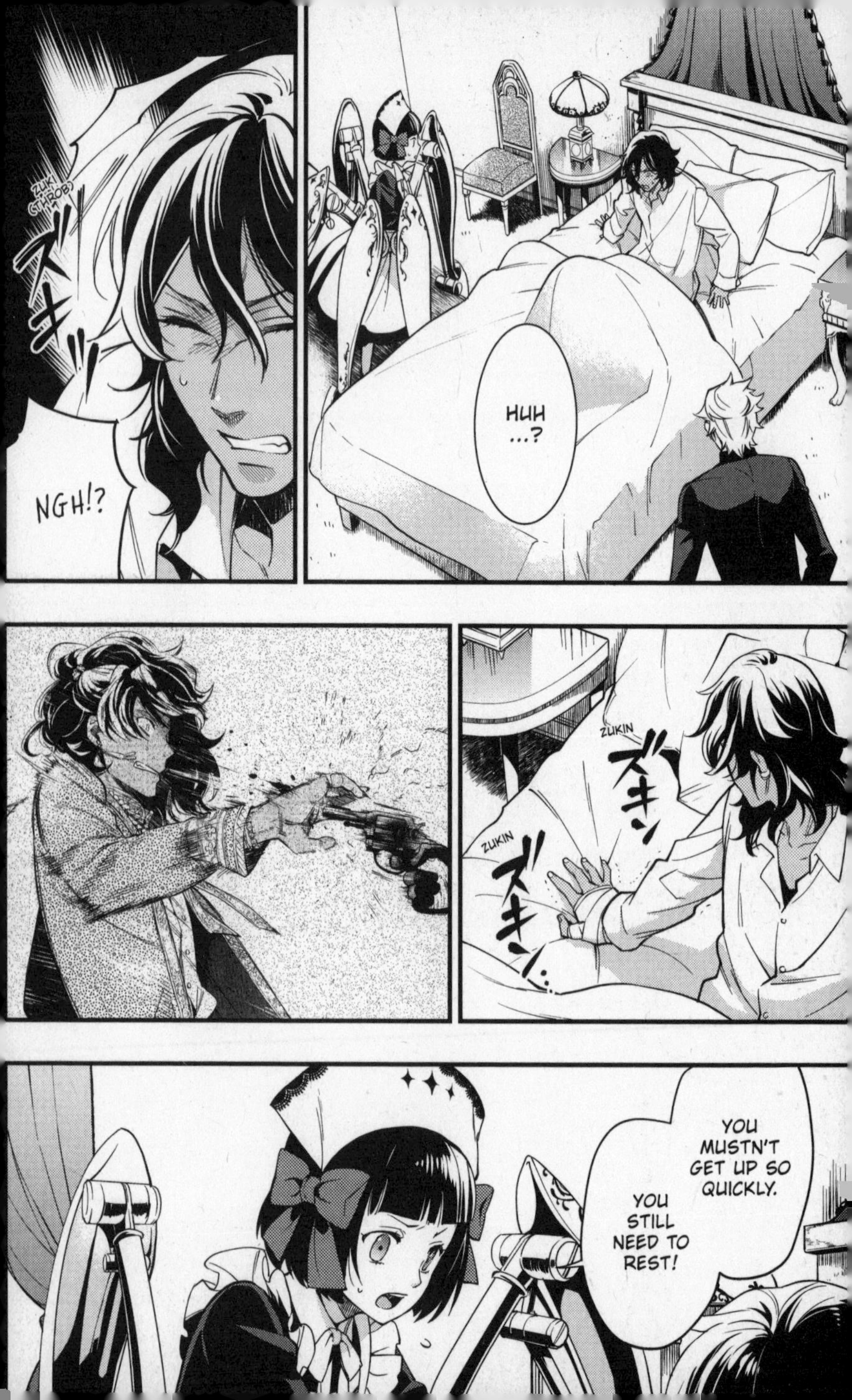
HUH ...?
ZUKI (THROB)
ズキッ
NGH!?
ZUKIN
ズキン
ZUKIN
ズキン
YOU MUSTN'T GET UP SO QUICKLY.
YOU STILL NEED TO REST!

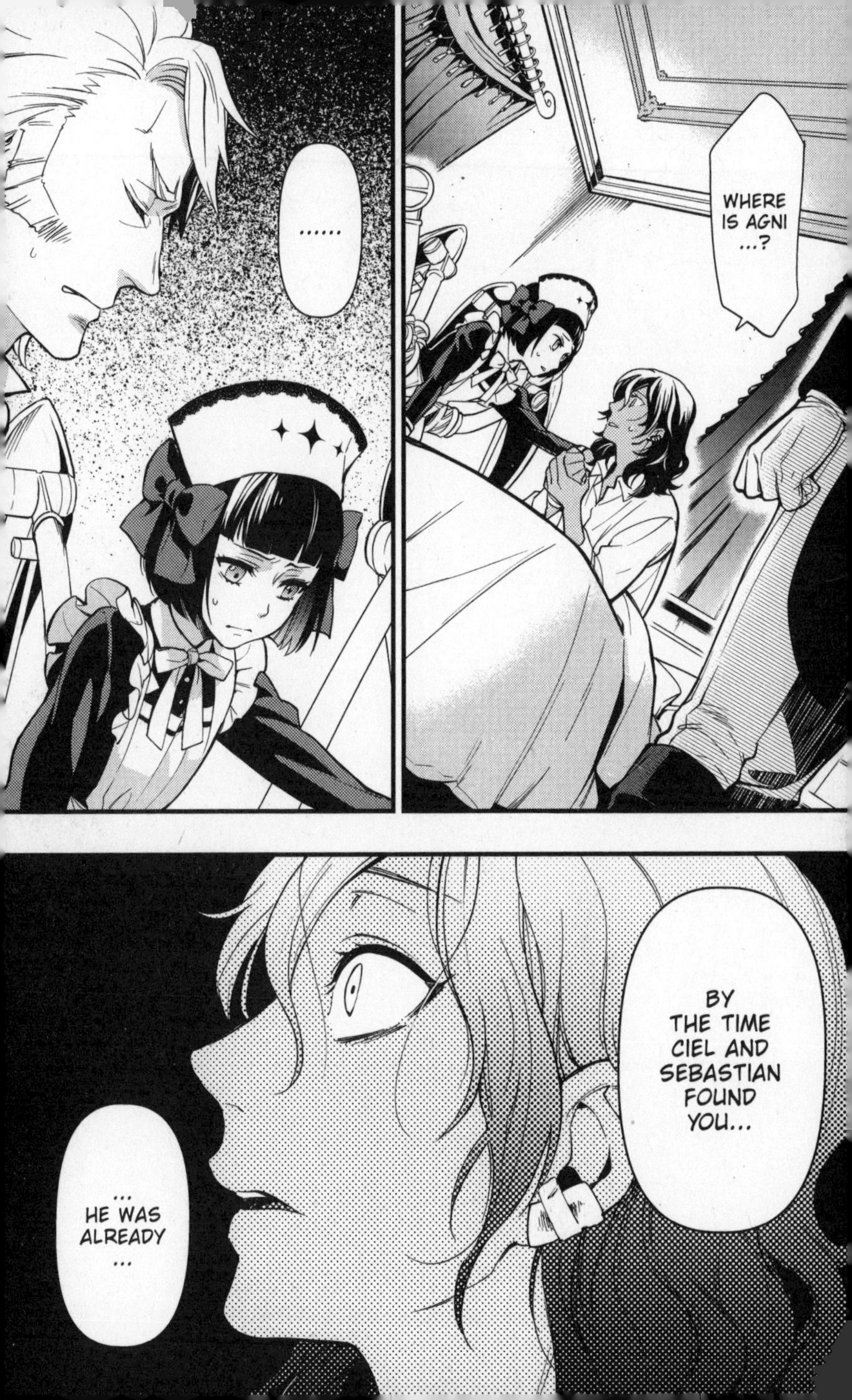
WHERE IS AGNI ...?
......
BY THE TIME CIEL AND SEBASTIAN FOUND YOU...
... HE WAS ALREADY ...

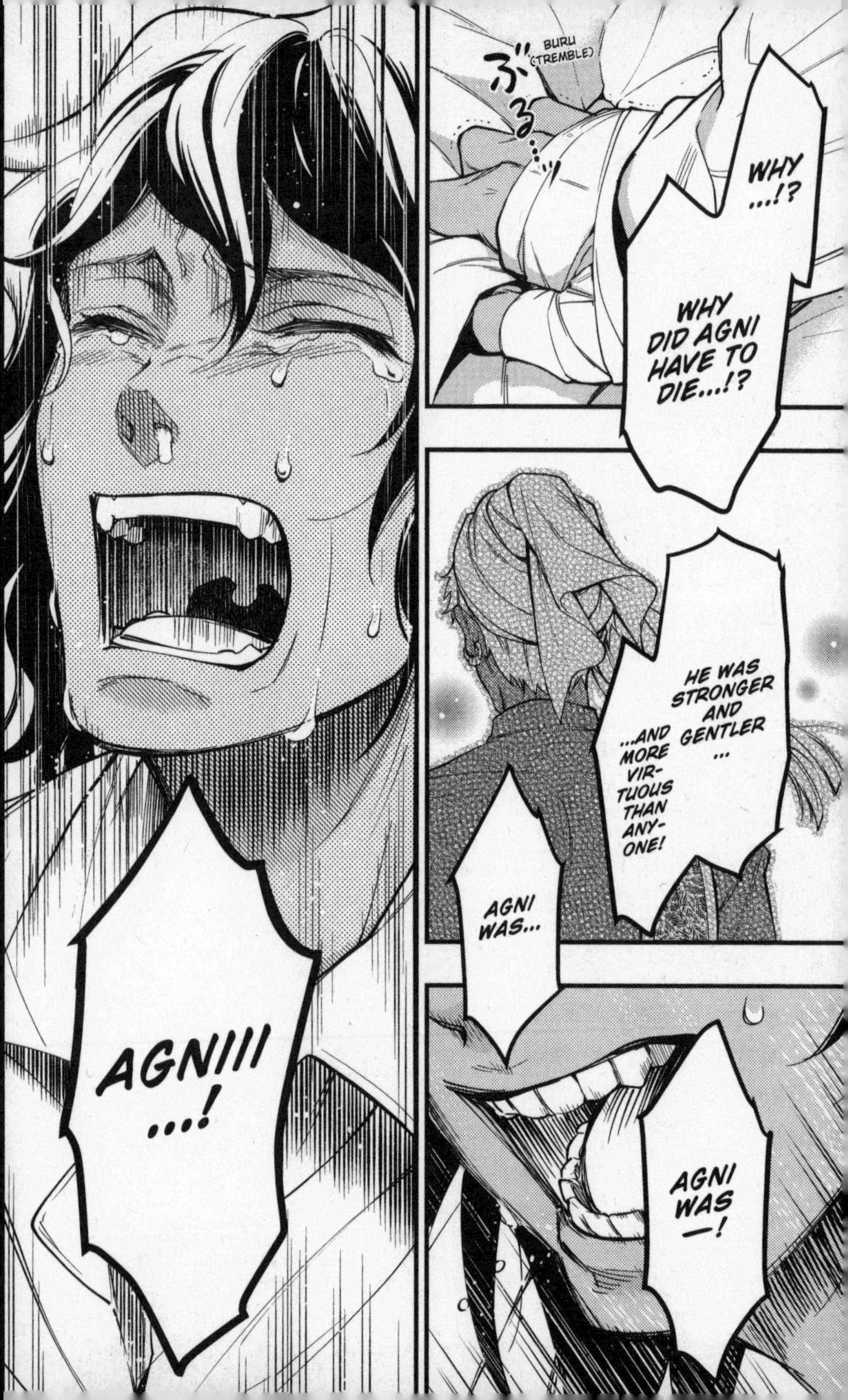
ぶる…
BURU (TREMBLE)
WHY ...!?
WHY DID AGNI HAVE TO DIE...!?
HE WAS STRONGER AND GENTLER ...
...AND MORE VIRTUOUS THAN ANYONE!
AGNI WAS...
AGNI WAS—!
AGNIII ...!

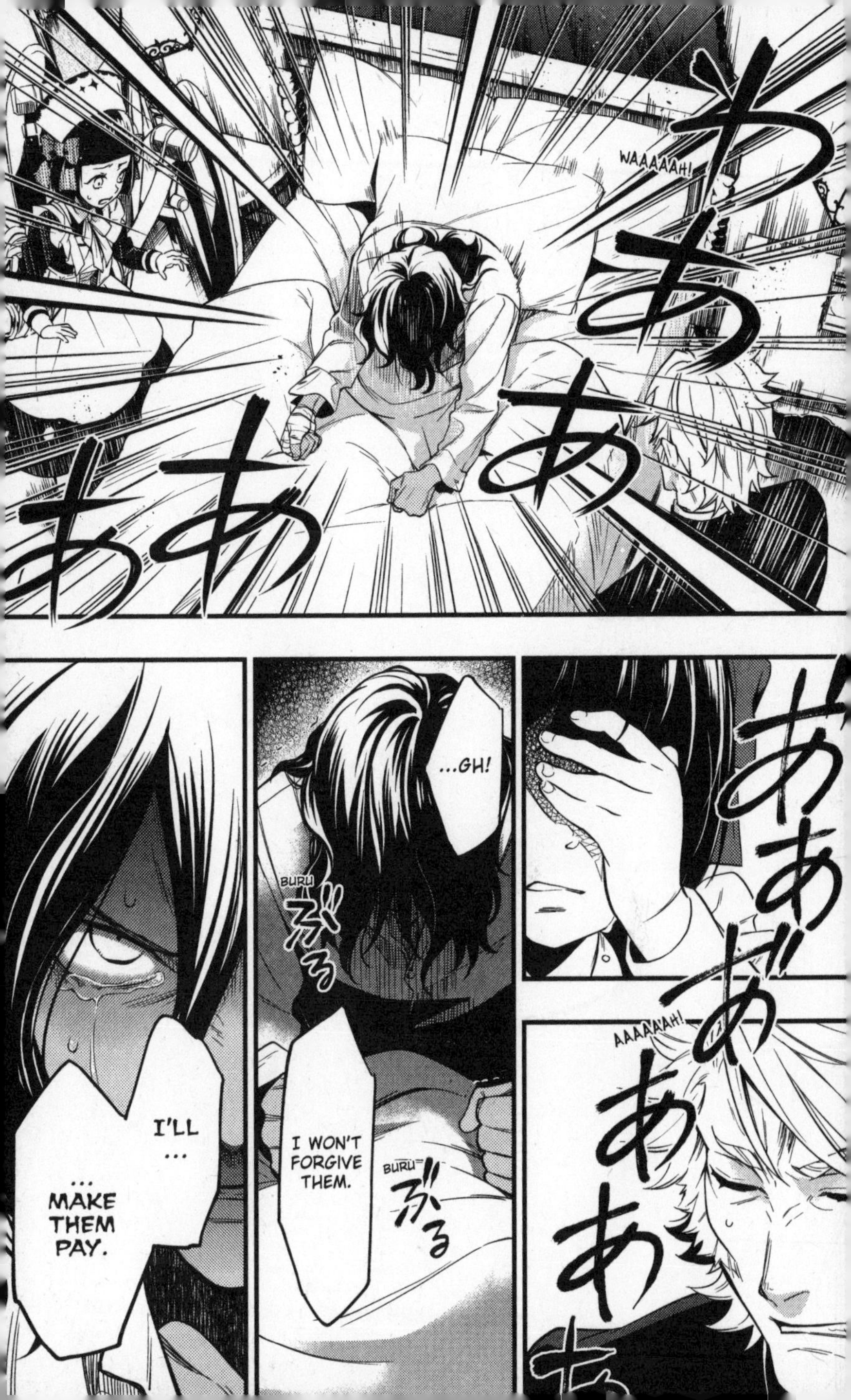
WAAAAAH!
AAAAAAH!
...GH!
BURU
ぶる
I WON'T FORGIVE THEM.
BURU
ぶる
I'LL ...
... MAKE THEM PAY.

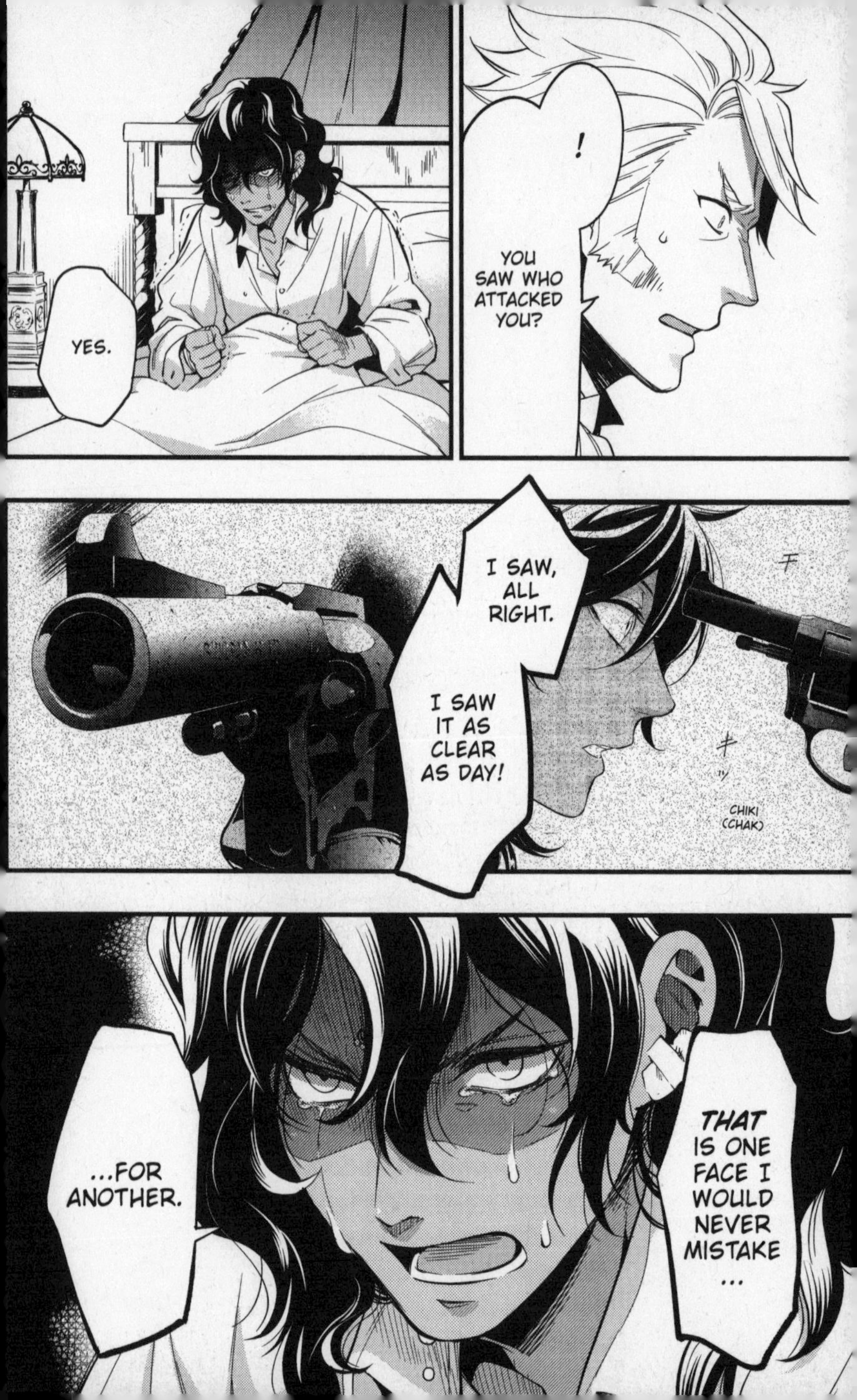
!
YOU SAW WHO ATTACKED YOU?
YES.
チキ
CHIKI (CHAK)
I SAW, ALL RIGHT.
I SAW IT AS CLEAR AS DAY!
THAT IS ONE FACE I WOULD NEVER MISTAKE ...
...FOR ANOTHER.

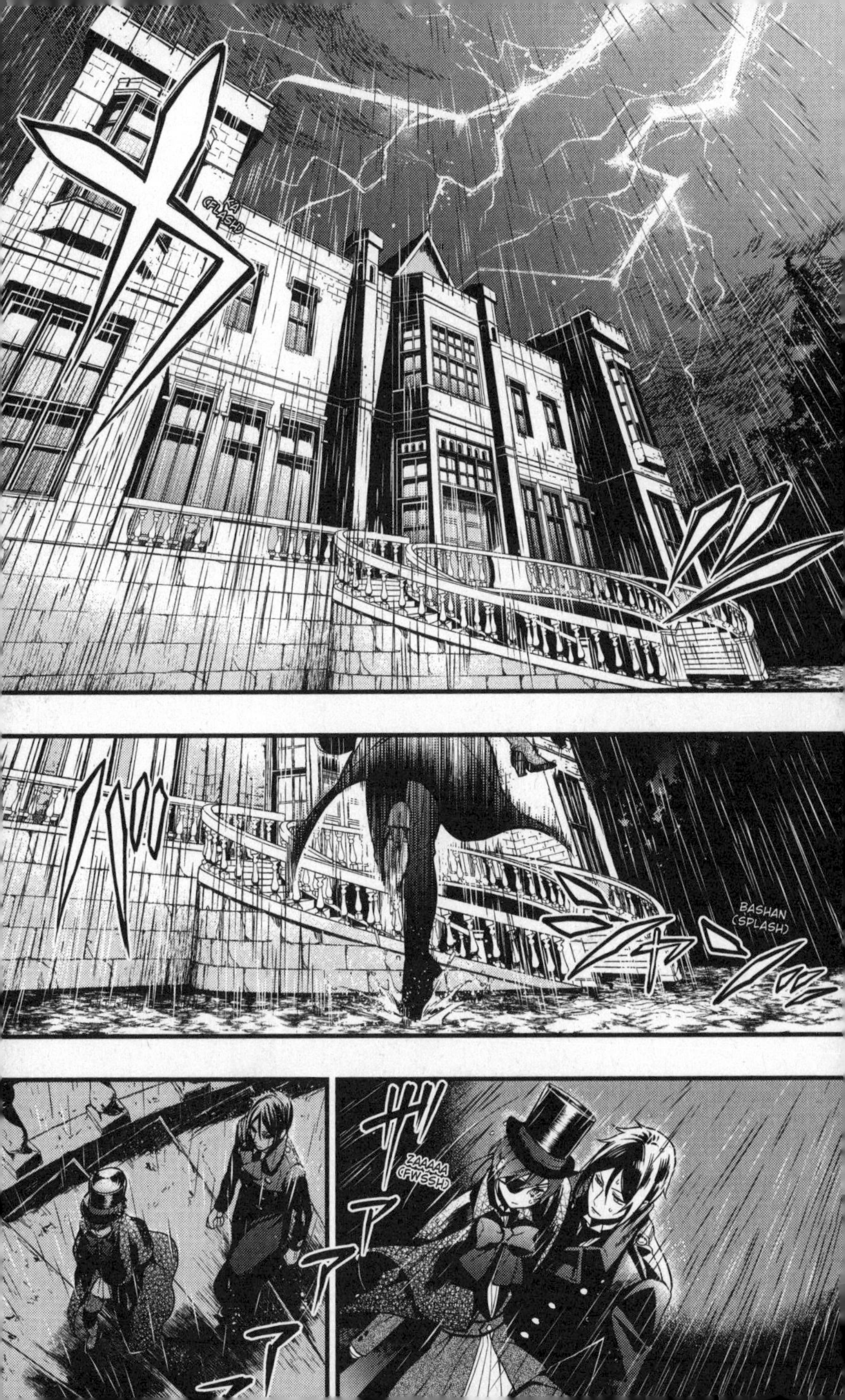
KA (FLASH)
BASHAN (SPLASH)
ZAAAAA (FWSSH)

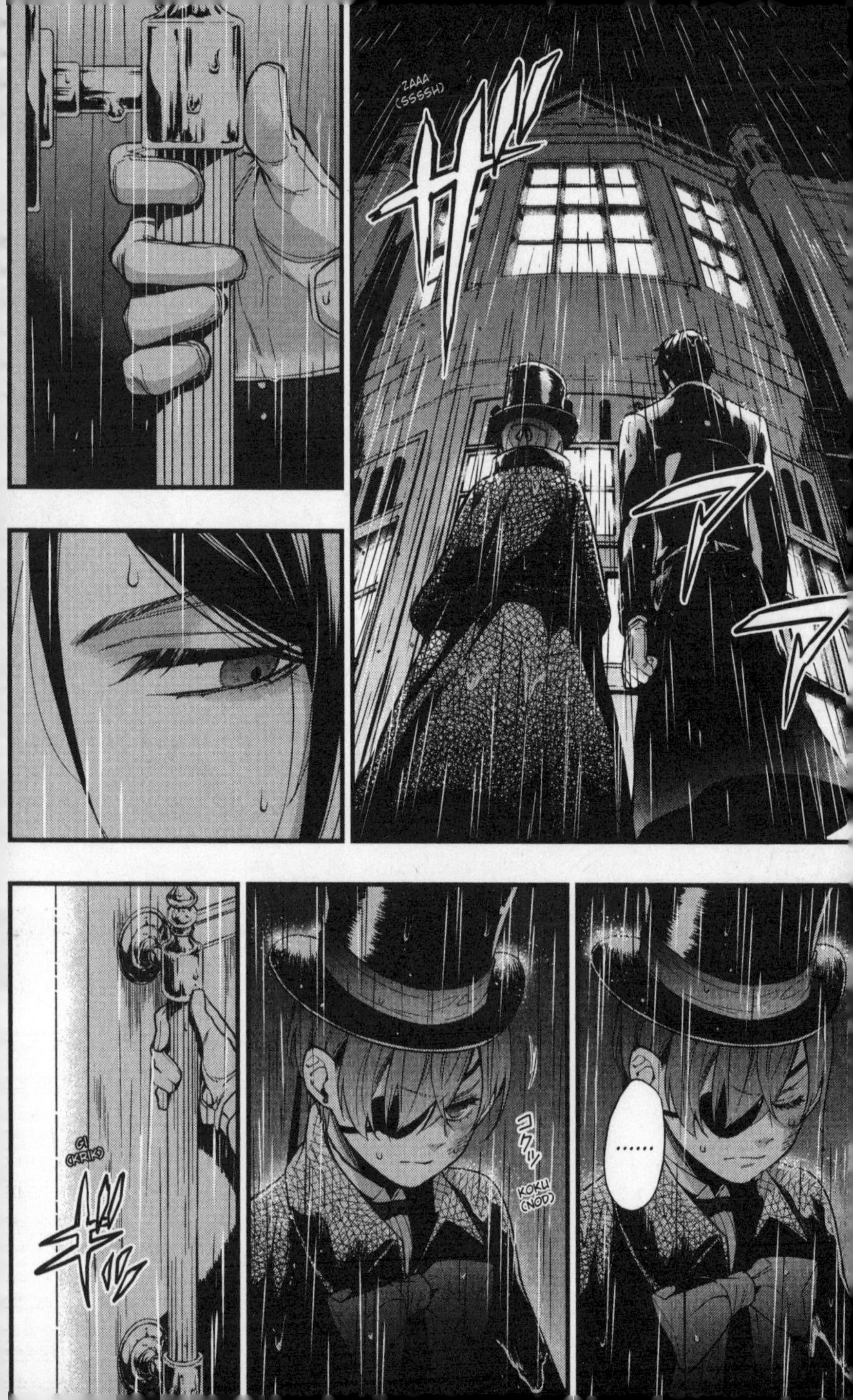
ZAAA (SSSSH)
......
KOKU (NOD)
GI (KRIK)

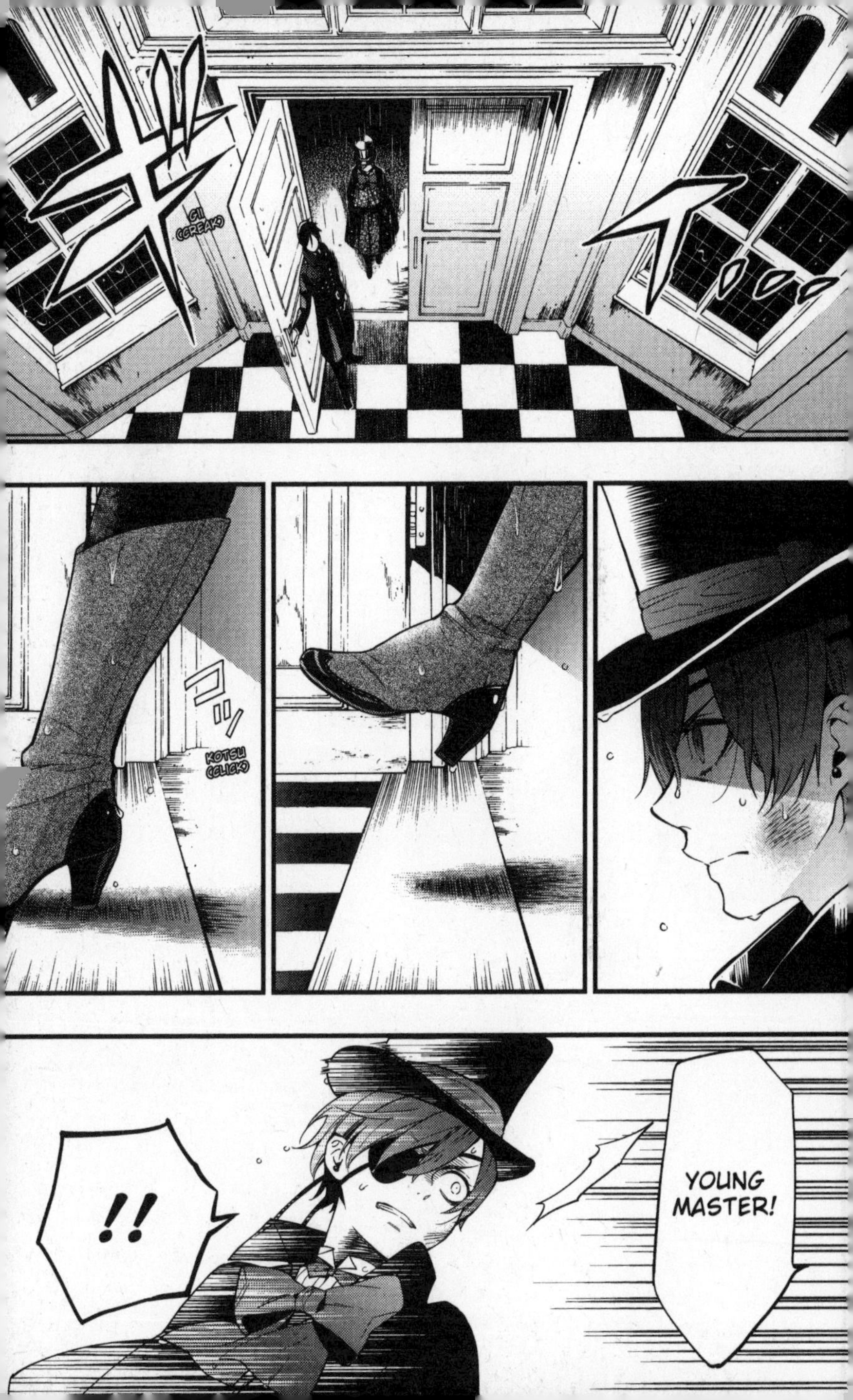
GII (CREAK)
KOTSU (CLICK)
YOUNG MASTER!
!!

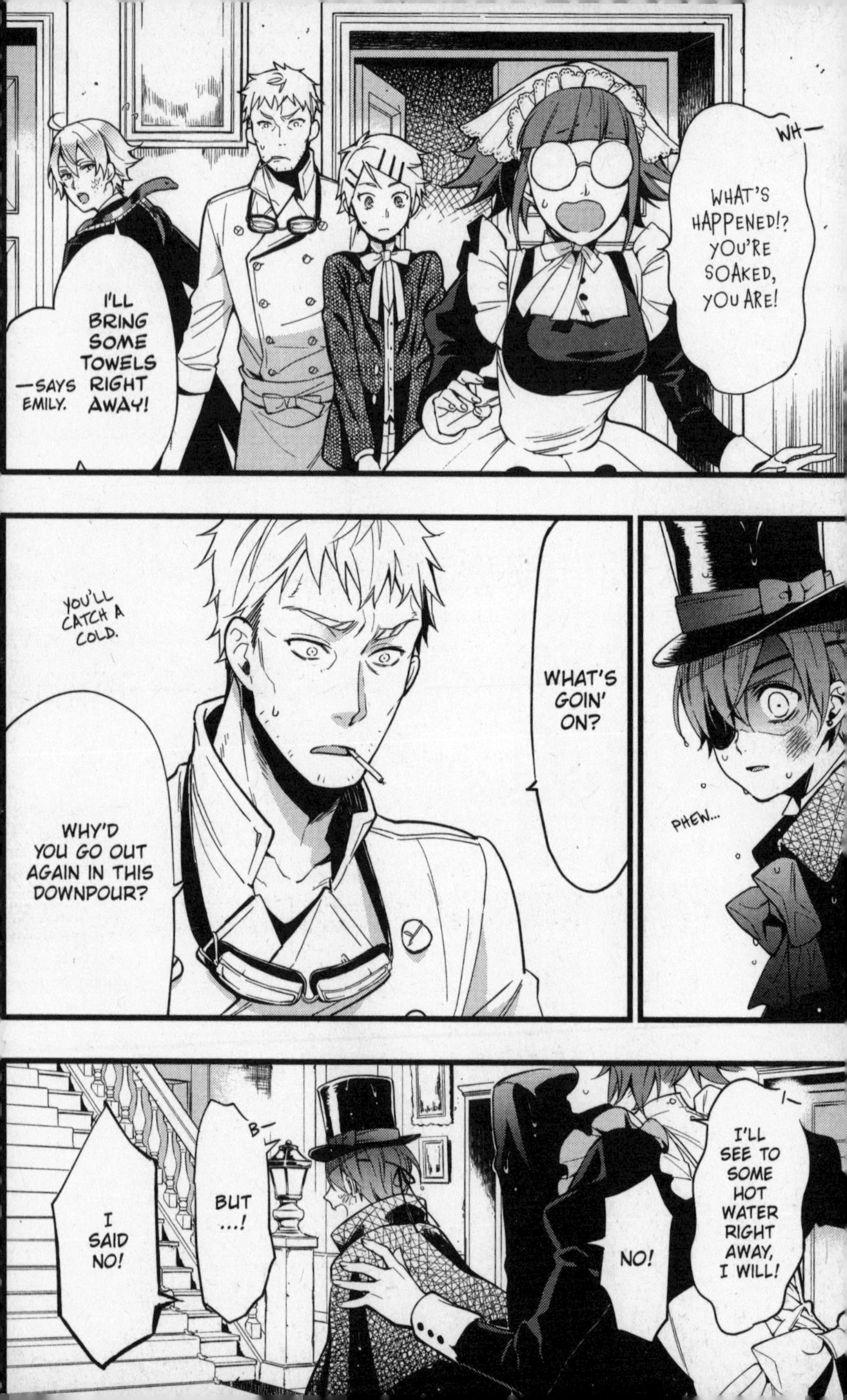
WH—
WHAT'S HAPPENED!? YOU'RE SOAKED, YOU ARE!
I'LL BRING SOME TOWELS RIGHT AWAY!
—SAYS EMILY.
PHEW...
WHAT'S GOIN' ON?
YOU'LL CATCH A COLD.
WHY'D YOU GO OUT AGAIN IN THIS DOWNPOUR?
I—
I'LL SEE TO SOME HOT WATER RIGHT AWAY, I WILL!
NO!
B—
BUT ...!
I SAID NO!

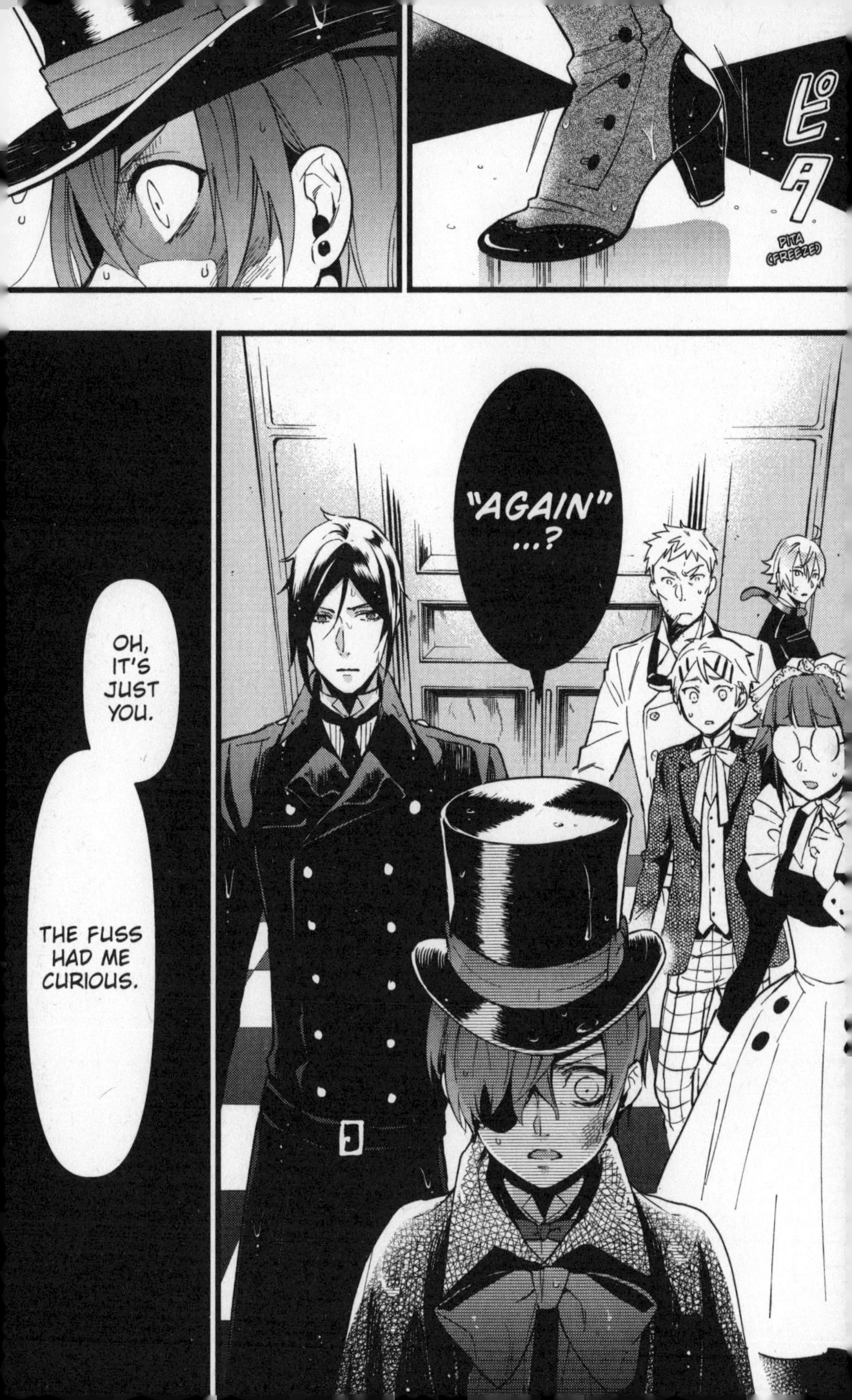
ピタ
PITA (FREEZED)
"AGAIN" ...?
OH, IT'S JUST YOU.
THE FUSS HAD ME CURIOUS.

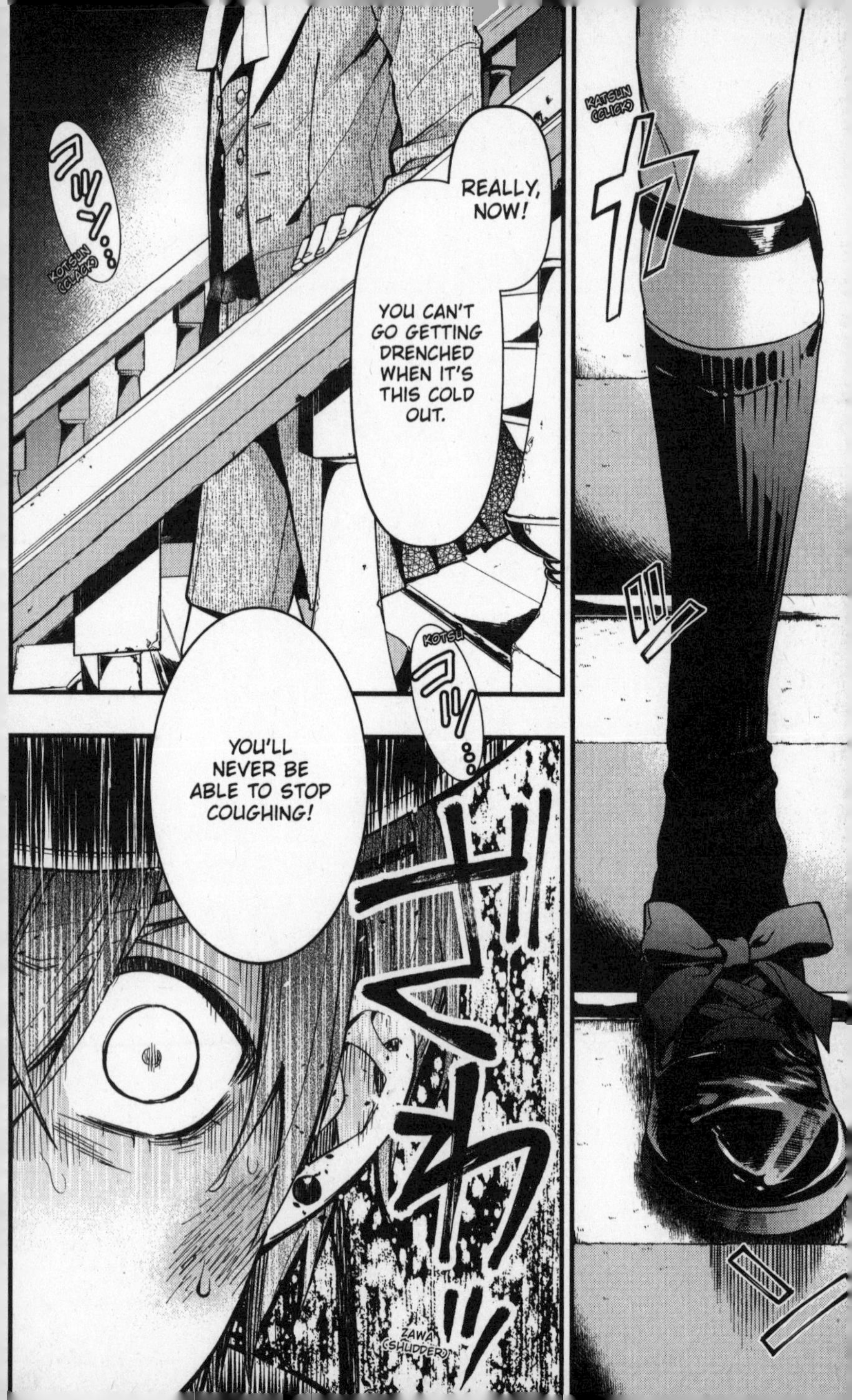
KATSUN (CLICK)
REALLY, NOW!
YOU CAN'T GO GETTING DRENCHED WHEN IT'S THIS COLD OUT.
KOTSUN (CLICK)
KOTSU
YOU'LL NEVER BE ABLE TO STOP COUGHING!
ZAWA (SHUDDER)

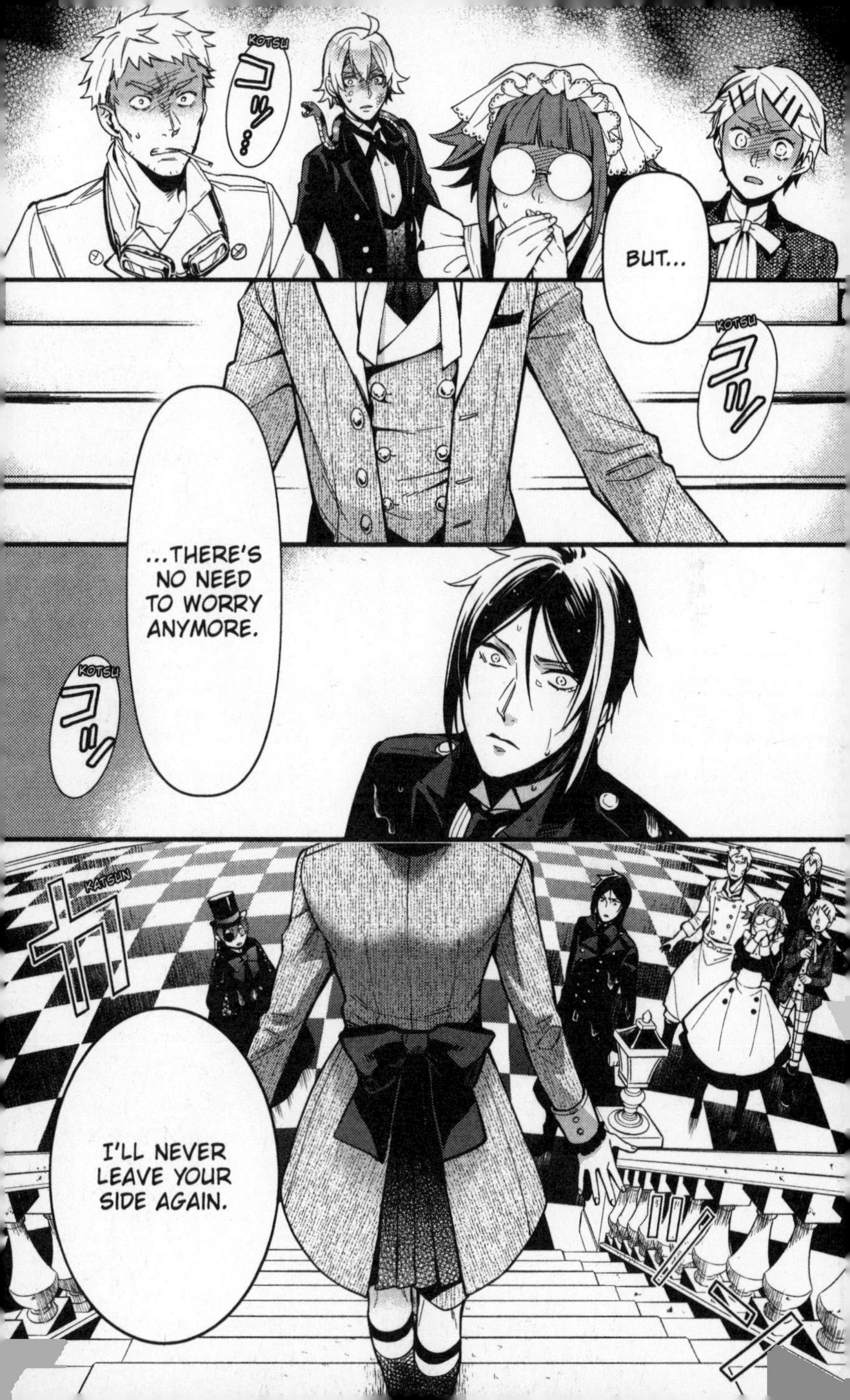
BUT...
KOTSU
KOTSU
...THERE'S NO NEED TO WORRY ANYMORE.
KOTSU
KATSUN
I'LL NEVER LEAVE YOUR SIDE AGAIN.

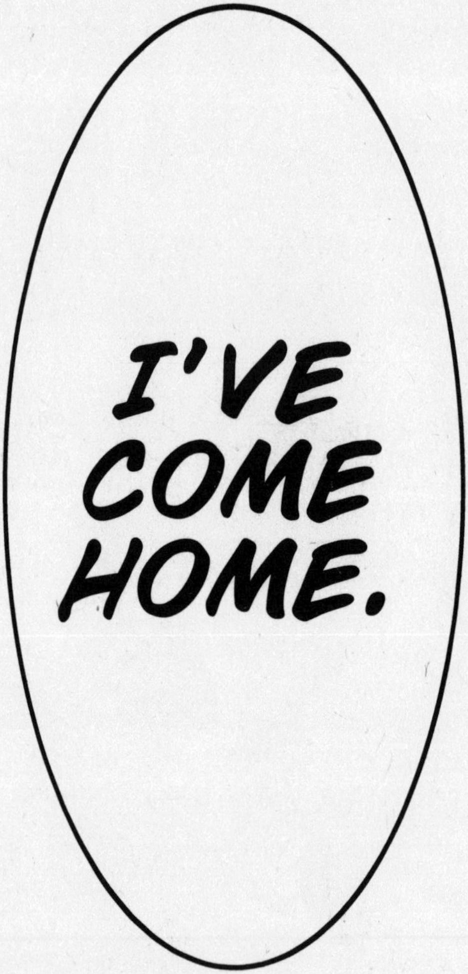
I'VE COME HOME.

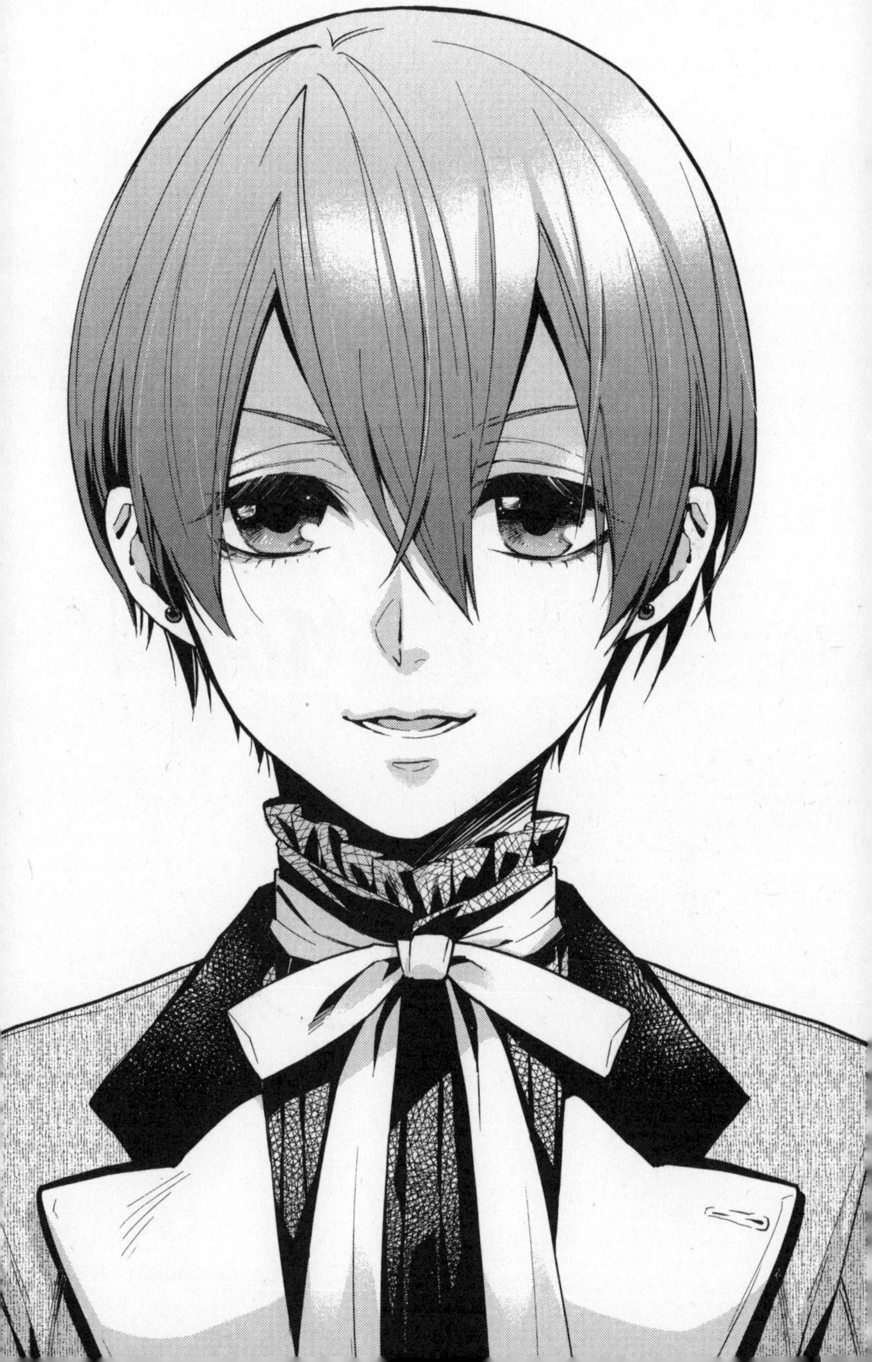

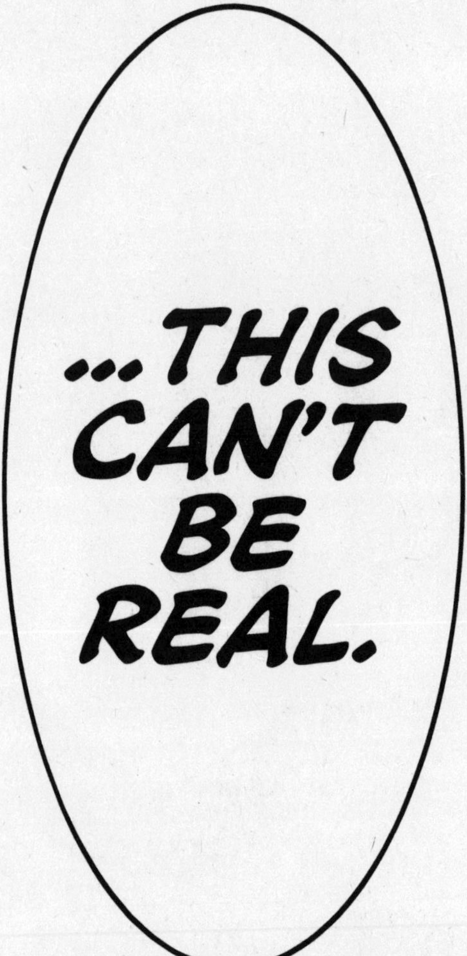
...THIS CAN'T BE REAL.

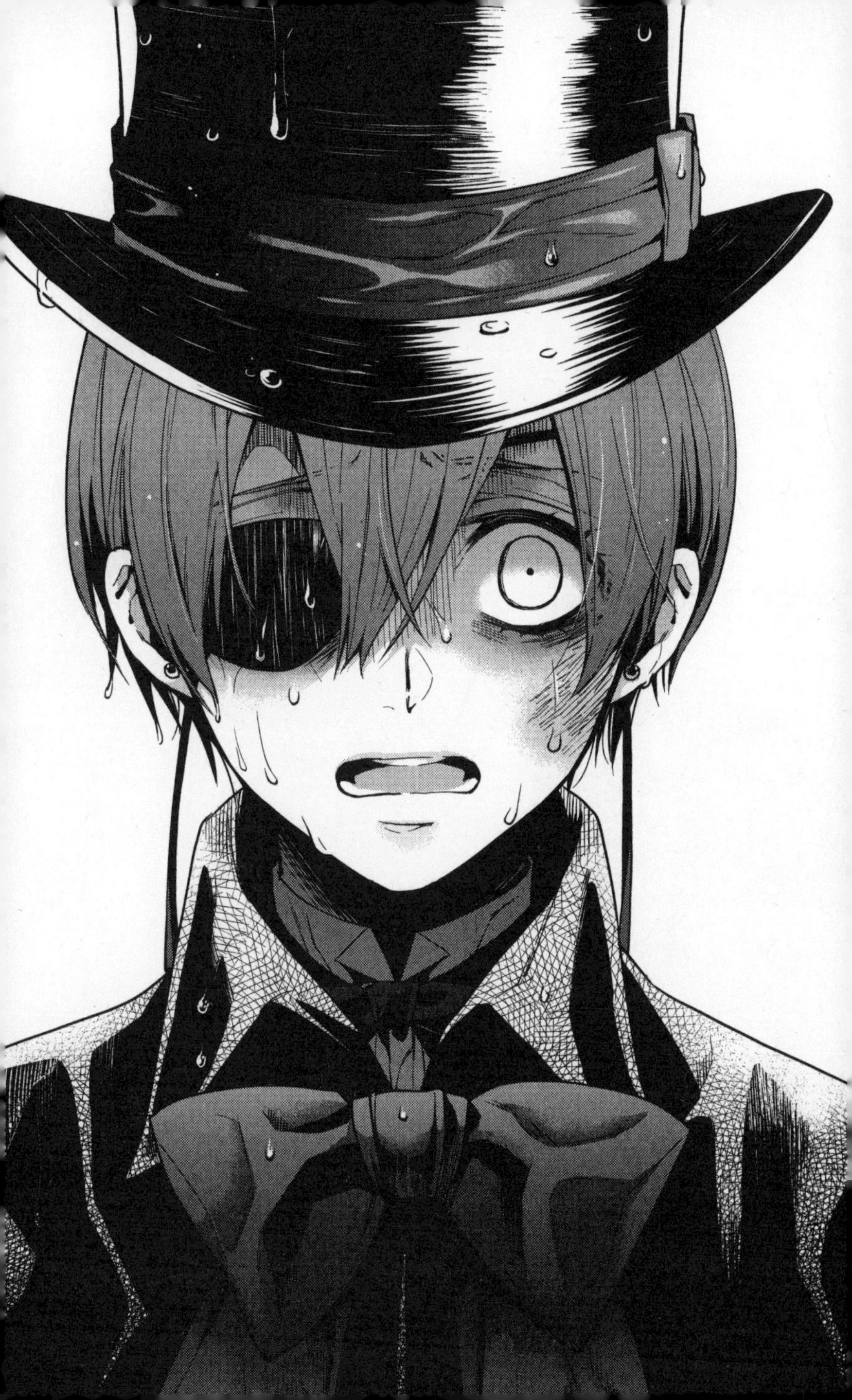

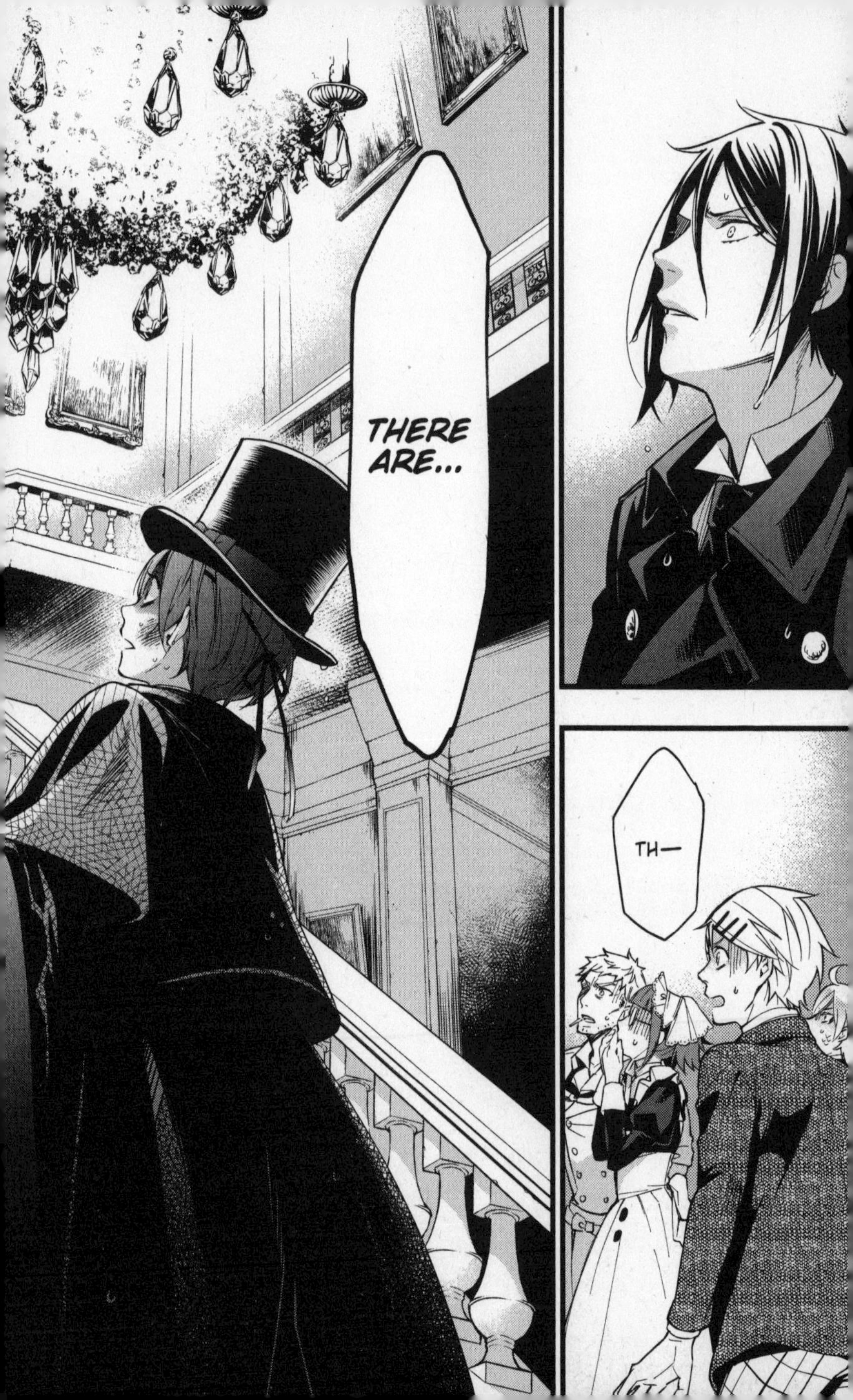
THERE ARE...
TH—

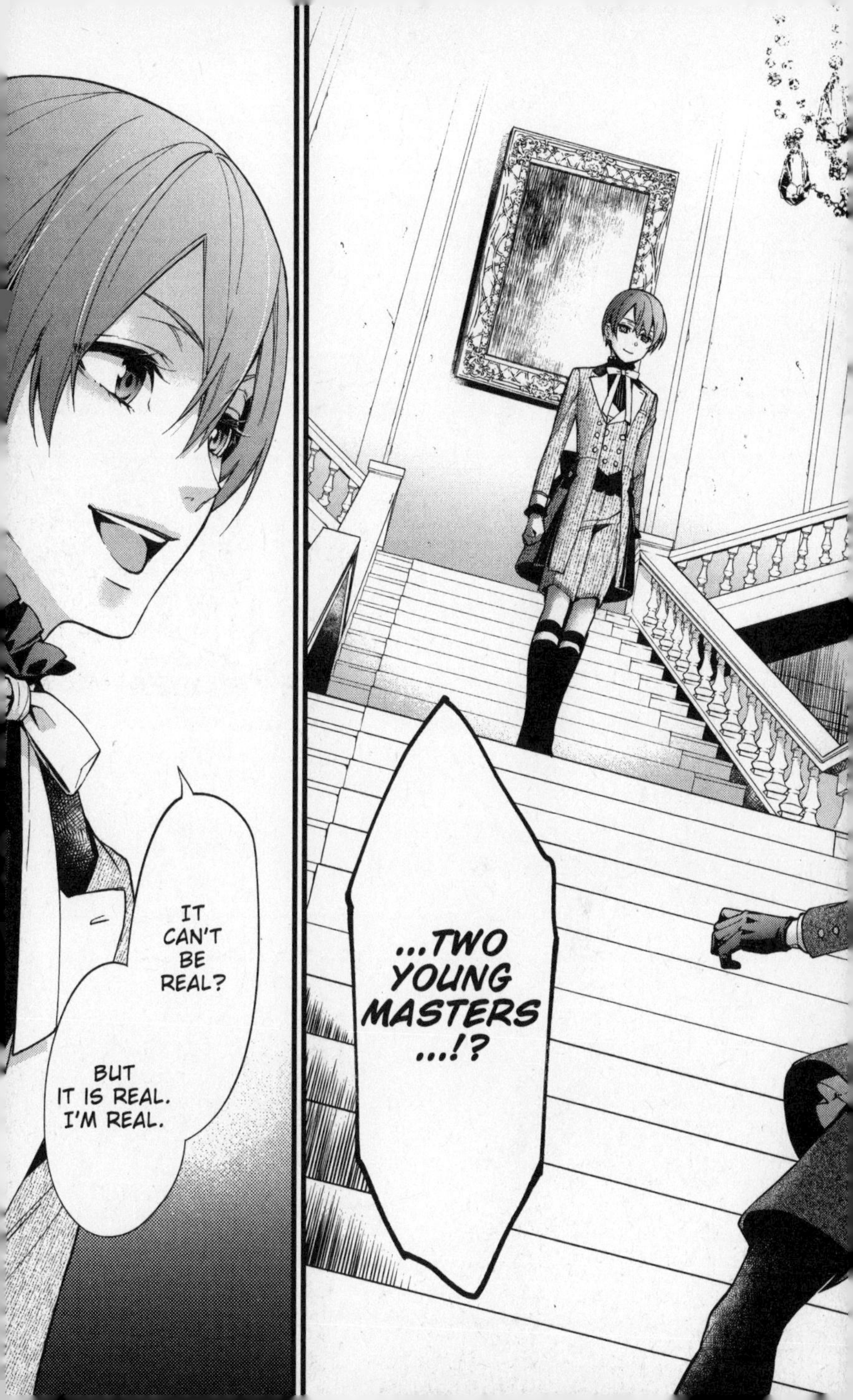
...TWO YOUNG MASTERS ...!?
IT CAN'T BE REAL?
BUT IT IS REAL. I'M REAL.

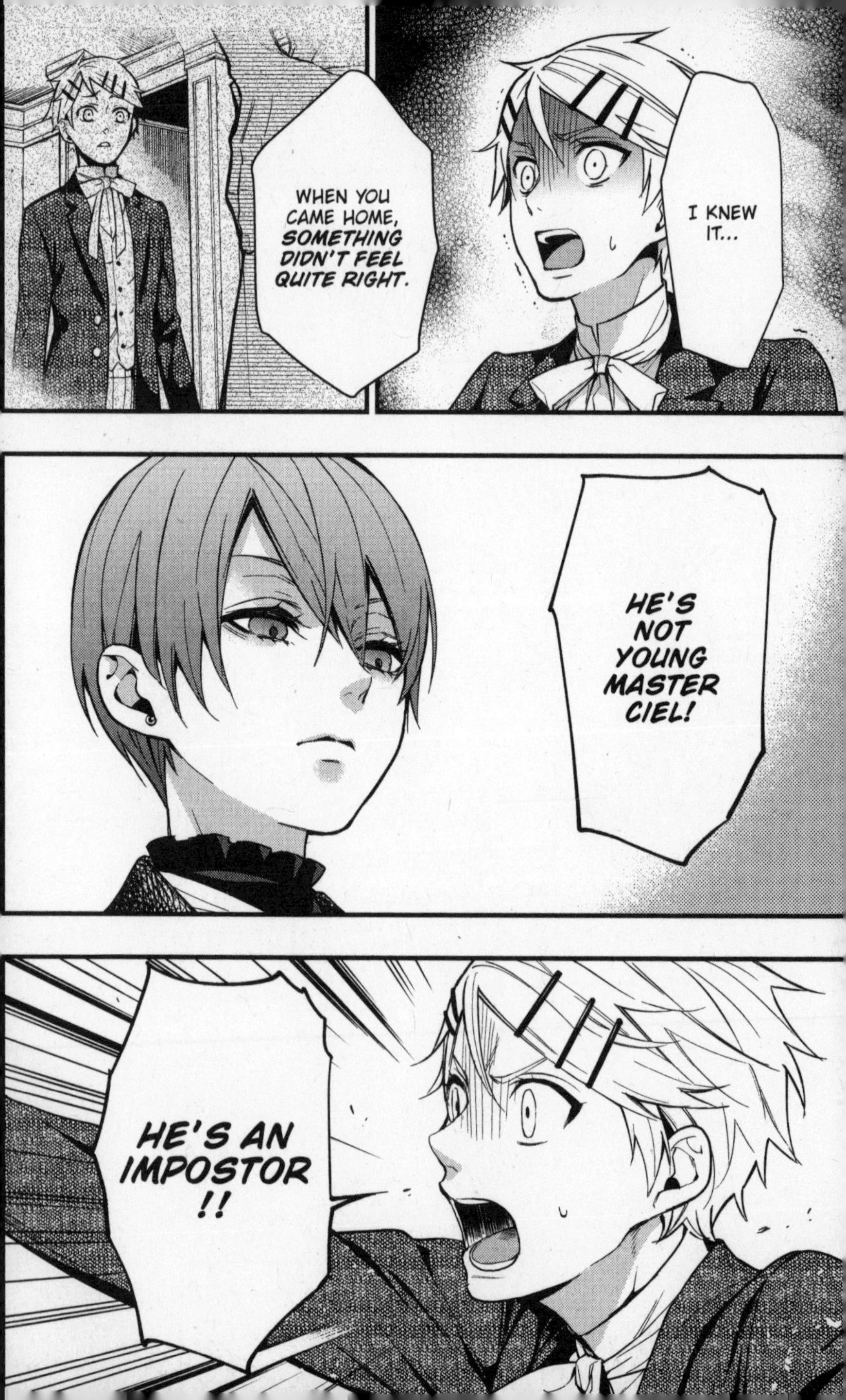
I KNEW IT...
WHEN YOU CAME HOME, SOMETHING DIDN'T FEEL QUITE RIGHT.
HE'S NOT YOUNG MASTER CIEL!
HE'S AN IMPOSTOR !!

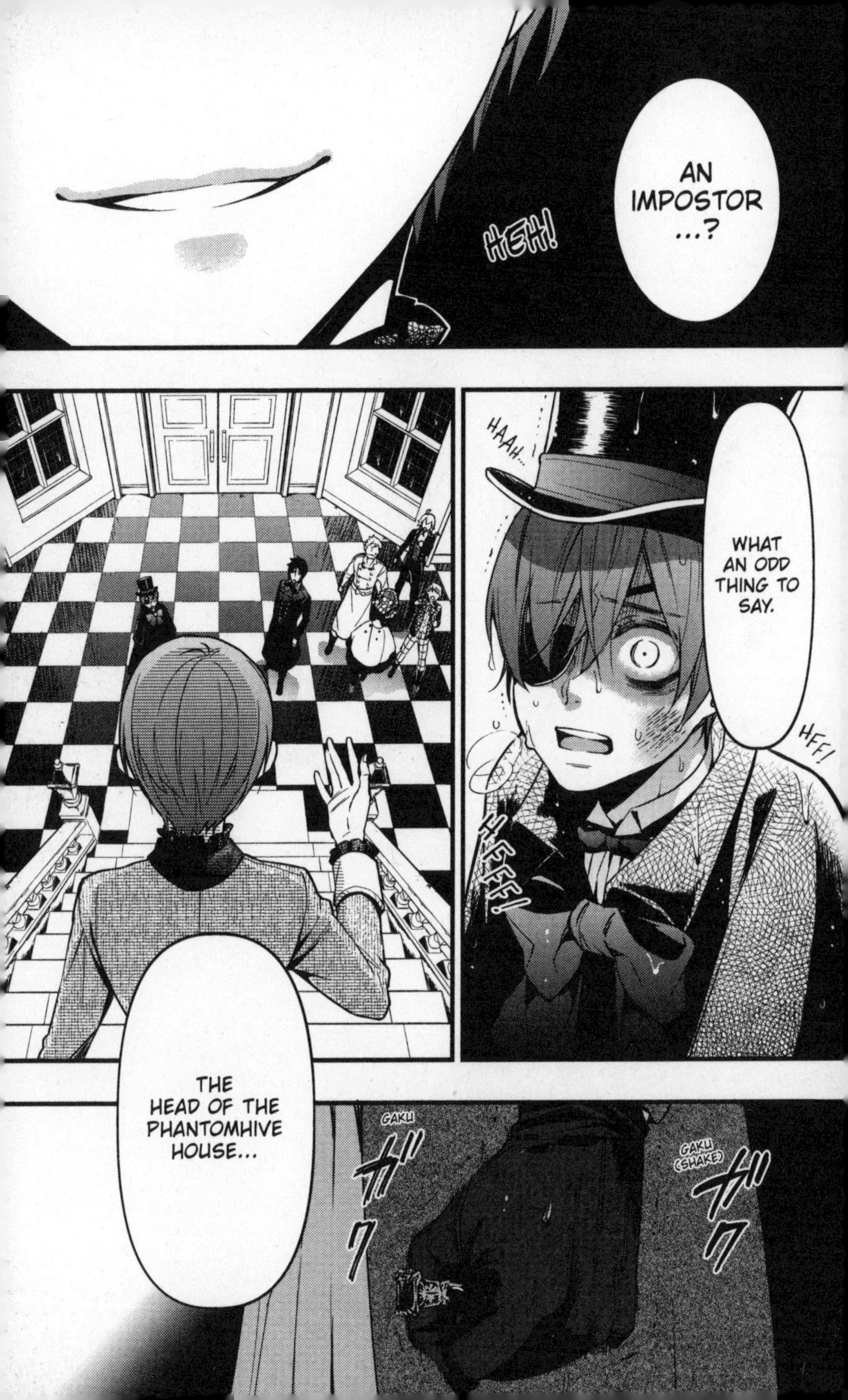
AN IMPOSTOR ...?
HEH!
HAAH...
WHAT AN ODD THING TO SAY.
HFF!
HFFF!
GAKU (SHAKE)
GAKU
THE HEAD OF THE PHANTOMHIVE HOUSE...

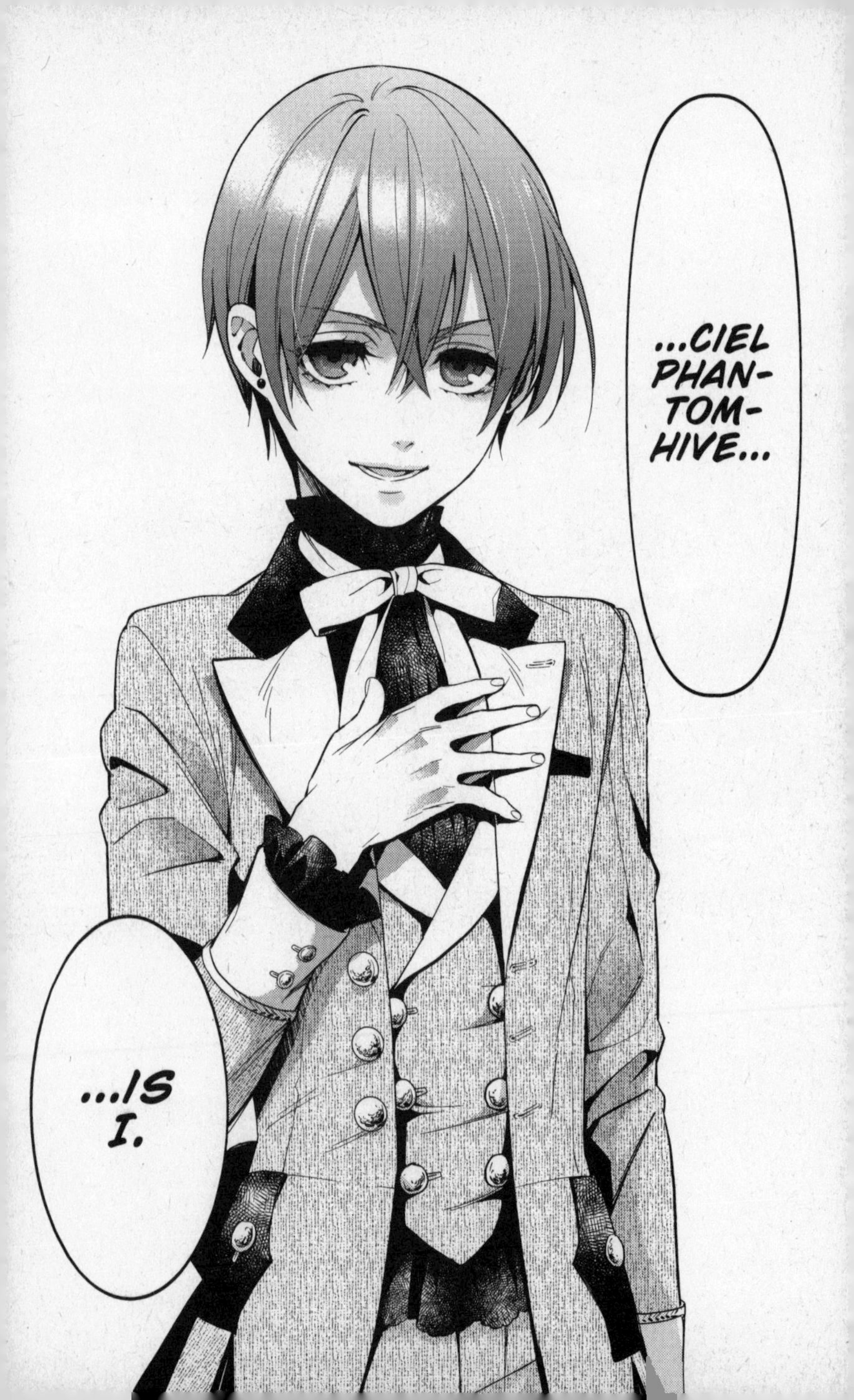
...CIEL PHAN-TOM-HIVE...
...IS I.

Black Butler

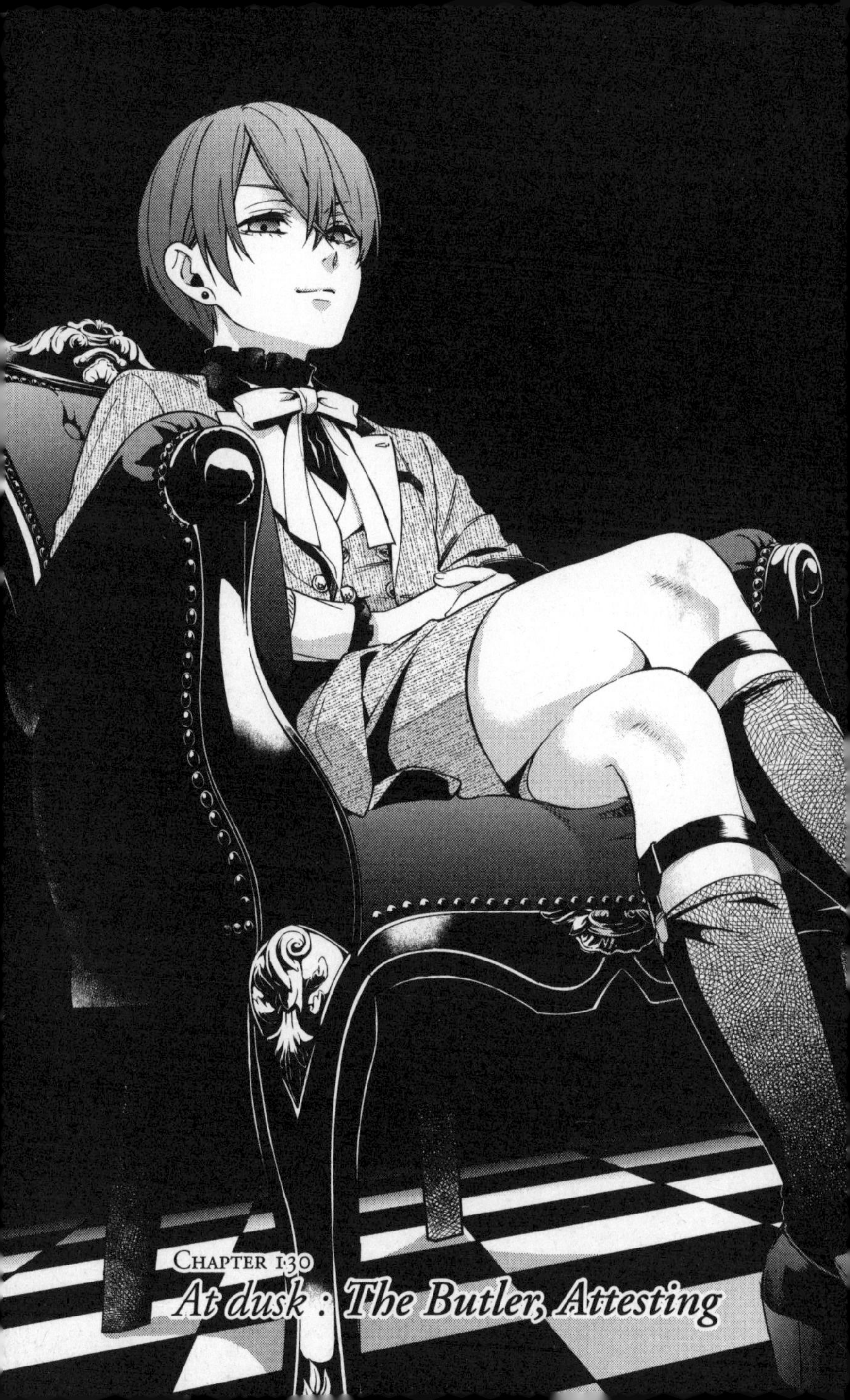
CHAPTER 130
At dusk : The Butler, Attesting

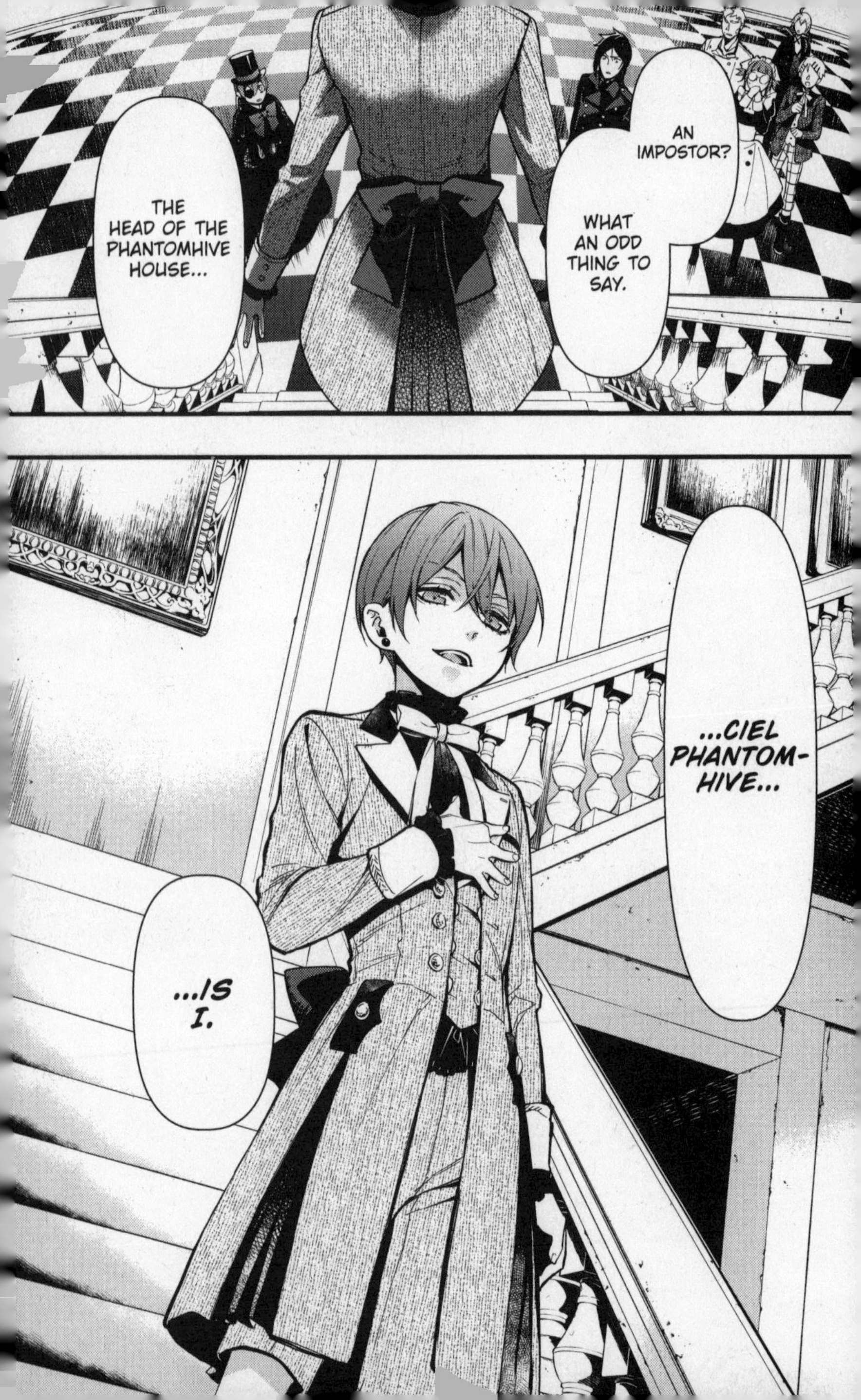
AN IMPOSTOR?
WHAT AN ODD THING TO SAY.
THE HEAD OF THE PHANTOMHIVE HOUSE...
...CIEL PHANTOM-HIVE...
...IS I.

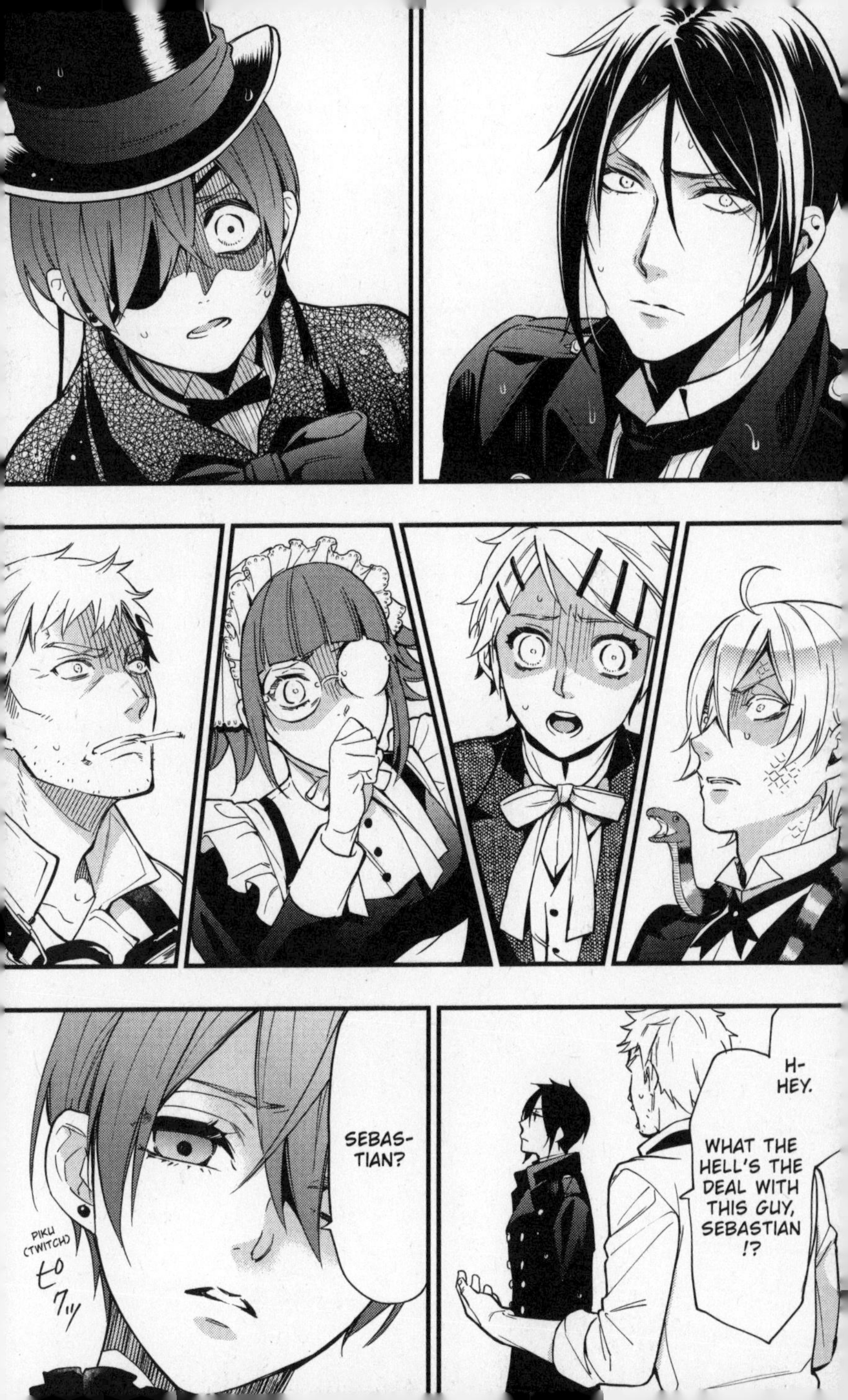
H-HEY.
WHAT THE HELL'S THE DEAL WITH THIS GUY, SEBASTIAN!?
SEBAS-TIAN?
PIKU (TWITCH)

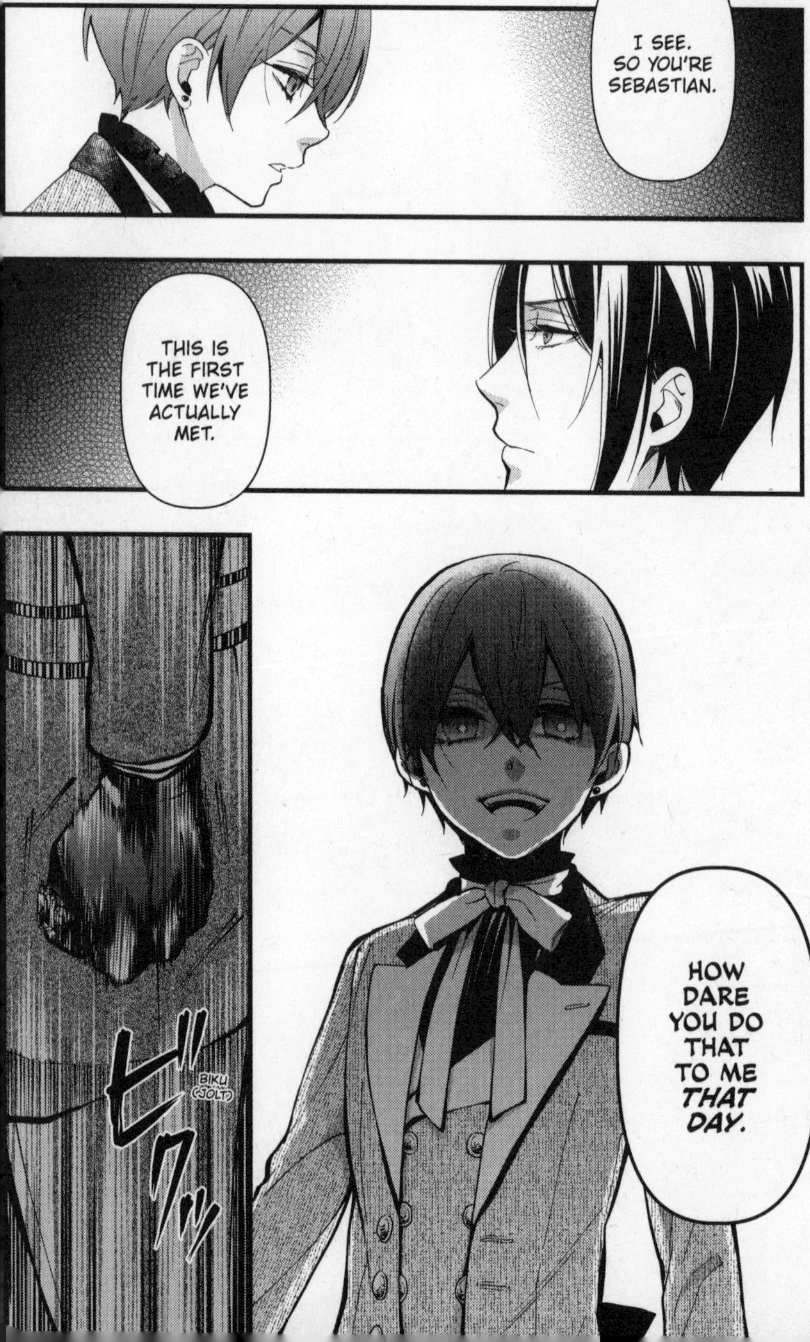
I SEE. SO YOU'RE SEBASTIAN.
THIS IS THE FIRST TIME WE'VE ACTUALLY MET.
HOW DARE YOU DO THAT TO ME *THAT DAY*.
ビクッ
BIKU (JOLT)

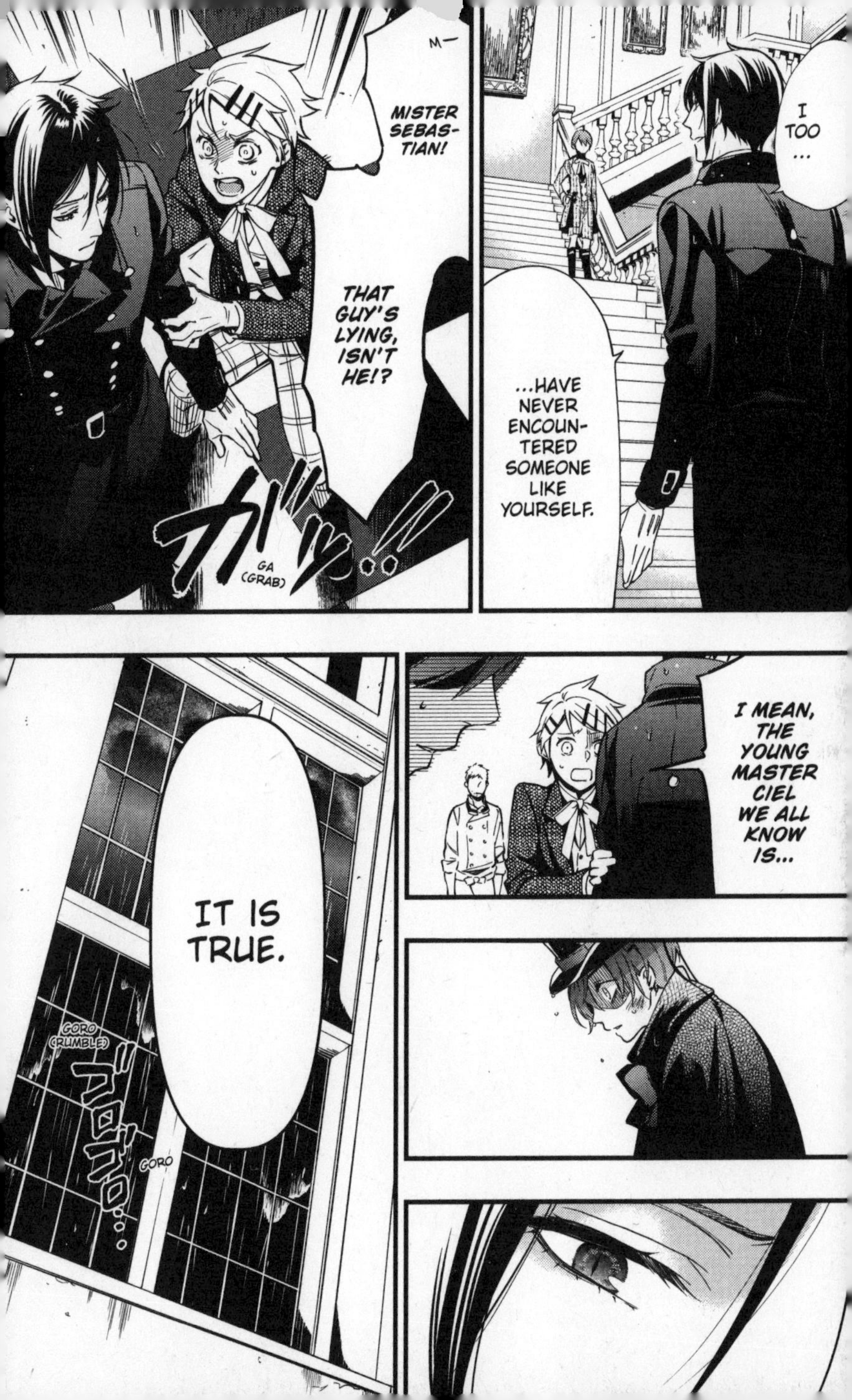
I TOO ...
...HAVE NEVER ENCOUNTERED SOMEONE LIKE YOURSELF.
M—
MISTER SEBASTIAN!
THAT GUY'S LYING, ISN'T HE!?
ガッ!!
GA (GRAB)
I MEAN, THE YOUNG MASTER CIEL WE ALL KNOW IS...
IT IS TRUE.
GORO (RUMBLE)
ゴロゴロ...
GORO

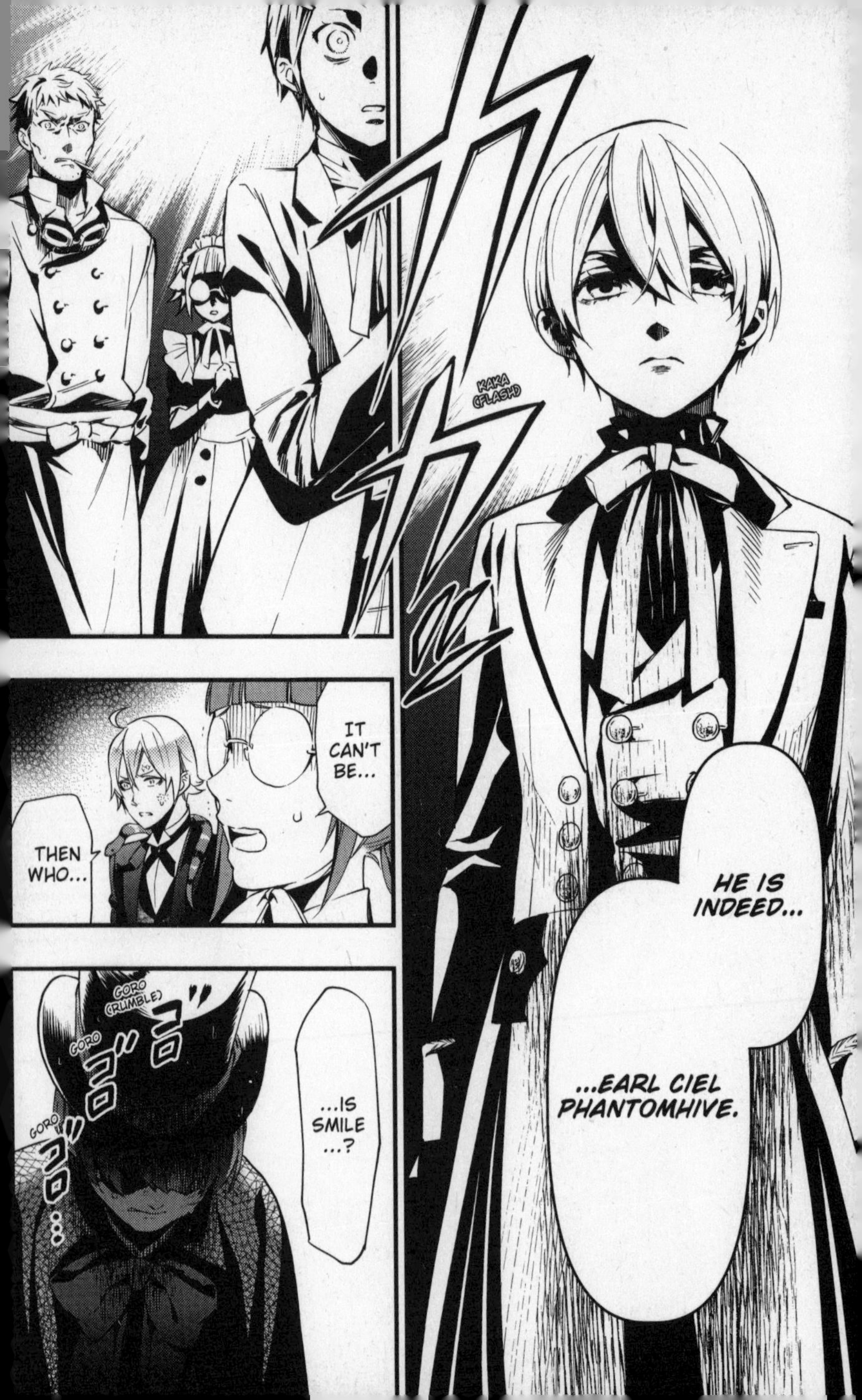
KAKA (FLASH)
HE IS INDEED...
...EARL CIEL PHANTOMHIVE.
IT CAN'T BE...
THEN WHO...
GORO (RUMBLE)
GORO
GORO
...IS SMILE ...?

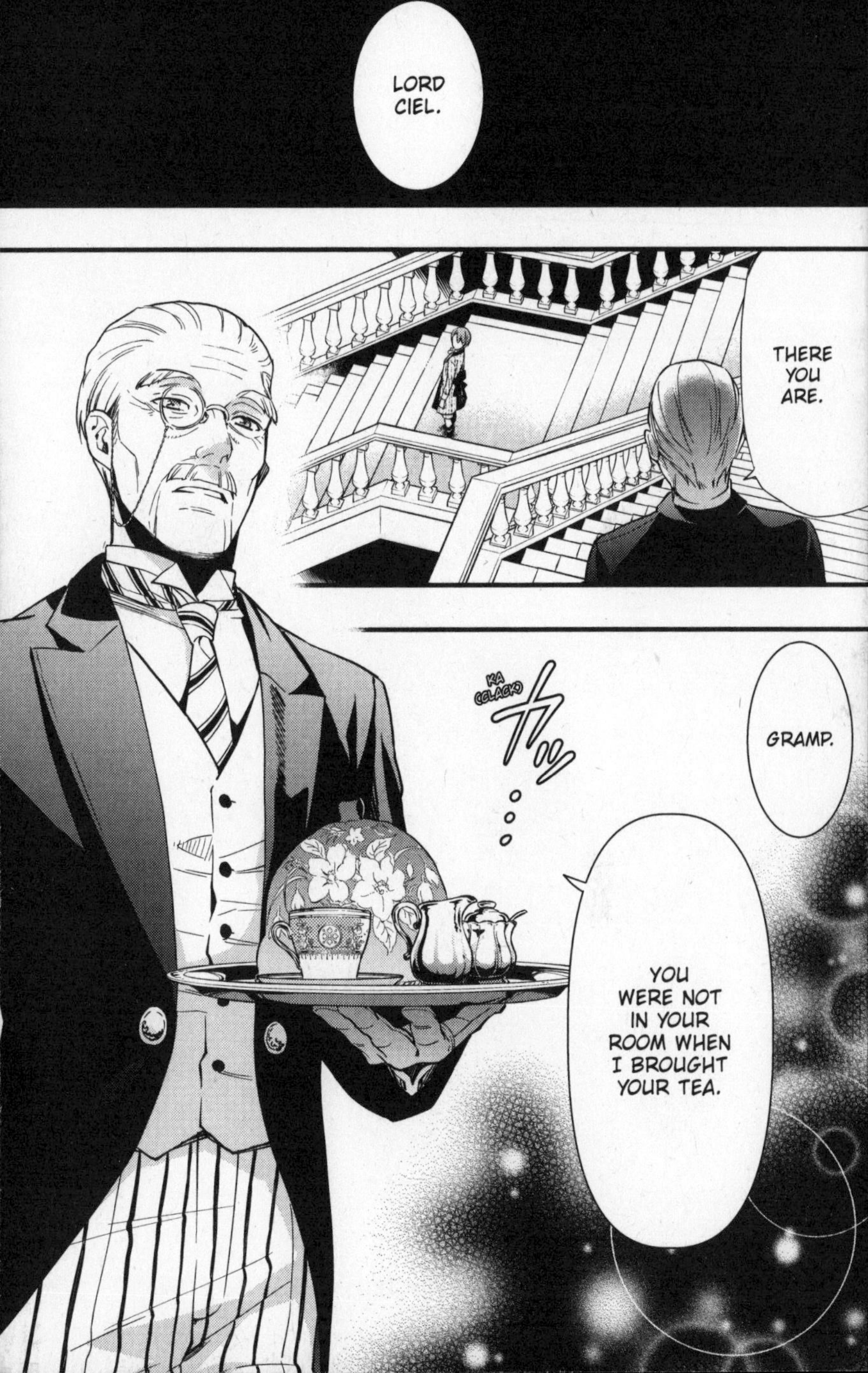
LORD CIEL.
THERE YOU ARE.
GRAMP.
KA (CLACK)
YOU WERE NOT IN YOUR ROOM WHEN I BROUGHT YOUR TEA.

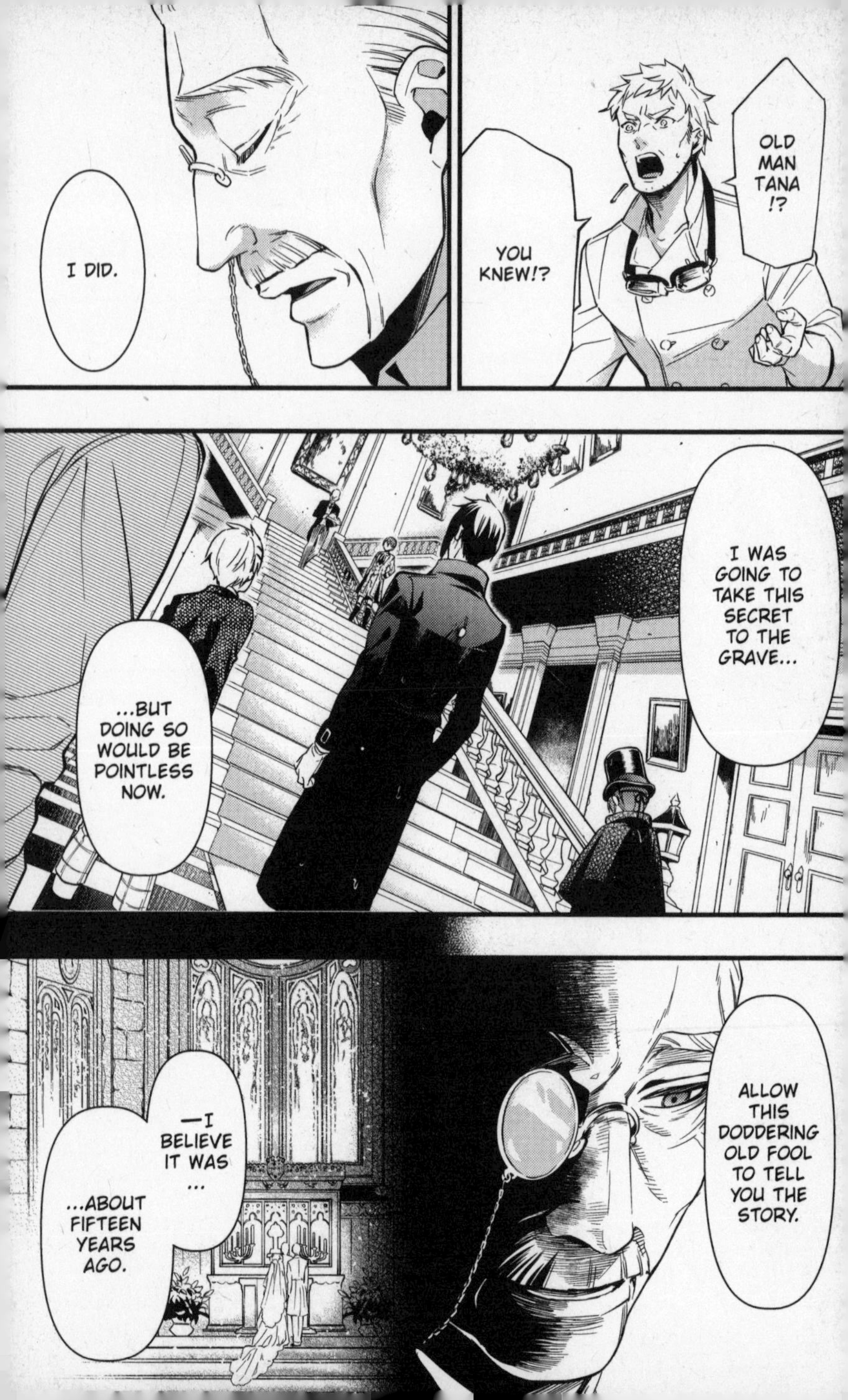
OLD MAN TANA!?
YOU KNEW!?
I DID.
I WAS GOING TO TAKE THIS SECRET TO THE GRAVE...
...BUT DOING SO WOULD BE POINTLESS NOW.
ALLOW THIS DODDERING OLD FOOL TO TELL YOU THE STORY.
—I BELIEVE IT WAS ...
...ABOUT FIFTEEN YEARS AGO.

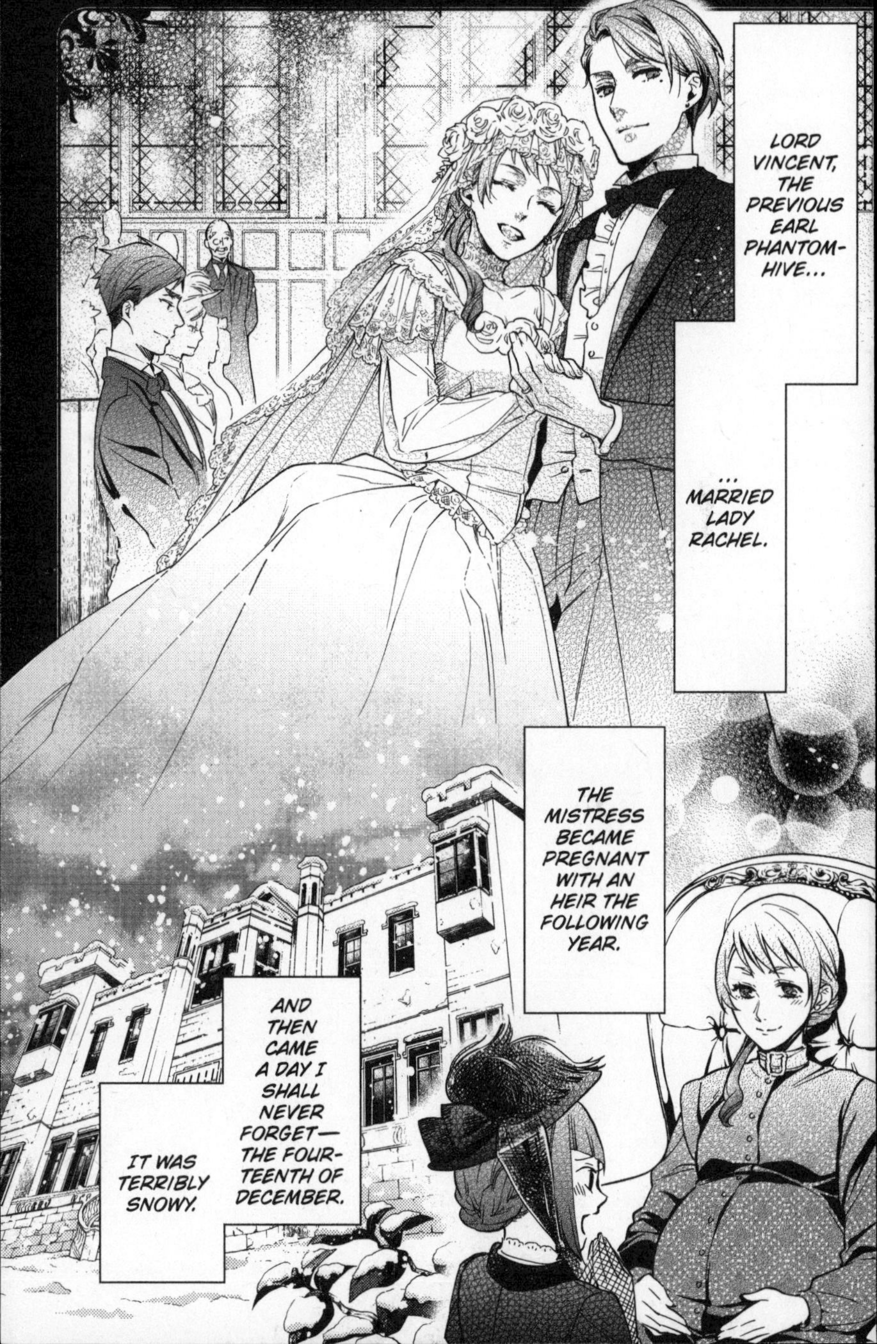
LORD VINCENT, THE PREVIOUS EARL PHANTOM-HIVE...
...MARRIED LADY RACHEL.
THE MISTRESS BECAME PREGNANT WITH AN HEIR THE FOLLOWING YEAR.
AND THEN CAME A DAY I SHALL NEVER FORGET—THE FOURTEENTH OF DECEMBER.
IT WAS TERRIBLY SNOWY.

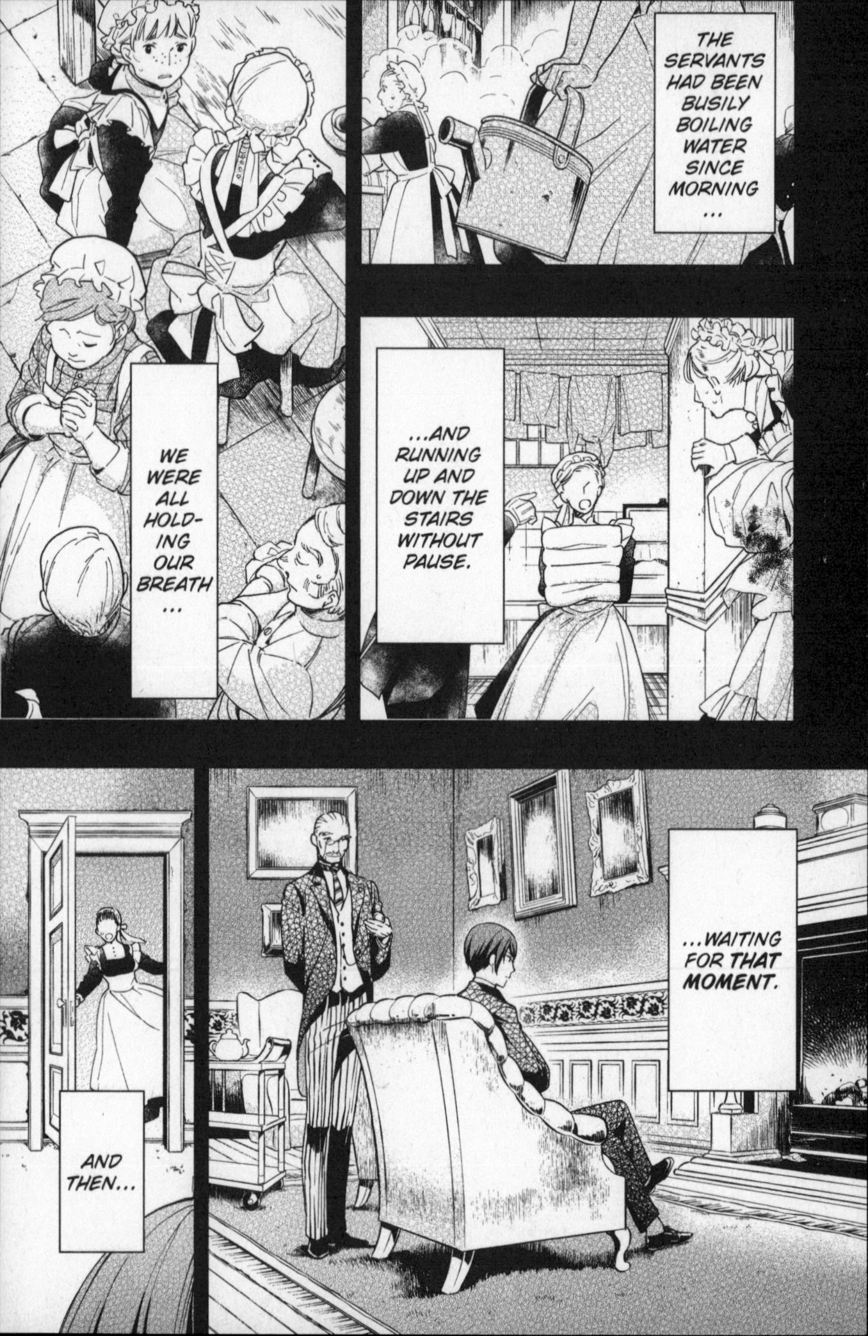
THE SERVANTS HAD BEEN BUSILY BOILING WATER SINCE MORNING...
...AND RUNNING UP AND DOWN THE STAIRS WITHOUT PAUSE.
WE WERE ALL HOLDING OUR BREATH...
...WAITING FOR THAT MOMENT.
AND THEN...

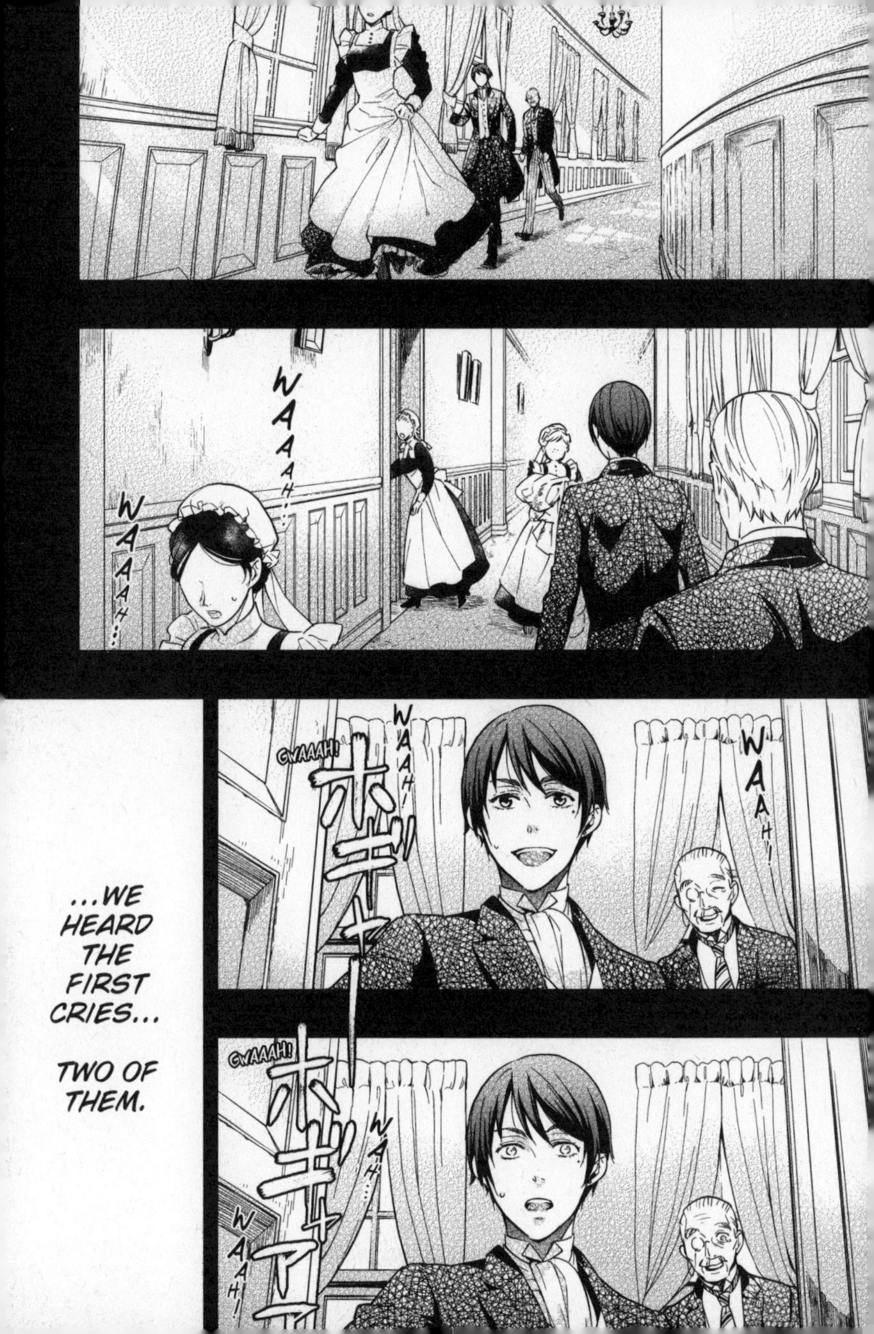

WAAAAH...
WAAAAH...
WAAAH!
WAAH!
GWAAAH!
ホギャ
...WE HEARD THE FIRST CRIES...
TWO OF THEM.
WAAH...
WAAAH!
GWAAAH!
ホギャア

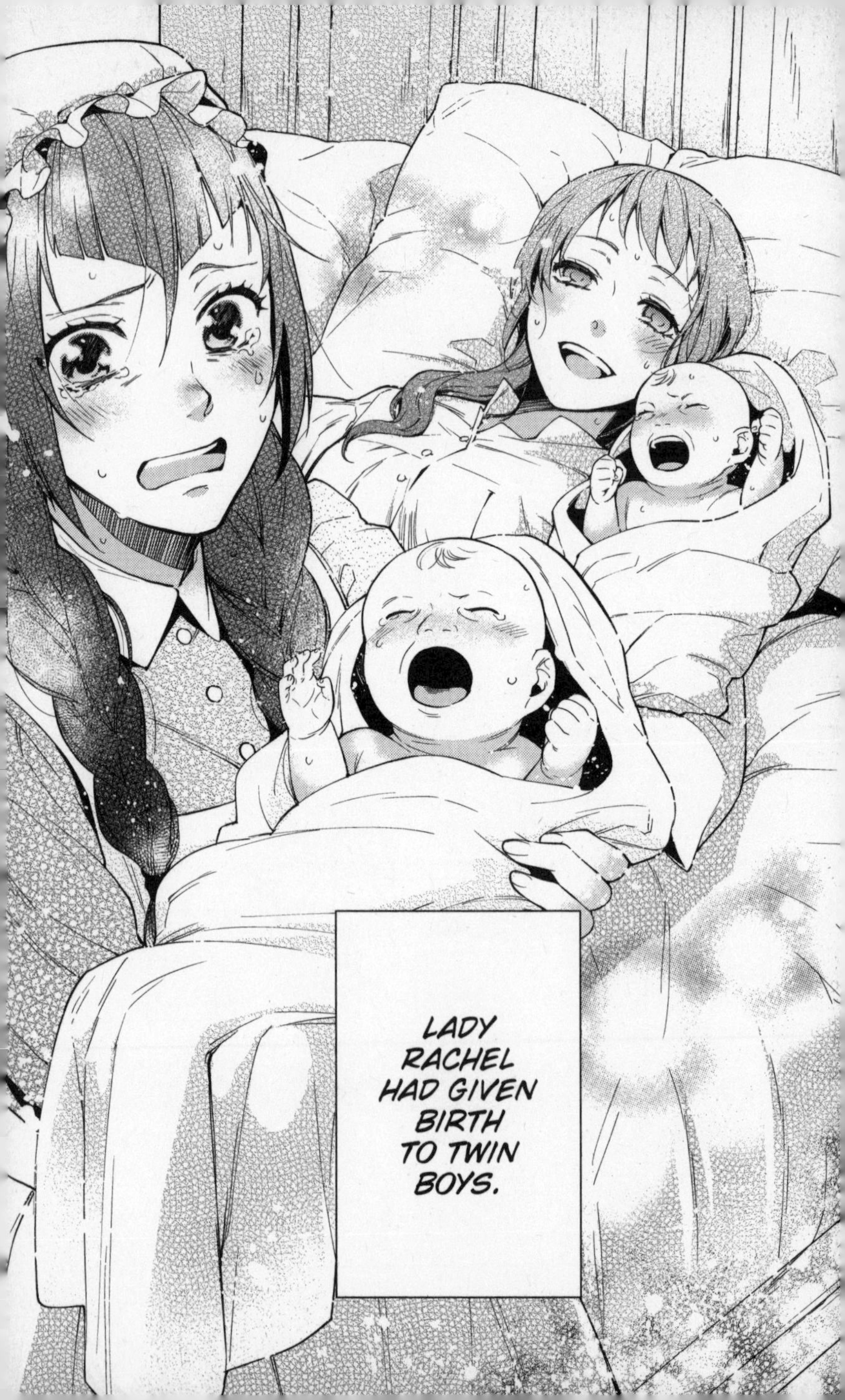
LADY RACHEL HAD GIVEN BIRTH TO TWIN BOYS.

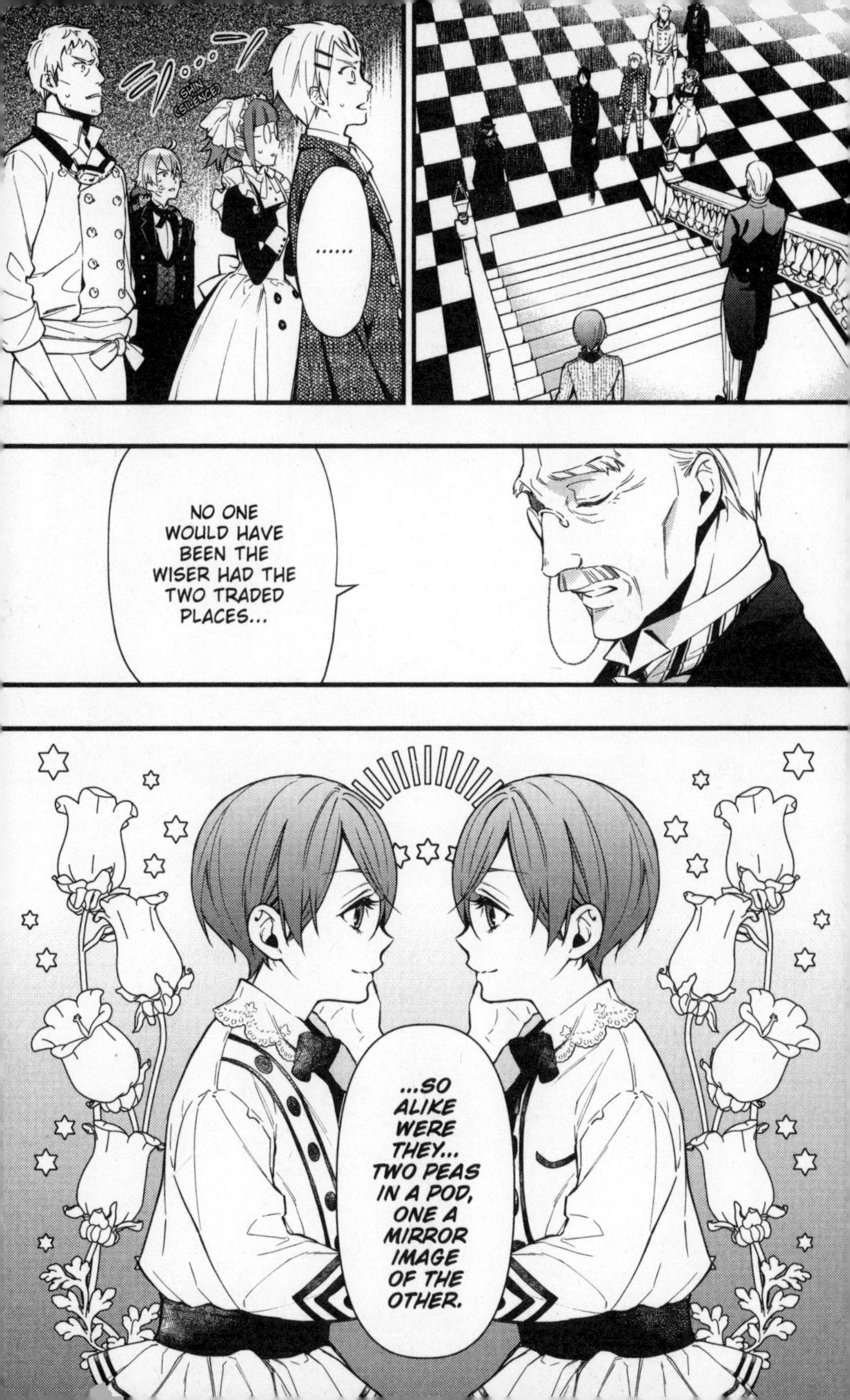
SHIN (SILENCE)
......
NO ONE WOULD HAVE BEEN THE WISER HAD THE TWO TRADED PLACES...
...SO ALIKE WERE THEY... TWO PEAS IN A POD, ONE A MIRROR IMAGE OF THE OTHER.

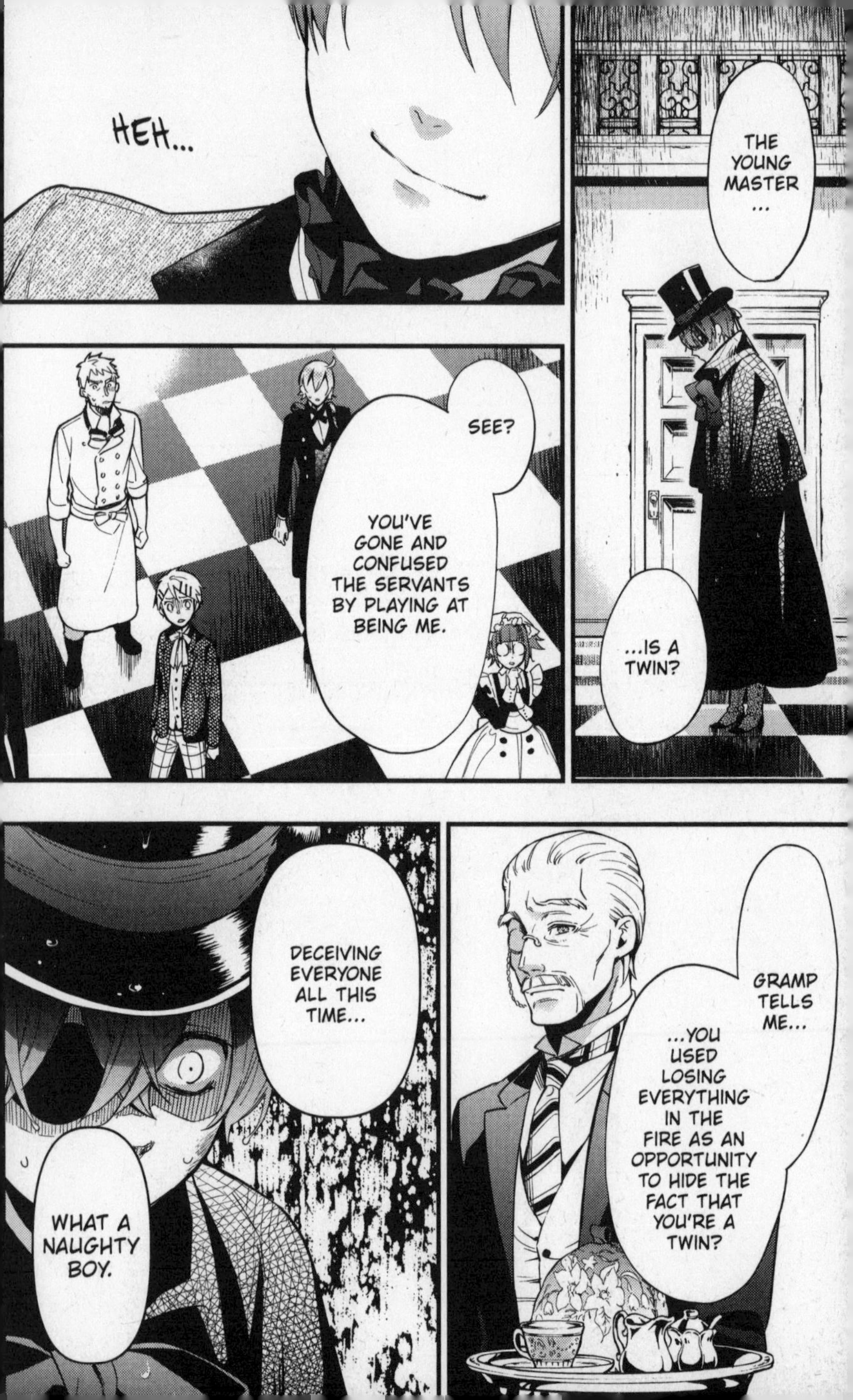
THE YOUNG MASTER...
...IS A TWIN?
HEH...
SEE?
YOU'VE GONE AND CONFUSED THE SERVANTS BY PLAYING AT BEING ME.
GRAMP TELLS ME...
...YOU USED LOSING EVERYTHING IN THE FIRE AS AN OPPORTUNITY TO HIDE THE FACT THAT YOU'RE A TWIN?
DECEIVING EVERYONE ALL THIS TIME...
WHAT A NAUGHTY BOY.

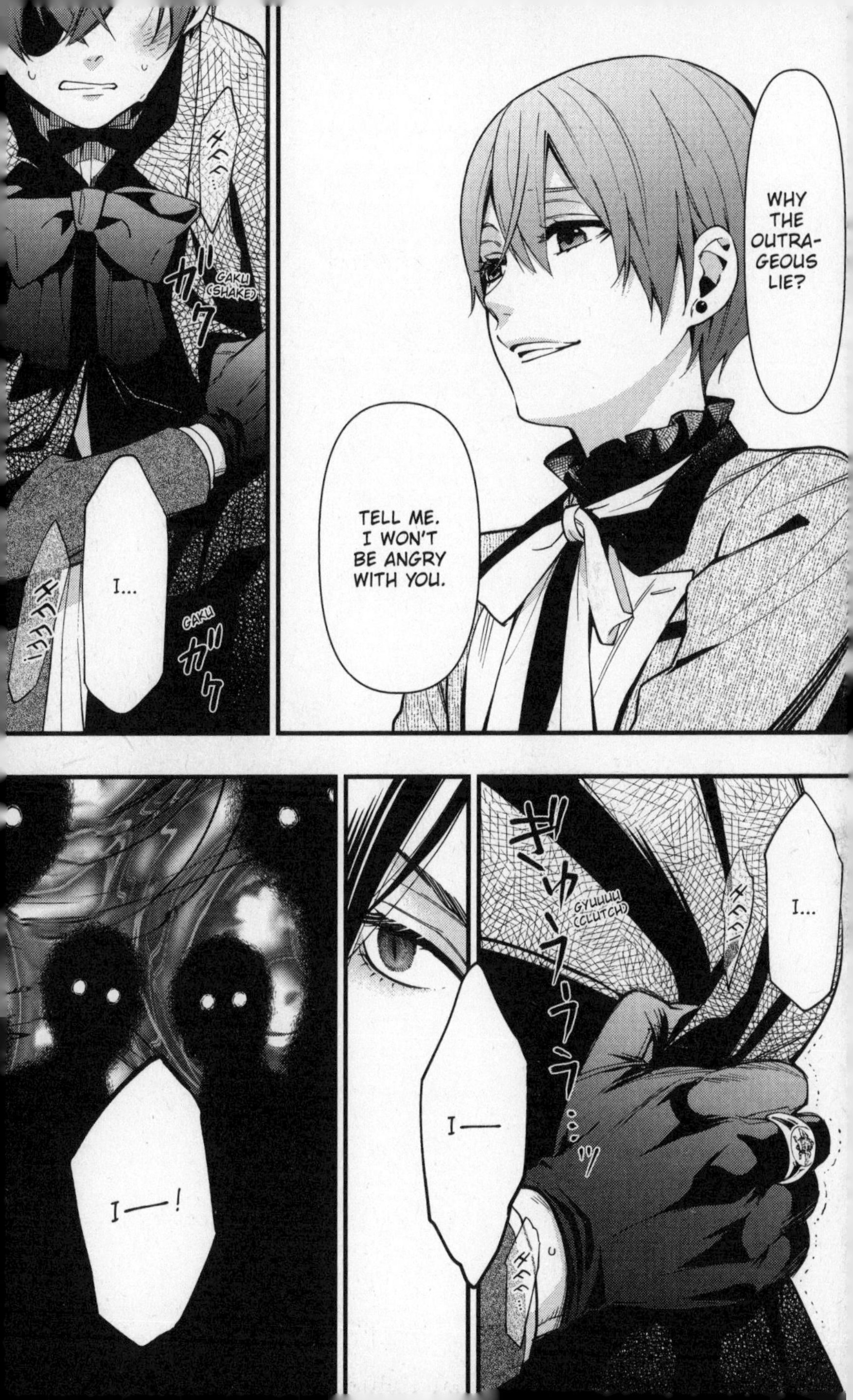
WHY THE OUTRA-GEOUS LIE?
TELL ME. I WON'T BE ANGRY WITH YOU.
GAKU (SHAKE)
I...
GAKU
I...
GYUUUU (CLUTCH)
I—
I—!

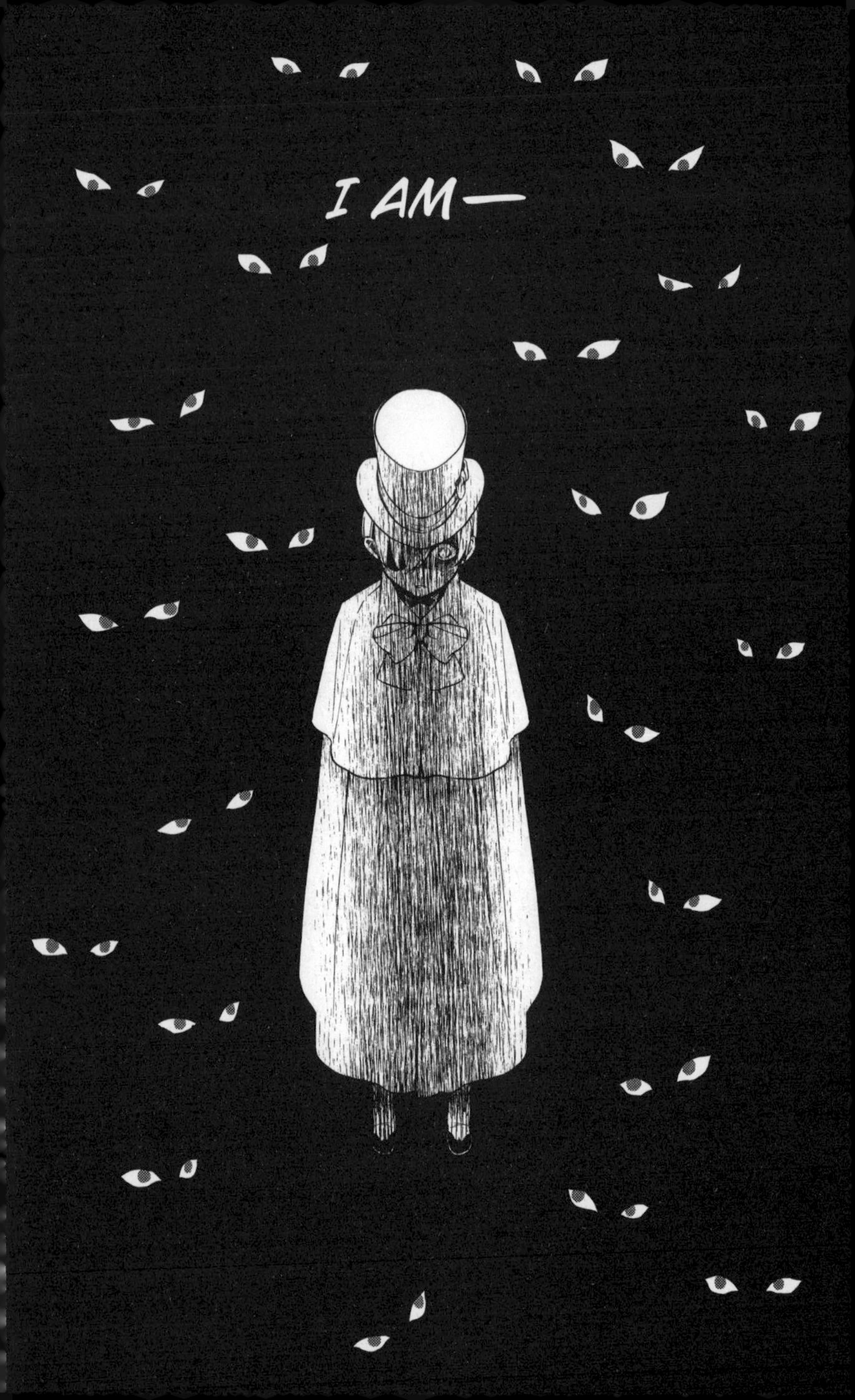
I AM—

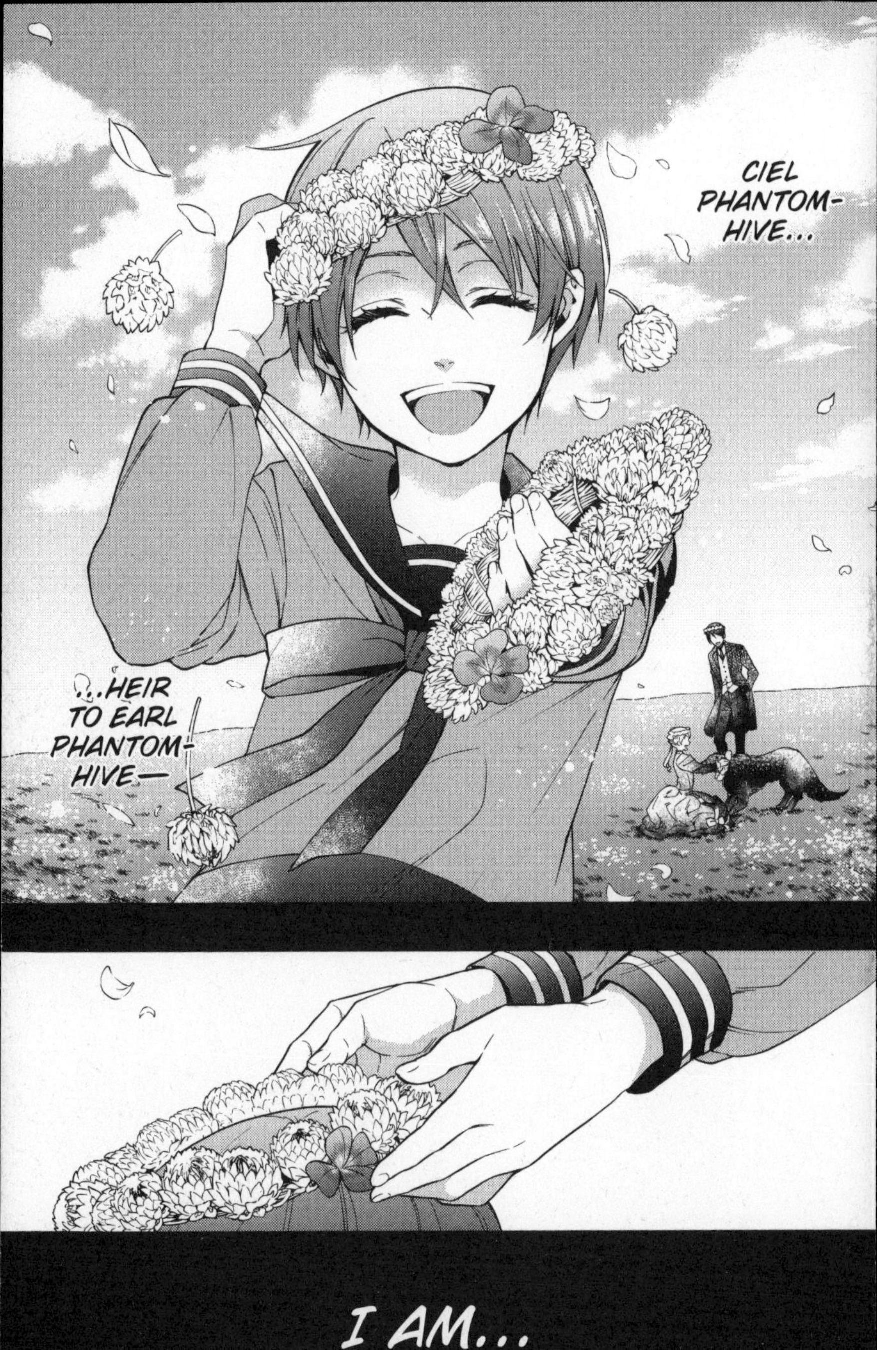
CIEL PHANTOM-HIVE...
...HEIR TO EARL PHANTOM-HIVE—
I AM...

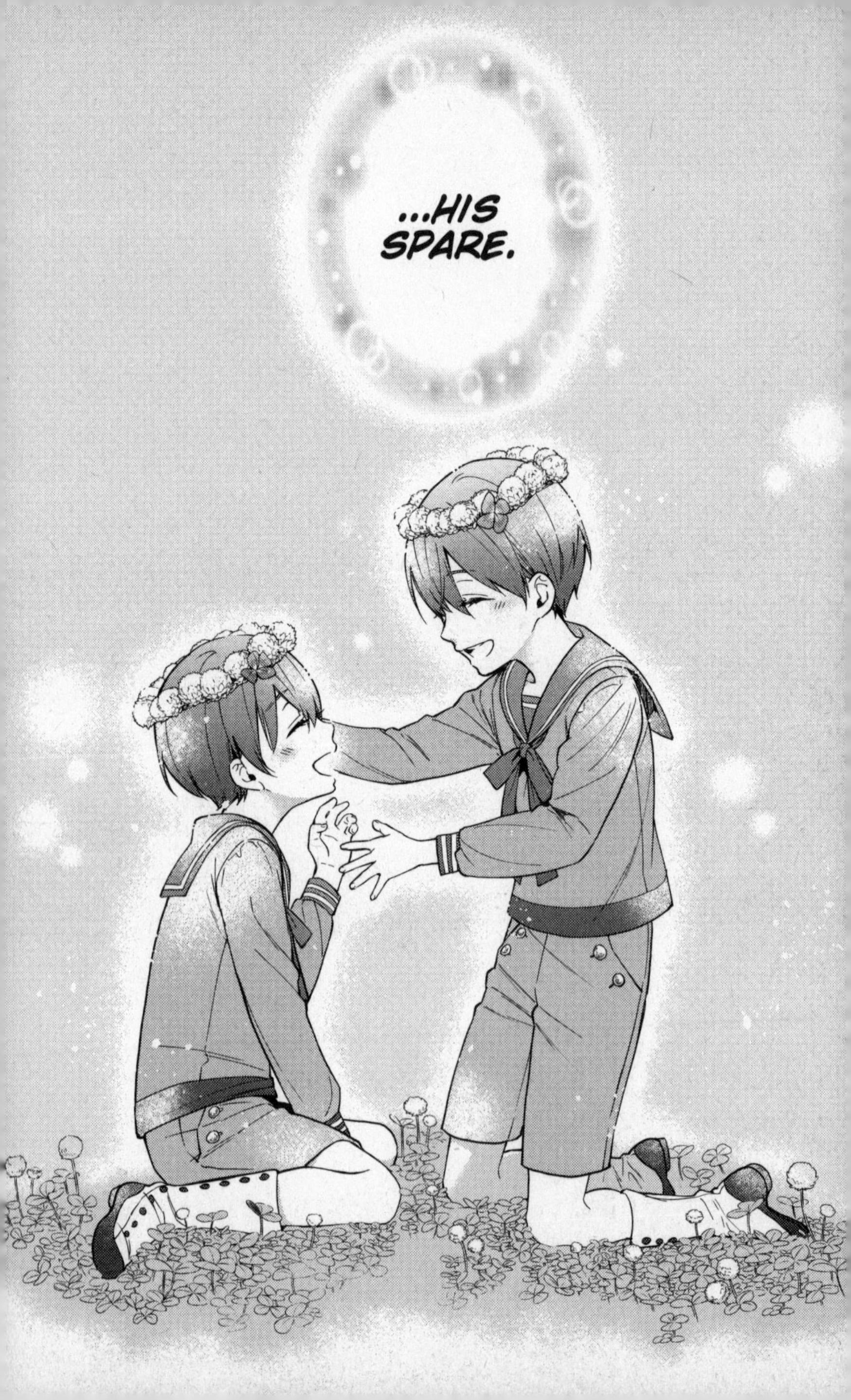
...HIS SPARE.

Black Butler

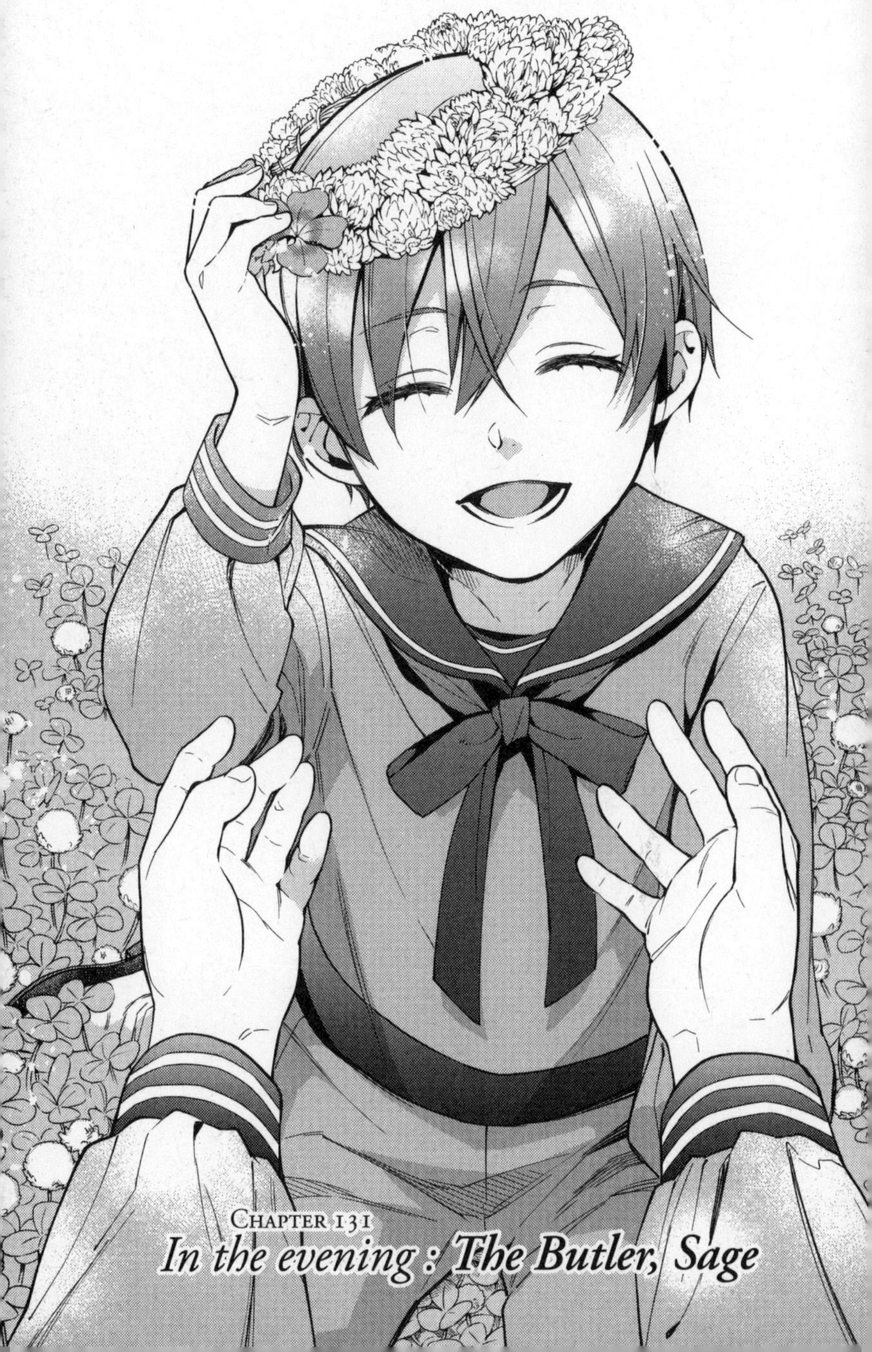

Chapter 131

In the evening : The Butler, Sage

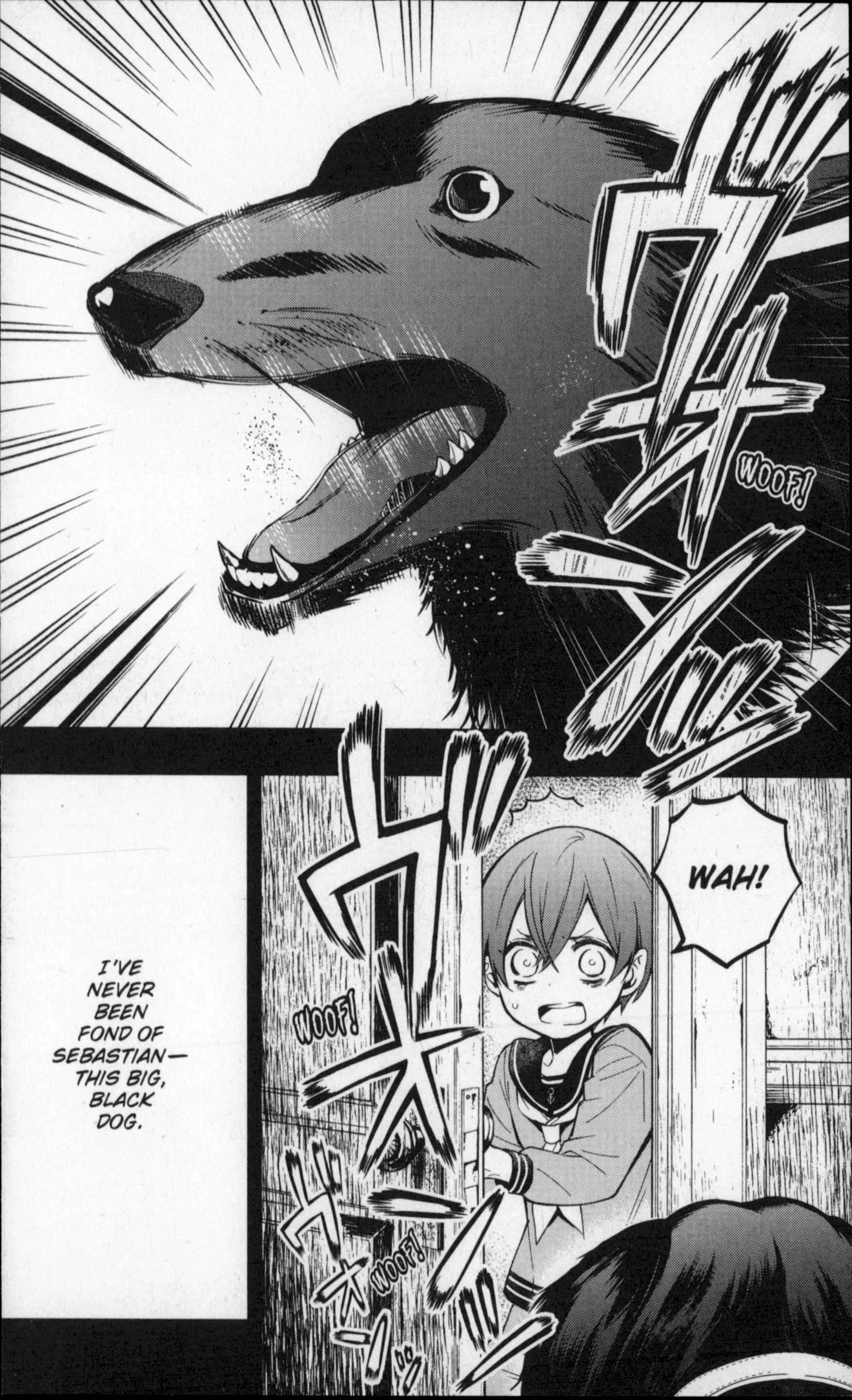
WOOF!
WAH!
WOOF!
WOOF!
I'VE NEVER BEEN FOND OF SEBASTIAN—THIS BIG, BLACK DOG.

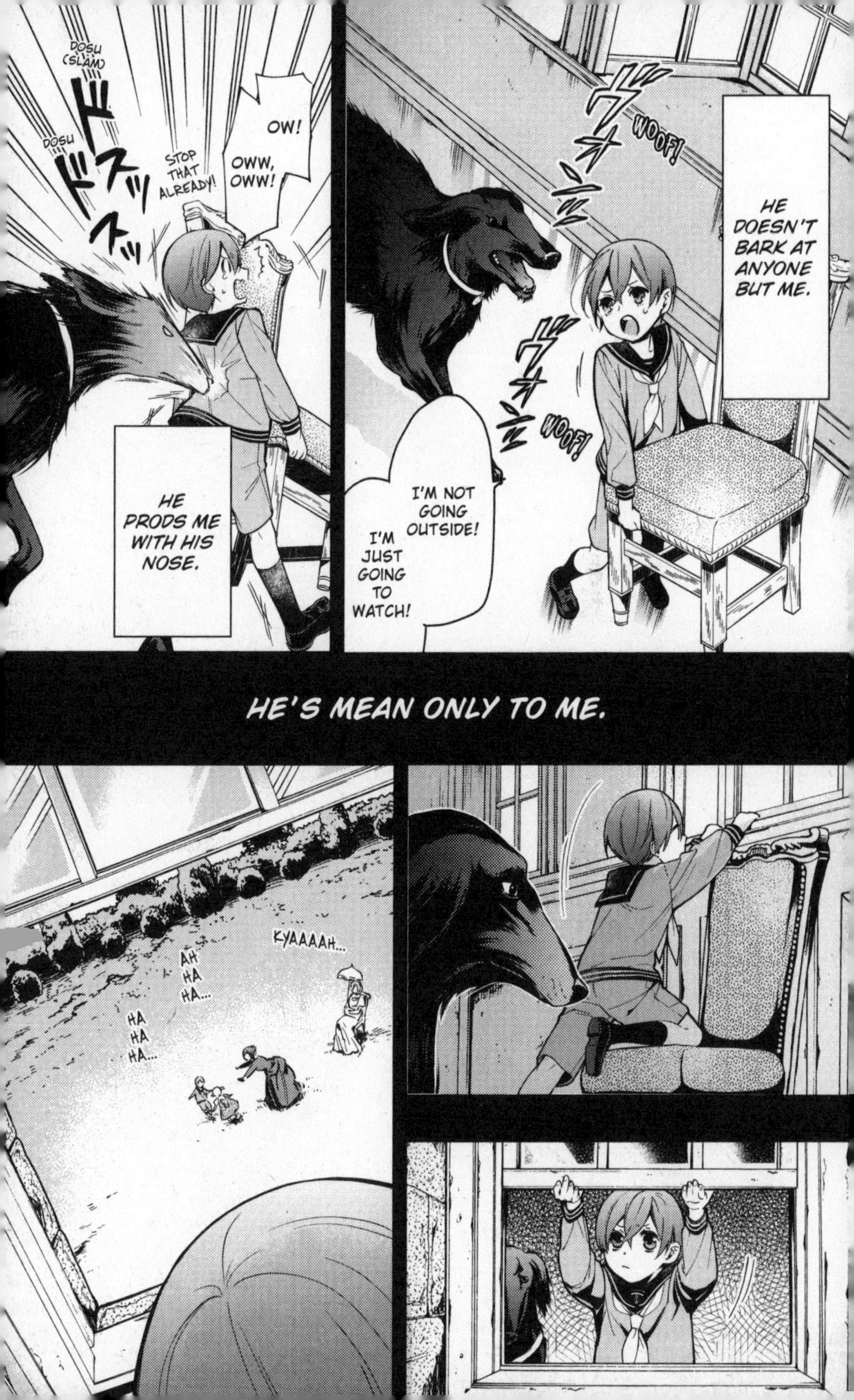
HE DOESN'T BARK AT ANYONE BUT ME.
WOOF!
WOOF!
I'M NOT GOING OUTSIDE!
I'M JUST GOING TO WATCH!
OW!
OWW, OWW!
STOP THAT ALREADY!
DOSU (SLAM)
DOSU
HE PRODS ME WITH HIS NOSE.
HE'S MEAN ONLY TO ME.
KYAAAAH...
AH HA HA...
HA HA HA...

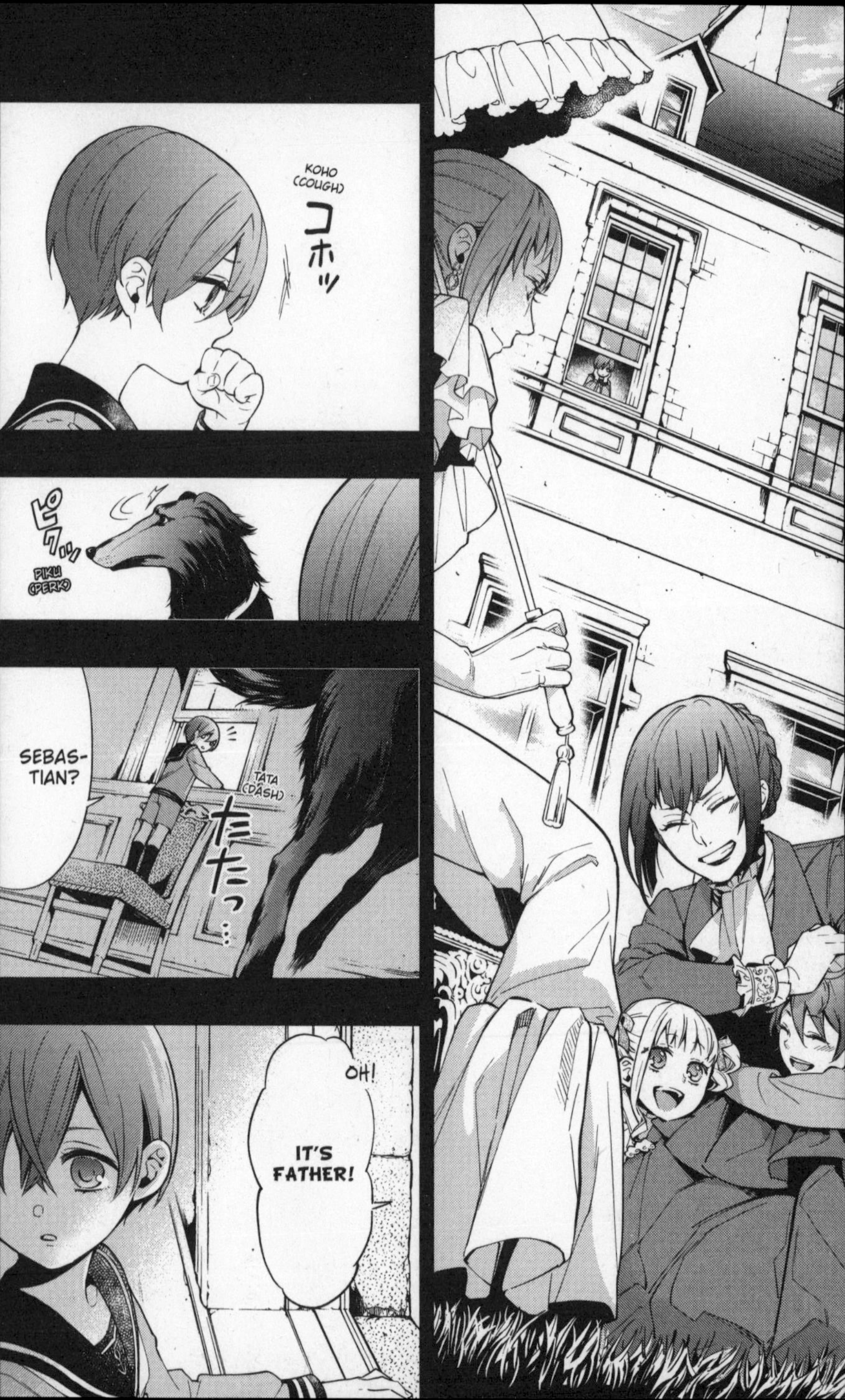

KOHO (COUGH)
コホッ
ピクッ
PIKU (PERK)
TATA (DASH)
たたっ…
SEBAS-TIAN?
OH!
IT'S FATHER!

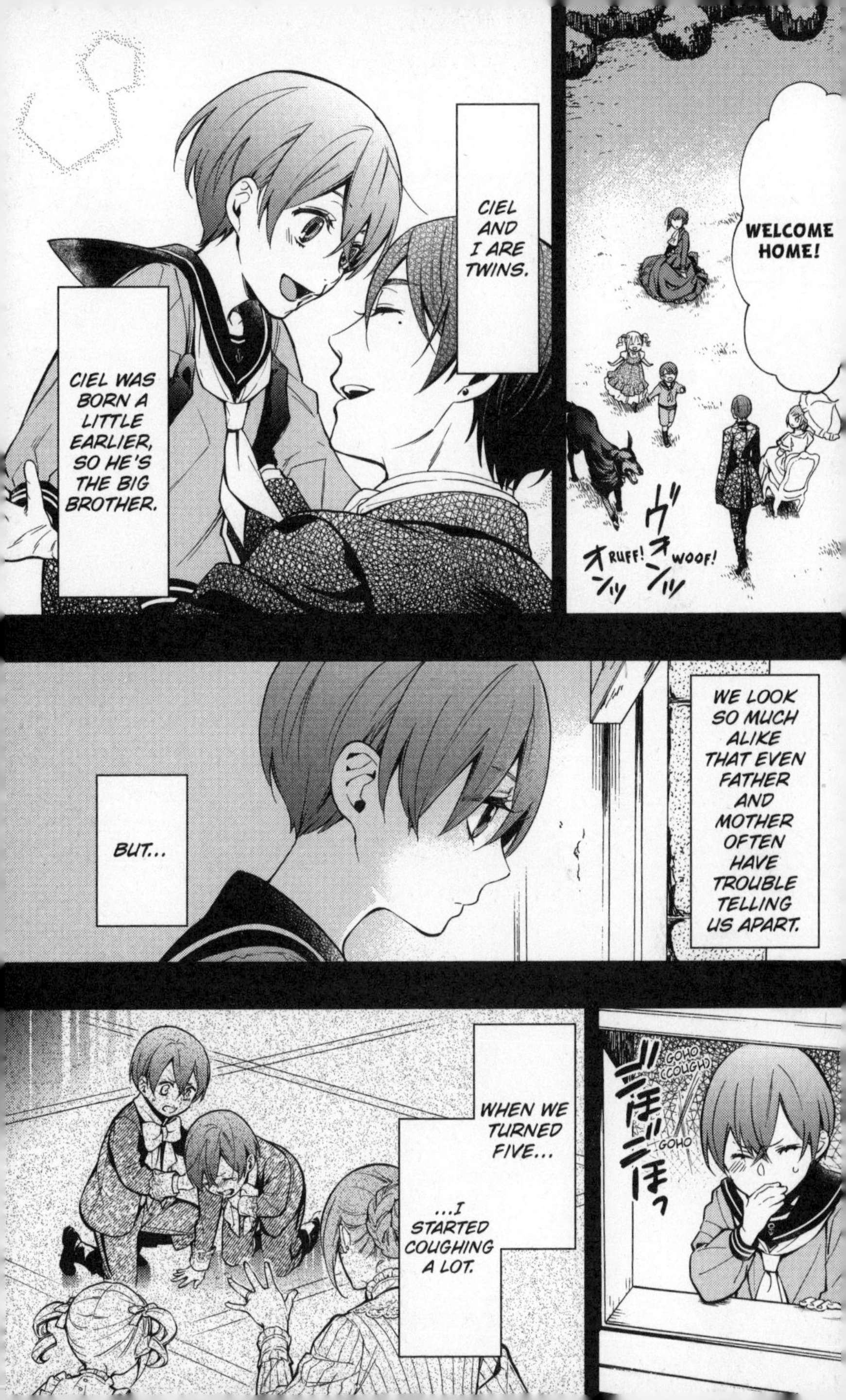
WELCOME HOME!
ヴォンッ WOOF!
オンッ RUFF!
CIEL AND I ARE TWINS.
CIEL WAS BORN A LITTLE EARLIER, SO HE'S THE BIG BROTHER.
WE LOOK SO MUCH ALIKE THAT EVEN FATHER AND MOTHER OFTEN HAVE TROUBLE TELLING US APART.
BUT...
ゴホ GOHO (COUGH)
ゴホッ GOHO
WHEN WE TURNED FIVE...
...I STARTED COUGHING A LOT.

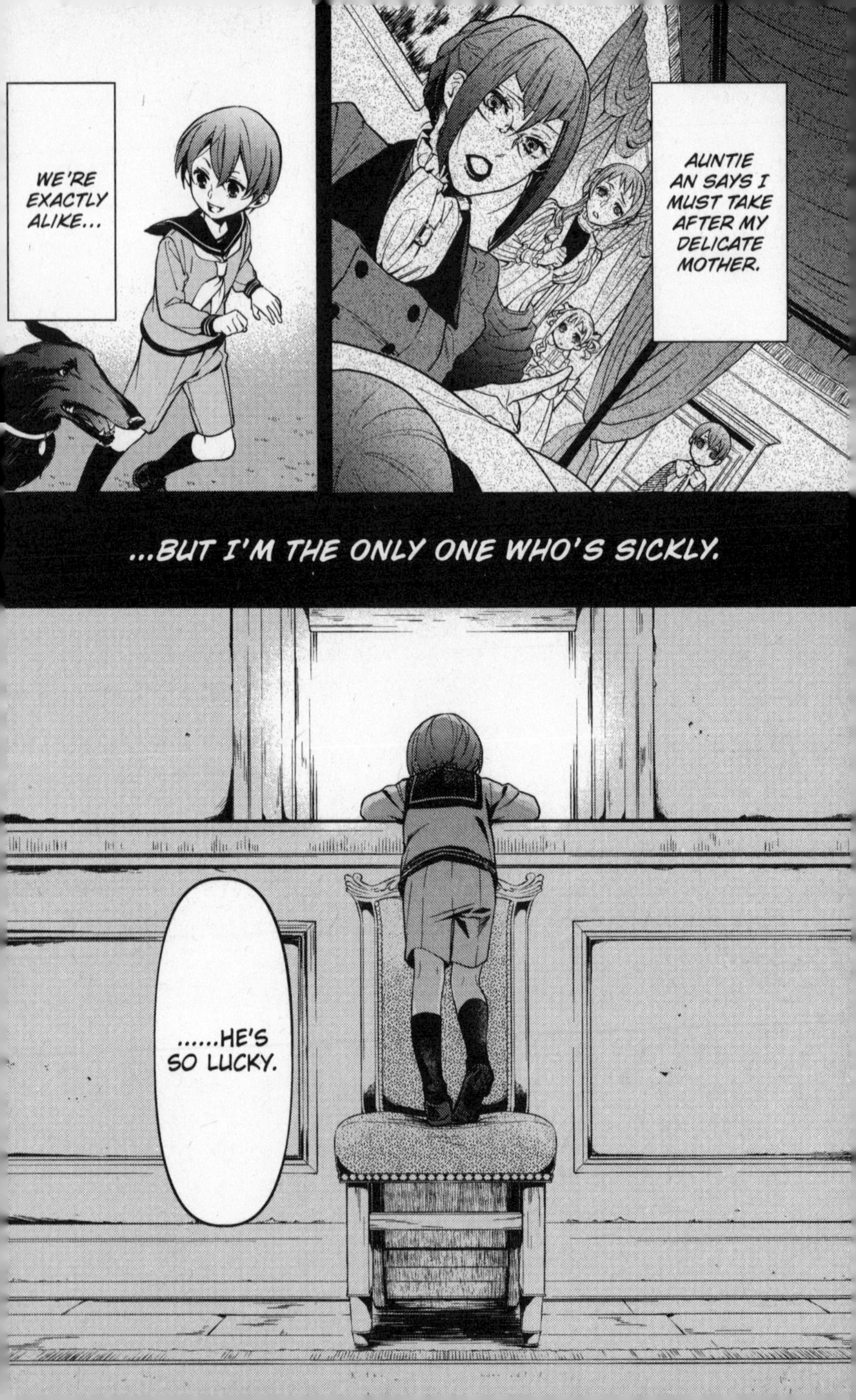
AUNTIE AN SAYS I MUST TAKE AFTER MY DELICATE MOTHER.
WE'RE EXACTLY ALIKE...
...BUT I'M THE ONLY ONE WHO'S SICKLY.
......HE'S SO LUCKY.

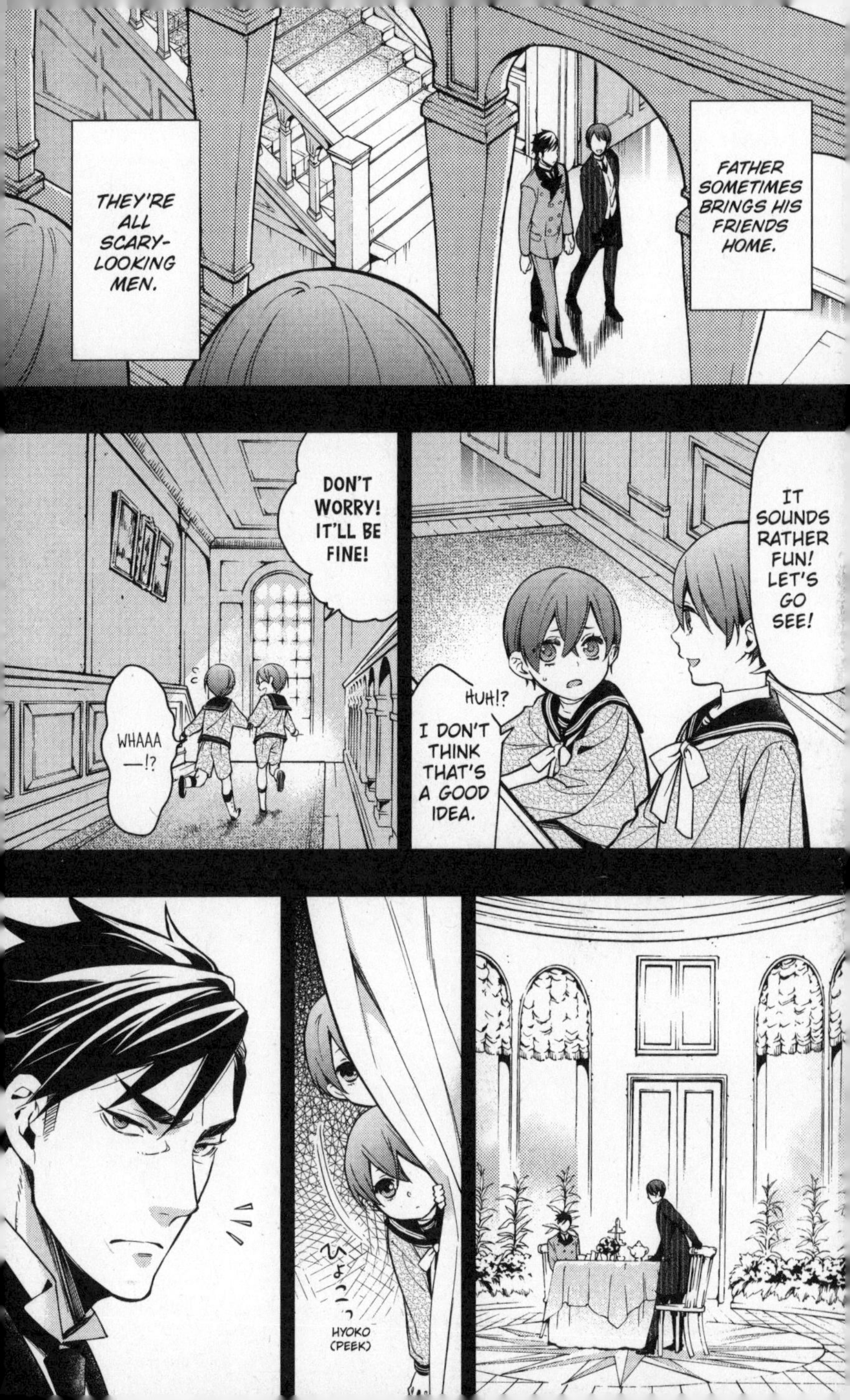
FATHER SOMETIMES BRINGS HIS FRIENDS HOME.
THEY'RE ALL SCARY-LOOKING MEN.
IT SOUNDS RATHER FUN! LET'S GO SEE!
HUH!?
I DON'T THINK THAT'S A GOOD IDEA.
DON'T WORRY! IT'LL BE FINE!
WHAAA—!?
ひょこっ
HYOKO (PEEK)

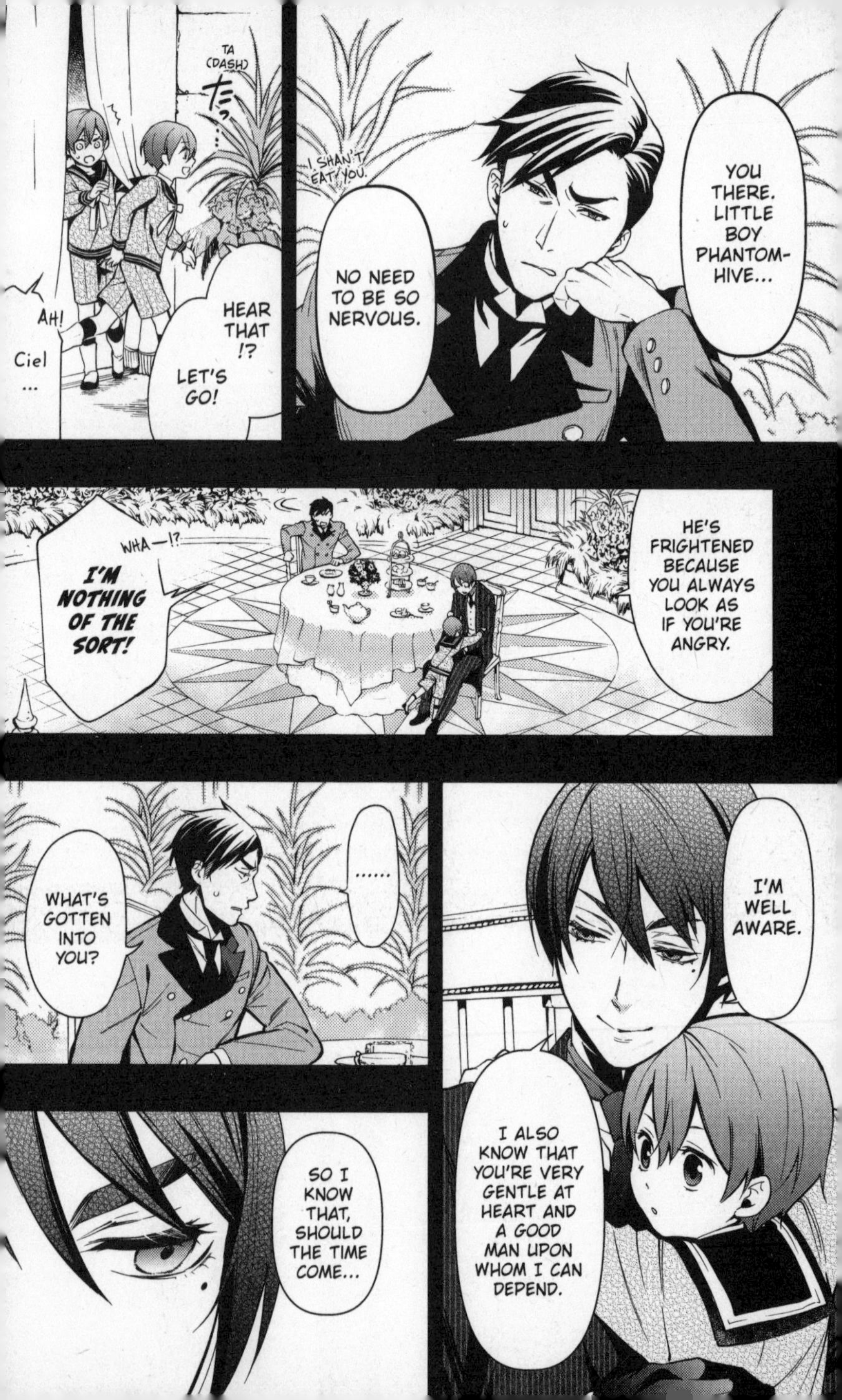
YOU THERE. LITTLE BOY PHANTOM-HIVE...
NO NEED TO BE SO NERVOUS.
I SHAN'T EAT YOU.
TA (DASH)
HEAR THAT!? LET'S GO!
AH!
Ciel ...
HE'S FRIGHTENED BECAUSE YOU ALWAYS LOOK AS IF YOU'RE ANGRY.
WHA—!?
I'M NOTHING OF THE SORT!
I'M WELL AWARE.
I ALSO KNOW THAT YOU'RE VERY GENTLE AT HEART AND A GOOD MAN UPON WHOM I CAN DEPEND.
......
WHAT'S GOTTEN INTO YOU?
SO I KNOW THAT, SHOULD THE TIME COME...

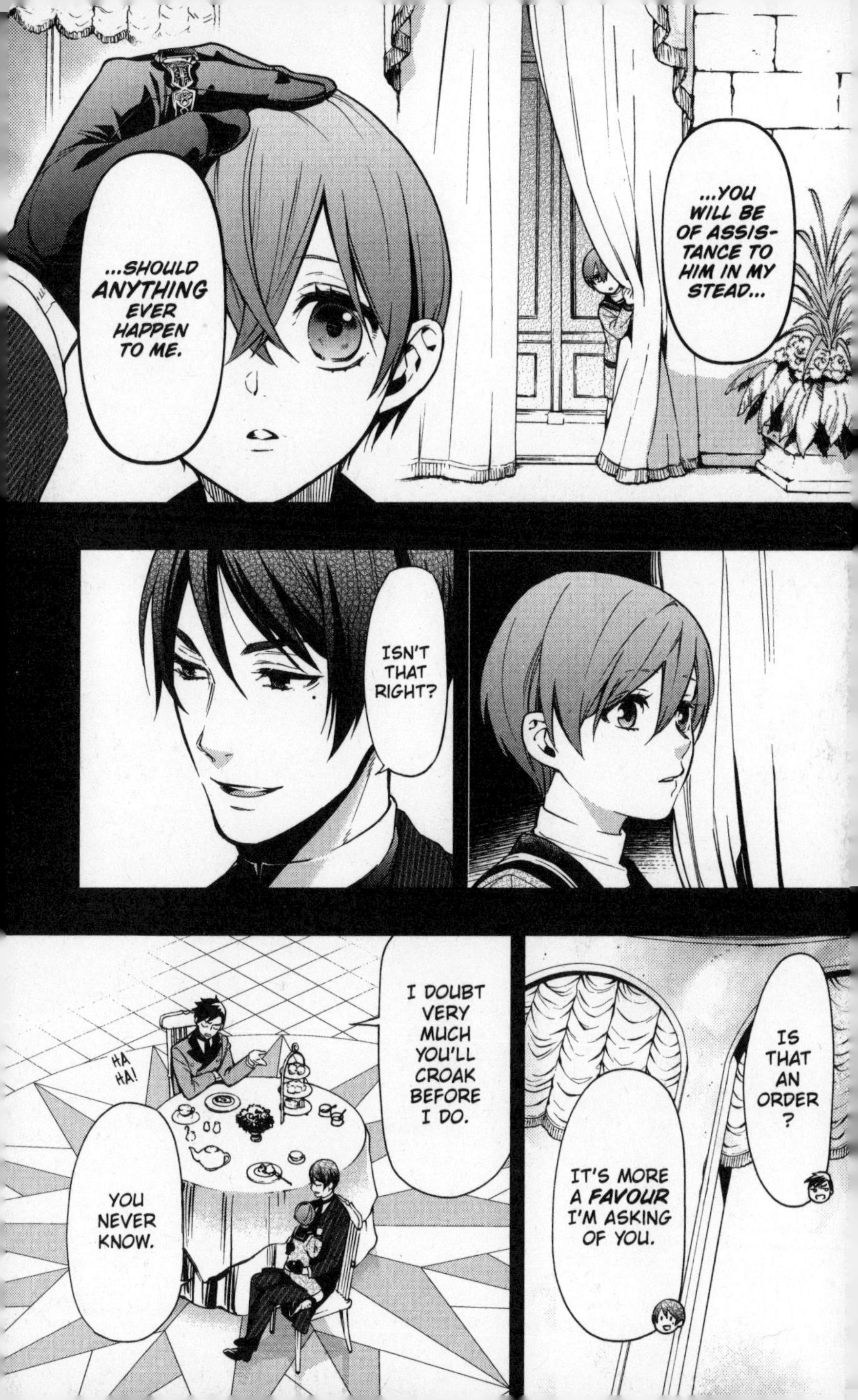
...YOU WILL BE OF ASSISTANCE TO HIM IN MY STEAD...
...SHOULD ANYTHING EVER HAPPEN TO ME.
ISN'T THAT RIGHT?
IS THAT AN ORDER?
IT'S MORE A FAVOUR I'M ASKING OF YOU.
I DOUBT VERY MUCH YOU'LL CROAK BEFORE I DO.
HA HA!
YOU NEVER KNOW.

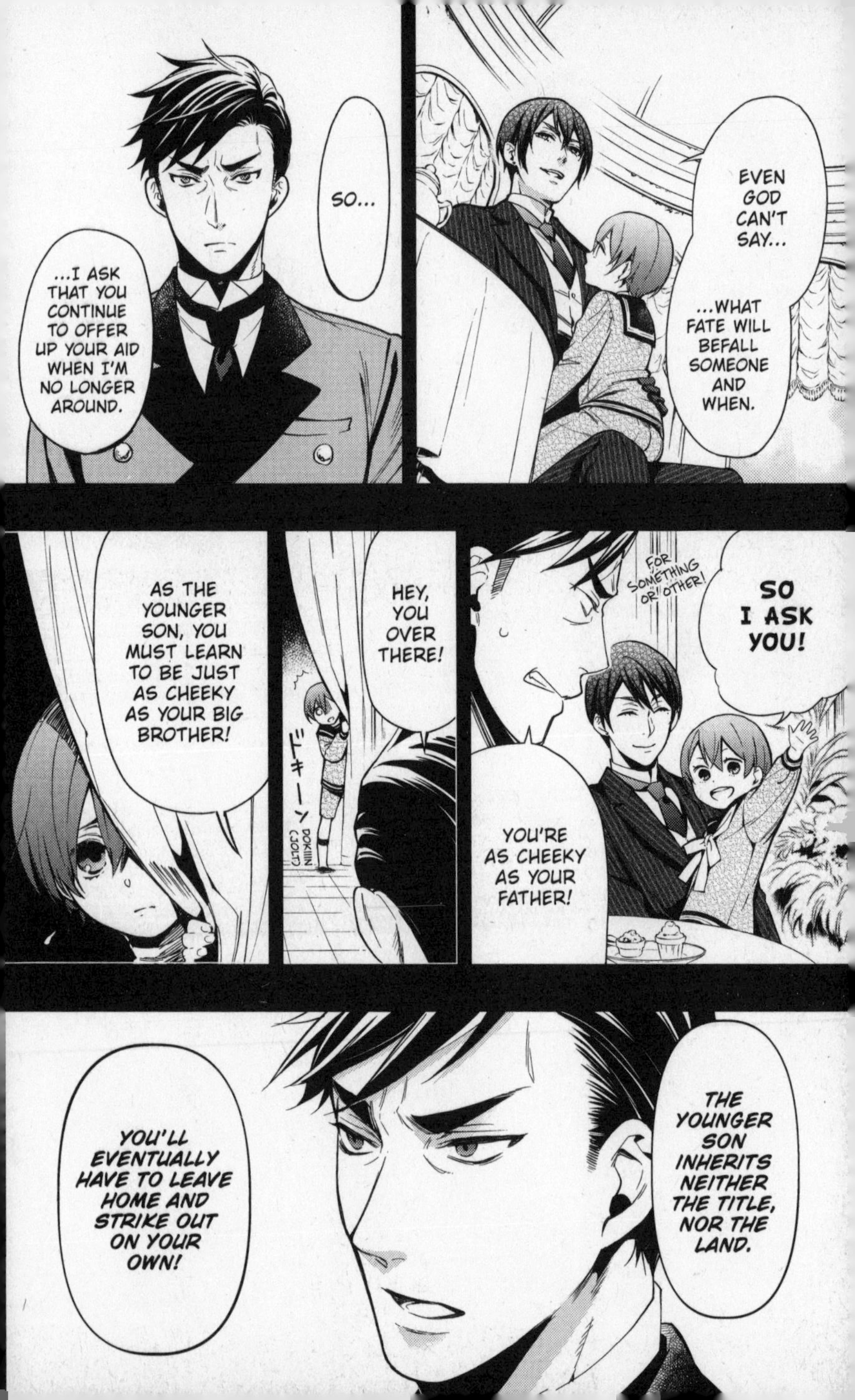
EVEN GOD CAN'T SAY...
...WHAT FATE WILL BEFALL SOMEONE AND WHEN.
SO...
...I ASK THAT YOU CONTINUE TO OFFER UP YOUR AID WHEN I'M NO LONGER AROUND.
SO I ASK YOU!
FOR SOMETHING OR OTHER!
YOU'RE AS CHEEKY AS YOUR FATHER!
HEY, YOU OVER THERE!
ドキーン
DOKIIIN (JOLT)
AS THE YOUNGER SON, YOU MUST LEARN TO BE JUST AS CHEEKY AS YOUR BIG BROTHER!
THE YOUNGER SON INHERITS NEITHER THE TITLE, NOR THE LAND.
YOU'LL EVENTUALLY HAVE TO LEAVE HOME AND STRIKE OUT ON YOUR OWN!

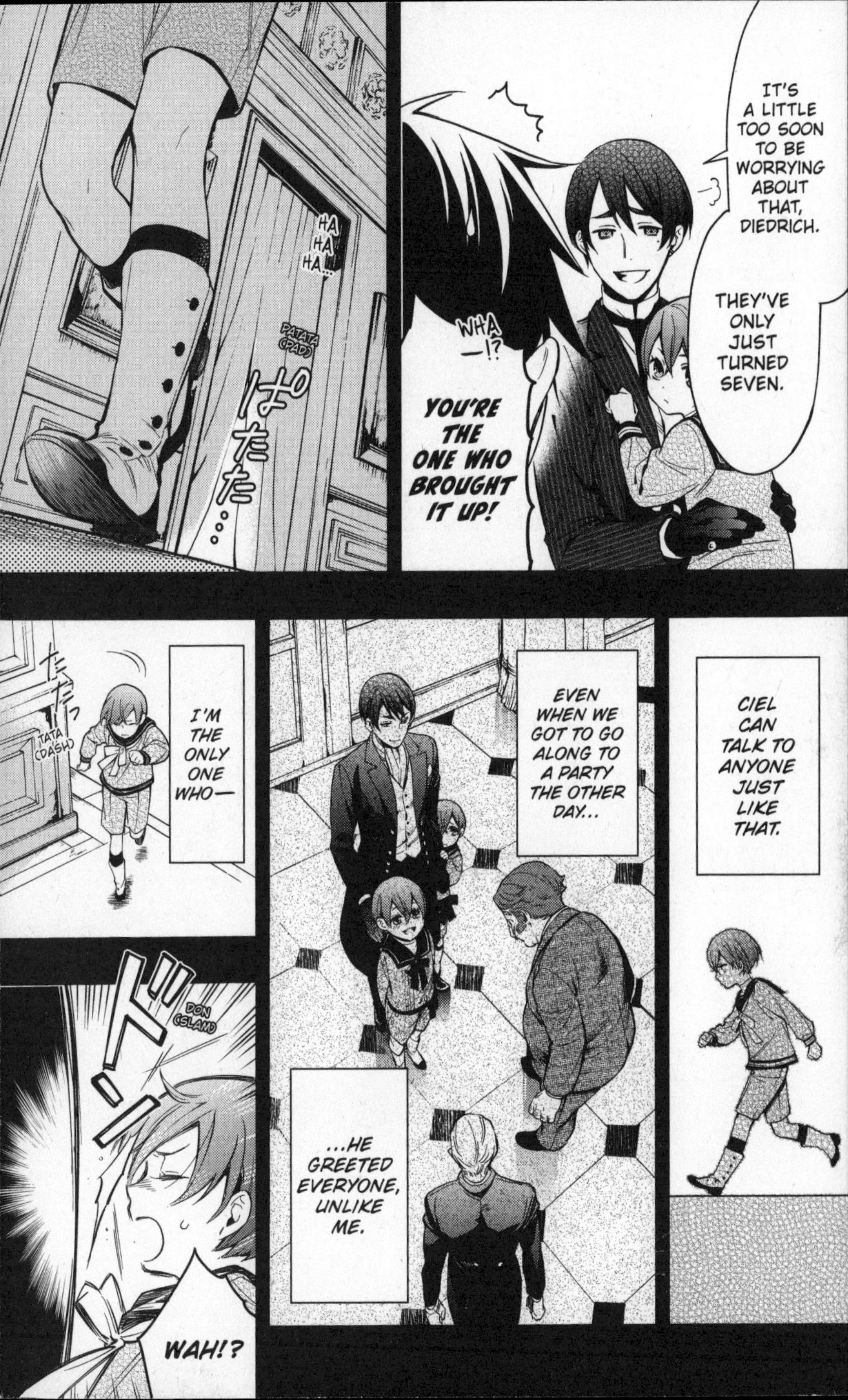
IT'S A LITTLE TOO SOON TO BE WORRYING ABOUT THAT, DIEDRICH.
THEY'VE ONLY JUST TURNED SEVEN.
WHA—!?
YOU'RE THE ONE WHO BROUGHT IT UP!
HA HA HA...
PATATA (PAD)
ぱたた…
CIEL CAN TALK TO ANYONE JUST LIKE THAT.
EVEN WHEN WE GOT TO GO ALONG TO A PARTY THE OTHER DAY...
...HE GREETED EVERYONE, UNLIKE ME.
TATA (DASH)
I'M THE ONLY ONE WHO—
DON (SLAM)
WAH!?

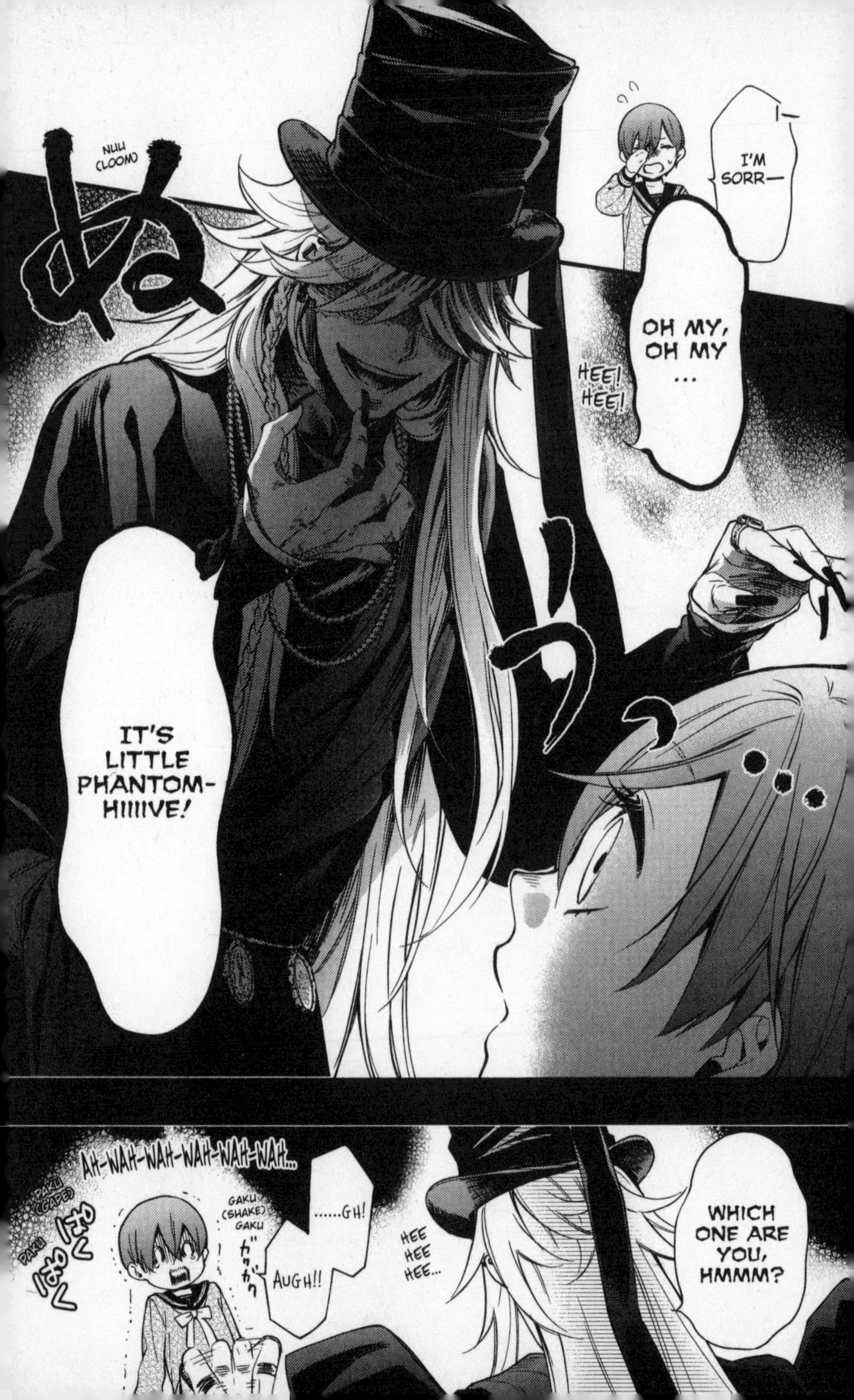
I—
I'M SORR—
OH MY, OH MY ...
HEE! HEE!
NUU (LOOM)
IT'S LITTLE PHANTOM-HIIIIIVE!
WHICH ONE ARE YOU, HMMM?
HEE HEE HEE...
AUGH!!
......GH!
GAKU (SHAKE) GAKU
AH-WAH-WAH-WAH-WAH-WAH...
PAKU (GAPE) PAKU

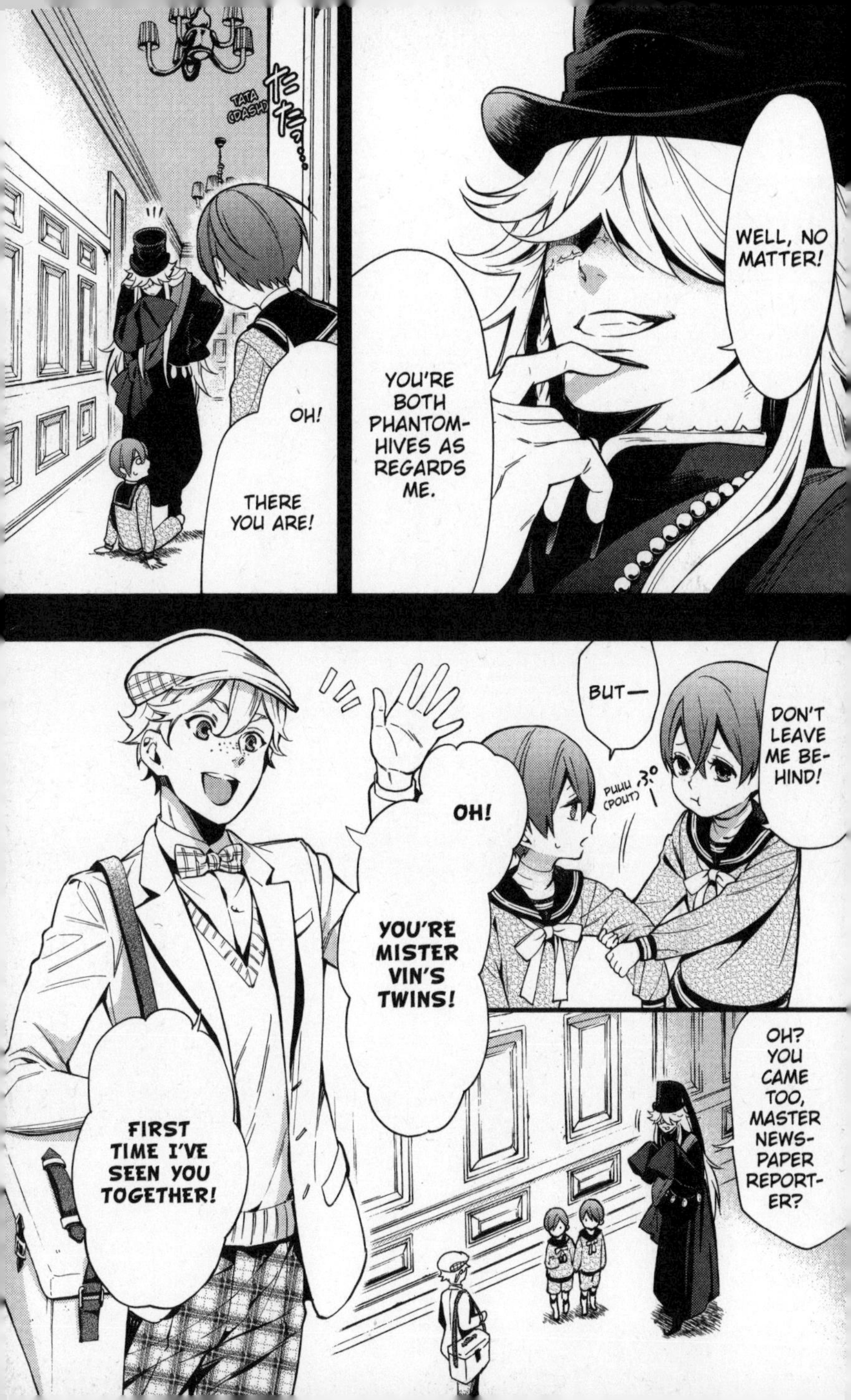

WELL, NO MATTER!
YOU'RE BOTH PHANTOM-HIVES AS REGARDS ME.
TATA (DASH)
OH!
THERE YOU ARE!
DON'T LEAVE ME BE-HIND!
BUT—
PUUU (POUT)
OH? YOU CAME TOO, MASTER NEWS-PAPER REPORT-ER?
OH!
YOU'RE MISTER VIN'S TWINS!
FIRST TIME I'VE SEEN YOU TOGETHER!

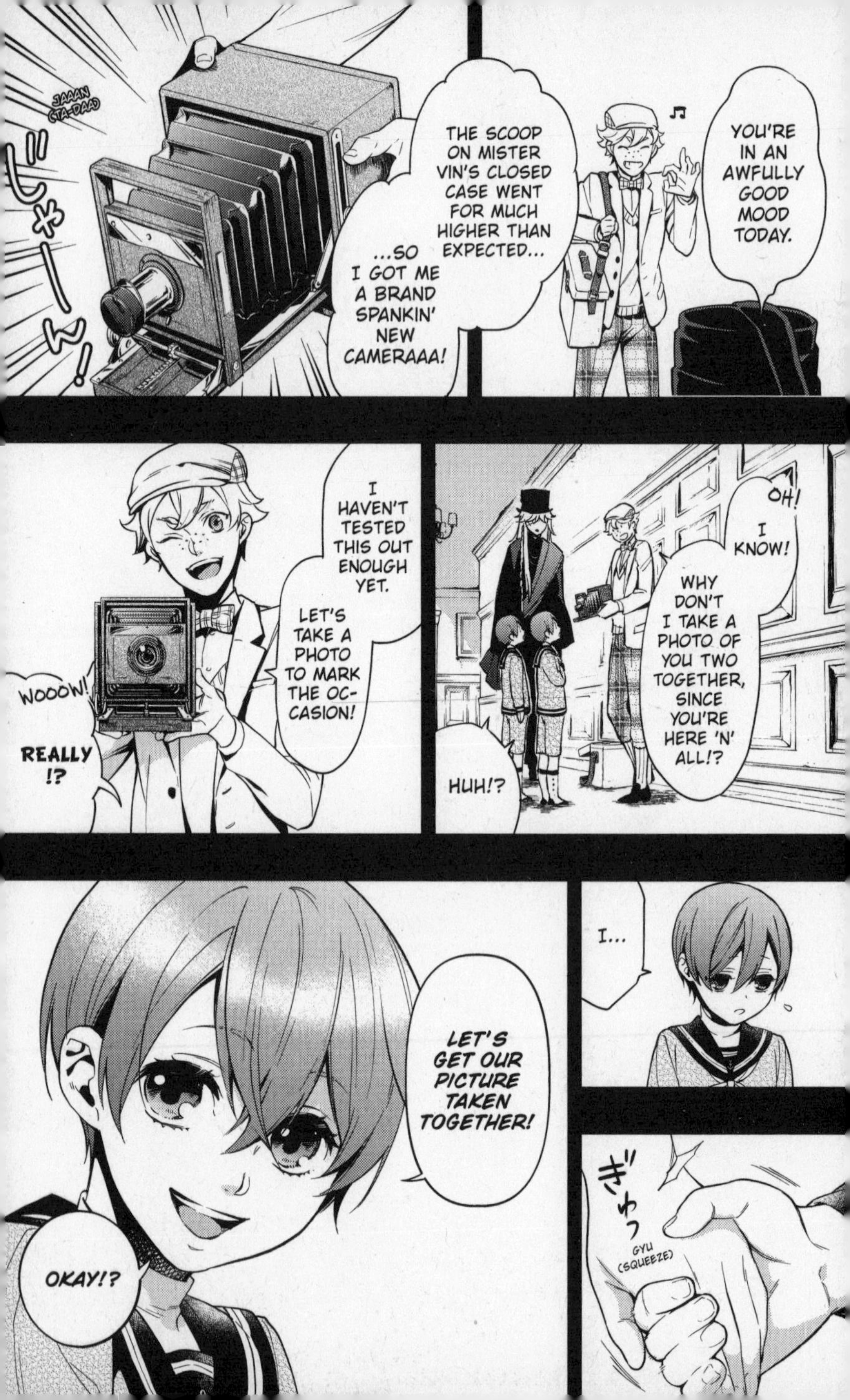
YOU'RE IN AN AWFULLY GOOD MOOD TODAY.
THE SCOOP ON MISTER VIN'S CLOSED CASE WENT FOR MUCH HIGHER THAN EXPECTED...
...SO I GOT ME A BRAND SPANKIN' NEW CAMERAAA!
じゃーん!
JAAAN (TA-DAA)
OH!
I KNOW!
WHY DON'T I TAKE A PHOTO OF YOU TWO TOGETHER, SINCE YOU'RE HERE 'N' ALL!?
HUH!?
I HAVEN'T TESTED THIS OUT ENOUGH YET.
LET'S TAKE A PHOTO TO MARK THE OC-CASION!
WOOOW!
REALLY!?
I...
ぎゅっ
GYU (SQUEEZE)
LET'S GET OUR PICTURE TAKEN TOGETHER!
OKAY!?

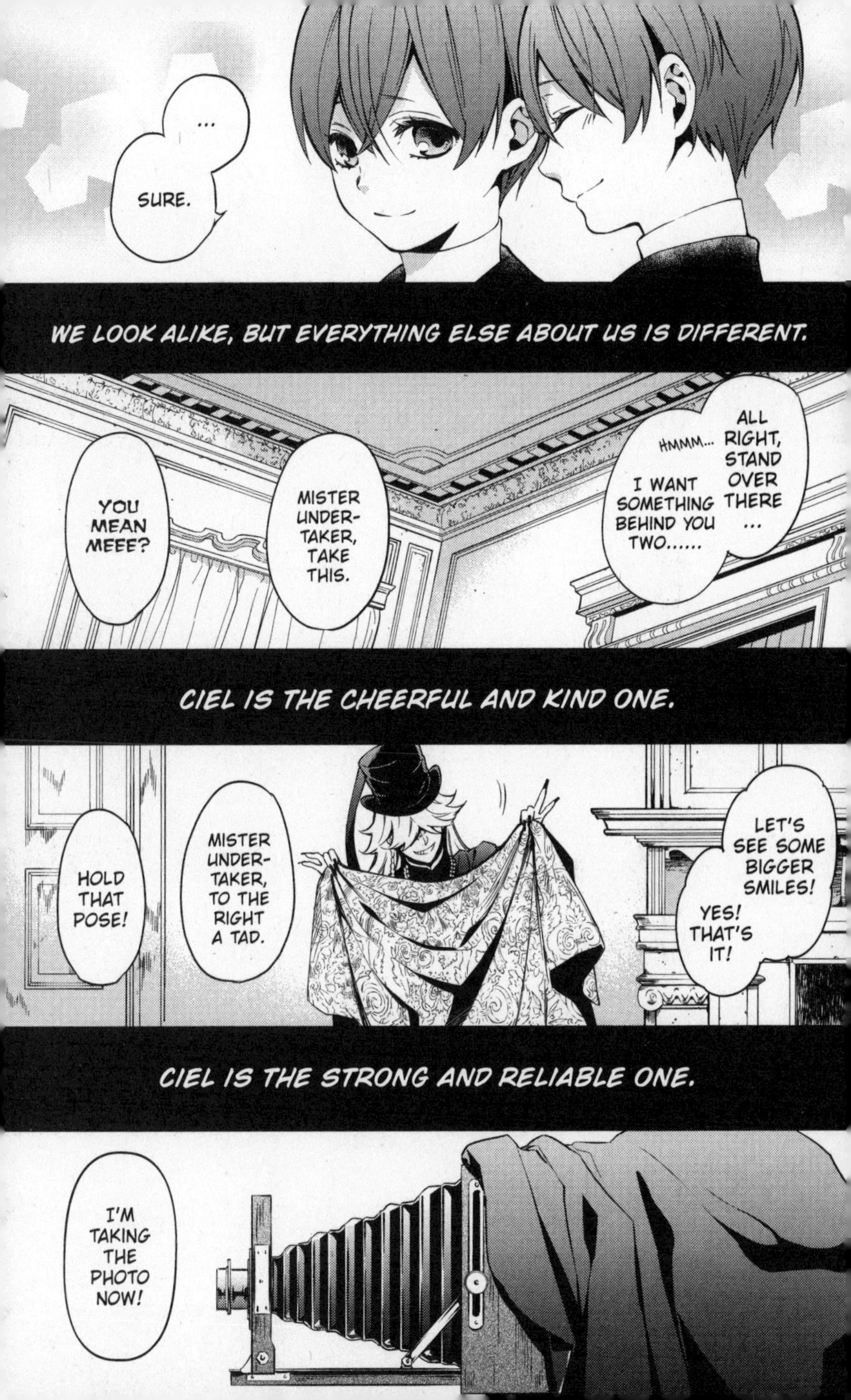
... SURE.
WE LOOK ALIKE, BUT EVERYTHING ELSE ABOUT US IS DIFFERENT.
ALL RIGHT, STAND OVER THERE ...
HMMM... I WANT SOMETHING BEHIND YOU TWO......
MISTER UNDERTAKER, TAKE THIS.
YOU MEAN MEEE?
CIEL IS THE CHEERFUL AND KIND ONE.
LET'S SEE SOME BIGGER SMILES! YES! THAT'S IT!
MISTER UNDERTAKER, TO THE RIGHT A TAD.
HOLD THAT POSE!
CIEL IS THE STRONG AND RELIABLE ONE.
I'M TAKING THE PHOTO NOW!

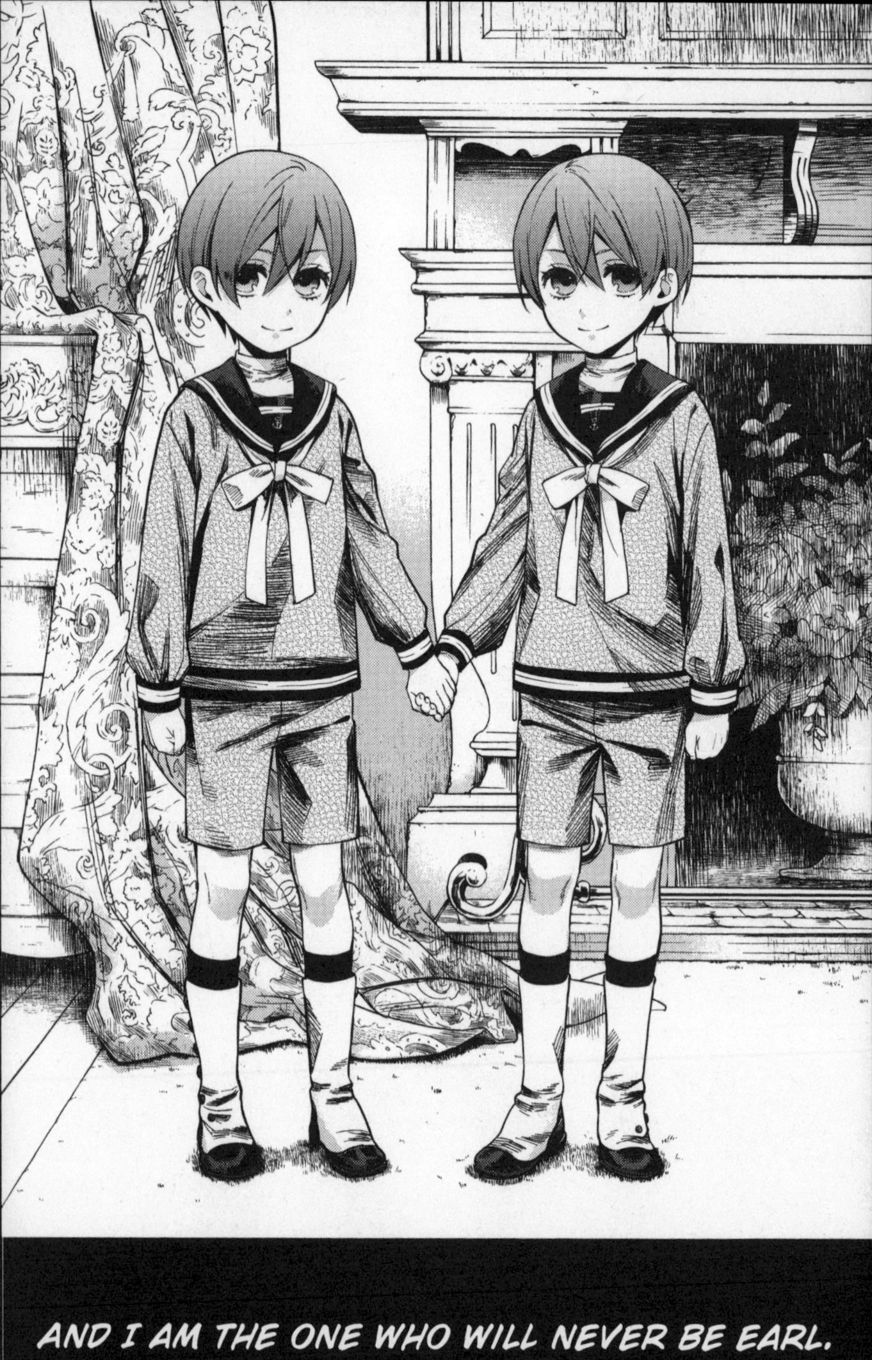
AND I AM THE ONE WHO WILL NEVER BE EARL.

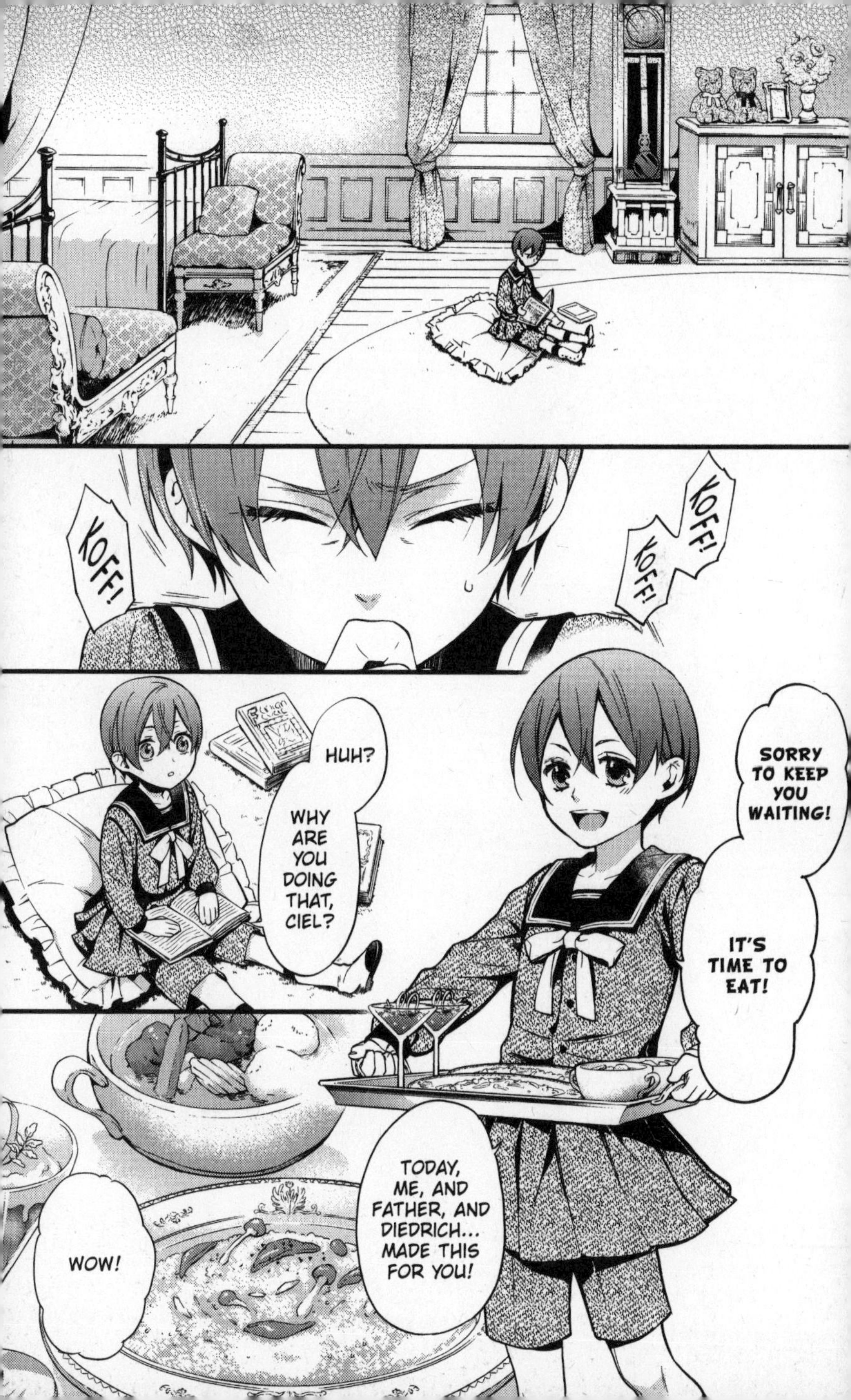
KOFF!
KOFF!
KOFF!
SORRY TO KEEP YOU WAITING!
IT'S TIME TO EAT!
HUH?
WHY ARE YOU DOING THAT, CIEL?
TODAY, ME, AND FATHER, AND DIEDRICH... MADE THIS FOR YOU!
WOW!

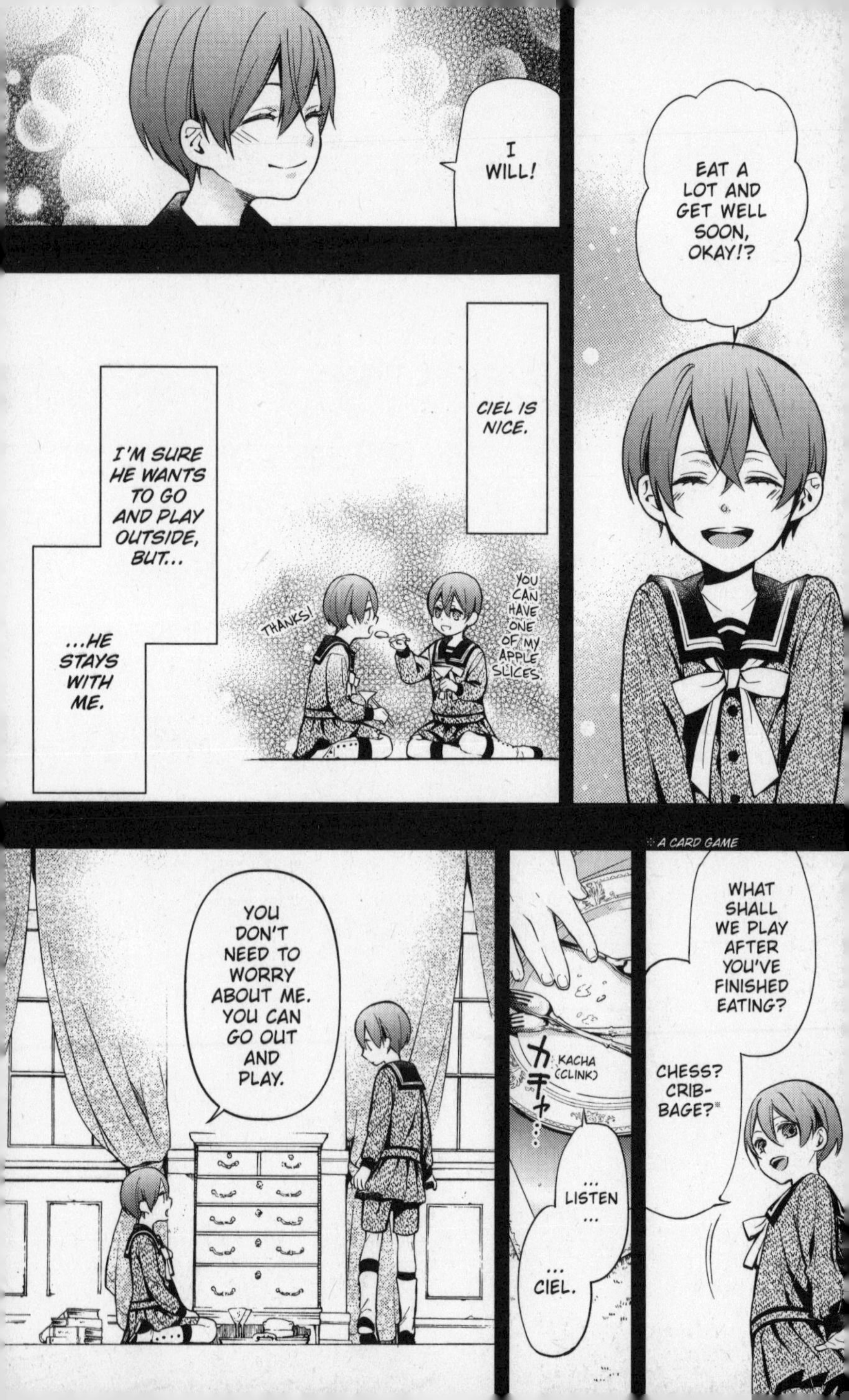
EAT A LOT AND GET WELL SOON, OKAY!?
I WILL!
CIEL IS NICE.
YOU CAN HAVE ONE OF MY APPLE SLICES.
THANKS!
I'M SURE HE WANTS TO GO AND PLAY OUTSIDE, BUT...
...HE STAYS WITH ME.
WHAT SHALL WE PLAY AFTER YOU'VE FINISHED EATING?
CHESS? CRIB-BAGE?※
※ A CARD GAME
KACHA (CLINK)
...LISTEN...
...CIEL.
YOU DON'T NEED TO WORRY ABOUT ME. YOU CAN GO OUT AND PLAY.

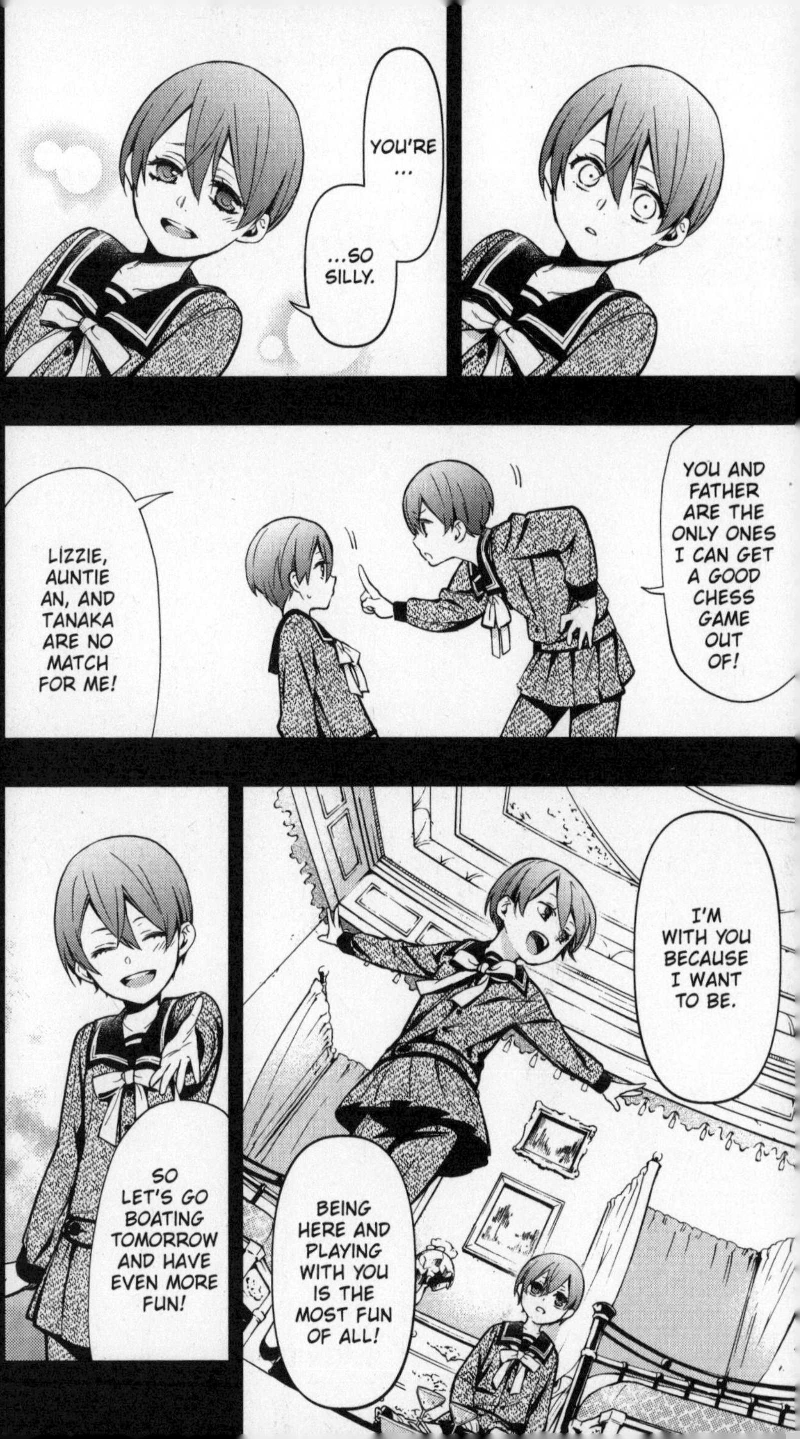
YOU'RE ...
...SO SILLY.
YOU AND FATHER ARE THE ONLY ONES I CAN GET A GOOD CHESS GAME OUT OF!
LIZZIE, AUNTIE AN, AND TANAKA ARE NO MATCH FOR ME!
I'M WITH YOU BECAUSE I WANT TO BE.
BEING HERE AND PLAYING WITH YOU IS THE MOST FUN OF ALL!
SO LET'S GO BOATING TOMORROW AND HAVE EVEN MORE FUN!

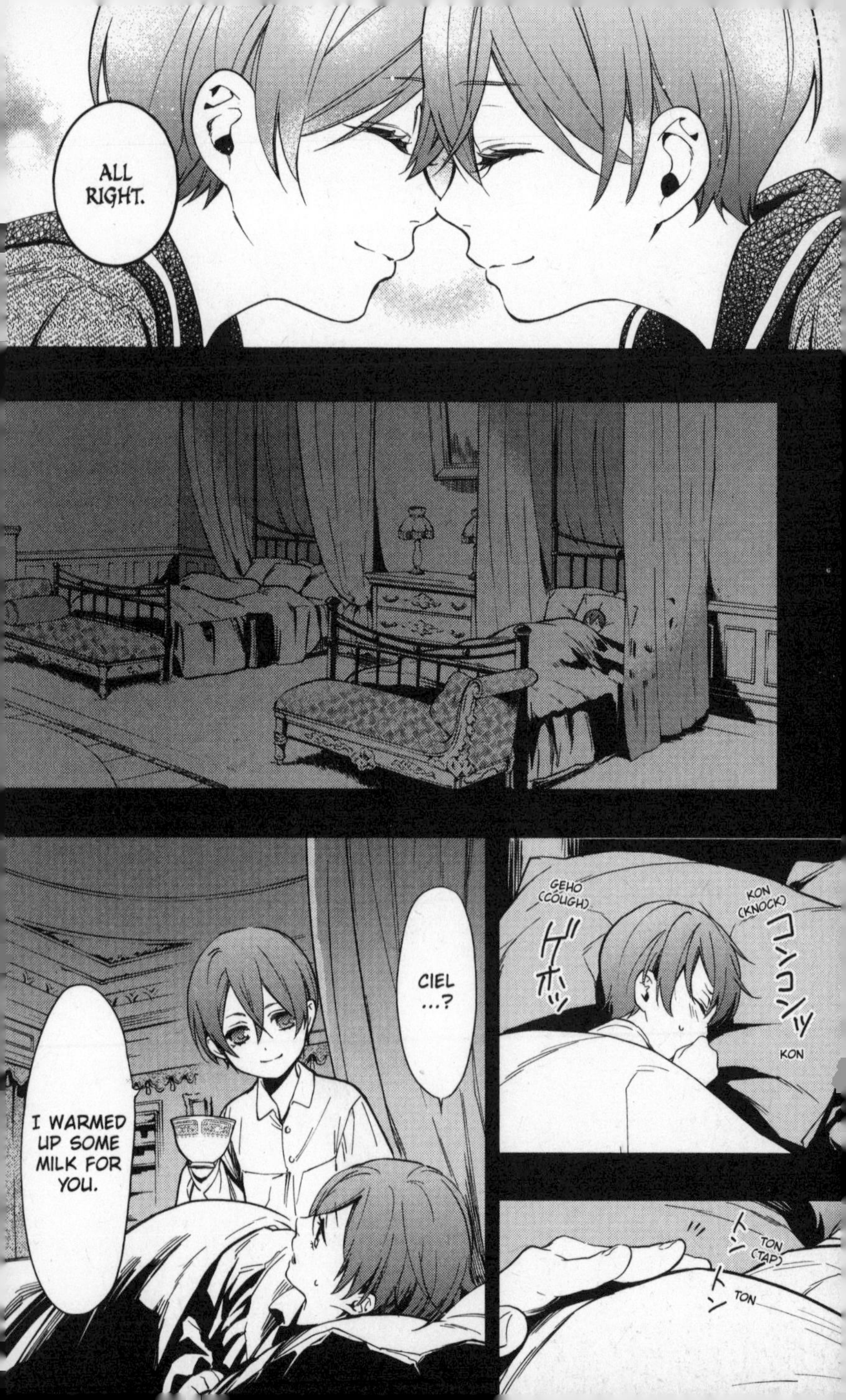
ALL RIGHT.
KON (KNOCK)
KON
GEHO (COUGH)
TON (TAP)
TON
CIEL ...?
I WARMED UP SOME MILK FOR YOU.

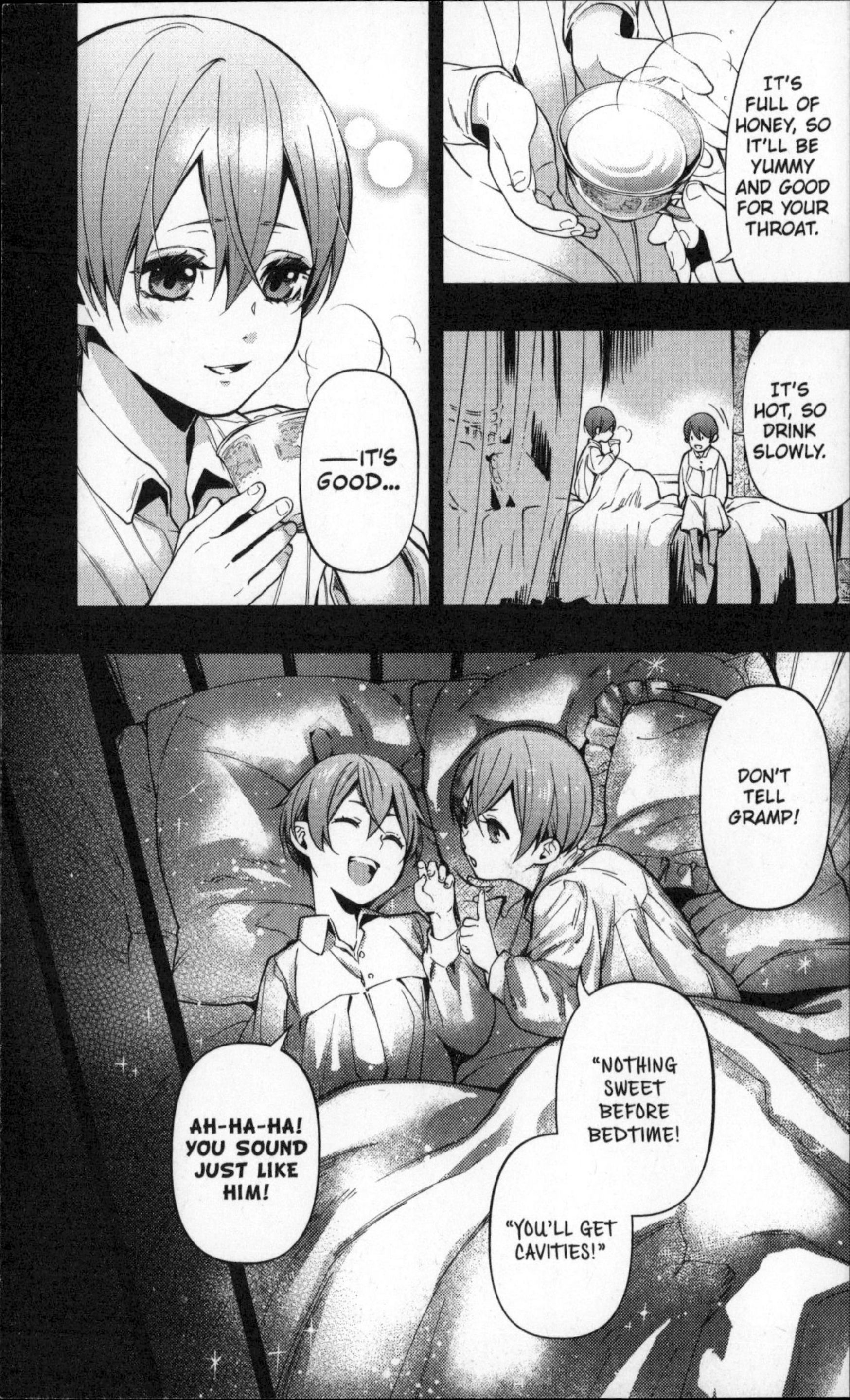
IT'S FULL OF HONEY, SO IT'LL BE YUMMY AND GOOD FOR YOUR THROAT.
IT'S HOT, SO DRINK SLOWLY.
—IT'S GOOD...
DON'T TELL GRAMP!
"NOTHING SWEET BEFORE BEDTIME!
"YOU'LL GET CAVITIES!"
AH-HA-HA! YOU SOUND JUST LIKE HIM!

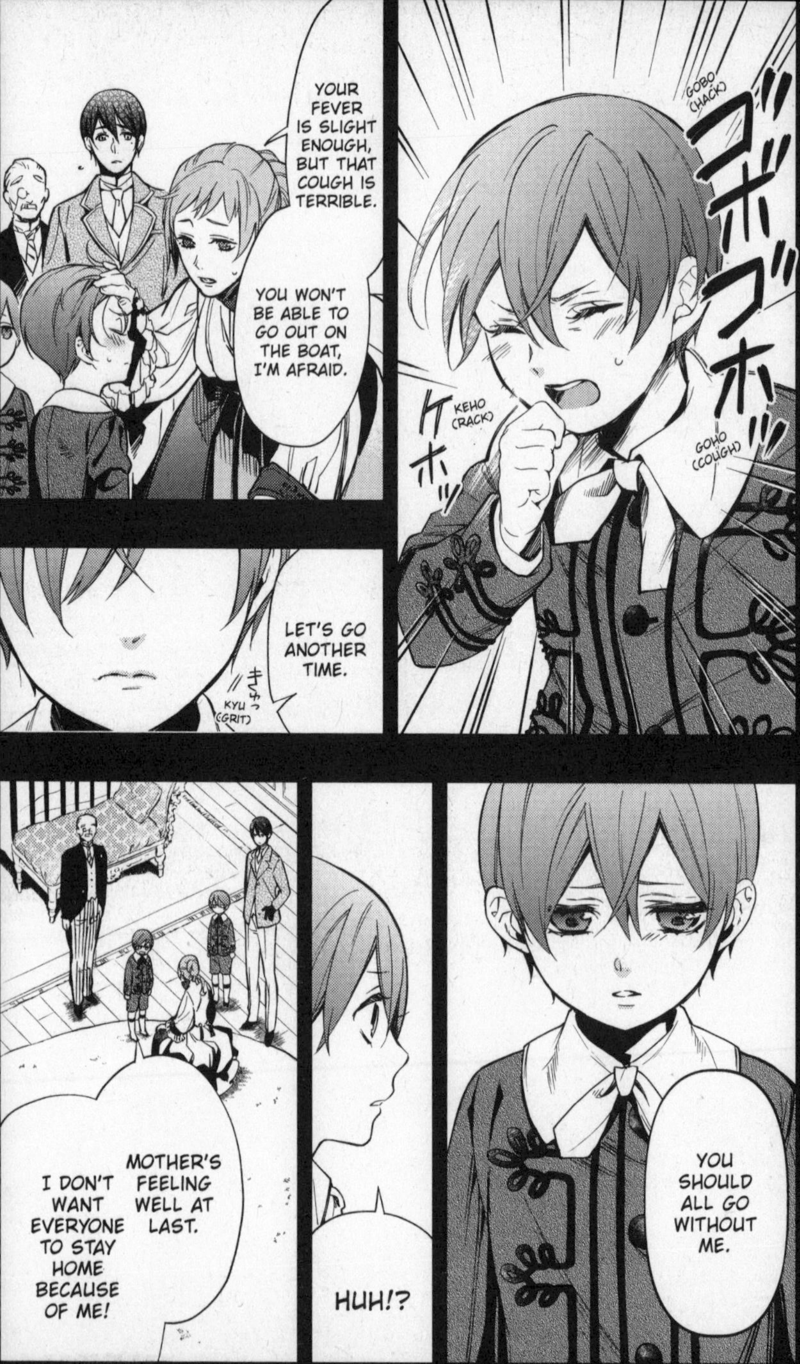
GOBO (HACK)
KEHO (RACK)
GOHO (COUGH)
YOUR FEVER IS SLIGHT ENOUGH, BUT THAT COUGH IS TERRIBLE.
YOU WON'T BE ABLE TO GO OUT ON THE BOAT, I'M AFRAID.
LET'S GO ANOTHER TIME.
KYU (GRIT)
YOU SHOULD ALL GO WITHOUT ME.
HUH!?
MOTHER'S FEELING WELL AT LAST.
I DON'T WANT EVERYONE TO STAY HOME BECAUSE OF ME!

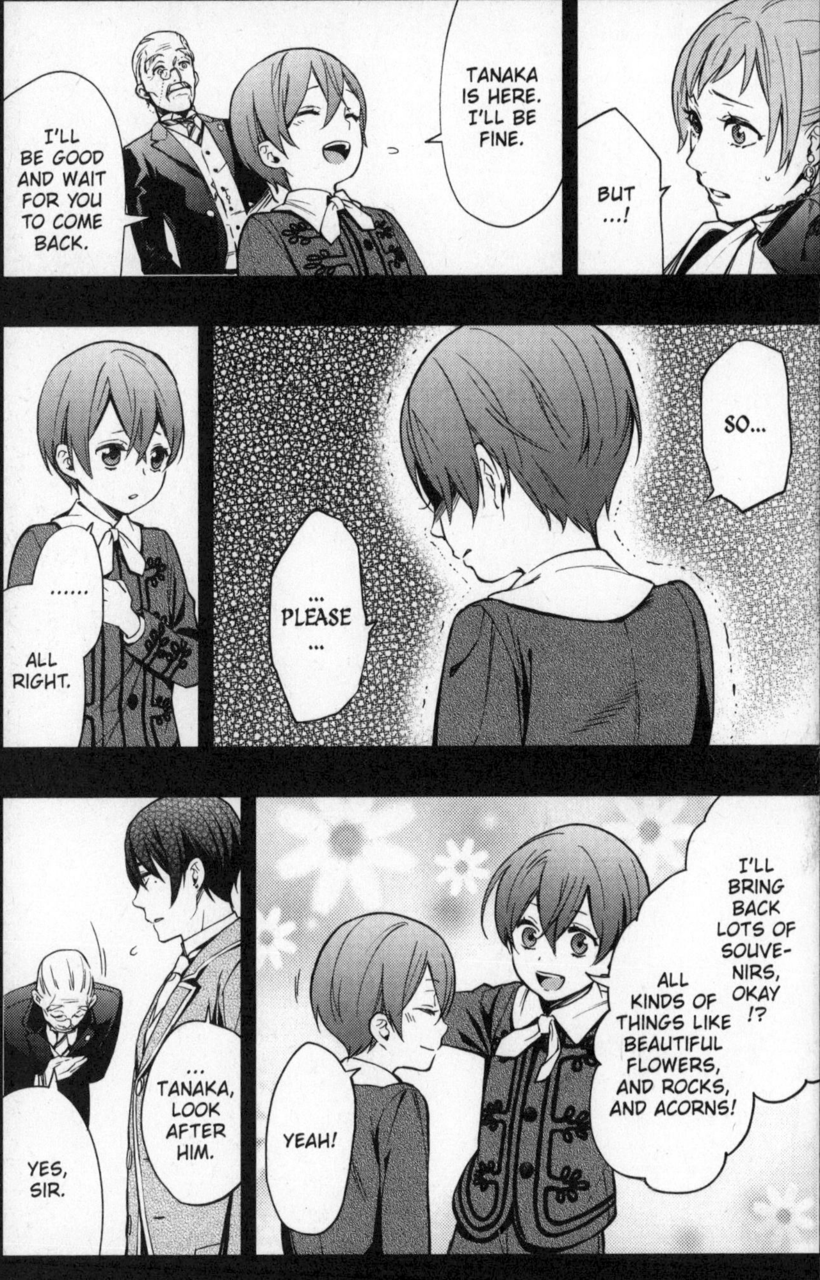
BUT ...!
TANAKA IS HERE. I'LL BE FINE.
I'LL BE GOOD AND WAIT FOR YOU TO COME BACK.
SO...
... PLEASE ...
......
ALL RIGHT.
I'LL BRING BACK LOTS OF SOUVE- NIRS, OKAY !?
ALL KINDS OF THINGS LIKE BEAUTIFUL FLOWERS, AND ROCKS, AND ACORNS!
YEAH!
... TANAKA, LOOK AFTER HIM.
YES, SIR.

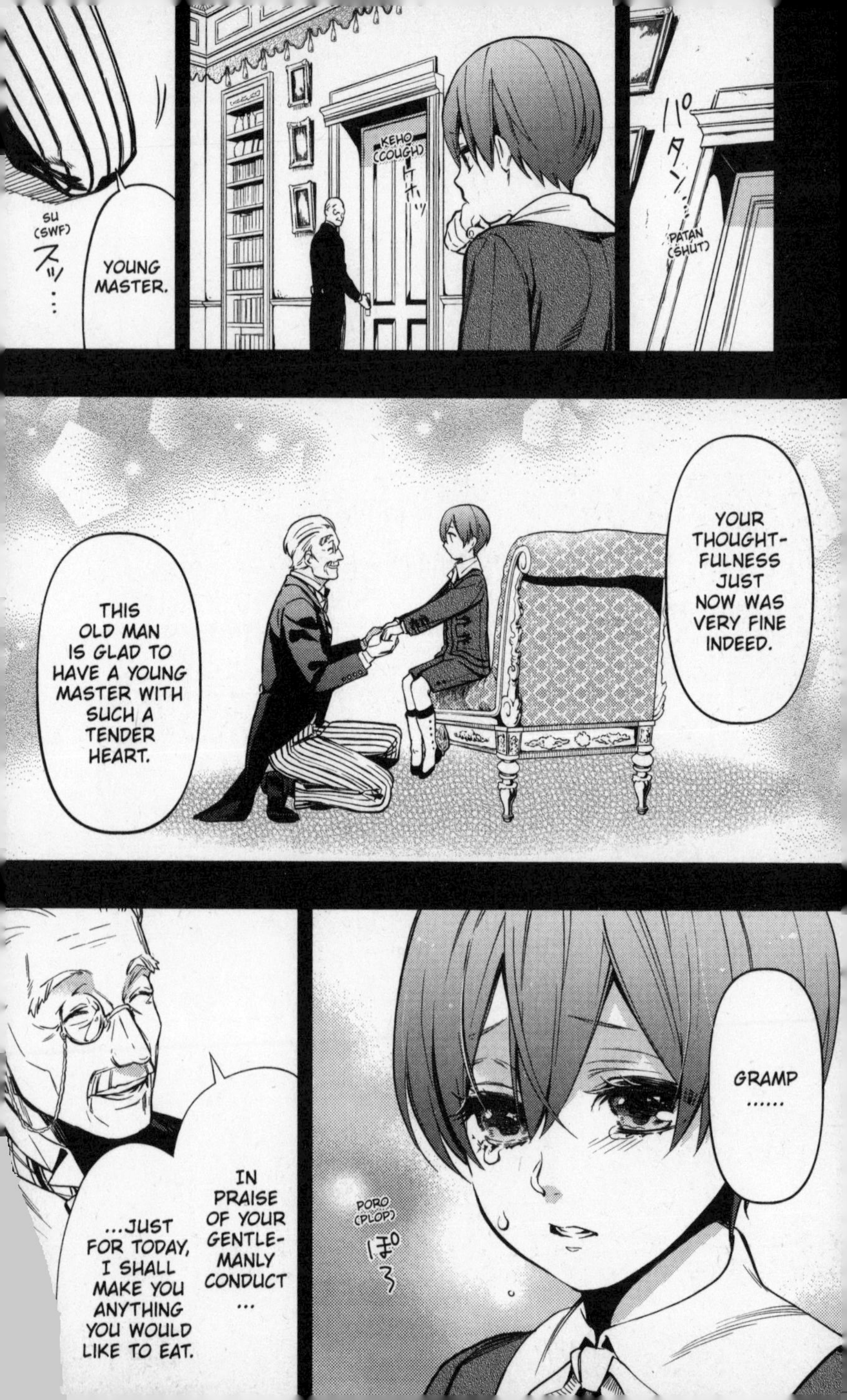
パタン…
PATAN (SHUT)
KEHO (COUGH)
ケホッ
YOUNG MASTER.
SU (SWF)
スッ…
YOUR THOUGHT-FULNESS JUST NOW WAS VERY FINE INDEED.
THIS OLD MAN IS GLAD TO HAVE A YOUNG MASTER WITH SUCH A TENDER HEART.
GRAMP ......
PORO (PLOP)
ぽろ
IN PRAISE OF YOUR GENTLE-MANLY CONDUCT ...
...JUST FOR TODAY, I SHALL MAKE YOU ANYTHING YOU WOULD LIKE TO EAT.

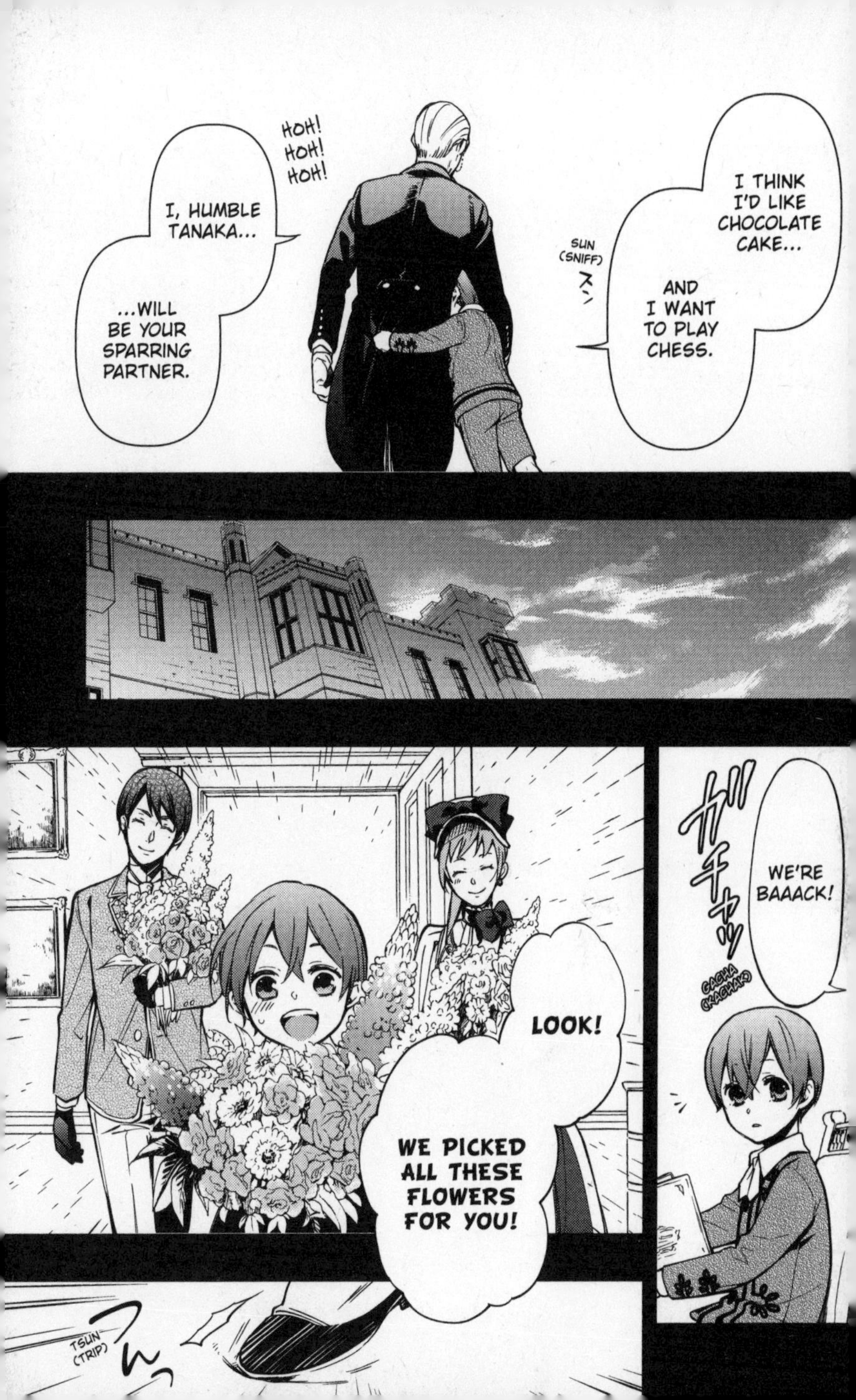

I THINK I'D LIKE CHOCOLATE CAKE...
AND I WANT TO PLAY CHESS.
SUN (SNIFF)
HOH! HOH! HOH!
I, HUMBLE TANAKA...
...WILL BE YOUR SPARRING PARTNER.
WE'RE BAAACK!
GACHA (KACHAK)
LOOK!
WE PICKED ALL THESE FLOWERS FOR YOU!
TSUN (TRIP)

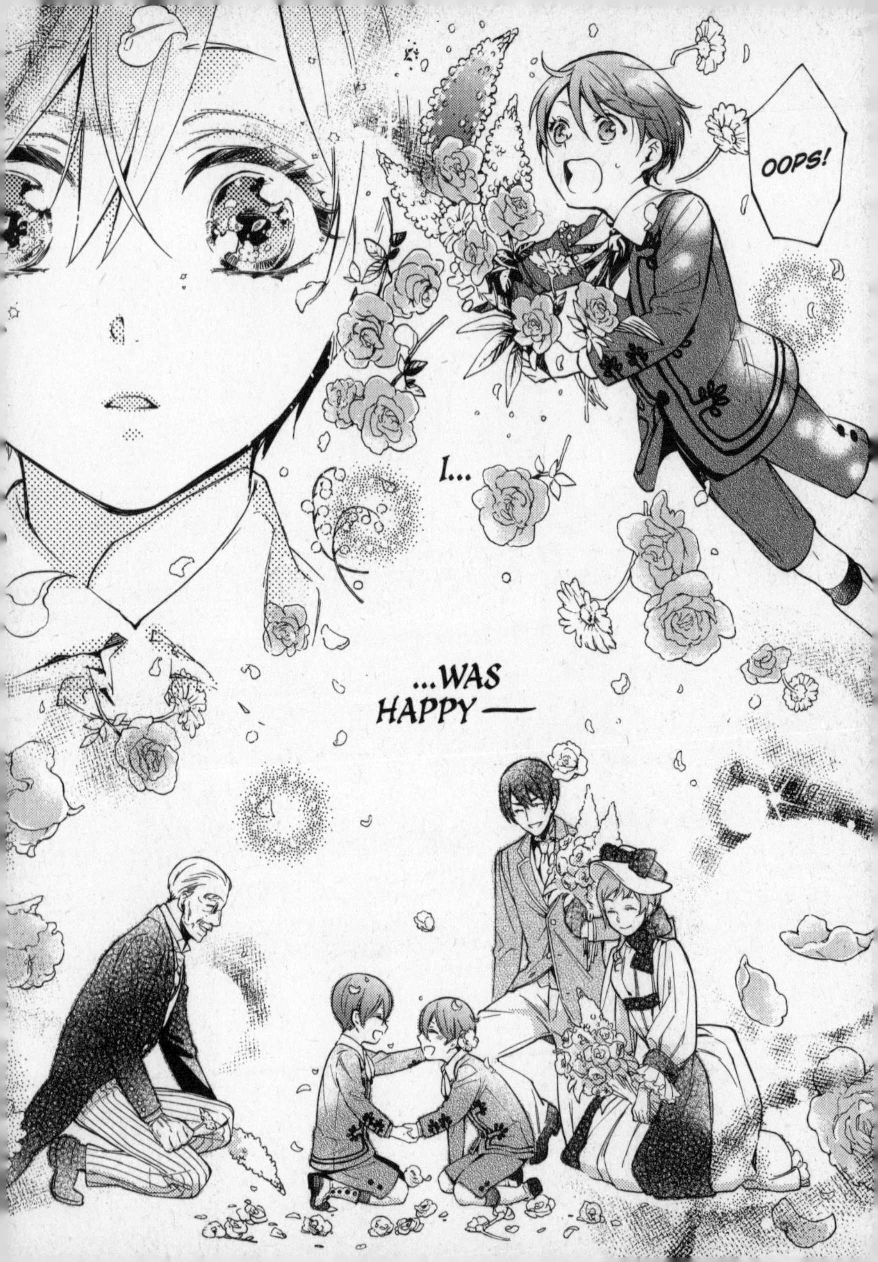
OOPS!
I...
...WAS HAPPY—

Black Butler

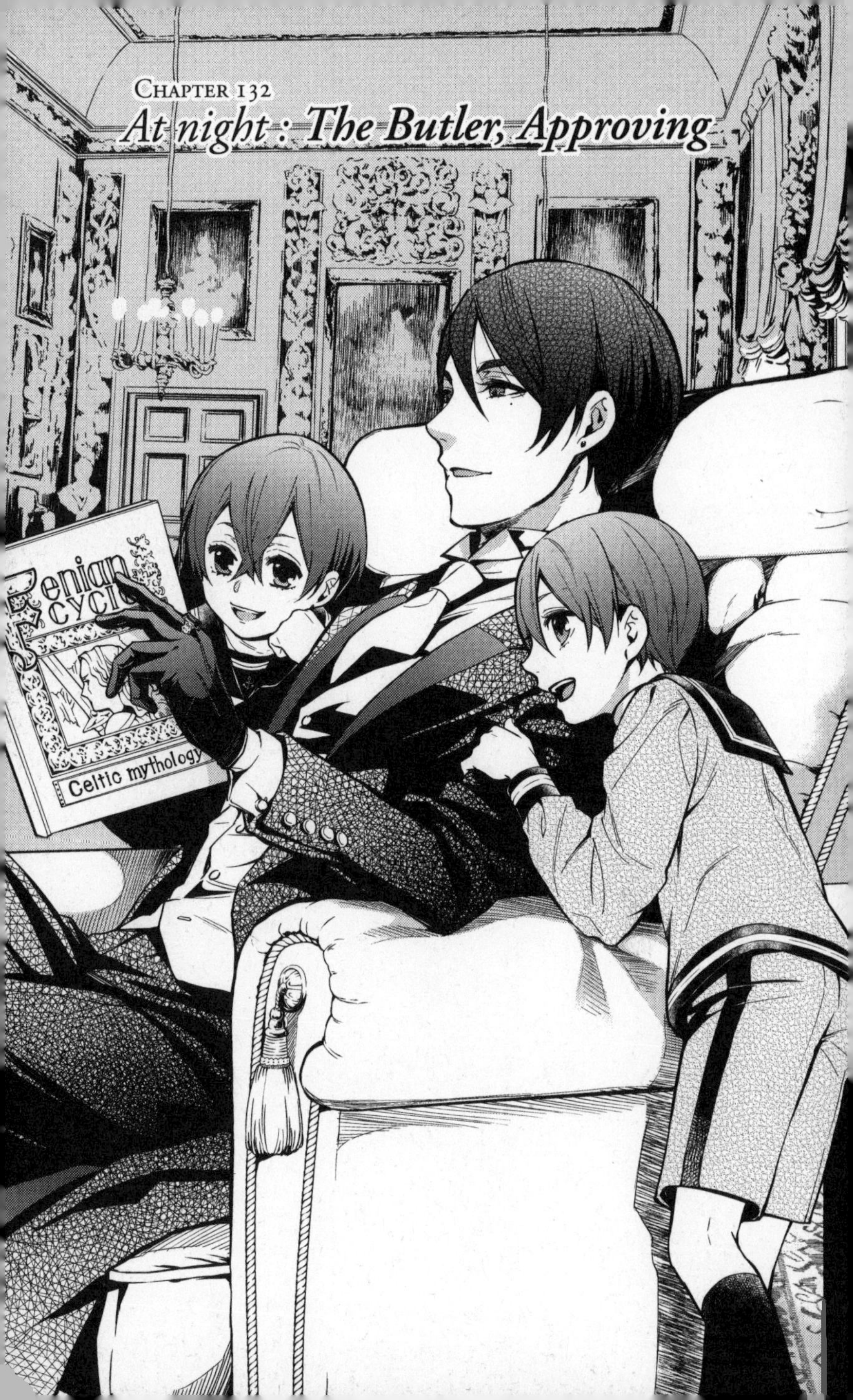
Chapter 132
At night : The Butler, Approving
Fenian Cycle
Celtic mythology

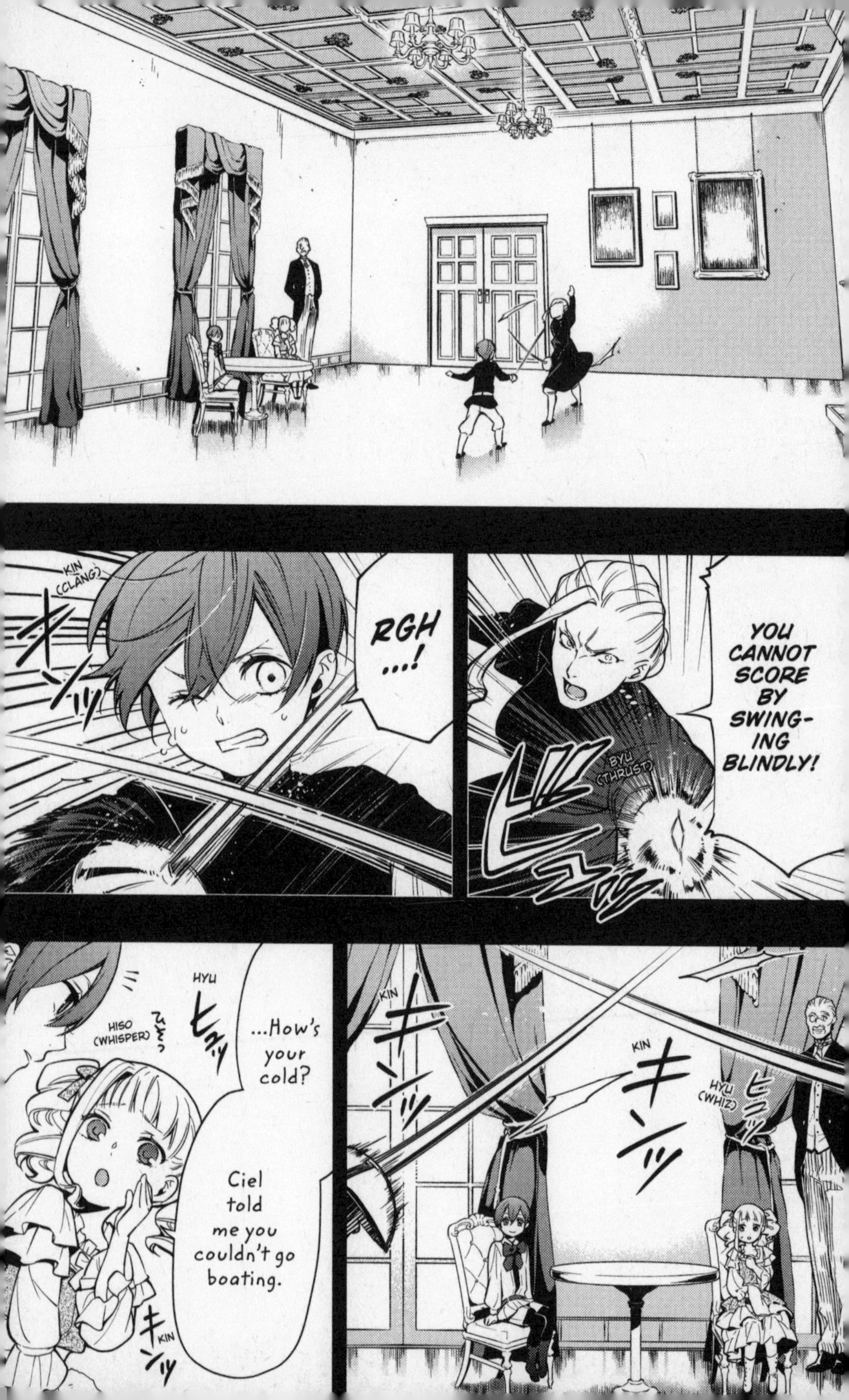
YOU CANNOT SCORE BY SWING-ING BLINDLY!
BYU (THRUST)
KIN (CLANG)
RGH ...!
HYU (WHIZ)
KIN
KIN
...How's your cold?
Ciel told me you couldn't go boating.
HYU
HISO (WHISPER)
KIN

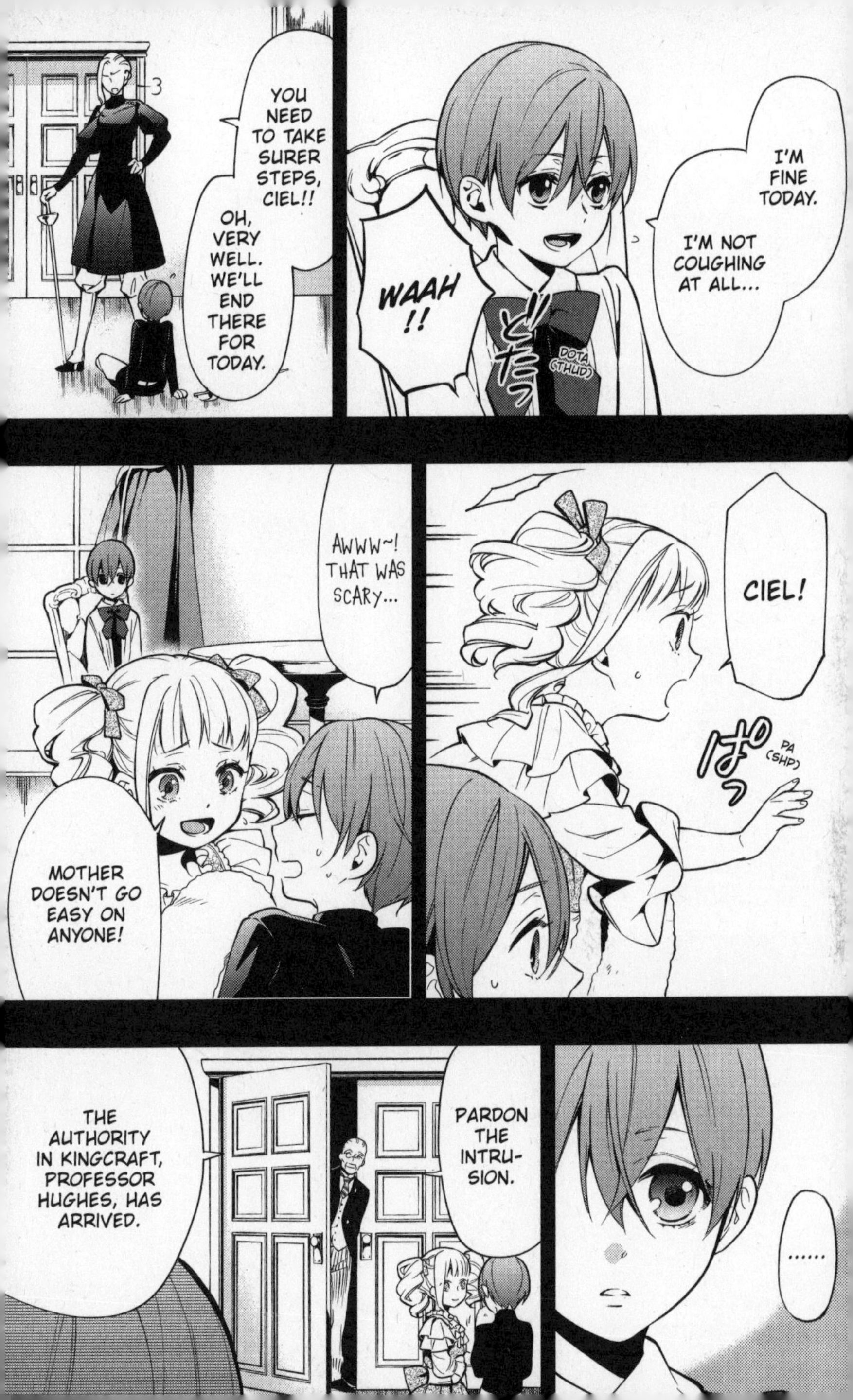
I'M FINE TODAY.
I'M NOT COUGHING AT ALL...
WAAH!!
DOTA (THUD)
YOU NEED TO TAKE SURER STEPS, CIEL!!
OH, VERY WELL. WE'LL END THERE FOR TODAY.
CIEL!
PA (SHP)
AWWW~! THAT WAS SCARY...
MOTHER DOESN'T GO EASY ON ANYONE!
......
PARDON THE INTRUSION.
THE AUTHORITY IN KINGCRAFT, PROFESSOR HUGHES, HAS ARRIVED.

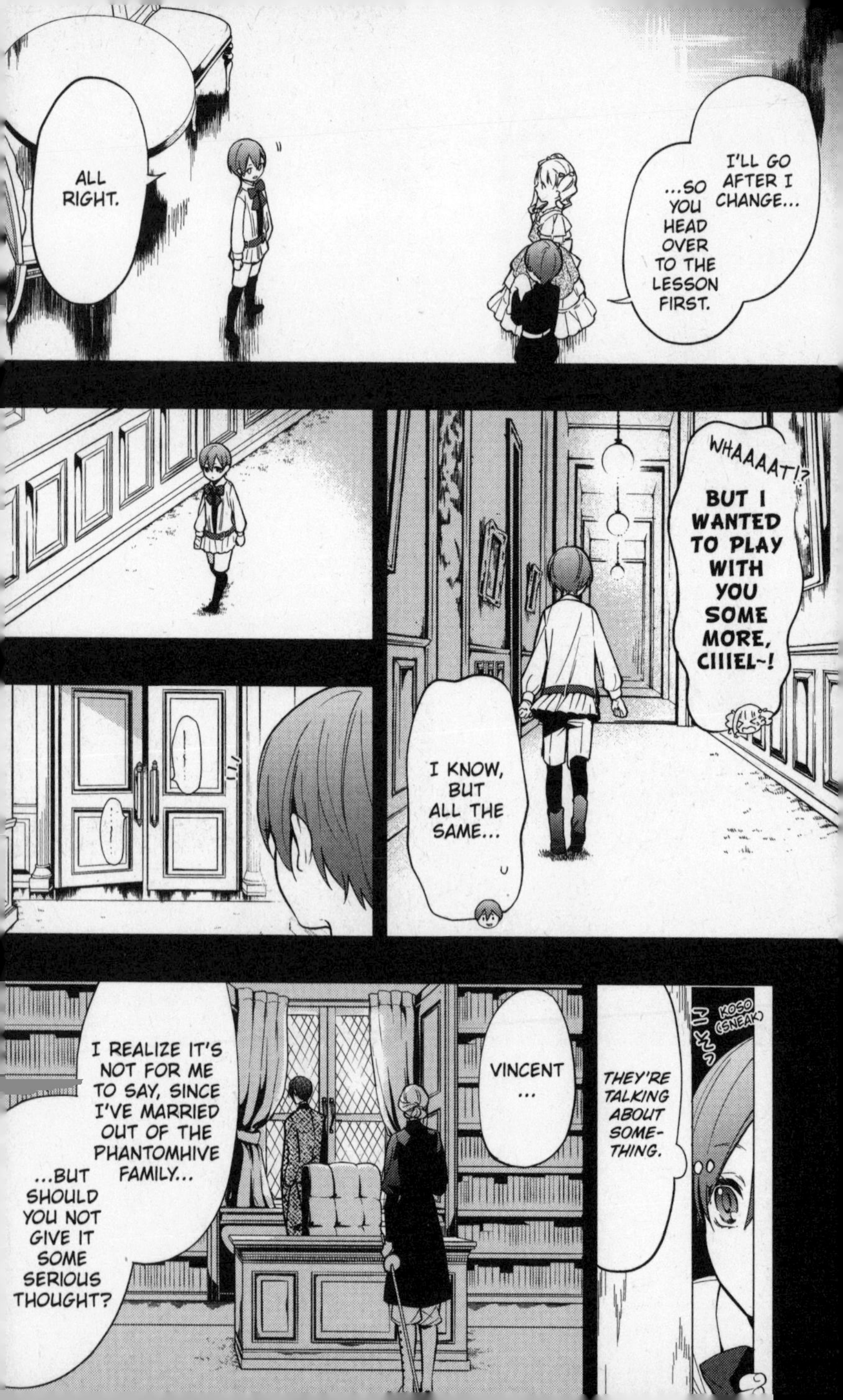
I'LL GO AFTER I CHANGE... ...SO YOU HEAD OVER TO THE LESSON FIRST.
ALL RIGHT.
WHAAAAT!? BUT I WANTED TO PLAY WITH YOU SOME MORE, CIIIEL~!
I KNOW, BUT ALL THE SAME...
KOSO (SNEAK)
THEY'RE TALKING ABOUT SOME-THING.
VINCENT...
I REALIZE IT'S NOT FOR ME TO SAY, SINCE I'VE MARRIED OUT OF THE PHANTOMHIVE FAMILY...
...BUT SHOULD YOU NOT GIVE IT SOME SERIOUS THOUGHT?

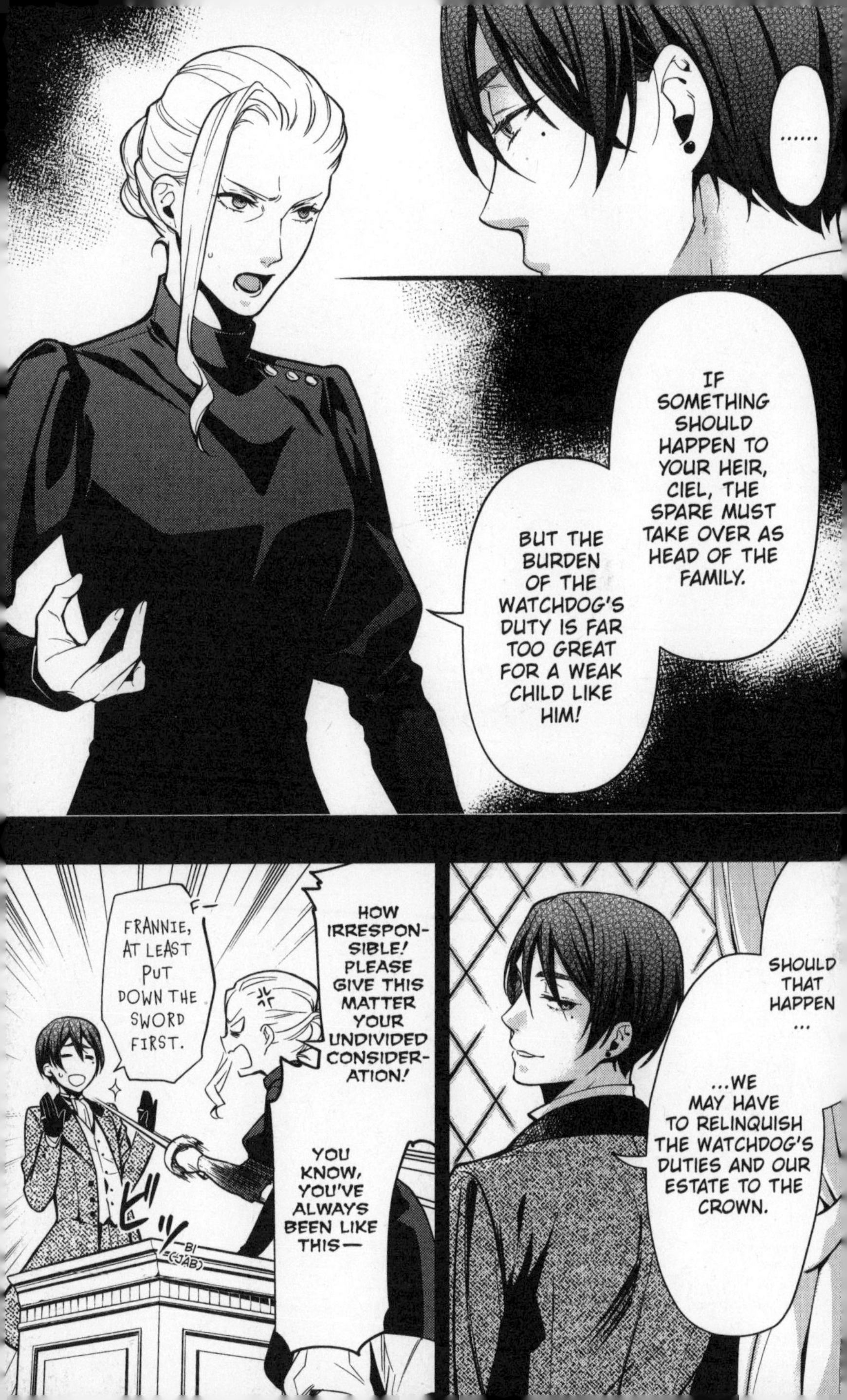
......
IF SOMETHING SHOULD HAPPEN TO YOUR HEIR, CIEL, THE SPARE MUST TAKE OVER AS HEAD OF THE FAMILY.
BUT THE BURDEN OF THE WATCHDOG'S DUTY IS FAR TOO GREAT FOR A WEAK CHILD LIKE HIM!
SHOULD THAT HAPPEN...
...WE MAY HAVE TO RELINQUISH THE WATCHDOG'S DUTIES AND OUR ESTATE TO THE CROWN.
HOW IRRESPONSIBLE! PLEASE GIVE THIS MATTER YOUR UNDIVIDED CONSIDERATION!
F—
FRANNIE, AT LEAST PUT DOWN THE SWORD FIRST.
YOU KNOW, YOU'VE ALWAYS BEEN LIKE THIS—
BI (JAB)

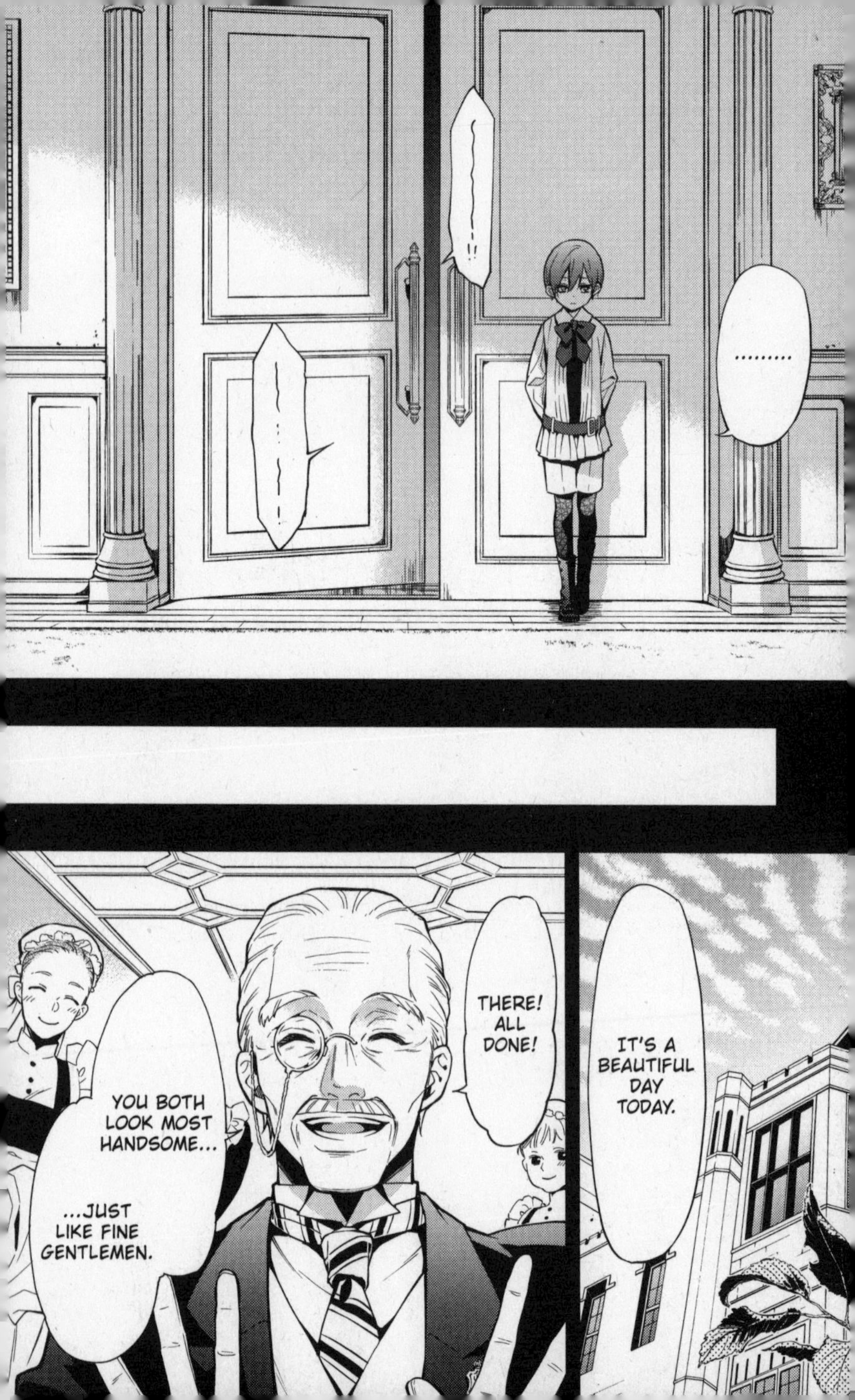
....
——!!
——
IT'S A BEAUTIFUL DAY TODAY.
THERE! ALL DONE!
YOU BOTH LOOK MOST HANDSOME...
...JUST LIKE FINE GENTLEMEN.

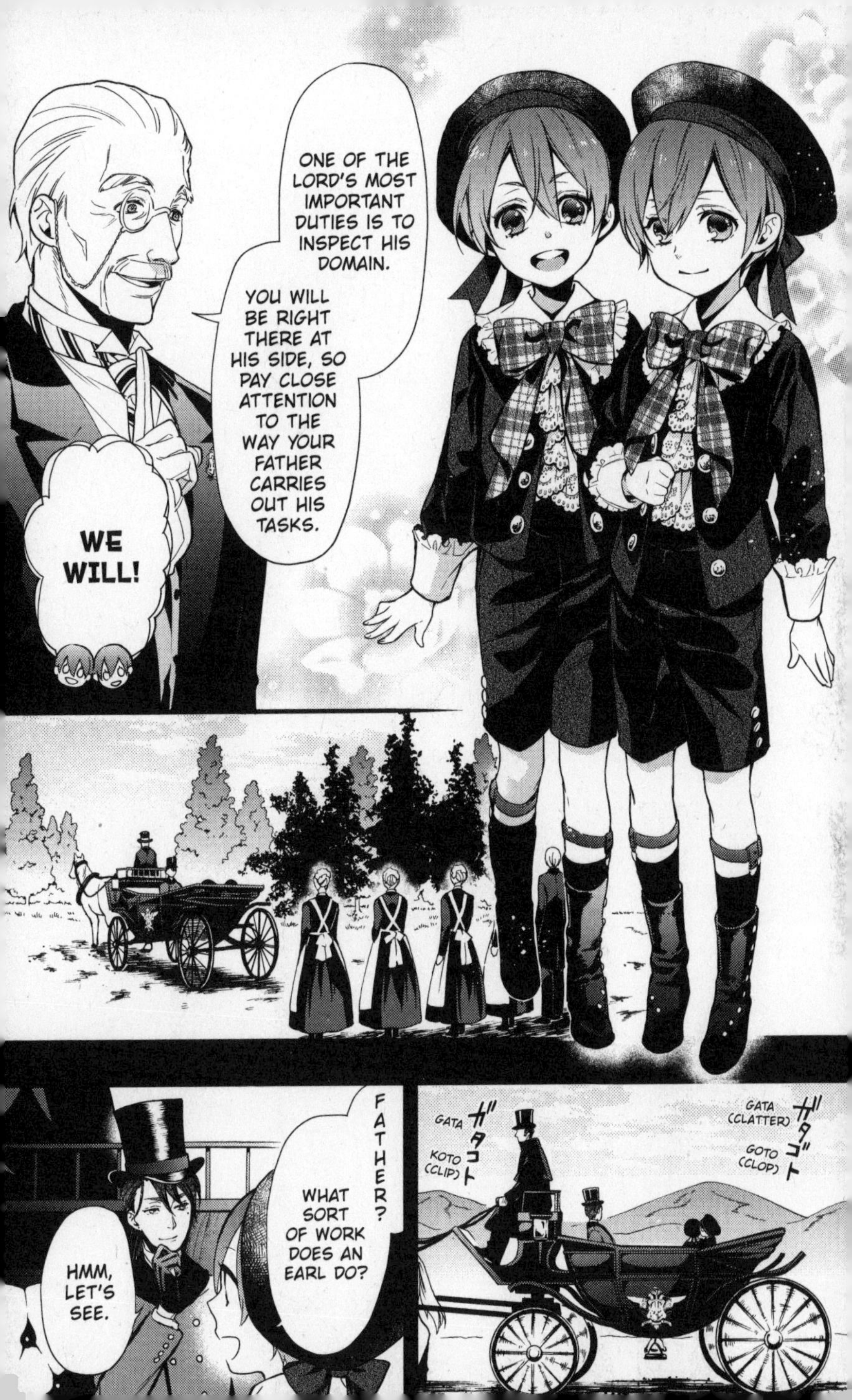
ONE OF THE LORD'S MOST IMPORTANT DUTIES IS TO INSPECT HIS DOMAIN.
YOU WILL BE RIGHT THERE AT HIS SIDE, SO PAY CLOSE ATTENTION TO THE WAY YOUR FATHER CARRIES OUT HIS TASKS.
WE WILL!
ガタ GATA (CLATTER)
ゴト GOTO (CLOP)
ガタ GATA
コト KOTO (CLIP)
FATHER?
WHAT SORT OF WORK DOES AN EARL DO?
HMM, LET'S SEE.

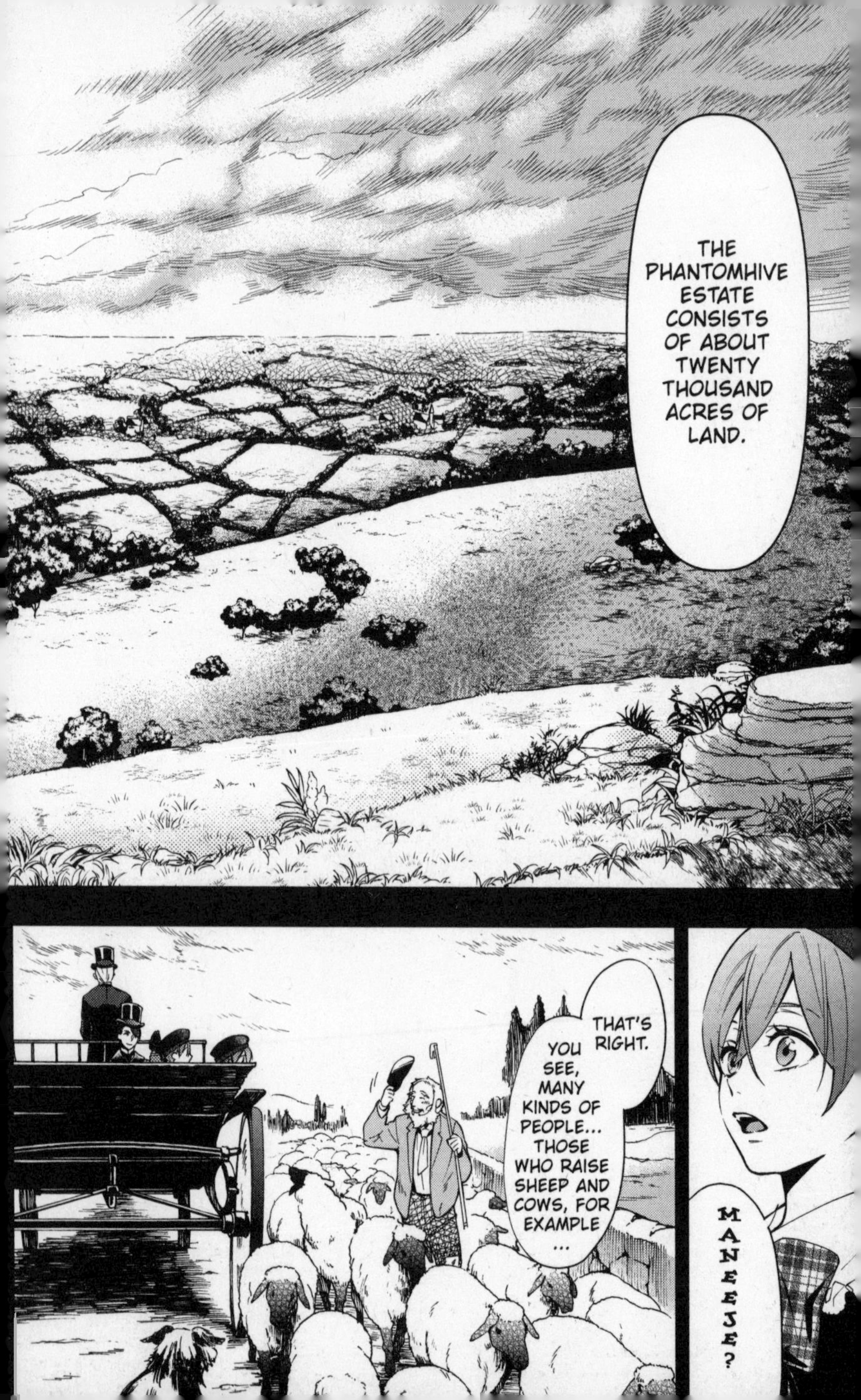
THE PHANTOMHIVE ESTATE CONSISTS OF ABOUT TWENTY THOUSAND ACRES OF LAND.
MANEEJE?
THAT'S RIGHT.
YOU SEE, MANY KINDS OF PEOPLE... THOSE WHO RAISE SHEEP AND COWS, FOR EXAMPLE...

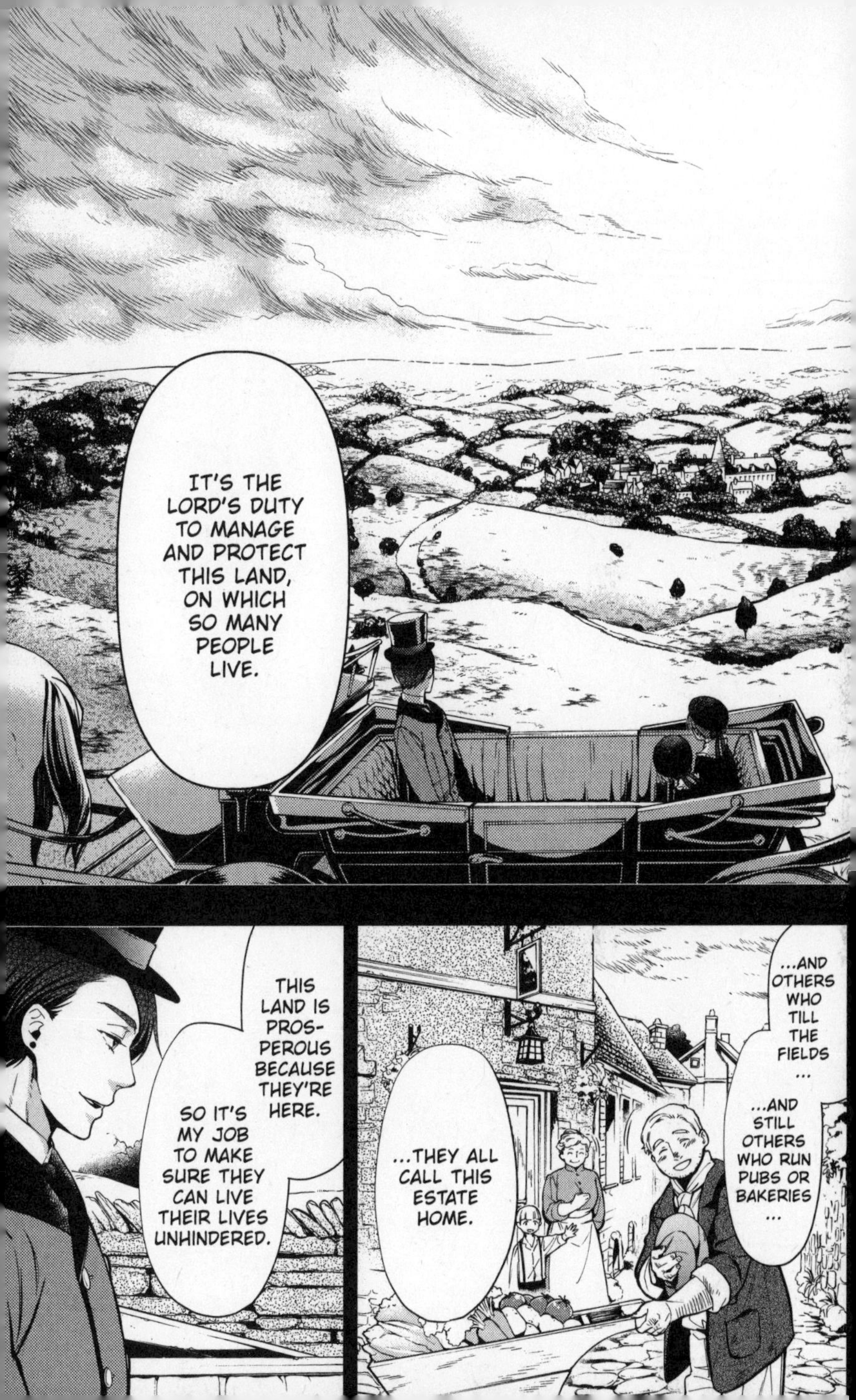
IT'S THE LORD'S DUTY TO MANAGE AND PROTECT THIS LAND, ON WHICH SO MANY PEOPLE LIVE.
...AND OTHERS WHO TILL THE FIELDS...
...AND STILL OTHERS WHO RUN PUBS OR BAKERIES...
...THEY ALL CALL THIS ESTATE HOME.
THIS LAND IS PROS-PEROUS BECAUSE THEY'RE HERE.
SO IT'S MY JOB TO MAKE SURE THEY CAN LIVE THEIR LIVES UNHINDERED.

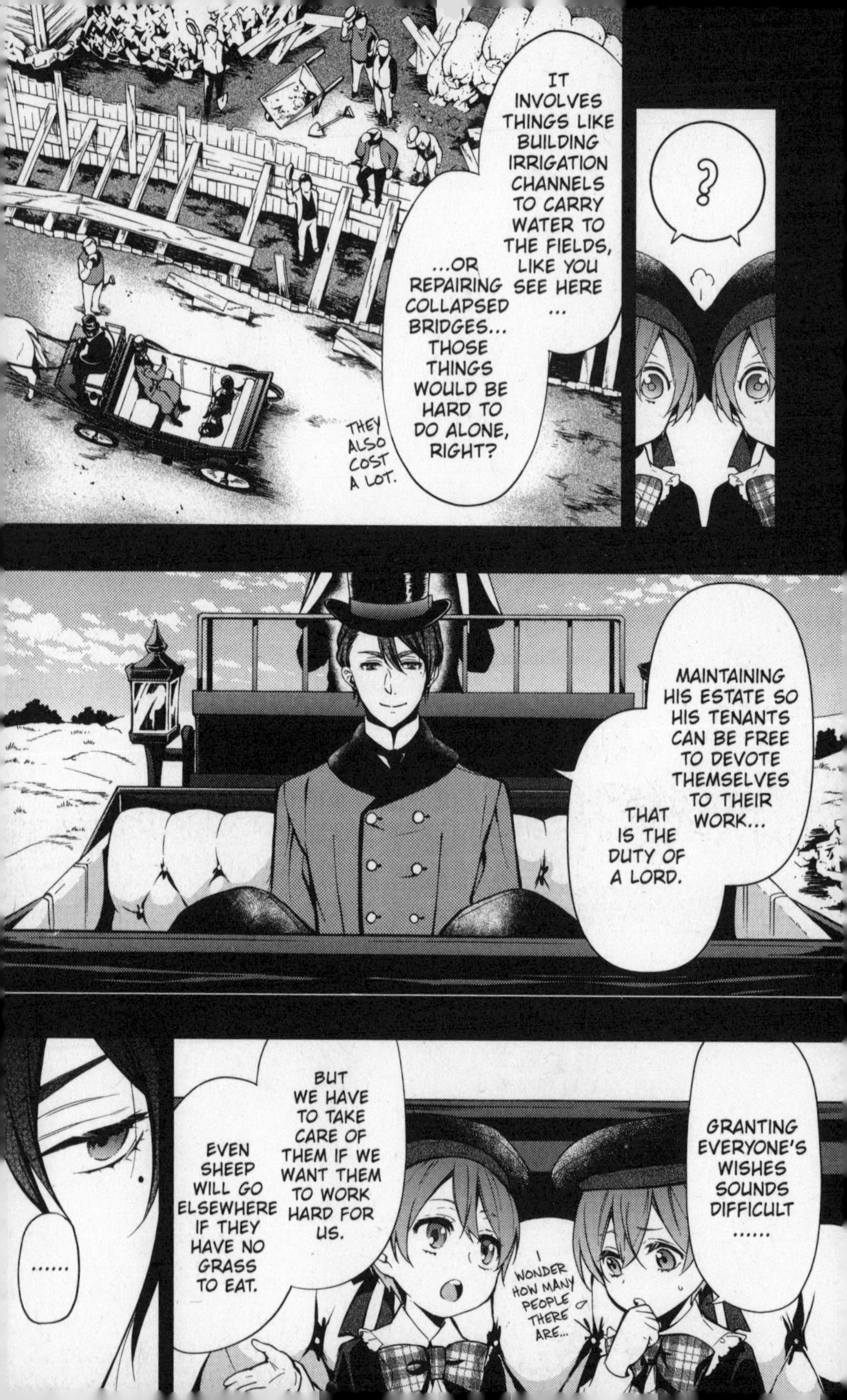
?
IT INVOLVES THINGS LIKE BUILDING IRRIGATION CHANNELS TO CARRY WATER TO THE FIELDS, LIKE YOU SEE HERE ...
...OR REPAIRING COLLAPSED BRIDGES... THOSE THINGS WOULD BE HARD TO DO ALONE, RIGHT?
THEY ALSO COST A LOT.
MAINTAINING HIS ESTATE SO HIS TENANTS CAN BE FREE TO DEVOTE THEMSELVES TO THEIR WORK...
THAT IS THE DUTY OF A LORD.
GRANTING EVERYONE'S WISHES SOUNDS DIFFICULT ......
I WONDER HOW MANY PEOPLE THERE ARE...
BUT WE HAVE TO TAKE CARE OF THEM IF WE WANT THEM TO WORK HARD FOR US.
EVEN SHEEP WILL GO ELSEWHERE IF THEY HAVE NO GRASS TO EAT.
......

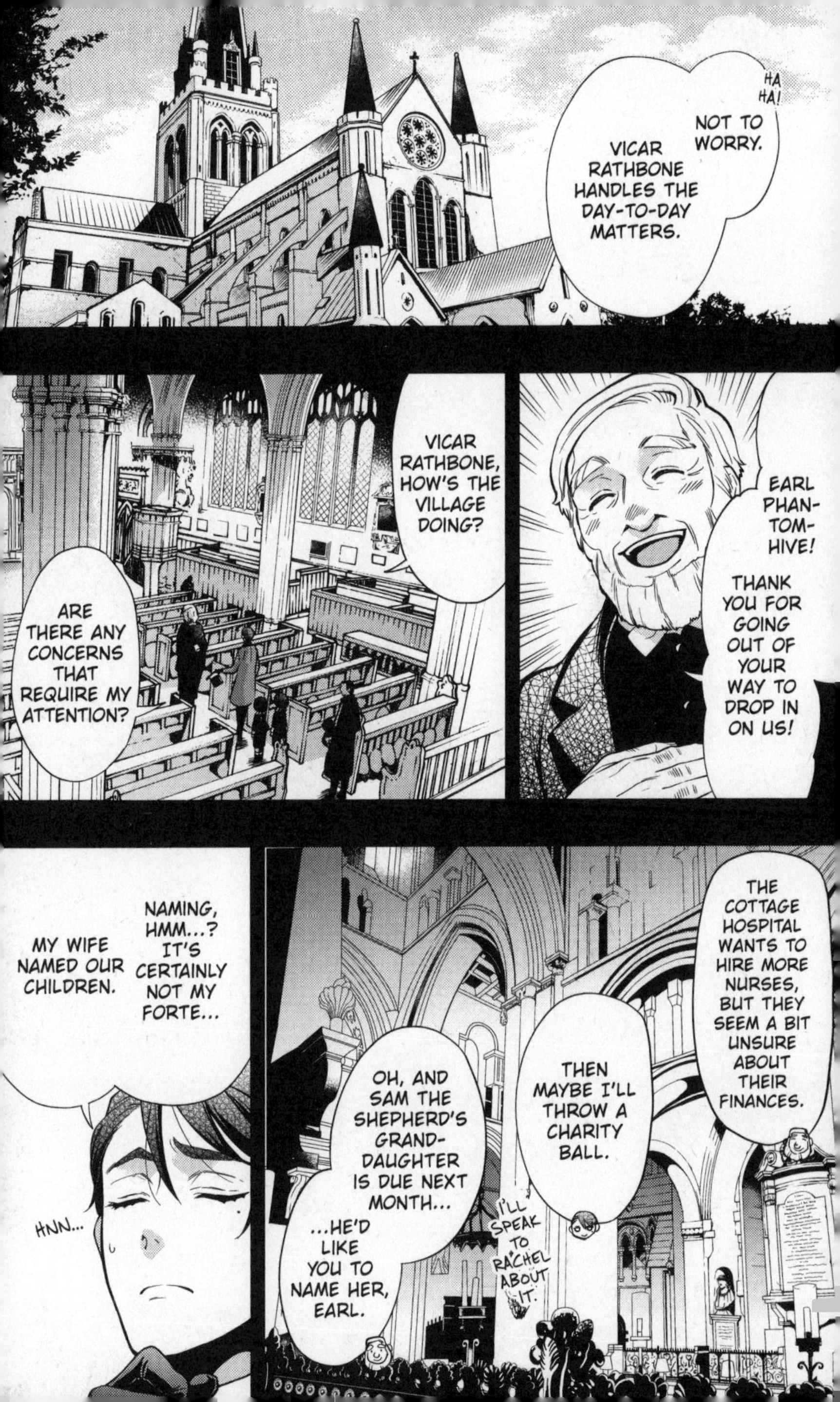

HA HA!
NOT TO WORRY.
VICAR RATHBONE HANDLES THE DAY-TO-DAY MATTERS.
EARL PHAN-TOM-HIVE!
THANK YOU FOR GOING OUT OF YOUR WAY TO DROP IN ON US!
VICAR RATHBONE, HOW'S THE VILLAGE DOING?
ARE THERE ANY CONCERNS THAT REQUIRE MY ATTENTION?
THE COTTAGE HOSPITAL WANTS TO HIRE MORE NURSES, BUT THEY SEEM A BIT UNSURE ABOUT THEIR FINANCES.
THEN MAYBE I'LL THROW A CHARITY BALL.
I'LL SPEAK TO RACHEL ABOUT IT.
OH, AND SAM THE SHEPHERD'S GRAND-DAUGHTER IS DUE NEXT MONTH...
...HE'D LIKE YOU TO NAME HER, EARL.
NAMING, HMM...? IT'S CERTAINLY NOT MY FORTE...
MY WIFE NAMED OUR CHILDREN.
HNN...

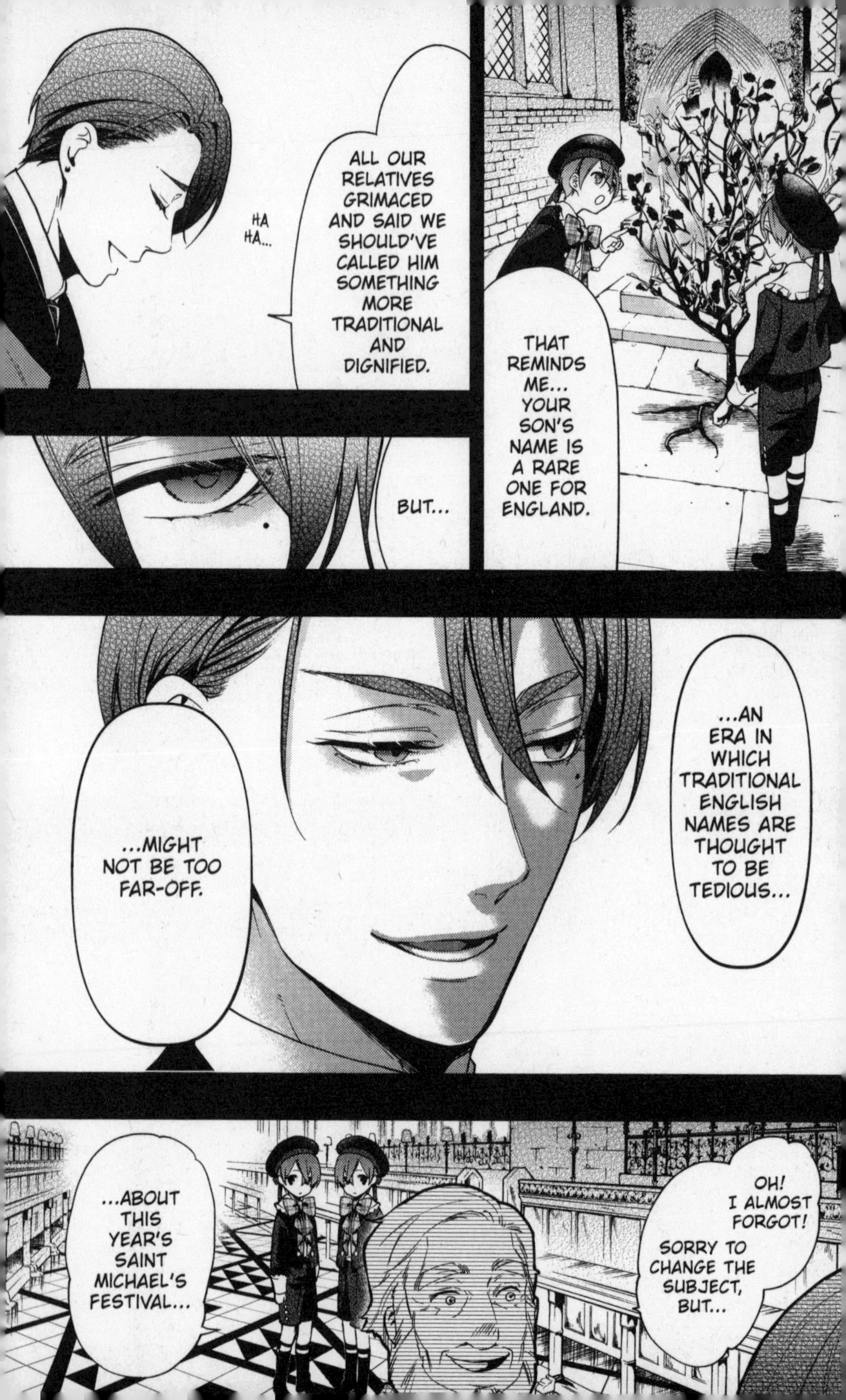
THAT REMINDS ME... YOUR SON'S NAME IS A RARE ONE FOR ENGLAND.
ALL OUR RELATIVES GRIMACED AND SAID WE SHOULD'VE CALLED HIM SOMETHING MORE TRADITIONAL AND DIGNIFIED.
HA HA...
BUT...
...AN ERA IN WHICH TRADITIONAL ENGLISH NAMES ARE THOUGHT TO BE TEDIOUS...
...MIGHT NOT BE TOO FAR-OFF.
OH! I ALMOST FORGOT!
SORRY TO CHANGE THE SUBJECT, BUT...
...ABOUT THIS YEAR'S SAINT MICHAEL'S FESTIVAL...

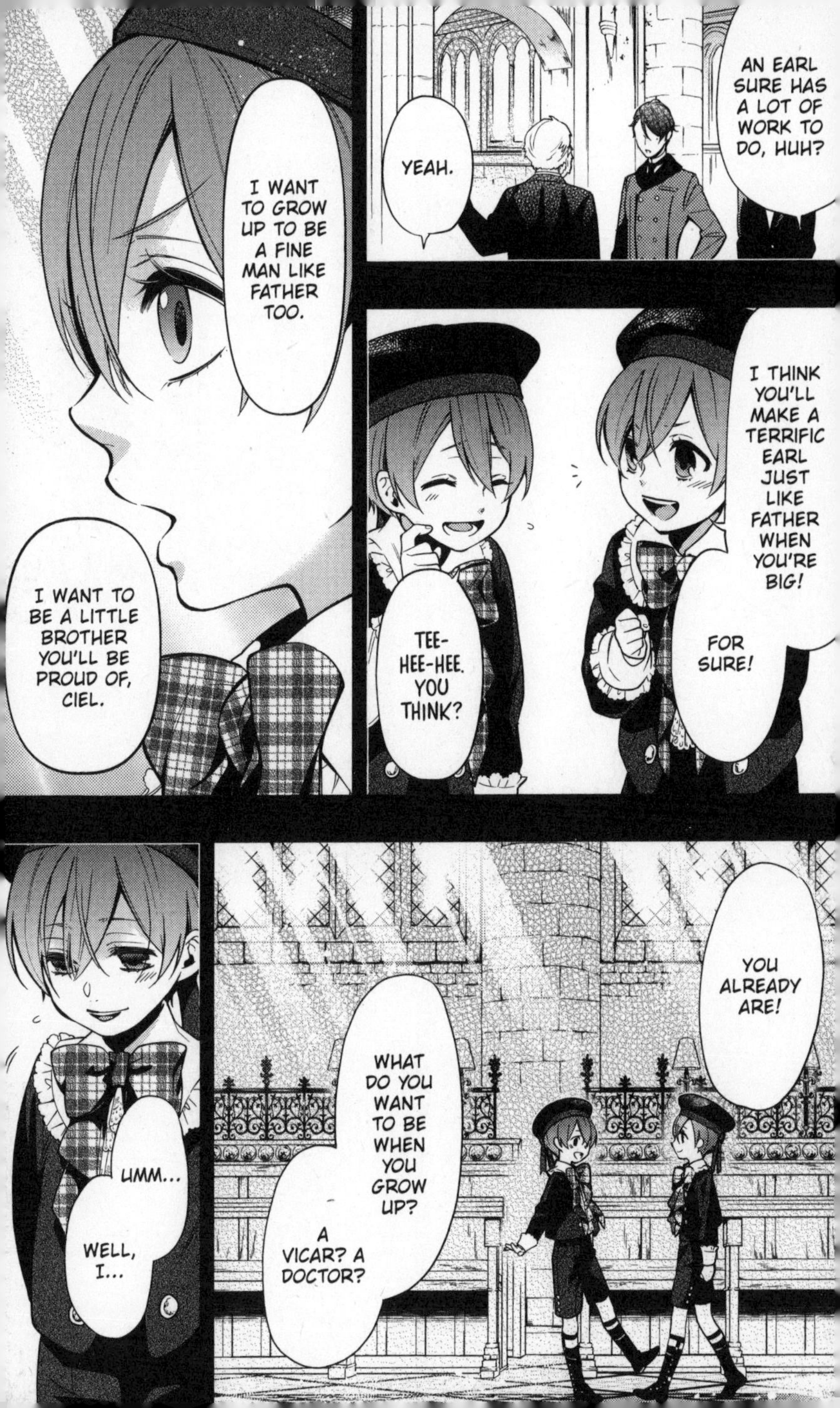
AN EARL SURE HAS A LOT OF WORK TO DO, HUH?
YEAH.
I THINK YOU'LL MAKE A TERRIFIC EARL JUST LIKE FATHER WHEN YOU'RE BIG!
FOR SURE!
TEE-HEE-HEE. YOU THINK?
I WANT TO GROW UP TO BE A FINE MAN LIKE FATHER TOO.
I WANT TO BE A LITTLE BROTHER YOU'LL BE PROUD OF, CIEL.
YOU ALREADY ARE!
WHAT DO YOU WANT TO BE WHEN YOU GROW UP?
A VICAR? A DOCTOR?
UMM...
WELL, I...

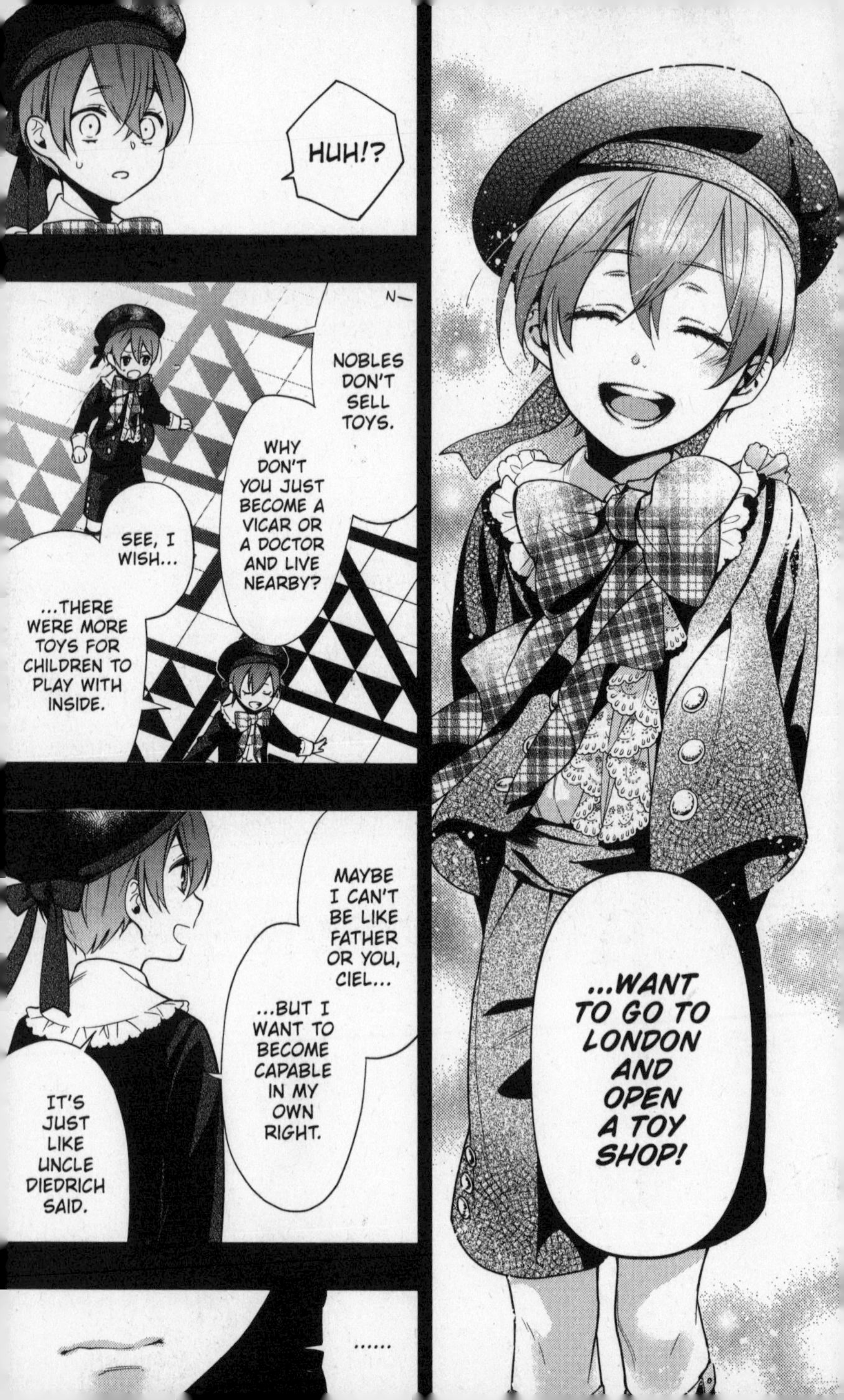
...WANT TO GO TO LONDON AND OPEN A TOY SHOP!
HUH!?
N—
NOBLES DON'T SELL TOYS.
WHY DON'T YOU JUST BECOME A VICAR OR A DOCTOR AND LIVE NEARBY?
SEE, I WISH...
...THERE WERE MORE TOYS FOR CHILDREN TO PLAY WITH INSIDE.
MAYBE I CAN'T BE LIKE FATHER OR YOU, CIEL...
...BUT I WANT TO BECOME CAPABLE IN MY OWN RIGHT.
IT'S JUST LIKE UNCLE DIEDRICH SAID.
......

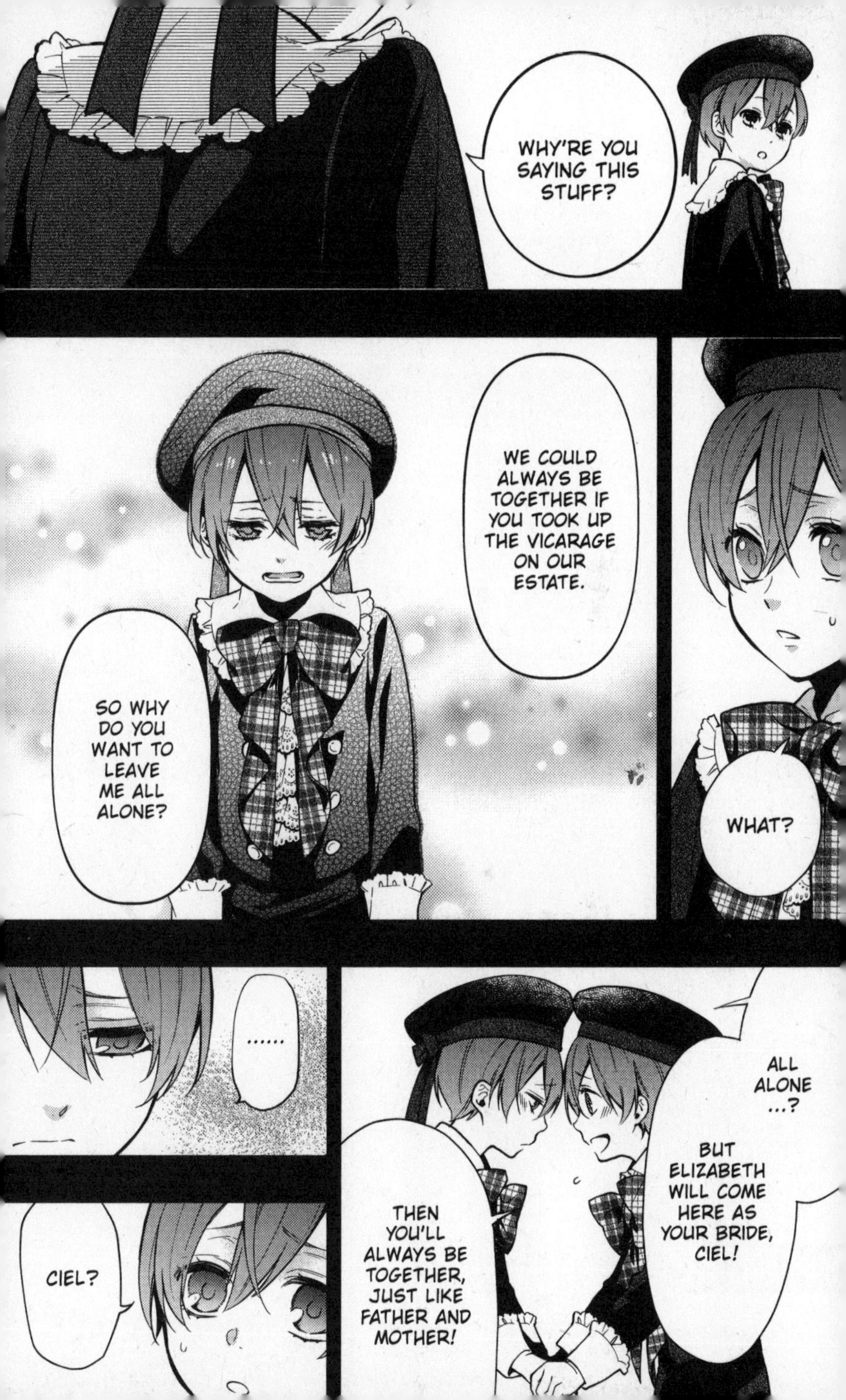
WHY'RE YOU SAYING THIS STUFF?
WHAT?
WE COULD ALWAYS BE TOGETHER IF YOU TOOK UP THE VICARAGE ON OUR ESTATE.
SO WHY DO YOU WANT TO LEAVE ME ALL ALONE?
ALL ALONE ...?
BUT ELIZABETH WILL COME HERE AS YOUR BRIDE, CIEL!
THEN YOU'LL ALWAYS BE TOGETHER, JUST LIKE FATHER AND MOTHER!
......
CIEL?

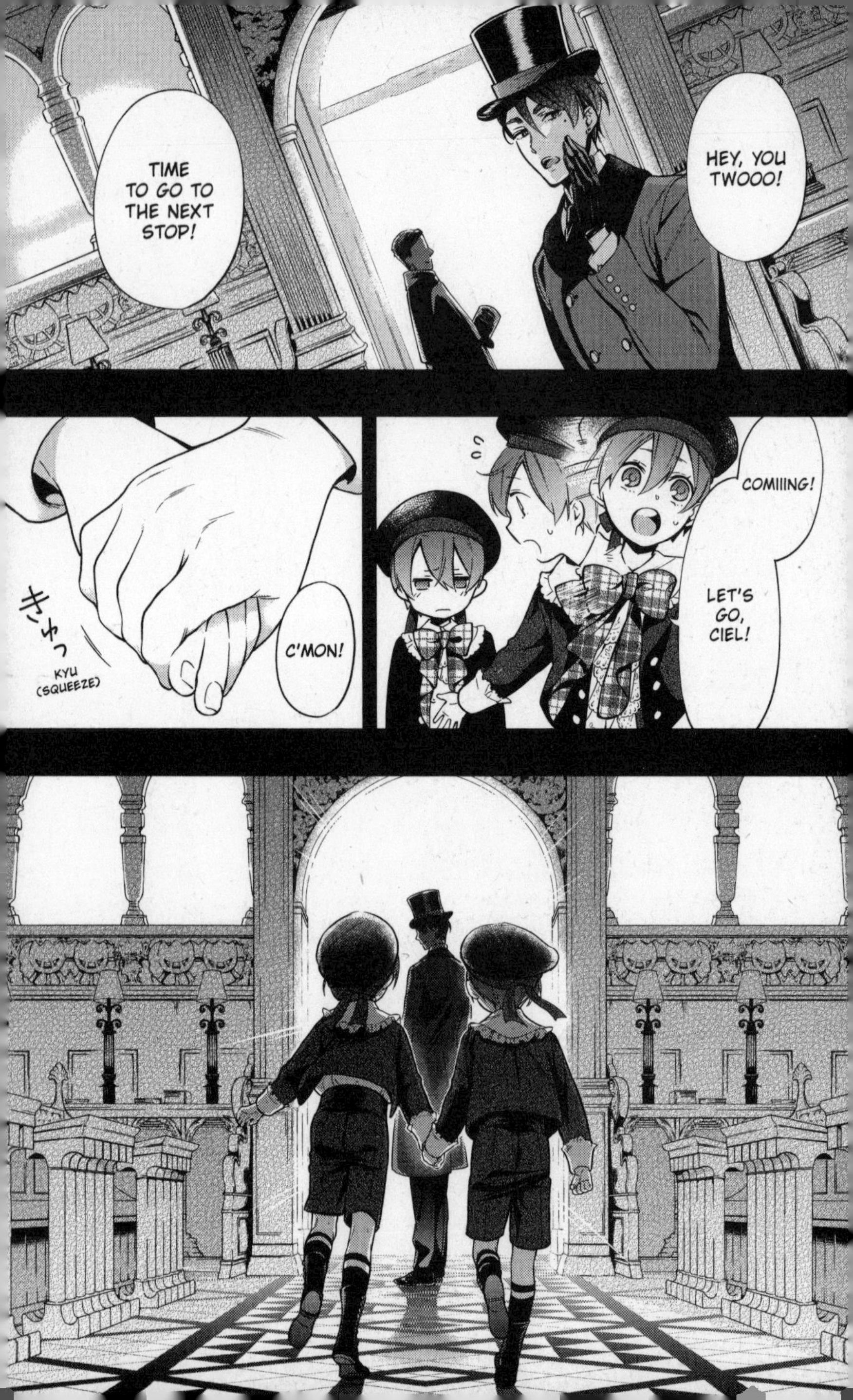
HEY, YOU TWOOO!
TIME TO GO TO THE NEXT STOP!
COMIIING!
LET'S GO, CIEL!
C'MON!
きゅっ
KYU (SQUEEZE)

Black Butler

Chapter 133

At midnight : The Butler, Vanished

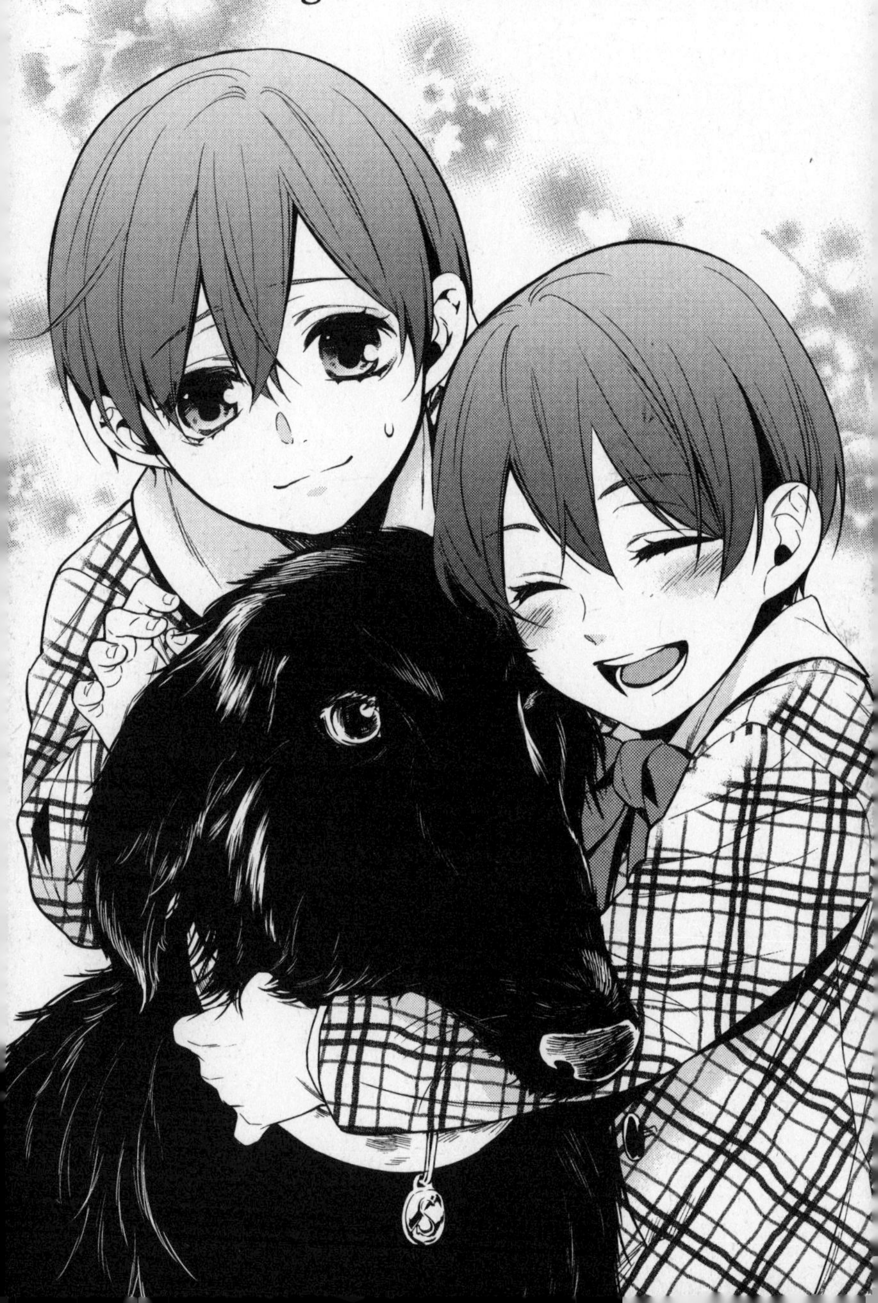

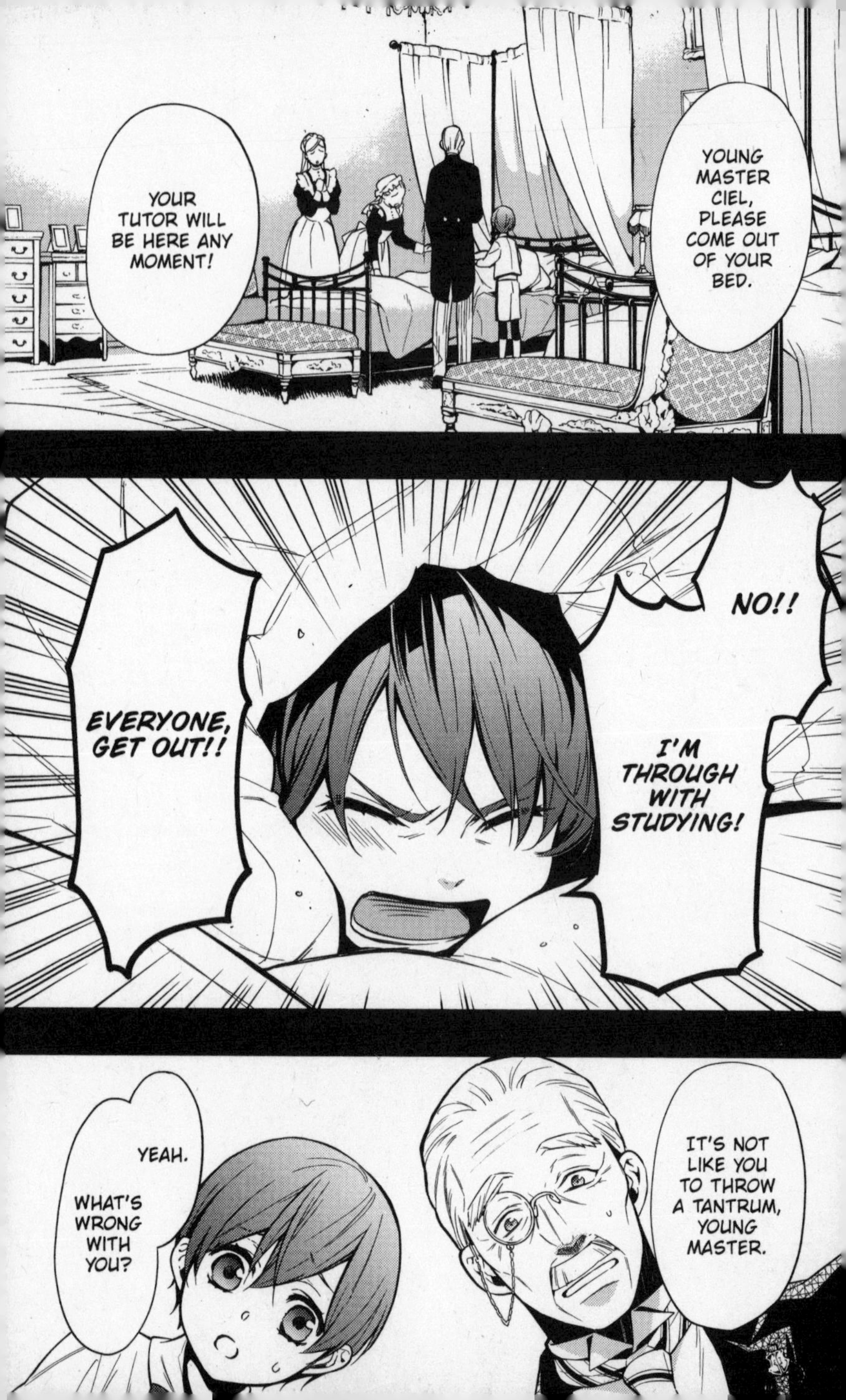
YOUNG MASTER CIEL, PLEASE COME OUT OF YOUR BED.
YOUR TUTOR WILL BE HERE ANY MOMENT!
NO!!
I'M THROUGH WITH STUDYING!
EVERYONE, GET OUT!!
IT'S NOT LIKE YOU TO THROW A TANTRUM, YOUNG MASTER.
YEAH.
WHAT'S WRONG WITH YOU?

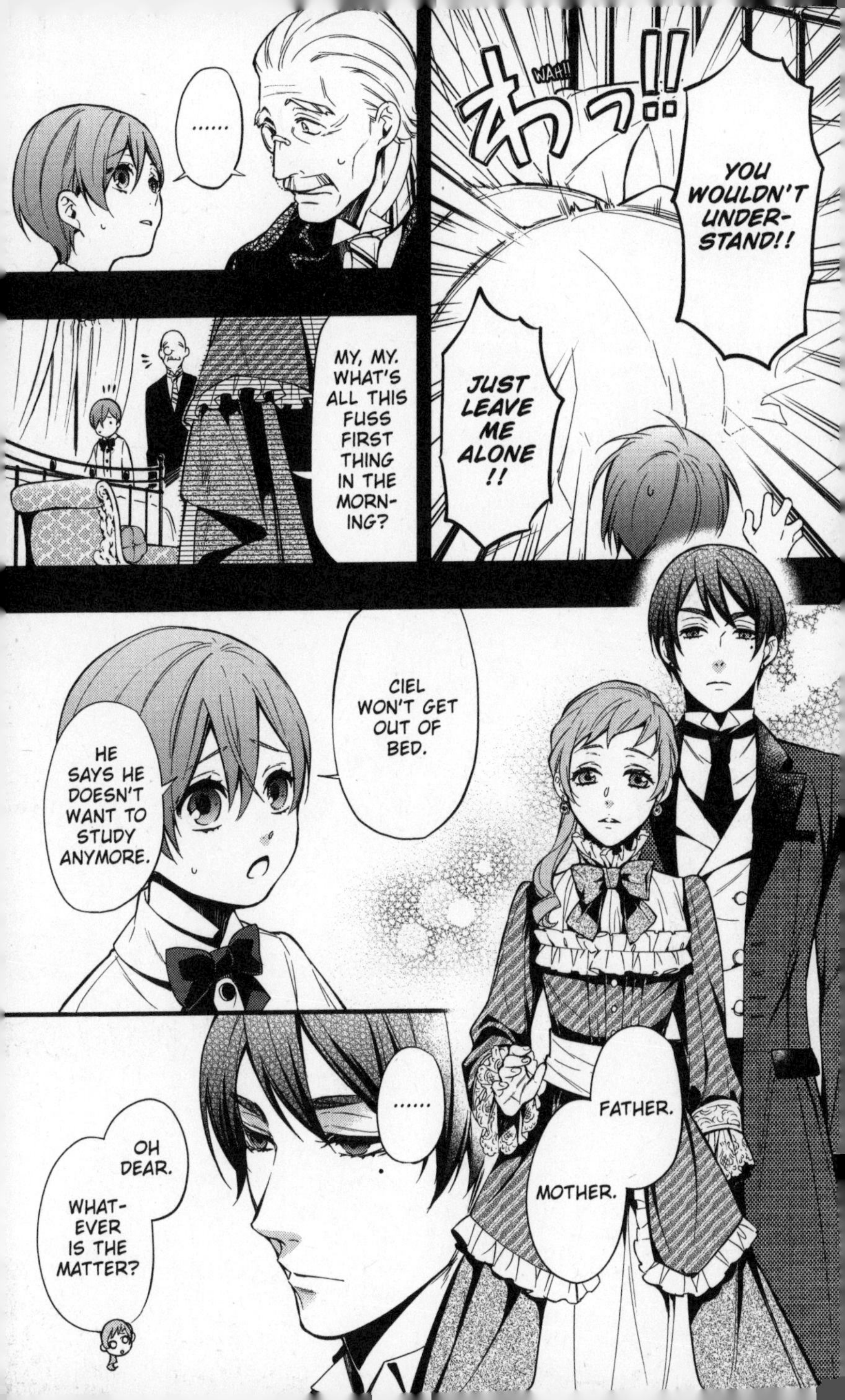
わっ!!
WAH!!
YOU WOULDN'T UNDERSTAND!!
JUST LEAVE ME ALONE!!
......
MY, MY. WHAT'S ALL THIS FUSS FIRST THING IN THE MORNING?
FATHER.
MOTHER.
CIEL WON'T GET OUT OF BED.
HE SAYS HE DOESN'T WANT TO STUDY ANYMORE.
......
OH DEAR.
WHATEVER IS THE MATTER?

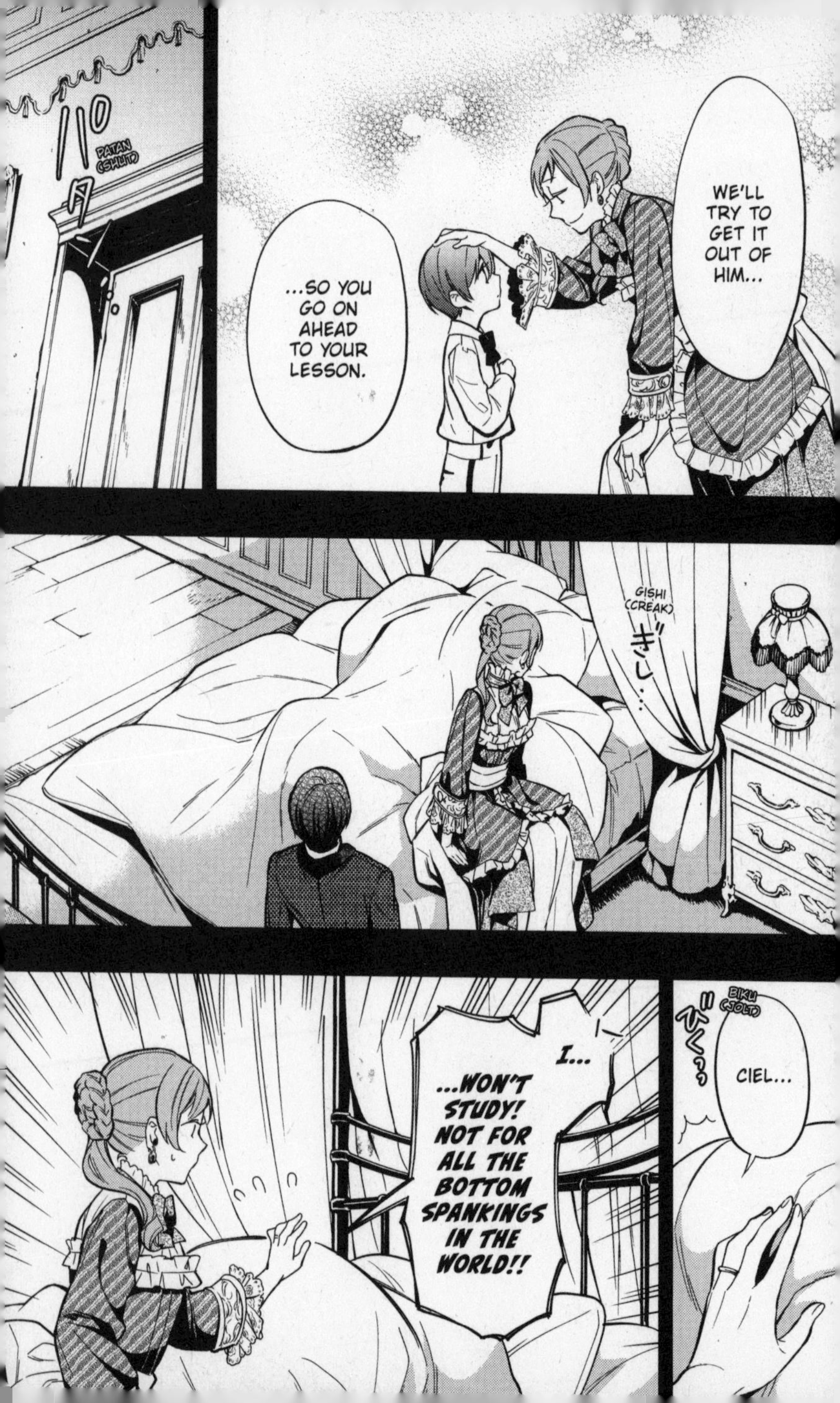
WE'LL TRY TO GET IT OUT OF HIM...
...SO YOU GO ON AHEAD TO YOUR LESSON.
PATAN (SHUT)
GISHI (CREAK)
BIKU (JOLT)
CIEL...
I...
...WON'T STUDY! NOT FOR ALL THE BOTTOM SPANKINGS IN THE WORLD!!

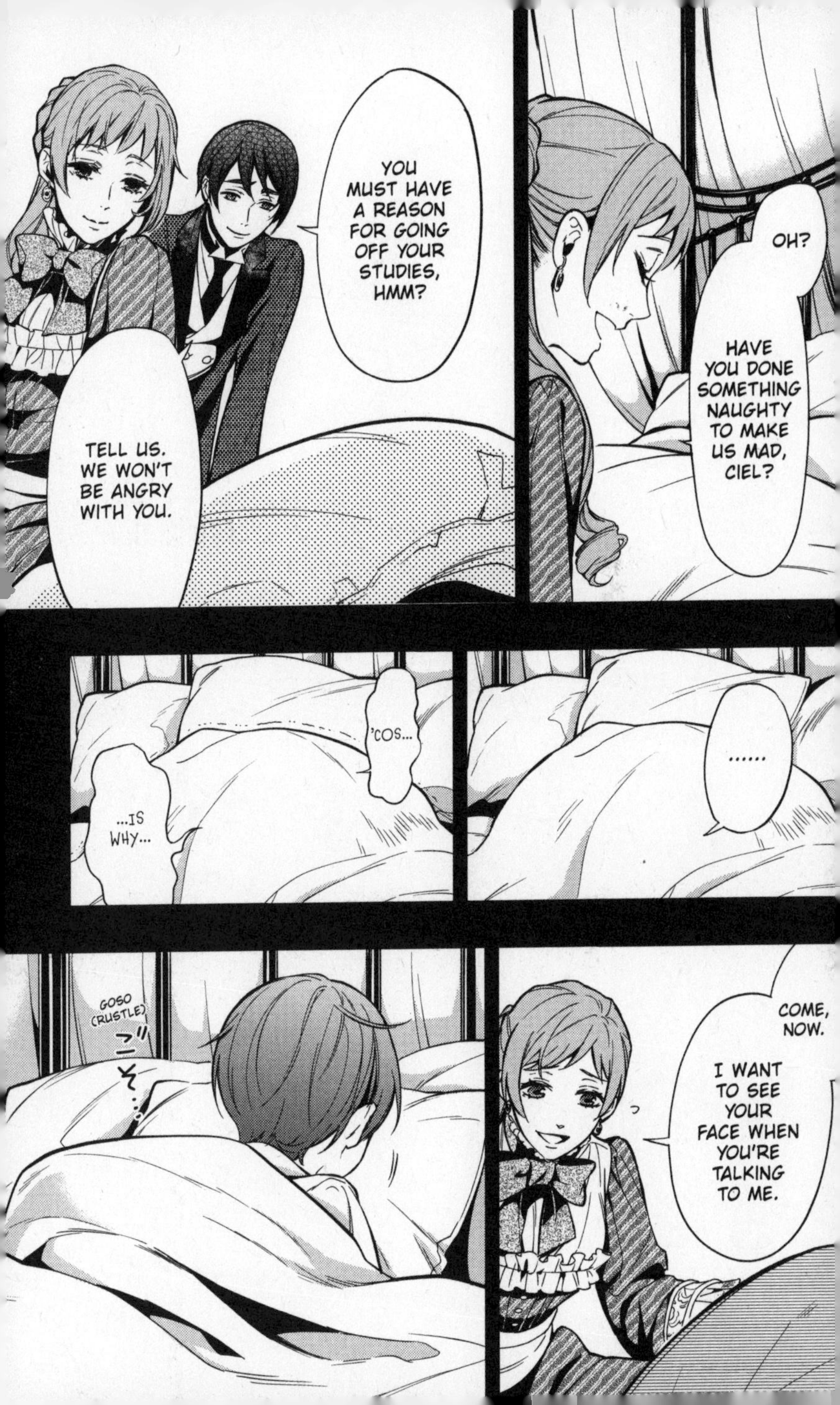
OH?
HAVE YOU DONE SOMETHING NAUGHTY TO MAKE US MAD, CIEL?
YOU MUST HAVE A REASON FOR GOING OFF YOUR STUDIES, HMM?
TELL US. WE WON'T BE ANGRY WITH YOU.
......
'COS...
...IS WHY...
COME, NOW.
I WANT TO SEE YOUR FACE WHEN YOU'RE TALKING TO ME.
GOSO (RUSTLE)

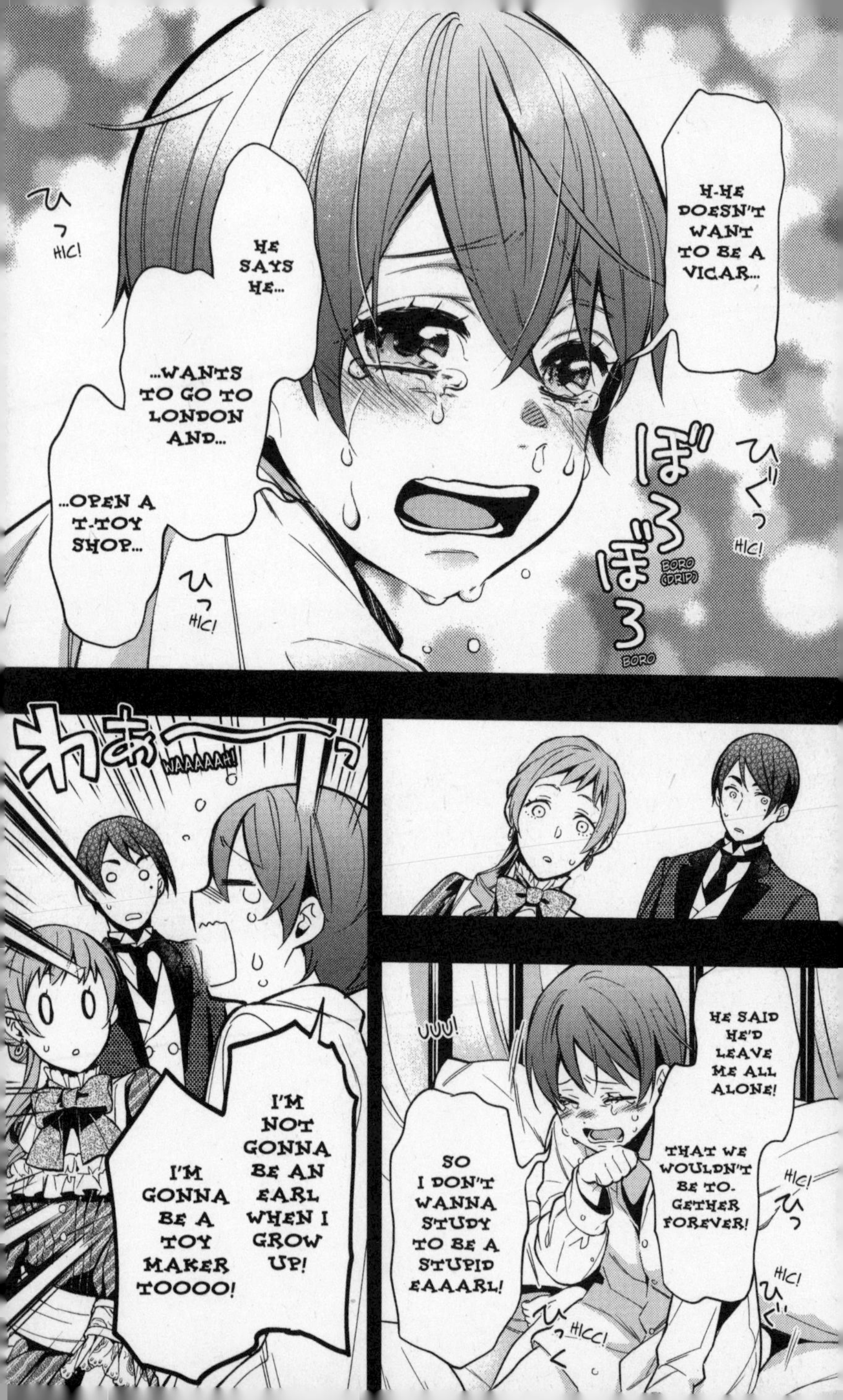

H-HE DOESN'T WANT TO BE A VICAR...
ひくっ HIC!
ぼろぼろ BORO (DRIP) BORO
HE SAYS HE...
...WANTS TO GO TO LONDON AND...
...OPEN A T-TOY SHOP...
ひっ HIC!
ひっ HIC!
HE SAID HE'D LEAVE ME ALL ALONE!
THAT WE WOULDN'T BE TO-GETHER FOREVER!
HIC! ひっ
HIC! ひぐ
UUU!
SO I DON'T WANNA STUDY TO BE A STUPID EAAARL!
ひっ HICC!
わあーっ WAAAAAH!
I'M NOT GONNA BE AN EARL WHEN I GROW UP!
I'M GONNA BE A TOY MAKER TOOOO!

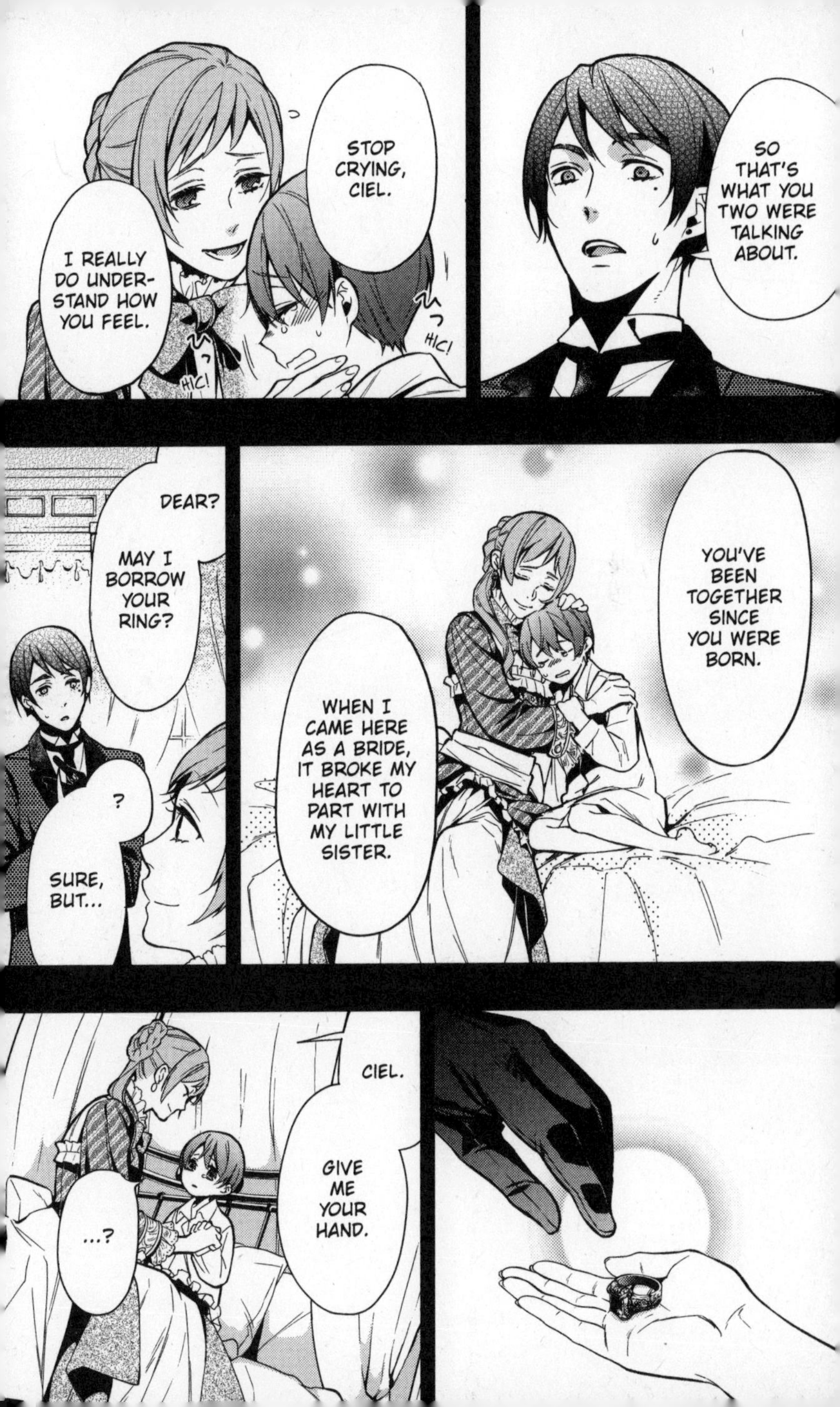
SO THAT'S WHAT YOU TWO WERE TALKING ABOUT.
STOP CRYING, CIEL.
HIC!
I REALLY DO UNDER-STAND HOW YOU FEEL.
HIC!
YOU'VE BEEN TOGETHER SINCE YOU WERE BORN.
WHEN I CAME HERE AS A BRIDE, IT BROKE MY HEART TO PART WITH MY LITTLE SISTER.
DEAR?
MAY I BORROW YOUR RING?
?
SURE, BUT...
CIEL.
GIVE ME YOUR HAND.
...?

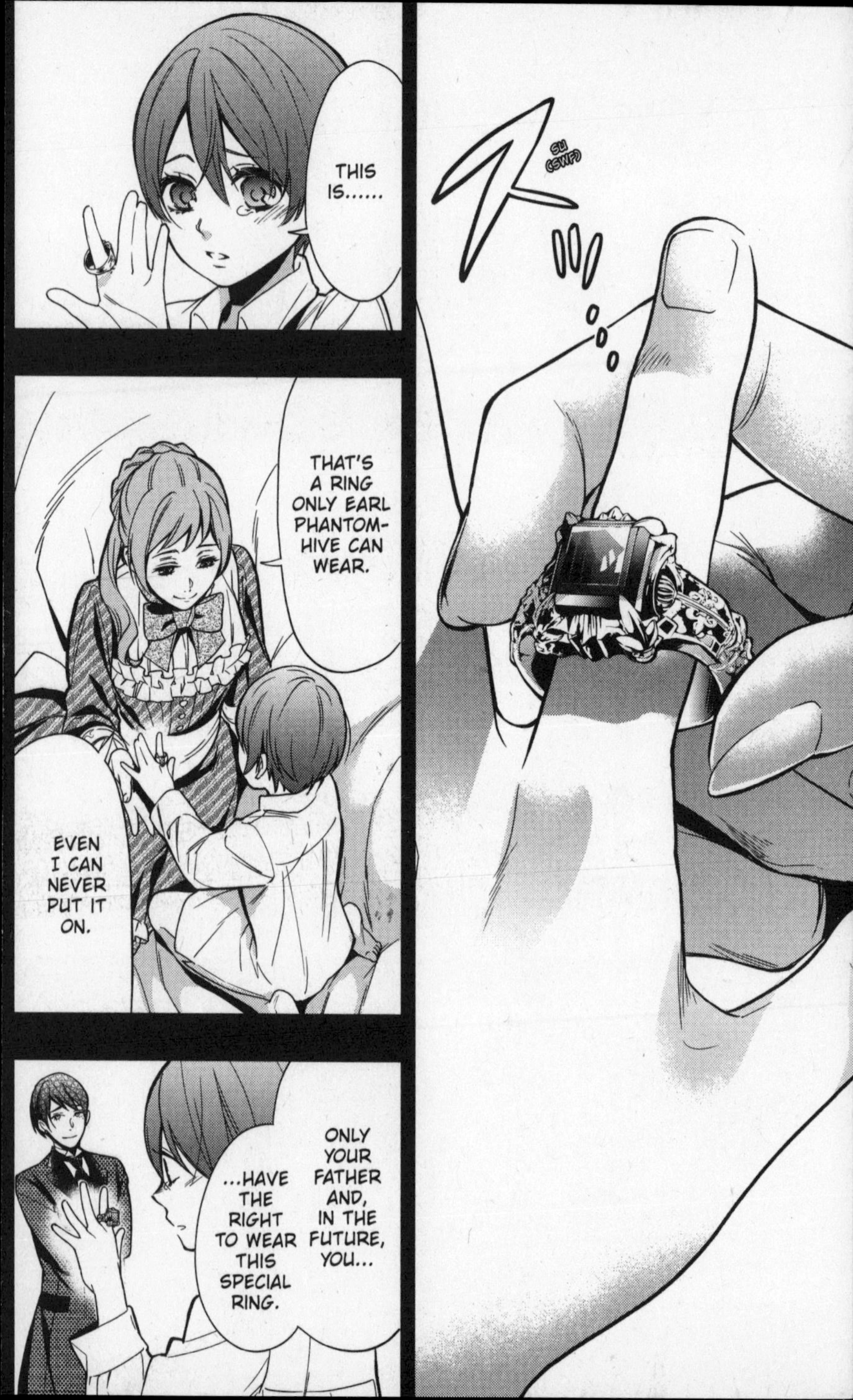
SU (SWP)
THIS IS......
THAT'S A RING ONLY EARL PHANTOM-HIVE CAN WEAR.
EVEN I CAN NEVER PUT IT ON.
ONLY YOUR FATHER AND, IN THE FUTURE, YOU...
...HAVE THE RIGHT TO WEAR THIS SPECIAL RING.

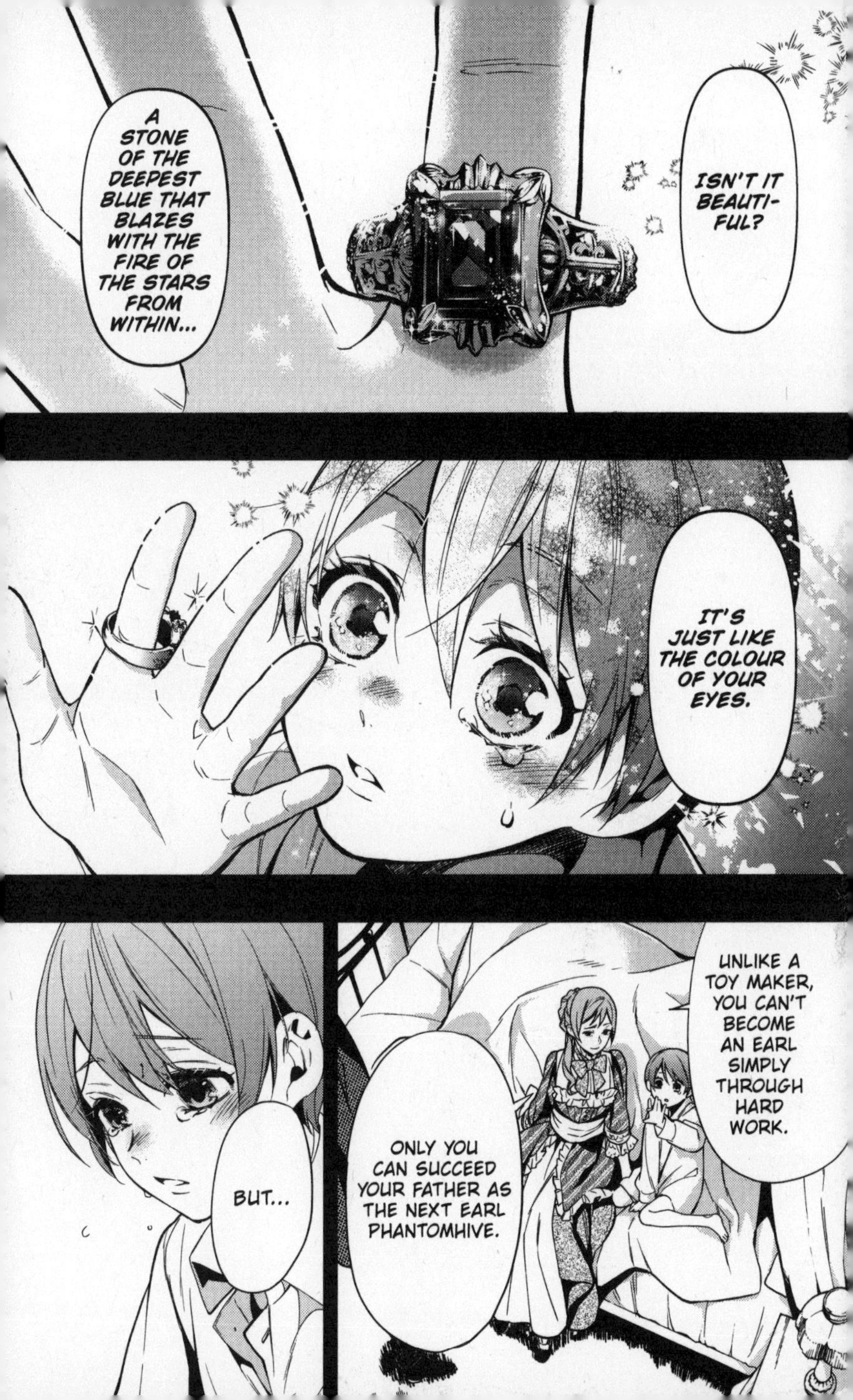
ISN'T IT BEAUTI-FUL?
A STONE OF THE DEEPEST BLUE THAT BLAZES WITH THE FIRE OF THE STARS FROM WITHIN...
IT'S JUST LIKE THE COLOUR OF YOUR EYES.
UNLIKE A TOY MAKER, YOU CAN'T BECOME AN EARL SIMPLY THROUGH HARD WORK.
ONLY YOU CAN SUCCEED YOUR FATHER AS THE NEXT EARL PHANTOMHIVE.
BUT...

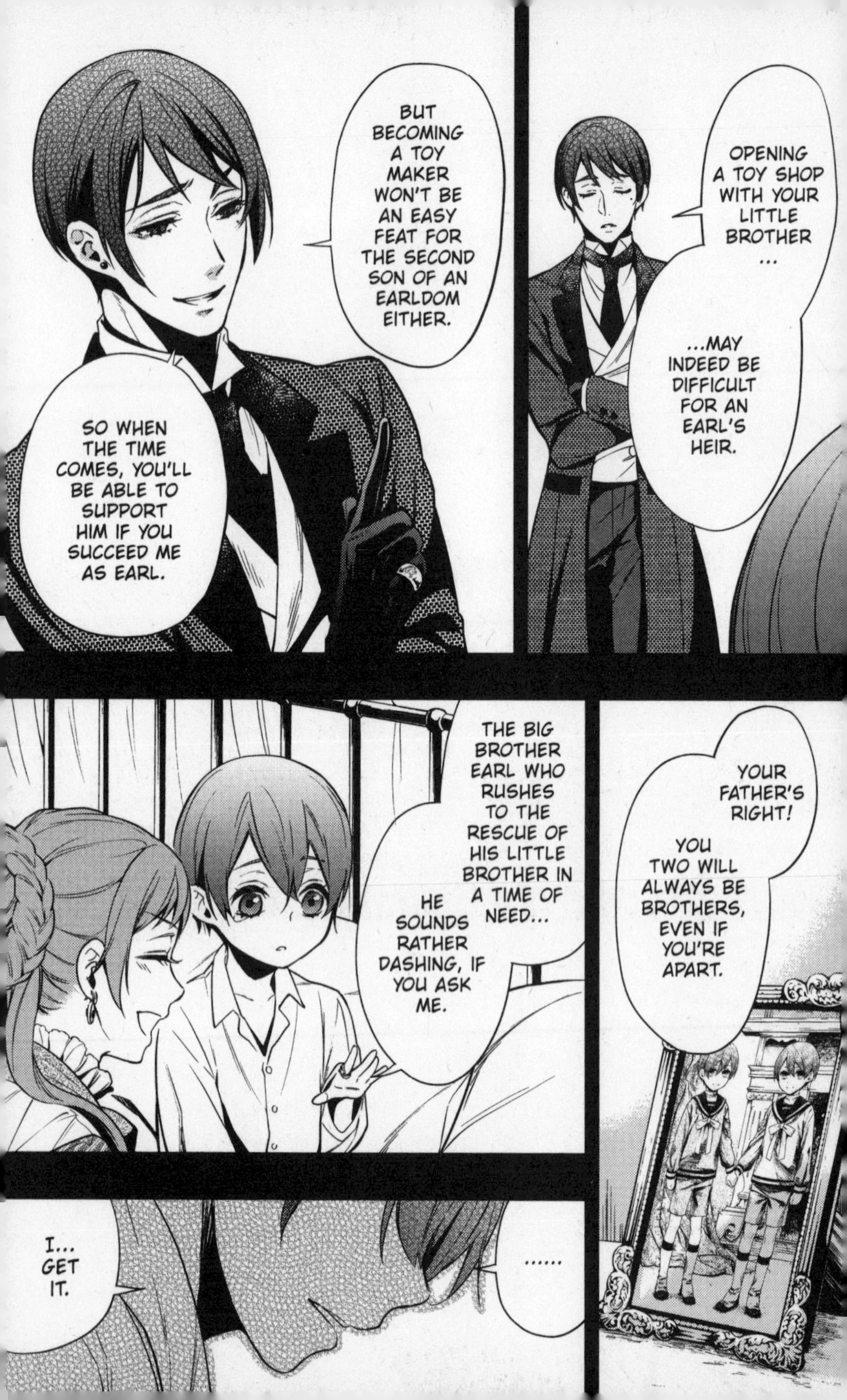
OPENING A TOY SHOP WITH YOUR LITTLE BROTHER ...
...MAY INDEED BE DIFFICULT FOR AN EARL'S HEIR.
BUT BECOMING A TOY MAKER WON'T BE AN EASY FEAT FOR THE SECOND SON OF AN EARLDOM EITHER.
SO WHEN THE TIME COMES, YOU'LL BE ABLE TO SUPPORT HIM IF YOU SUCCEED ME AS EARL.
YOUR FATHER'S RIGHT!
YOU TWO WILL ALWAYS BE BROTHERS, EVEN IF YOU'RE APART.
THE BIG BROTHER EARL WHO RUSHES TO THE RESCUE OF HIS LITTLE BROTHER IN A TIME OF NEED...
HE SOUNDS RATHER DASHING, IF YOU ASK ME.
......
I... GET IT.

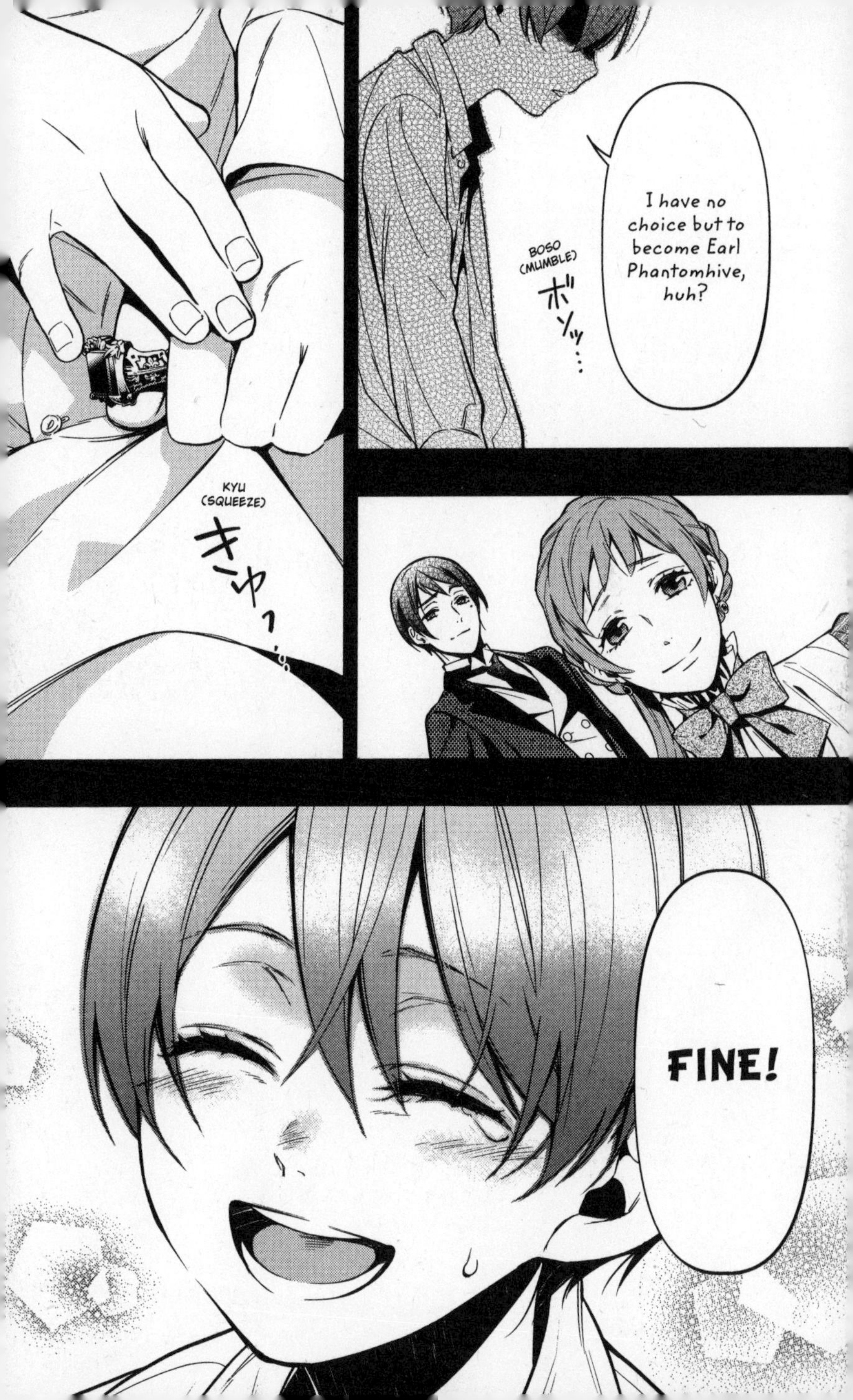
I have no choice but to become Earl Phantomhive, huh?
BOSO (MUMBLE)
ボソッ…
KYU (SQUEEZE)
きゅっ
FINE!

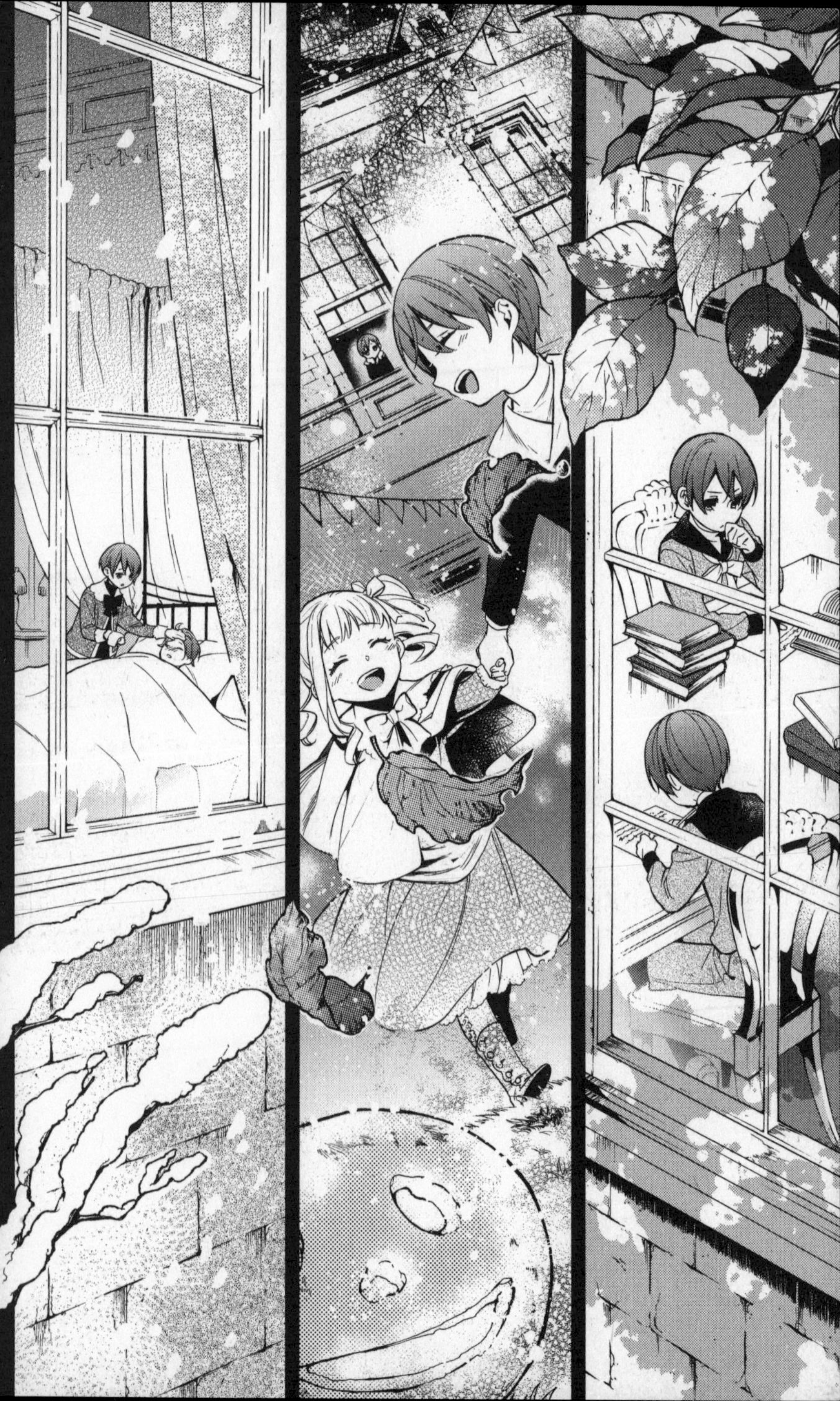

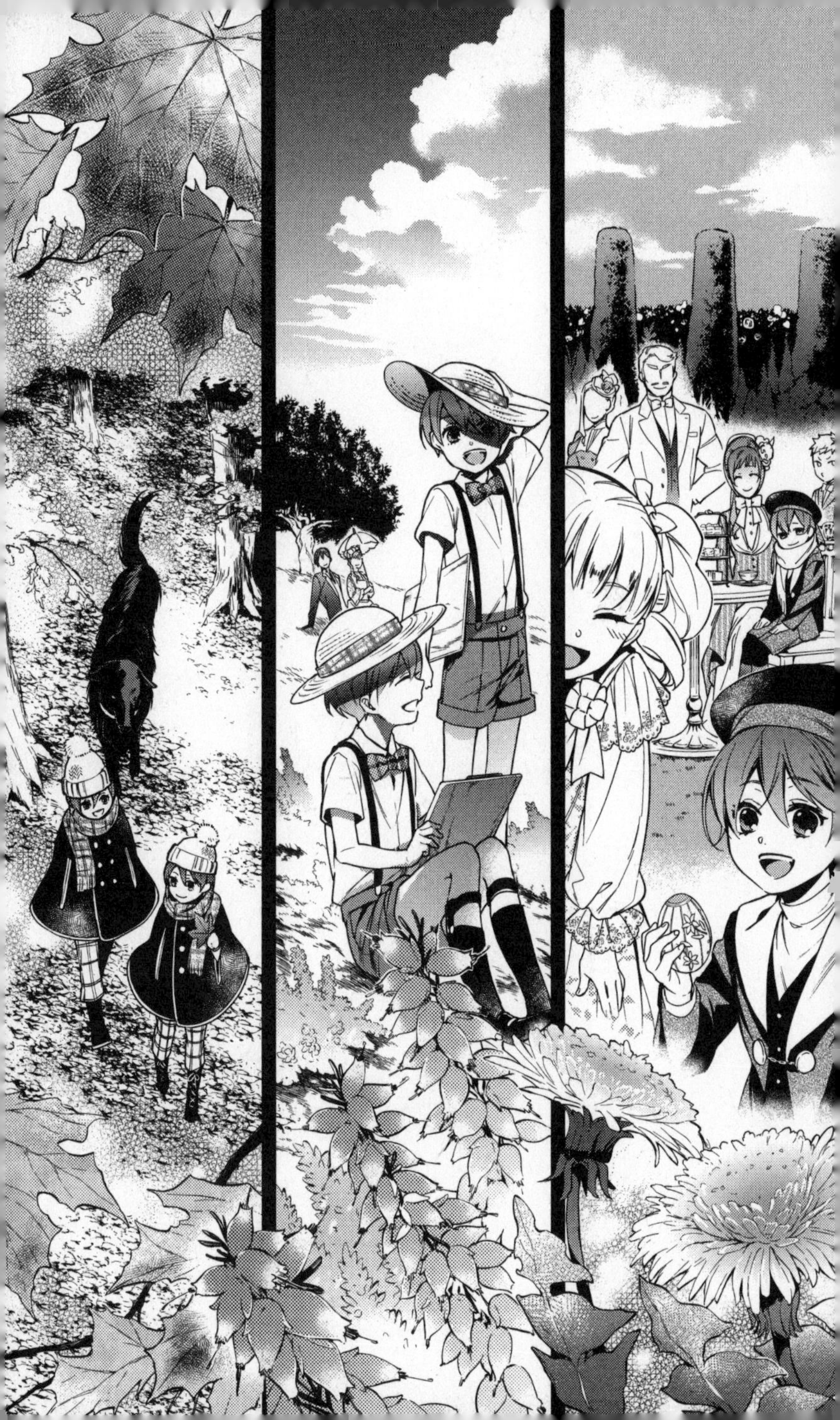

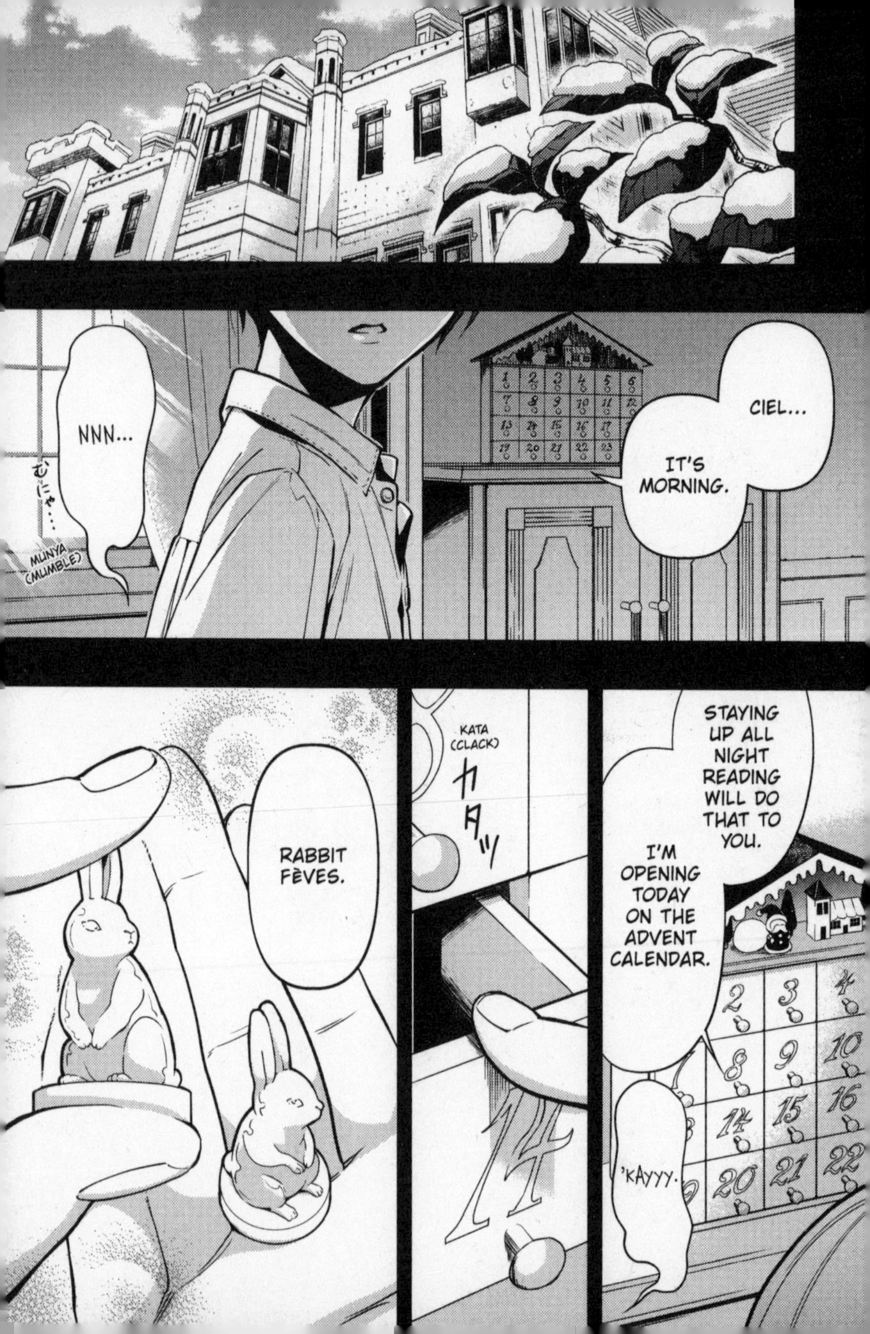
CIEL...
IT'S MORNING.
NNN...
むにゃ…
MUNYA (MUMBLE)
STAYING UP ALL NIGHT READING WILL DO THAT TO YOU.
I'M OPENING TODAY ON THE ADVENT CALENDAR.
'KAYYY.
カタッ
KATA (CLACK)
RABBIT FÈVES.

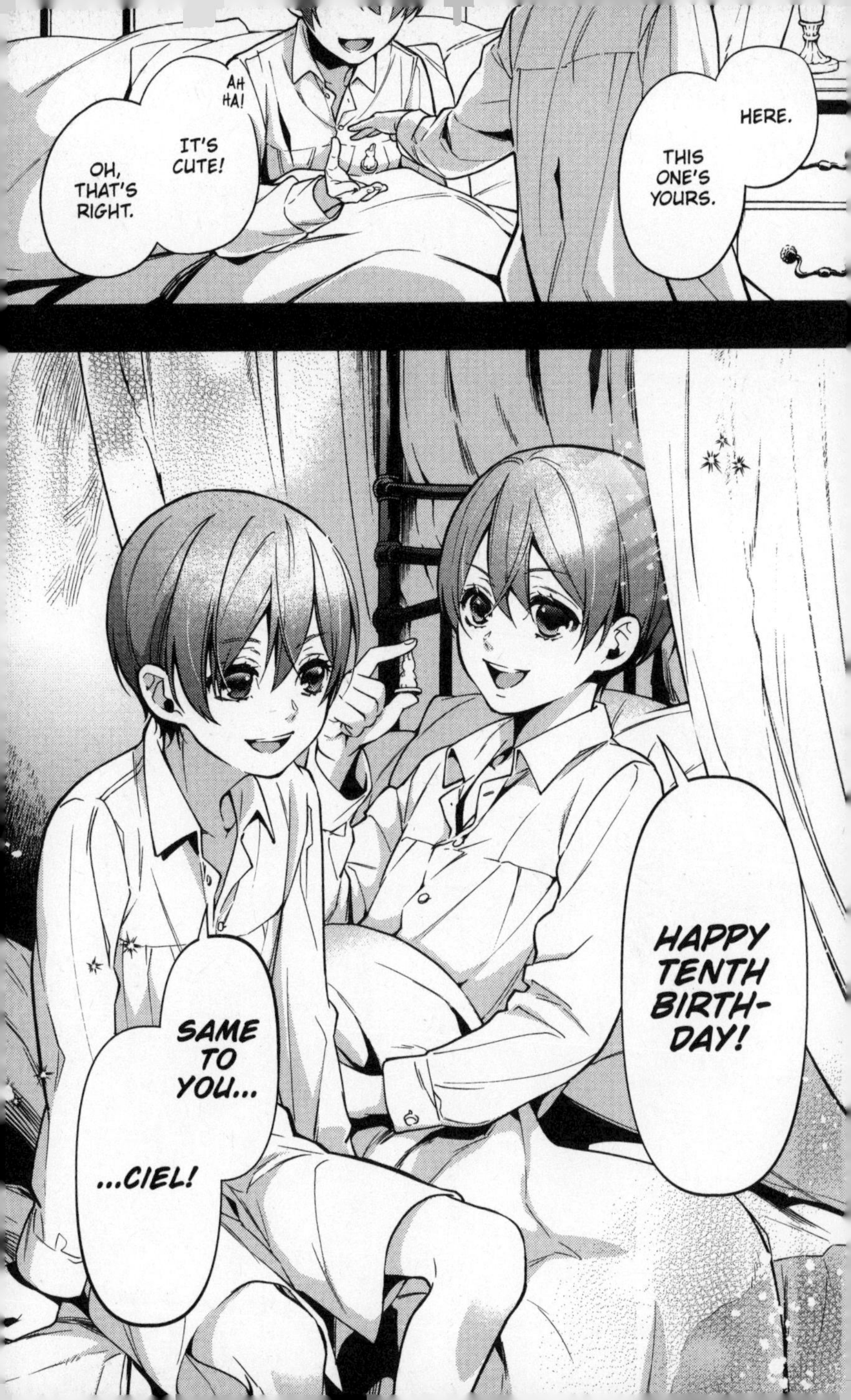
HERE.
THIS ONE'S YOURS.
AH HA!
IT'S CUTE!
OH, THAT'S RIGHT.
HAPPY TENTH BIRTH-DAY!
SAME TO YOU...
...CIEL!

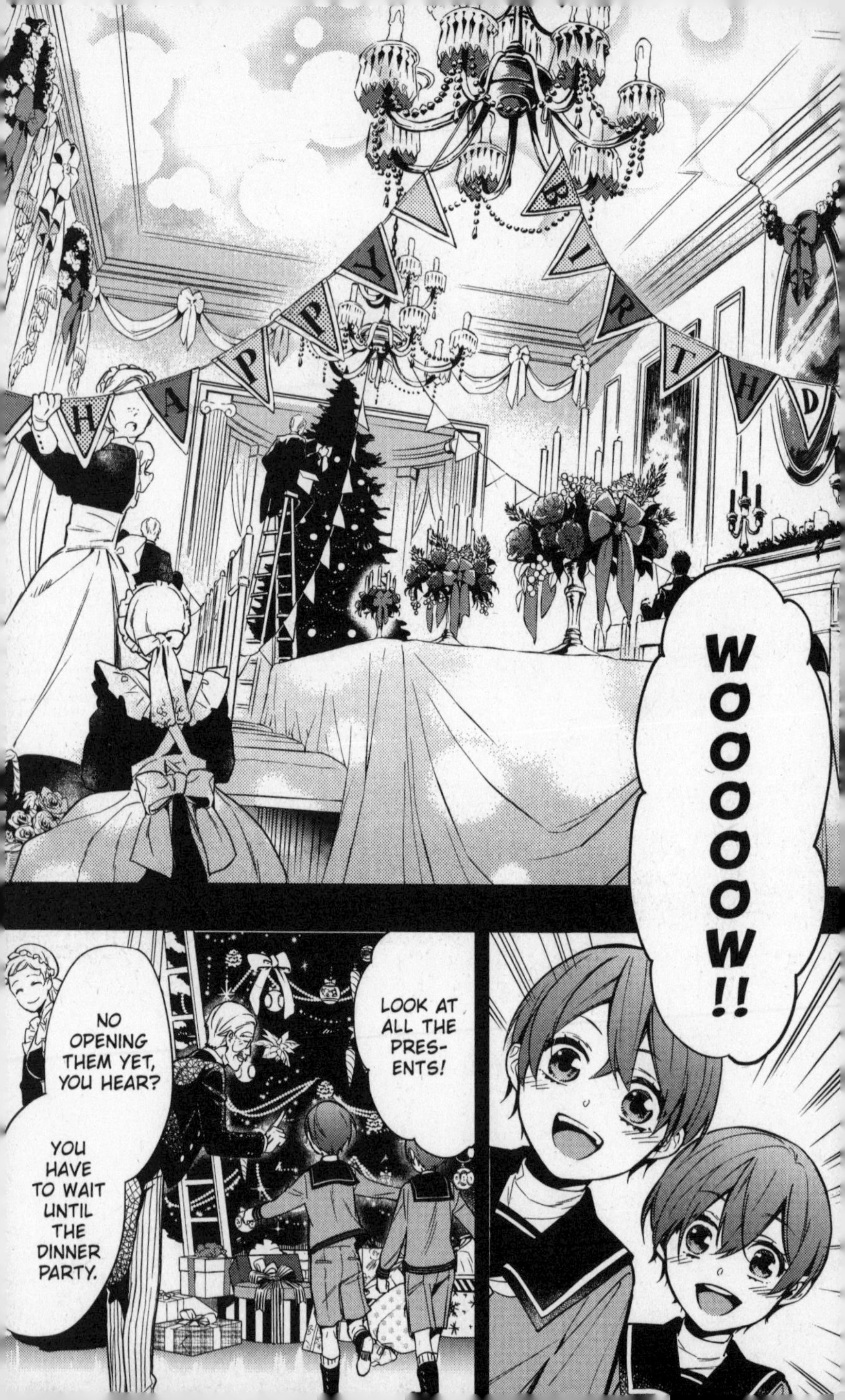
HAPPY BIRTHD
WOOOOOOW!!
LOOK AT ALL THE PRES-ENTS!
NO OPENING THEM YET, YOU HEAR?
YOU HAVE TO WAIT UNTIL THE DINNER PARTY.

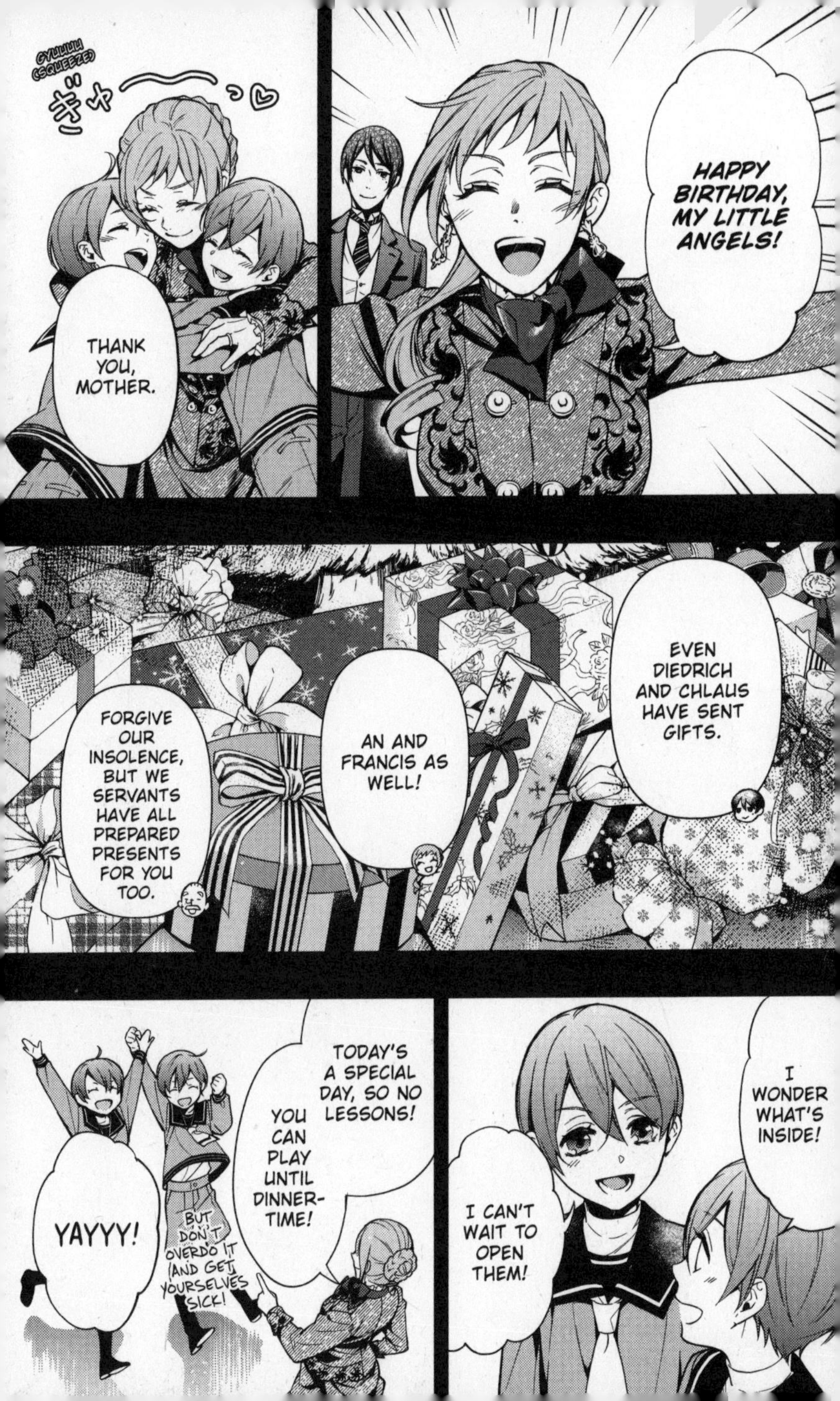
HAPPY BIRTHDAY, MY LITTLE ANGELS!
GYUUUUU (SQUEEZE)
ぎゅーっ♡
THANK YOU, MOTHER.
EVEN DIEDRICH AND CHLAUS HAVE SENT GIFTS.
AN AND FRANCIS AS WELL!
FORGIVE OUR INSOLENCE, BUT WE SERVANTS HAVE ALL PREPARED PRESENTS FOR YOU TOO.
I WONDER WHAT'S INSIDE!
I CAN'T WAIT TO OPEN THEM!
TODAY'S A SPECIAL DAY, SO NO LESSONS!
YOU CAN PLAY UNTIL DINNER-TIME!
BUT DON'T OVERDO IT AND GET YOURSELVES SICK!
YAYYY!

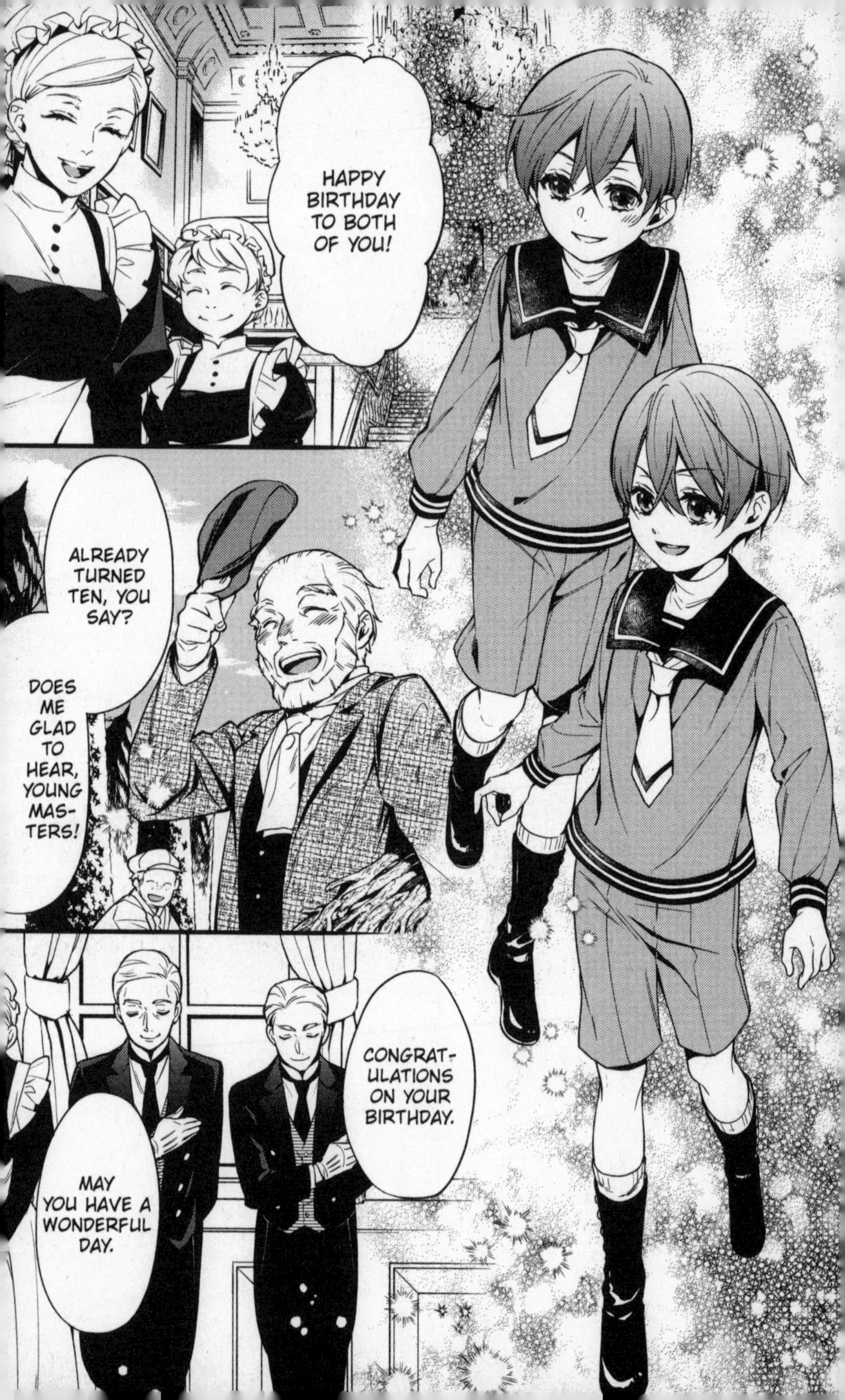
HAPPY BIRTHDAY TO BOTH OF YOU!
ALREADY TURNED TEN, YOU SAY?
DOES ME GLAD TO HEAR, YOUNG MAS-TERS!
CONGRAT-ULATIONS ON YOUR BIRTHDAY.
MAY YOU HAVE A WONDERFUL DAY.

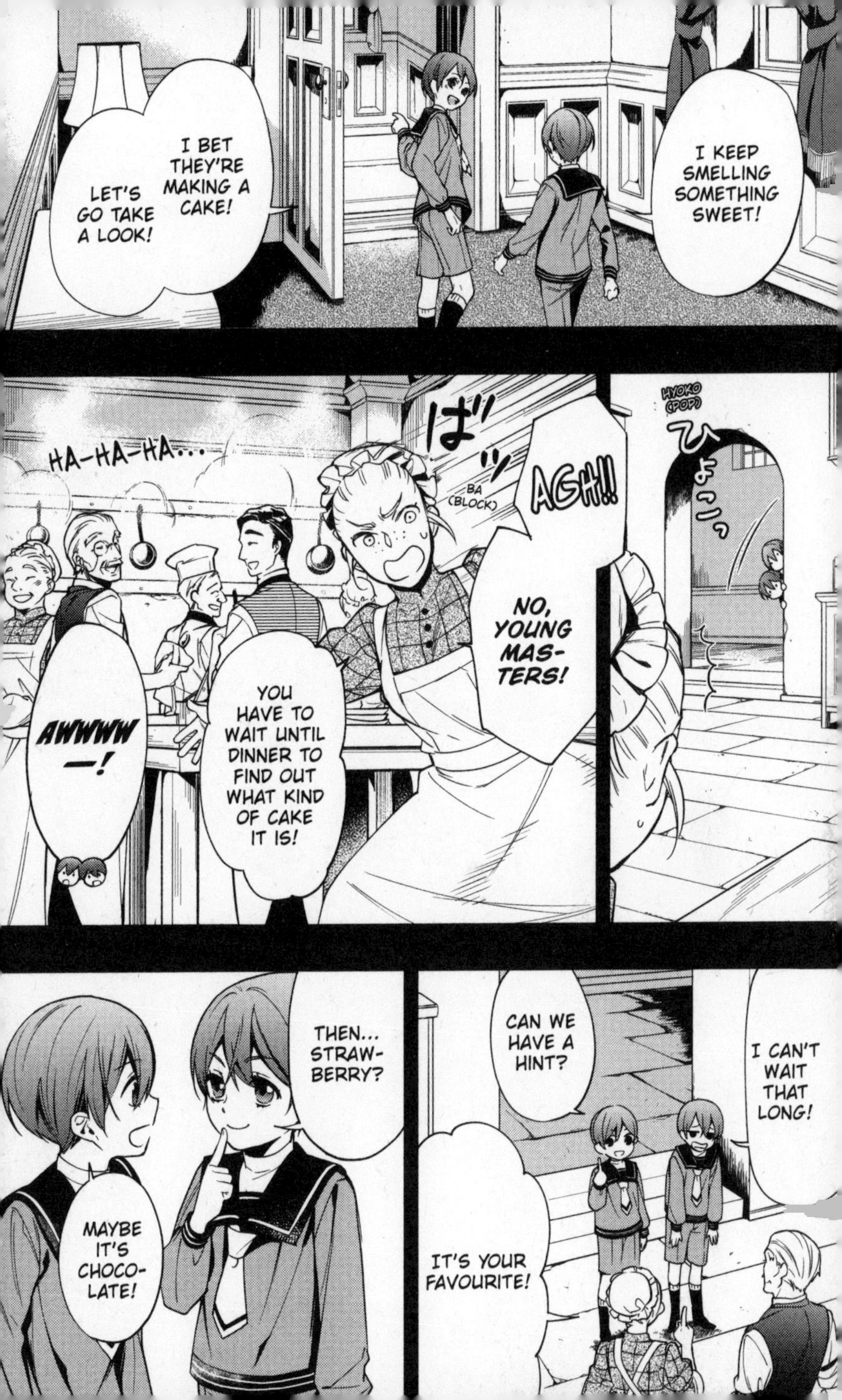
I KEEP SMELLING SOMETHING SWEET!
I BET THEY'RE MAKING A CAKE!
LET'S GO TAKE A LOOK!
HYOKO (POP)
ひょこっ
ばッ
BA (BLOCK)
AGH!!
NO, YOUNG MAS-TERS!
YOU HAVE TO WAIT UNTIL DINNER TO FIND OUT WHAT KIND OF CAKE IT IS!
AWWWW—!
HA-HA-HA...
I CAN'T WAIT THAT LONG!
CAN WE HAVE A HINT?
IT'S YOUR FAVOURITE!
THEN... STRAW-BERRY?
MAYBE IT'S CHOCO-LATE!

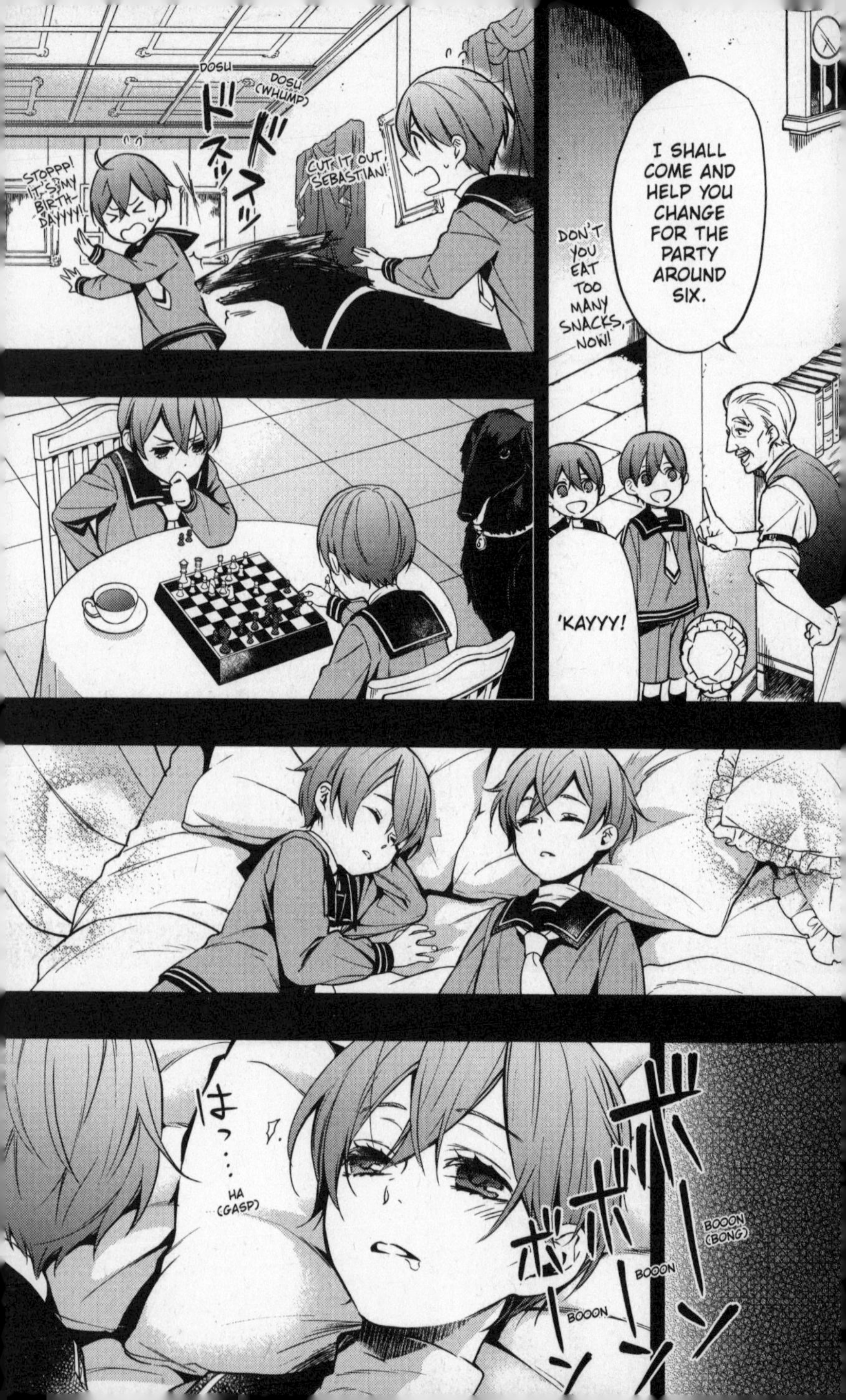
I SHALL COME AND HELP YOU CHANGE FOR THE PARTY AROUND SIX.
DON'T YOU EAT TOO MANY SNACKS, NOW!
'KAYYY!
DOSU (WHUMP)
DOSU
CUT IT OUT, SEBASTIAN!
STOPPP! IT'S MY BIRTHDAYYY!
BOOON (BONG)
BOOON
BOOON
HA (GASP)

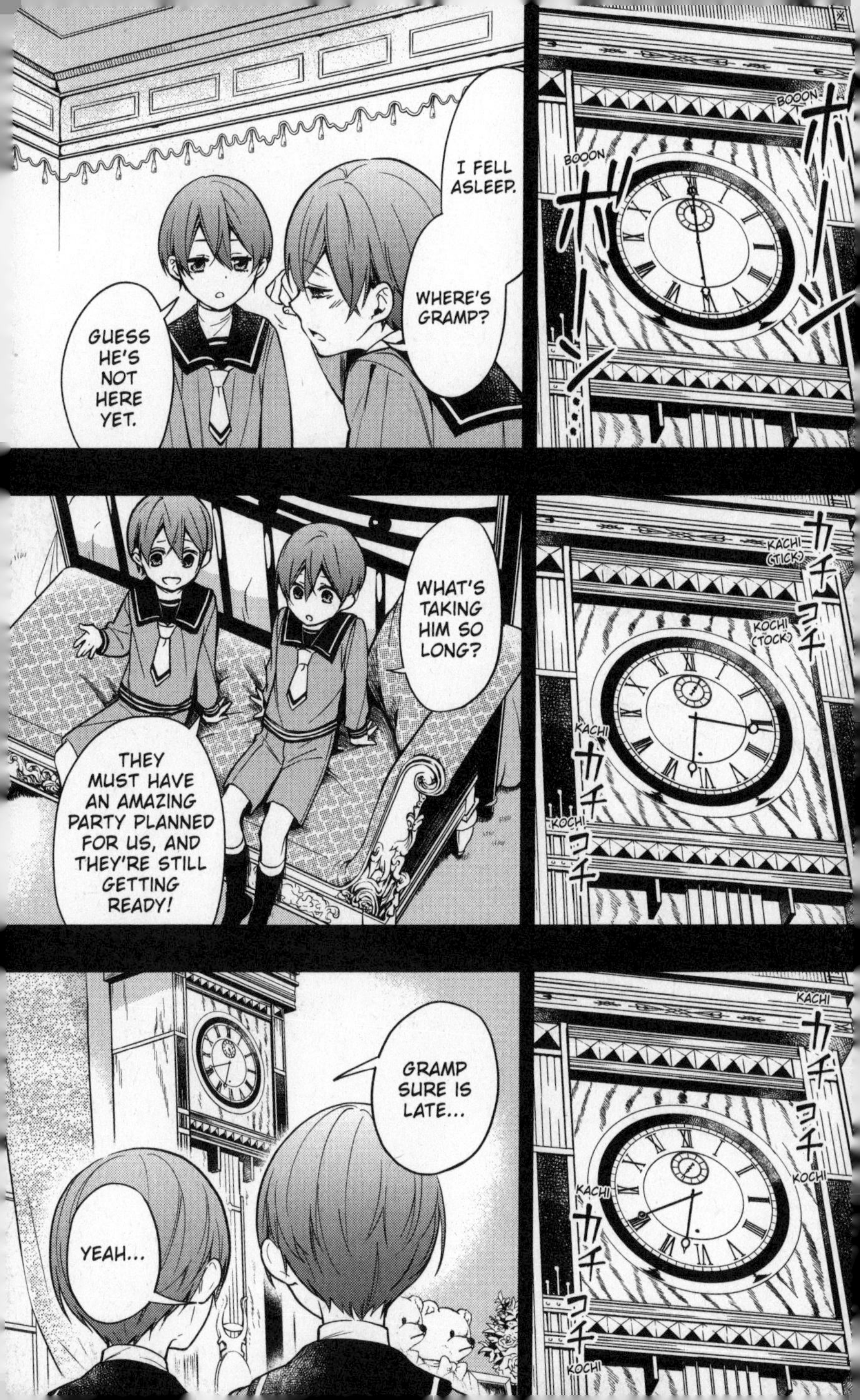
BOOON
ボーン
BOOON
ボーン
I FELL ASLEEP.
WHERE'S GRAMP?
GUESS HE'S NOT HERE YET.
KACHI (TICK)
カチ
KOCHI (TOCK)
コチ
KACHI
カチ
KOCHI
コチ
WHAT'S TAKING HIM SO LONG?
THEY MUST HAVE AN AMAZING PARTY PLANNED FOR US, AND THEY'RE STILL GETTING READY!
KACHI
カチ
KOCHI
コチ
KACHI
カチ
KOCHI
コチ
GRAMP SURE IS LATE...
YEAH...

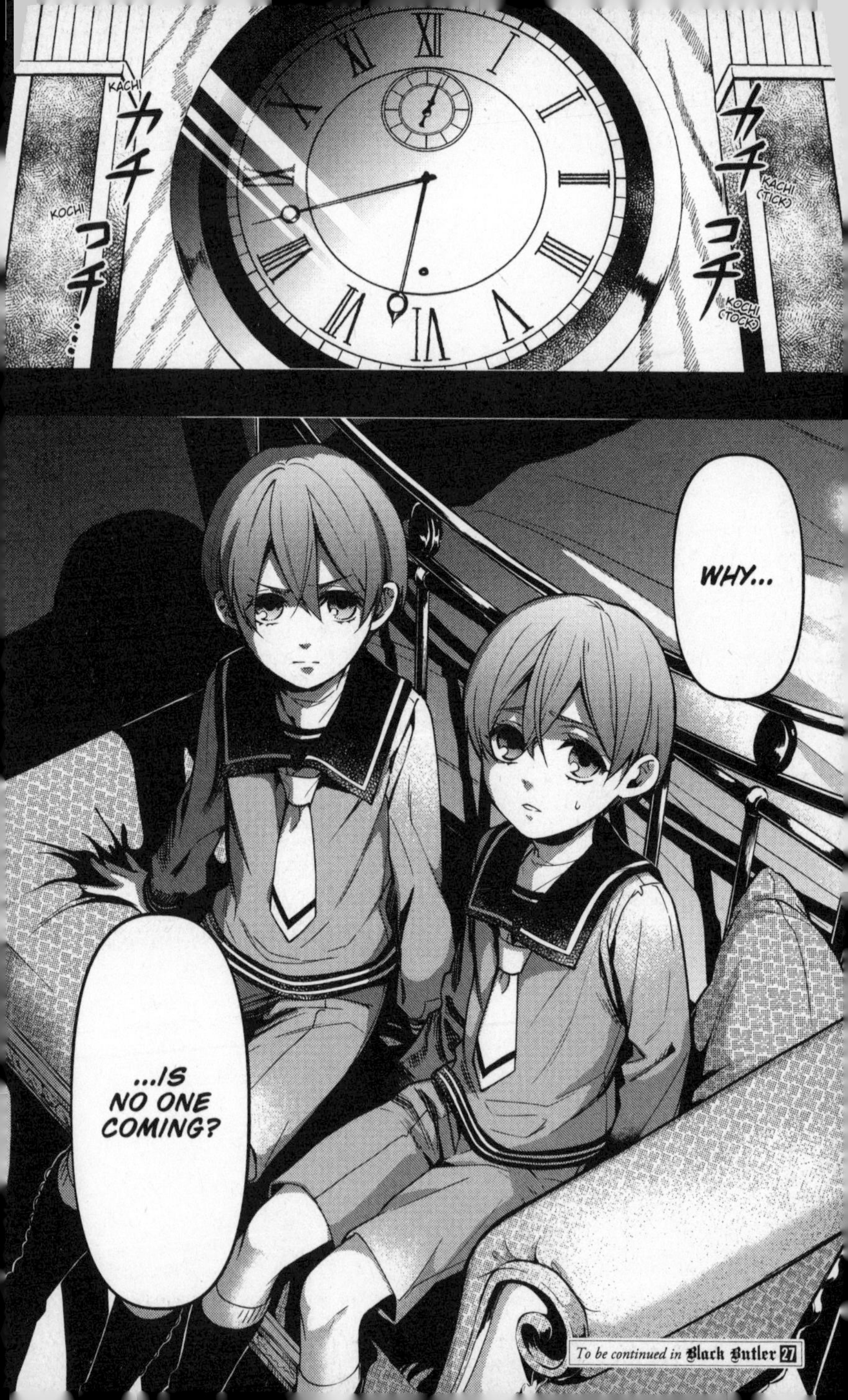
カチ
KACHI (TICK)
コチ
KOCHI (TOCK)
カチ
KACHI
コチ…
KOCHI
WHY...
...IS NO ONE COMING?
To be continued in Black Butler 27

Black Butler

黒執事

Downstairs

Wakana Haduki
7
Tsuki Sorano
Chiaki Nagaoka
Sanihiko
Seira
Natsume

*

Takeshi Kuma

*

Yana Toboso

Adviser

Rico Murakami

Special thanks to You!

Translation Notes

INSIDE BACK COVER
Black Santa, Red Santa
In European folklore, red-suited Saint
Nicholas is the Santa who bestows gifts
upon good children, while Krampus, a
horned demon and sometimes companion of
Saint Nicholas, visits horrors upon naughty
children. Krampus is occasionally depicted
carrying a sack into which he stuffs bad
boys and girls for eating and other nefarious
purposes, as Sebastian is doing.

PAGE 19
Hansom cab
A hansom cab is a two-wheeled carriage
pulled by a single horse and seating up to
two passengers. The earlier model of hansom
cab had an open front, so passengers got wet
if it rained. Later, hansoms had half doors
that protected the passengers' feet and legs.

PAGE 124
Cribbage
Cribbage is a card game developed in
seventeenth century England. The objective
of the game is to reach the target score of
121 points. Scores are kept on a cribbage
board.

PAGE 137
Kingcraft
Now an archaic term, kingcraft is the art of
ruling as a monarch, or the study thereof. It
typically involves lessons in diplomacy and
political intrigue.

PAGE 145
Vicar Rathbone
Sebastian appeared as Vicar Rathbone in
Volume 10 of *Black Butler*.

PAGE 166
Fève
A *fève* (literally "bean") is a small porcelain
figure or trinket often baked into king cakes
(*galette des rois*), which are eaten in France
during the Christmas holiday.

Yana Toboso

AUTHOR'S NOTE

There have been a lot of celebrations going on around me lately, since many people close to me have gotten married or have had children.

These milestones don't feel quite real, but enough time must have passed to turn events I thought were far off in the future into events that are happening now.

And with that, here's Volume 26.

BLACK BUTLER ㉖

YANA TOBOSO

Translation: Tomo Kimura
Lettering: Bianca Pistillo

KUROSHITSUJI Vol. 26 © 2017 Yana Toboso / SQUARE ENIX CO., LTD. First published in Japan in 2017 by SQUARE ENIX CO., LTD. English translation rights arranged with SQUARE ENIX CO., LTD. and Yen Press, LLC through Tuttle-Mori Agency, Inc.

Yen Press
1290 Avenue of the Americas
New York, NY 10104

Visit us!
† yenpress.com
† facebook.com/yenpress
† twitter.com/yenpress
† yenpress.tumblr.com
† instagram.com/yenpress

First Yen Press Edition: August 2018
The chapters in this volume were originally published as ebooks by Yen Press.

Yen Press is an imprint of Yen Press, LLC.
The Yen Press name and logo are trademarks of Yen Press, LLC.

The publisher is not responsible for websites (or their content) that are not owned by the publisher.

Library of Congress Control Number: 2010525567

ISBNs: 978-1-9753-5475-6 (paperback)
        978-1-9753-5476-3 (ebook)

10 9 8 7 6 5 4 3 2 1

WOR

Printed in the United States of America